The Secret Cuban Missile Crisis Documents

THE SECRET CUBAN MISSILE CRISIS DOCUMENTS

Central Intelligence Agency

INTRODUCTION BY
Graham T. Allison, Jr.

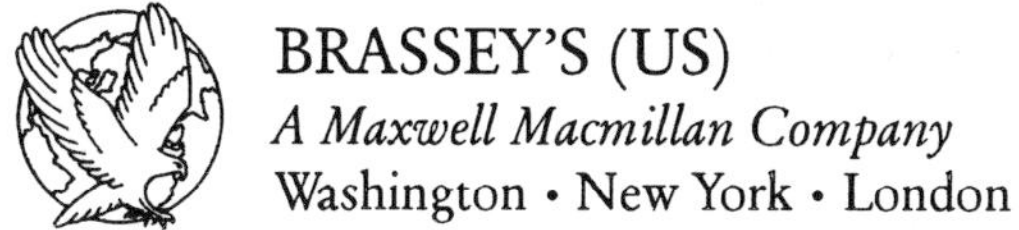
BRASSEY'S (US)
A Maxwell Macmillan Company
Washington • New York • London

First Brassey's (US) edition 1994

Brassey's (US)

Editorial Offices
Brassey's (US)
8000 Westpark Drive
First Floor
McLean, Virginia 22102

Order Department
Brassey's Book Orders
c/o Macmillan Publishing Co.
100 Front Street, Box 500
Riverside, New Jersey 08075

Brassey's (US) is a Maxwell Macmillan Company. Brassey's (US) books are available at special discounts for bulk purchases for sales promotions, premiums, fund-raising, or educational use through the Special Sales Director, Macmillan Publishing Company, 866 Third Avenue, New York, New York 10022.

Library of Congress Cataloging-in-Publication Data

The Secret Cuban missile crisis documents / Central Intelligence
Agency. — 1st Brassey's (US) ed.
p. cm.
ISBN 0-02-881082-1 (hardcover). — ISBN 0-02-881083-X (softcover)
1. Cuban Missile Crisis, 1962—Sources. I. United States.
Central Intelligence Agency.
E841.S43 1994
972.9106'4—dc20

10 9 8 7 6 5 4 3 2 1

Printed in the United States of America

Publisher's Note

Brassey's (US) is pleased to publish commercially this important collection from the Central Intelligence Agency's files and archive. Our purpose is to make more readily available to the general public these recently declassified U.S. government documents about one of the most important times in human history, when the world stood on the edge of nuclear war. As the publisher, I have unique memories of that time when my wife left for safety in Alabama while I flew numerous 24-hour airborne alert sorties over the polar ice cap as the pilot of a B-52G loaded with nuclear weapons targeted on the Soviet Union. I will never forget the oriental music I heard as the Soviets tried to jam our radios so we would not receive a "go" code if President Kennedy felt forced to that decision.

Today our world seems safer, and former Soviet adversaries have become valued friends and colleagues. But it is important to remember the history of the Cuban Missile Crisis so we never get as close to the nuclear edge again. We are thus pleased to provide a historical context for the CIA documents with the following article by the expert on this crisis, Graham T. Allison, Jr., JFK School of Government, Harvard University. This article was recently published as one of 786 in Brassey's *International Military and Defense Encyclopedia.*

Introduction*

The Cuban Missile Crisis of October 1962 is the classic nuclear crisis. For thirteen days, President John F. Kennedy and Chairman Nikita Khrushchev contemplated choices that could have led to war, even nuclear war. At the time, Kennedy estimated the risks of war as "between one-in-three and even." Khrushchev spoke of "the smell of burning" in the air. Cloudy though it is, the missile crisis remains the best window available for scholars and policymakers who want to pursue questions about nuclear confrontation and superpower crisis management.

The missile crisis ranks among the most studied events of all time. About no analogous event is so much information available. This includes firsthand memoirs by participants, tens of thousands of pages of highly classified documents that have been made public, and even secret audio tapes of the most private deliberations at the top levels of the U.S. government during these events—all accessible during the lifetime of the participants who can be cross-examined. While Soviet perceptions, motivations, and decision-making processes remain unclear, *glasnost* has made more information available, including interviews with Soviet participants, than scholars have had about any equivalent decisions of the Soviet government.

Answers to Ranke's questions of "what really happened," whether in the middle of the crisis or elsewhere, do not depend solely on the evidence available. Conceptual frameworks that analysts bring to their inquiry, assumptions historians make, and categories they use in framing questions shape what are accepted as satisfactory answers. The missile crisis has provided fertile ground for competing arguments not only about the crisis itself, but also about larger questions of theories of foreign policy analysis and crisis management. These

*Excerpted from Brassey's *International Military and Defense Encyclopedia*

debates, however, are not likely to improve on President Kennedy's own conclusion about the missile crisis; namely, that the "ultimate decision remains impenetrable to the observer—often, indeed, to the decider himself . . . there will always be the dark and tangled stretches in the decision-making process—mysterious even to those who may be most intimately involved."

The Facts

The thirteen days of the crisis began on 14 October 1962 when the United States discovered that the Soviet Union was in the midst of a secret attempt to deploy strategic nuclear missiles to Cuba. A U.S. high-altitude U-2 overflight of Cuba took photographs that provided clear evidence of an ambitious Soviet deployment of 48 medium-range ballistic missiles (MRBMs, range 1,100 nautical miles) and 24 intermediate-range ballistic missiles (IRBMs, range 2,200 nautical miles) at four separate sites in Cuba. The U.S. government's reaction was, in the words of the president's brother, Atty. Gen. Robert Kennedy, one of "shocked incredulity." Never before had the Soviet Union stationed nuclear weapons outside Soviet territory. Khrushchev had given Kennedy the most solemn private pledges that the Soviet Union would not undertake any such action. Relying on these assurances, Kennedy had rebutted charges made by Republican opponents in the midterm congressional elections by drawing a bright line that declared Soviet installation of significant offensive capabilities in Cuba, specifically including strategic missiles, "unacceptable."

Thus, from the outset, President Kennedy determined that the missiles must be removed. The question, then, was *how* the missiles could be eliminated without war. To assist him in assessing the predicament and fashioning a response, the president assembled his most trusted advisers as the Executive Committee (Excomm) of the National Security Council. Since the Soviet government was unaware that its clandestine initiative had been uncovered, the president and his advisers had the luxury of a week for private deliberation. In the beginning, the president and most of his advisers favored a direct air strike to destroy the missiles. After full analysis of the pros and cons of this and other options, Kennedy chose a naval quarantine of all Soviet arms shipments to Cuba as the initial response.

On Monday, 22 October, the president announced to the Soviet Union, the American public, and the world the U.S. discovery of the Soviet deception and the U.S. response with a naval quarantine. U.S. forces worldwide were raised to alert status. President Kennedy's speech warned the Soviet Union that any attack from Cuba would be met with a "full retaliatory response." (In an initial private letter, Khrushchev assured Kennedy that the Soviet Union, not Cuba, had full control of the missiles in Cuba.)

There ensued a week of public and private bargaining. U.S. allies in Europe and Latin America supported the American position that the Soviet initiative was illegal and unacceptable, and that the missiles had to be withdrawn. The U.S. naval quarantine went into effect on Wednesday. Soviet ships tested the blockade. Ships carrying additional Soviet missiles, specifically the *Poltava*, approached the blockade line but then stopped. While U.S. intelligence was not certain of the presence of nuclear warheads on Cuba, the U.S. government had to act as if they were there. (By the late 1980s, Soviet sources had confirmed the presence of twenty nuclear warheads on the island.)

On Thursday, the U.S. government received a letter from the Soviet government proposing to withdraw the missiles in response to an American pledge not to invade Cuba. Before the United States was able to respond, a second letter arrived on Friday, raising the ante: U.S. missiles in Turkey were the price demanded for Soviet missiles in Cuba. The U.S. government responded to the first proposal, without reference to the second. U.S. officials argued both in the Excomm and publicly that the United States could not trade away missiles deployed for the defense of a North Atlantic Treaty Organization (NATO) ally in the context of a crisis. On Saturday, a Soviet surface-to-air missile (SAM) in Cuba shot down a U.S. U-2 flying over Cuba. Reversing a previous decision to retaliate against SAM sites that attacked U.S. forces, President Kennedy paused. Arguments in the Excomm became bitter. The president decided to communicate to Khrushchev a clear warning that unless he announced withdrawal of the missiles immediately, the United States would take unilateral action to eliminate them. Most members of the Excomm expected the president to authorize an air strike against the missiles in Cuba at the meeting scheduled for Sunday morning. Most of the participants anticipated a Soviet response against U.S. missiles in Turkey or in Berlin, or elsewhere. Thus, as they left "Black Saturday," they wondered whether they would live to see another week. Some of the participants' families left Washington, D.C.

At 9:00 Sunday morning, Washington time, Chairman Khrushchev's announcement that the missiles would be withdrawn was broadcast live from Moscow.

The Context

The larger context in which these thirteen days occurred includes three ongoing competitions between the United States and the Soviet Union. The overriding competition was, of course, the Cold War. Regaining the initiative in the Cold War had, in effect, been Kennedy's principal theme in the presidential campaign of 1960. Attacking the Republican administration's complacency in meeting Soviet threats, Kennedy pointed to the "missile gap," the "space gap," and Soviet successes in the Caribbean and Southeast Asia. His inaugural speech as president sounded the trumpet, pledging Americans would "pay any price, bear any burden . . . to assure the success of liberty."

Two weeks before Kennedy's own inauguration, Khrushchev announced that the Soviet Union would vigorously support "wars of national liberation." The Kennedy administration read this as a virtual declaration of war in the developing world. Fidel Castro's Cuba illustrated the subtlety of Soviet tactics. Having come to power in 1958 as a nonaligned revolutionary, Castro had increasingly allied himself with the Soviets, in a violation of the Monroe Doctrine. Like the Eisenhower administration before it, the Kennedy administration declared the Castro government "illegitimate." In April 1961, the Kennedy administration sponsored a halfhearted invasion of Cuba by 1,500 Cuban exiles directed by the CIA (the Bay of Pigs incident). This effort was decisively defeated by Castro. After first attempting to deny U.S. involvement, Kennedy accepted full responsibility for the failure. In the aftermath, U.S. covert actions against Castro increased significantly, including several attempts to assassinate him.

The third strand of the broader context was the competition for nuclear advantage. Through the 1950s, the United States maintained a significant nuclear superiority. This posture offset Soviet conventional advantages in Europe and provided the backdrop for the Eisenhower administration's doctrine of "massive retaliation." After the Soviet launch of Sputnik, Khrushchev touted massive increases in Soviet missile-launched nuclear capabilities. Kennedy targeted this emerging "missile gap" as a major issue in the 1960 presidential campaign; for the first time, the Soviet Union would exercise nuclear advantage over the United States.

After taking office, the administration soon learned that the Soviet Union had failed to exploit its potential to build missiles in the way Khrushchev had threatened. Nonetheless, the U.S. rapidly expanded its own deployment of nuclear weapons. By late 1961, the United States was deliberately communicating to the Soviet Union that the Soviets were on the short end of a missile gap.

In fact, by late 1962, U.S. advantages were approaching a capacity for what has been called a "splendid first strike"—namely, an attack after which the Soviet Union could have been incapable of responding with a major attack on the United States. (During the crisis, the United States estimated that the Soviets had 75 operational intercontinental ballistic missiles [ICBMs]; subsequent U.S. estimates reduced this number to 44 operational launchers. More recent Soviet information indicates that the Soviet government may not have been confident of the capacity even of these 44 weapons.)

Central Questions

The central questions about the missile crisis are three: (1) Why did the Soviet Union deploy missiles in Cuba? (2) Why did the United States respond with the blockade? and (3) Why did the Soviet Union withdraw the missiles? Answers to each have been, and remain, a matter of continuing debate.

The issue of why the Soviet government had attempted such an unexpected and dangerous initiative arose at the first meeting of the Excomm. They identified five hypotheses: (1) bargaining barter—Khrushchev deployed the missiles as a chip that could be traded for U.S. missiles in Turkey, or Berlin, or something else; (2) diverting trap—if this lightning rod drew U.S. fire, the Soviet Union could take the occasion to move against Berlin (as it had moved against Hungary in 1956 when the world was diverted by the Franco-British action at Suez); (3) Cuban defense—fearing a follow-up to the abortive Bay of Pigs invasion, Moscow moved to assure the defense of its Cuban ally; (4) Cold War politics—the missile crisis posed "the supreme probe of American intentions and resolve"; that is, if the United States failed to respond, U.S. cowardice would be exposed and the Soviet Union could act boldly elsewhere; (5) missile power—facing a real missile gap in terms of intercontinental strategic missiles, Moscow chose the only short-term fix available to redress its strategic nuclear inferiority.

The Excomm considered arguments for and against each of these hypotheses, examining specific evidence about the Soviet deployment. Thus, for example, the hypothesis of Cuban defense was rejected by the Excomm, and has generally been rejected by subsequent analyses, on the grounds that the Soviet Union could have achieved this objective more efficiently and at less risk without deploying strategic nuclear weapons. Soviet troops armed with conventional weapons would have sufficed. Certainly Cuban defense would not require IRBMs that threaten New York and Strategic Air Command (SAC) bases in Nebraska in addition to the MRBM threat against Washington.

Scholarly attempts to answer this question have pointed more broadly to the array of factors that must have influenced Soviet decision making. Yet even these analyses have tended to resolve the competing hypotheses with conclusions about "the objective" or "the primary objective" of the Soviet government—on the assumption that the various objectives of relevant individuals in the Soviet government can appropriately be summarized as if the Soviet government were a unitary rational actor.

Other scholars, employing different assumptions, have argued that individuals in the Soviet government must have been moved by different considerations: Khrushchev perhaps by his preoccupation with possible U.S. military action against Cuba; other members of the Politburo, spurred by the Soviet Strategic Rocket Forces, were more concerned about Soviet strategic inferiority. Evidence from the Soviet Union gives these analyses additional plausibility and color.

In his memoirs, Khrushchev states that his overriding concern was what he believed to be the impending American military invasion of Cuba. Other Soviet sources (including Sergei Mikoyan, on the basis of conversations with his father Anastos Mikoyan, at the time the first deputy premier) emphasize the following: Khrushchev's impulsiveness, which led him to make decisions without an adequate assessment of the risks; the origin of the idea during Khrushchev's visit to the Crimea where he was struck by equivalent U.S. deployments just across the Black Sea in Turkey; a real fear by Khrushchev and other Soviet leaders that a U.S. military invasion of Cuba was imminent; and a general concern about strategic nuclear inferiority. In the spirit of *glasnost*, Soviet participants in these events later offered accounts of the decision-making process from which the deployment emerged.

Why the United States chose to respond to Soviet missiles in Cuba with a blockade has generated less debate. The historical record shows that the Excomm considered options ranging from doing nothing to a major air strike and invasion. The explanation the U.S. government gave at the time for its choice has been widely accepted in subsequent analyses. Essentially, the argument is that the costs and risks of other alternatives simply exceeded those of the blockade. The blockade was a golden mean between inaction and aggression; firm enough to communicate determination but still not so precipitous as a strike. It placed on Khrushchev the burden of choice for the next step. It capitalized on U.S. naval superiority in the region and emphasized the advantages of U.S. conventional arms if further steps were required.

The general acceptance of this official explanation is a reminder of the three perils all historians face. First, it is no accident that the concepts of rationality, rationale, and rationalization have a common root. Had the U.S. government chosen a different option, it would have provided an explanation for that choice, emphasizing the benefits of an air strike or doing nothing versus the costs and risks of the other alternatives. Reasons given to explain and justify an action are not identical with causes. Second, after an episode, there is a powerful temptation for participants to adjust their positions and even their memories about their own views and about the merits of arguments at the time. As a result, the sharper edges of arguments are blunted. Third, after a decision that produces successful results, it becomes harder to visualize real, reasonable alternatives. The certainty of what was chosen and what occurred thus overwhelms the uncertainties the actors faced when making decisions.

Subsequent analyses have noted the number of additional causal factors that shaped the selection of the blockade. The fact that U.S. intelligence discovered the missiles during the process of deployment, rather than two weeks later, after deployment had been completed, provided the opportunity to choose an option like blockade. Had the missiles already been operational, such a choice would have been irrelevant. Similarly, while the costs and risks of any surgical air strike may have outweighed, on balance, the potential benefits, in this specific instance, the U.S. Air Force estimated that it would not be able to assure destruction of all Soviet missiles. That estimate, based upon standard U.S. Air Force estimating procedures, turned out to have mistakenly assumed that the Soviet missiles were "mobile." During the second week of the crisis, after this mistake was corrected, the option of a surgical air strike became live again as part of the deliberations. Similarly, finer-grained analyses give greater weight to the sharp differences among individual members of the Excomm. Robert Kennedy once observed, "The fourteen people involved were very significant. . . . If six of them had been president of the U.S., I think that the world might have been blown up." Discounting exaggeration, one should nonetheless note differences among Secretary of Defense Robert McNamara, who judged the Soviet missiles of no military significance and thus was prepared to tolerate them; the presidential assistant for national security affairs McGeorge Bundy, who appears to have favored a private diplomatic approach to Khrushchev rather than risk a public confrontation; Robert Kennedy, who was impressed by the "Tojo analogy," unable to explain to himself or others how a great and good power could initiate a surprise air strike on a small island nation; and the former secretary of state Dean Acheson who wrote: "As I saw it at the time, and still believe, the decision to resort to the blockade was a decision to postpone the issue at the expense of time within which the nuclear weapons might be made operational." Competing groups in the Excomm were labeled "hawks" and "doves," terms that entered the political vocabulary thereafter.

Explorations of why Khrushchev withdrew the missiles have tended to follow naturally from accounts of the merits of the blockade. The blockade signaled a willingness to use local nonnuclear forces but left open a "staircase of ascending steps in the use of force." In the background was overwhelming U.S. nuclear superiority. Having no real alternative, Khrushchev withdrew.

Competing analyses of the Soviet withdrawal of missiles reject the hypothesis that the blockade worked. They focus instead on the events of the final Saturday of the crisis and specifically on Kennedy's partially public and partially undisclosed decision to present Khrushchev with a combination of stick and carrot. The stick consisted of the threat to bomb the missiles if Khrushchev did not act immediately to remove them. The carrot was an arrangement that had both a public and a private clause. The public clause was a pledge not to invade Cuba or support invasions of Cuba. The private clause promised removal of U.S. missiles from Turkey after the crisis was successfully resolved. The private arrangement was known only to the president, his brother, the assistant for national security affairs, the secretary of defense, and the secretary of state. Denied by the U.S. government publicly, it was not even hinted to other members of the Excomm. Not until the twentieth anniversary of the crisis, after scholars had pointed to the likelihood of such an understanding, did those party to the private pledge acknowledge this arrangement.

Graham T. Allison, Jr.
John F. Kennedy School of Government
Harvard University

CIA Documents on the Cuban Missile Crisis 1962

Foreword

The Central Intelligence Agency is pleased to declassify and publish this collection of documents on the Cuban Missile Crisis, as the First Intelligence History Symposium marks the thirtieth anniversary of that event. We hope that both the Symposium and this volume will help fill the large gaps in information previously available on the role of intelligence in this crisis. The volume and Symposium are both products of CIA's new program of openness, which Robert Gates, Director of Central Intelligence (DCI), announced in his speech to the Oklahoma Press Association last February.

To help carry out this openness program, the Center for the Study of Intelligence, CIA's focal point for research and publication on intelligence since 1975, has been reorganized, expanded in size and mission, and placed in the Office of the DCI. The Center now includes the CIA History Staff, first formed in 1951, and a new Historical Review Group, which has increased both the scope and pace of the program to declassify historical records that DCI William Casey established in 1985.

Dr. Mary S. McAuliffe, Deputy Chief of the History Staff, has located and compiled the documents in this collection. Dr. McAuliffe, who has recently completed a study of John A. McCone's tenure as DCI, graduated from Principia College, took a Ph.D. in history from the University of Maryland, and taught at Iowa State University before joining CIA and the History Staff in 1986. She is the author of *Crisis on the Left: Cold War Politics and American Liberals, 1947-1954* (Amherst, MA: University of Massachusetts Press, 1978).

The Historical Review Group declassified the documents that Dr. McAuliffe selected, using new guidelines prepared by a special CIA task force and approved by the DCI last spring. We are especially grateful to the principal reviewer who handled this difficult process—including coordination with other departments and agencies—with great skill and dispatch. We should also acknowledge the invaluable help of our History Assistant, Ms. Diane Marvin, and of the members of the Directorate of Intelligence's Design Center and Publication Center, and of the Directorate of Administration's Printing and Photography Group, who prepared and produced this book with remarkable speed and virtuosity.

A number of documents in this collection have been excerpted, some to reduce their length, and others to speed the declassification of missile crisis information by omitting irrelevant material. When the Historical Review Group systematically reviews these and other missile crisis records for declassification and release to the National Archives, we expect that most of the material omitted for reasons of length or relevance in our published excerpts will be declassified and made available to the public.

J. Kenneth McDonald
Chief, History Staff

11 September 1992

CIA Documents on the Cuban Missile Crisis 1962

Preface

The collection in this volume includes many of CIA's most important documents on the Cuban missile crisis. It contains the "honeymoon cables" that Director of Central Intelligence (DCI) John A. McCone sent to Headquarters from France a month before the missile crisis, as well as McCone's notes taken during the National Security Council Executive Committee meetings at the height of the crisis. It also includes intelligence memorandums and estimates, briefing papers, Cuban refugee reports, and memorandums on Operation MONGOOSE, the clandestine program aimed at destabilizing the Castro regime. Many of the evaluations of the missile threat contained here draw upon IRONBARK material, whose source was Soviet Col. Oleg Penkovsky.

To the degree possible, the documents in this volume are organized according to the date of subject matter, so that a February 1963 document discussing a September 1962 event will appear among September 1962 documents. In general, support documents follow documents that summarize a sequence of events.

To conserve space and speed declassification, excerpts have been taken from some of the lengthier entries. In some cases, the summary or conclusion section of a document has been excerpted, while in others, material on topics unrelated to Cuba or the missile crisis has been omitted. All such instances have been noted in the Contents list and in the documents' headings.

All the documents in this volume have been subject to declassification review, and portions of some have been deleted for security reasons.

In the weeks immediately preceding the missile crisis, DCI McCone was frequently out of town. During these times, his Deputy Director of Central Intelligence (DDCI), Lt. Gen. Marshall S. Carter, served as Acting Director. McCone was away from Washington on his honeymoon in France from the evening of 23 August through 23 September 1962. He left for Los Angeles on business on the evening of 11 October 1962, coming back late on 14 October. He returned to the West Coast on the afternoon of 15 October, immediately following news of the death of his stepson. The discovery of missiles in Cuba brought him back to Washington on the evening of 16 October, where he remained for the rest of the crisis.

It should be noted that these documents, many of them written hastily during a time of national emergency, contain occasional errors. McCone's 19 October 1962 memorandum for the file (Document 63), for example, confuses the days of the week, although not the dates, of the first crisis meetings that he attended.

Much has been written on the missile crisis during the 30 years that have elapsed since those 13 days in October, but the unavailability of classified material has left many questions still unanswered. The CIA History Staff hopes that the publication of this volume, and the further releases that follow, will make possible a more complete understanding of this complex and deeply troubling event.

Mary S. McAuliffe
Deputy Chief, History Staff

Persons Mentioned

Brief Titles and Descriptions as of October 1962

Acheson, Dean	Former Secretary of State
Alsop, Joseph	Columnist
Alsop, Stewart	Columnist
Anderson, Adm. George W., Jr., USN	Chief of Naval Operations
Ball, George W.	Under Secretary of State
Bohlen, Charles E.	Newly appointed Ambassador to France, former Ambassador to the Soviet Union
Bowles, Chester	President's Special Representative and Adviser on African, Asian and Latin American Affairs
Bundy, McGeorge	Special Assistant to the President for National Security Affairs
Cannon, Representative Clarence (D-MO)	Chairman, House Appropriations Committee
Carroll, Lt. Gen. Joseph F., USAF	Director, Defense Intelligence Agency
Carter, Lt. Gen. Marshall S., USA	Deputy Director of Central Intelligence
Castro, Fidel	Prime Minister of Cuba
Charyk, Joseph V.	Under Secretary of the Air Force
Cline, Ray S.	Deputy Director for Intelligence, CIA

Dillon, C. Douglas	Secretary of the Treasury
Dirksen, Senator Everett M. (R-IL)	Senate Minority Leader
Donovan, James B.	New York lawyer representing the Cuban Families Committee in efforts to release prisoners captured at the Bay of Pigs invasion, 1961
Eisenhower, Gen. Dwight D.	Former President of the United States
Elder, Walter	Executive Assistant to the Director of Central Intelligence
Forrestal, Michael V.	National Security Council staff member
Fulbright, Senator J. William (D-AR)	Chairman, Senate Foreign Relations Committee
Gilpatric, Roswell L.	Deputy Secretary of Defense
Graybeal, Sidney N.	Chief, Offensive Missiles Division, Office of Scientific Intelligence, CIA
Grogan, Col. Stanley J., USA (Retired)	Assistant to the DCI for Public Affairs
Gromyko, Andrei A.	Soviet Foreign Minister
Halleck, Representative Charles A. (R-IN)	House Minority Leader
Harvey, William K.	Chief, Task Force W (CIA unit tasked with carrying out Operation MONGOOSE)
Hayden, Senator Carl (D-AZ)	President Pro Tempore of the Senate and Chairman, Senate Appropriations Committee

Helms, Richard M.	Deputy Director for Plans, CIA
Hickenlooper, Senator Bourke B. (R-IA)	Chairman, Senate Republican Policy Committee
Hilsman, Roger, Jr.	Director, Bureau of Intelligence and Research, Department of State
Johnson, Clarence (Kelly)	Chief aircraft designer, Lockheed Aircraft
Johnson, Lyndon B.	Vice President of the United States
Johnson, U. Alexis	Deputy Under Secretary of State for Political Affairs
Karamessines, Thomas H.	Assistant Deputy Director for Plans, CIA
Kaysen, Carl	Deputy Special Assistant to the President for National Security Affairs
Keating, Senator Kenneth B. (R-NY)	Senator who warned of missiles in Cuba
Kennedy, John F.	President of the United States
Kennedy, Robert F.	Attorney General
Kent, Sherman	Chairman, Board of National Estimates, CIA
Khrushchev, Nikita S.	First Secretary, Central Committee CPSU and Soviet Premier
Killian, James R., Jr.	President of MIT and Chairman, President's Foreign Intelligence Advisory Board
Kirkpatrick, Lyman B.	Executive Director, CIA
Knoche, E. Henry	Executive Assistant to the Deputy Director of Central Intelligence

Knox, William E.	President, Westinghouse International
Krock, Arthur	Columnist, *The New York Times*
Lansdale, Brig. Gen. Edward G., USAF	Assistant for Special Operations to the Secretary of Defense and head of Operation MONGOOSE
Lawrence, David	Editor and columnist, *U.S. News & World Report*
Lemnitzer, Gen. Lyman L., USA	Chairman, Joint Chiefs of Staff until 1 October 1962
Lovett, Robert A.	Former Secretary of Defense
Lundahl, Arthur C.	Director, National Photographic Interpretation Center
Mansfield, Senator Mike (D-MT)	Senate Majority Leader
Martin, Edwin M.	Assistant Secretary of State for Inter-American Affairs
McCloy, John J.	Coordinator of US disarmament activities and member of the US Delegation to the United Nations during the missile crisis
McCone, John A.	Director of Central Intelligence
McNamara, Robert S.	Secretary of Defense
Miskovsky, M. C.	Assistant General Counsel, CIA
Norstad, Gen. Lauris, USAF	Supreme Allied Commander, Europe (SACEUR) and Commander in Chief, US European Command
Parker, Col. David Stewart, USA	Deputy Director, National Photographic Interpretation Center

Parrott, Thomas A.	Executive Secretary, NSC Special Group
Reber, James Q.	Chairman, Committee on Overhead Reconnaissance
Rostow, Walt W.	Counselor and Chairman of Policy Planning Council, State Department
Rusk, Dean	Secretary of State
Russell, Bertrand	British philosopher and author
Russell, Senator Richard B. (D-GA)	Chairman, Senate Armed Services Committee
Saltonstall, Senator Leverett (R-MA)	Chairman, Senate Republican Conference
Scott, Paul	Columnist
Scoville, Herbert (Pete), Jr.	Deputy Director for Research, CIA
Smathers, Senator George A. (D-FL)	Secretary, Senate Democratic Conference
Sorensen, Theodore	Special Counsel to the President
Stevenson, Adlai E.	US Representative to the UN and Representative in the Security Council
Sweeney, Gen. Walter C., Jr., USAF	Commander in Chief, Tactical Air Command
Taylor, Gen. Maxwell D., USA	President's Military Representative until 1 October 1962; thereafter Chairman, Joint Chiefs of Staff
Thompson, Llewellyn E., Jr.	Former Ambassador to the Soviet Union

Tidwell, William A.	Assistant to Deputy Director for Intelligence (Planning), CIA
U Thant	Secretary-General of the United Nations
Vinson, Representative Carl (D-GA)	Chairman, House Armed Services Committee
Warner, John S.	Legislative Counsel, CIA
Wheelon, Albert D.	Chairman, Guided Missile & Astronautics Intelligence Committee
Wiesner, Jerome B.	Science Adviser to the President
Wilson, Don	Deputy Director, USIA

Acronyms and Abbreviations

AG	Attorney General
ALPHA-66	Cuban exile group
BNE	Board of National Estimates, CIA
CHICKADEE	Special information handling channel for nondocumentary material generated by Col. Oleg Penkovsky
CINCARIB	Commander in Chief, Caribbean
CINCEUR	Commander in Chief, Europe
CINCLANT	Commander in Chief, Atlantic
COMINT	Communications Intelligence
COMOR	Committee on Overhead Reconnaissance
COS	Chief of Station
DCI	Director of Central Intelligence
DDCI	Deputy Director of Central Intelligence
DD/I	Deputy Director for Intelligence
DD/P	Deputy Director for Plans
DD/R	Deputy Director for Research
DIA	Defense Intelligence Agency
DOD	Department of Defense
DRE	Cuban Student Directorate (Cuban student exile group)
ELINT	Electronic Intelligence
FI	Foreign Intelligence
5412 Committee	Oversight committee of the National Security Council; also referred to as the Special Group

GCI	Ground Control Intercept
GMAIC	Guided Missile and Astronautics Intelligence Committee
ICBM	Intercontinental ballistic missile
IL 28	Soviet jet light bomber
IRBM	Intermediate-range ballistic missile
IRONBARK	Special information handling channel for documentary material generated by Col. Oleg Penkovsky
JAEIC	Joint Atomic Energy Intelligence Committee
JCS	Joint Chiefs of Staff
MiG 21	Soviet jet fighter
MONGOOSE	Operation MONGOOSE
MRBM	Medium-range ballistic missile
MT	Megatons
NATO	North Atlantic Treaty Organization
NIE	National Intelligence Estimate
NORAD	North American Air Defense Command
NPIC	National Photographic Interpretation Center
NSA	National Security Agency
NSAM	National Security Action Memorandum
NSC	National Security Council
OAS	Organization of American States
OCI	Office of Current Intelligence, CIA
OD	Operating Directive
ONE	Office of National Estimates, CIA

OSI	Office of Scientific Intelligence, CIA
PFIAB	President's Foreign Intelligence Advisory Board
PI	Photointerpreter
POL	Petroleum, oil, and lubricants
PSALM	Special information handling channel for material related to presence of Soviet missiles in Cuba
RF-101	Low altitude reconnaissance aircraft (US)
SA-2	See SAM
SAC	Strategic Air Command
SACEUR	Supreme Allied Commander, Europe
SAM	Surface-to-air missile
SHAPE	Supreme Headquarters, Allied Powers, Europe
SNIE	Special National Intelligence Estimate
SS-4	See MRBM
SS-5	See IRBM
SecDef	Secretary of Defense
Special Group (Augmented)	National Security Council committee with oversight over Operation MONGOOSE
Special Group	Oversight committee of the National Security Council; also referred to as the 5412 Committee
TFW	Task Force W (special CIA unit tasked with carrying out Operation MONGOOSE)
U-2	High-altitude reconnaissance aircraft (US)
UN	United Nations
USIA	United States Information Agency
USIB	United States Intelligence Board

Contents

Part II: Crisis, 16-28 October 1962

PART I

PRELUDE TO CRISIS

Sudden surge in supply of Soviet materiel and personnel to Cuba . . . McCone warns high administration officials, including the President, that the Soviets may be placing medium-range ballistic missiles there . . . CIA U-2 overflights discover surface-to-air missile sites in Cuba . . . McCone warns that SAMs may serve to protect a later emplacement of medium-range missiles . . . Efforts continue to win release of Bay of Pigs prisoners . . . Discovery of medium-range ballistic missile sites in Cuba . . .

1. *Maps of Cuban overflights, August-October 1962*

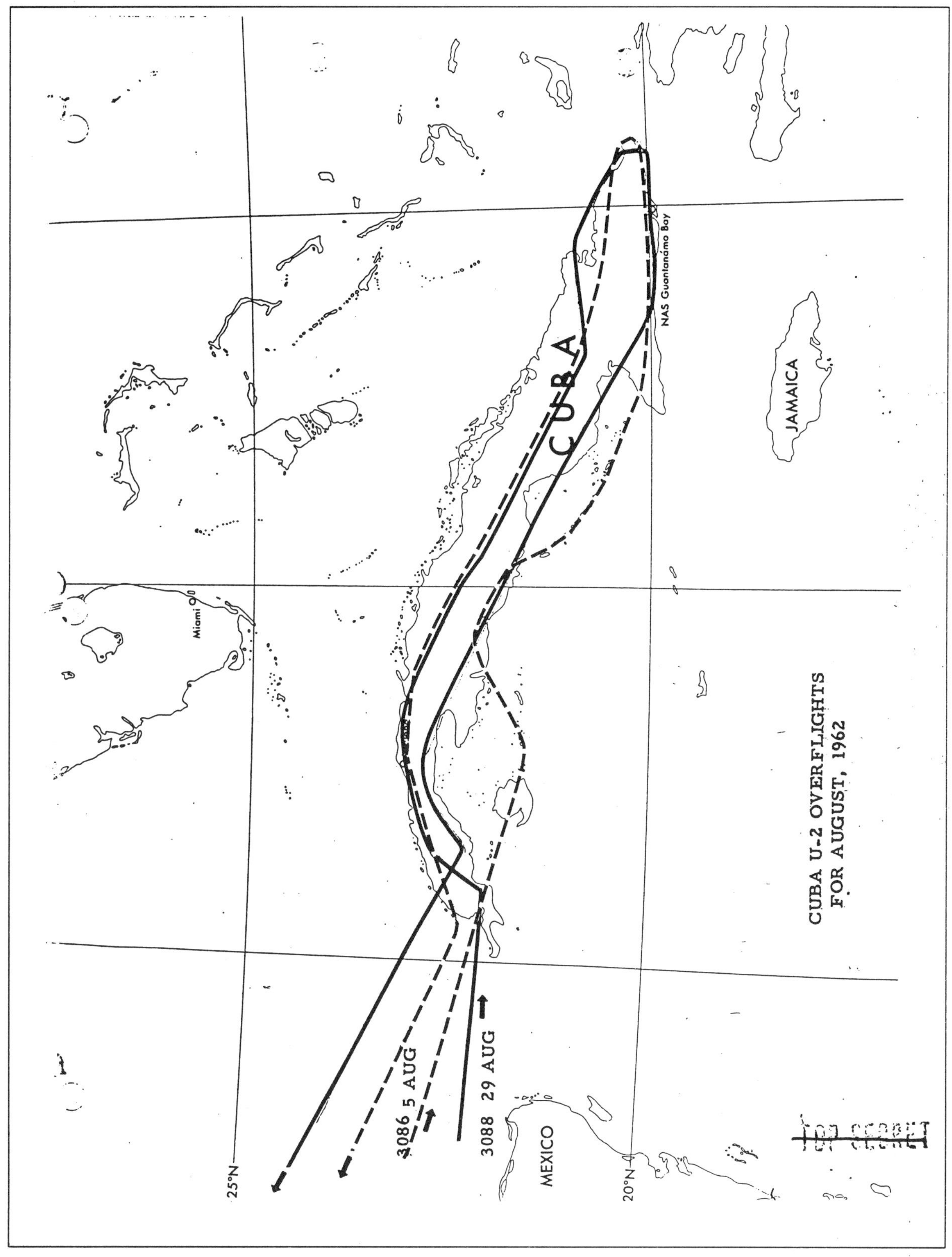

1. *(Continued)*

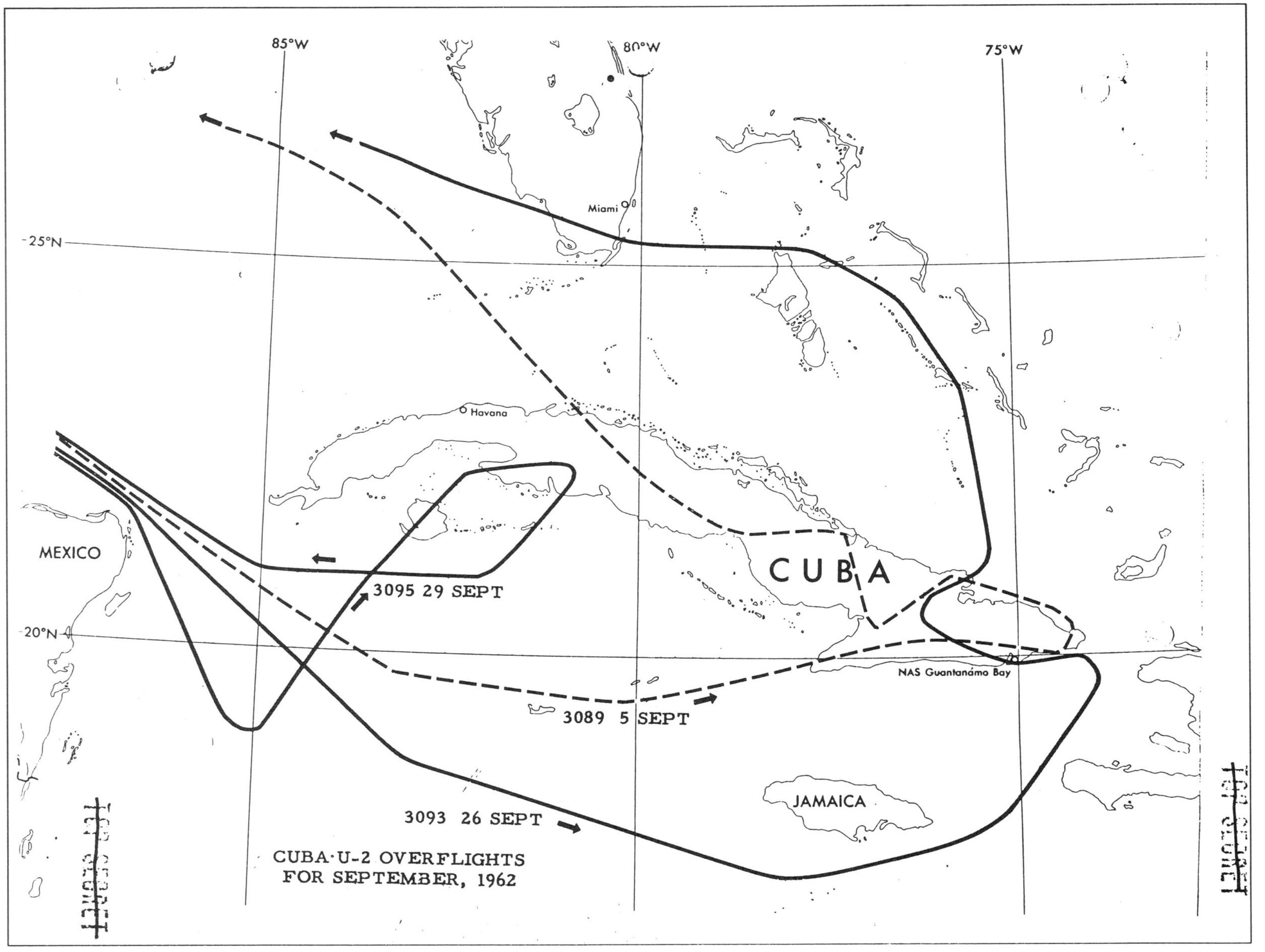
TOP SECRET
85°W
80°W
75°W
25°N
20°N
Miami
Havana
MEXICO
CUBA
NAS Guantanamo Bay
3095 29 SEPT
3089 5 SEPT
JAMAICA
3093 26 SEPT
CUBA·U-2 OVERFLIGHTS
FOR SEPTEMBER, 1962
TOP SECRET

1. *(Continued)*

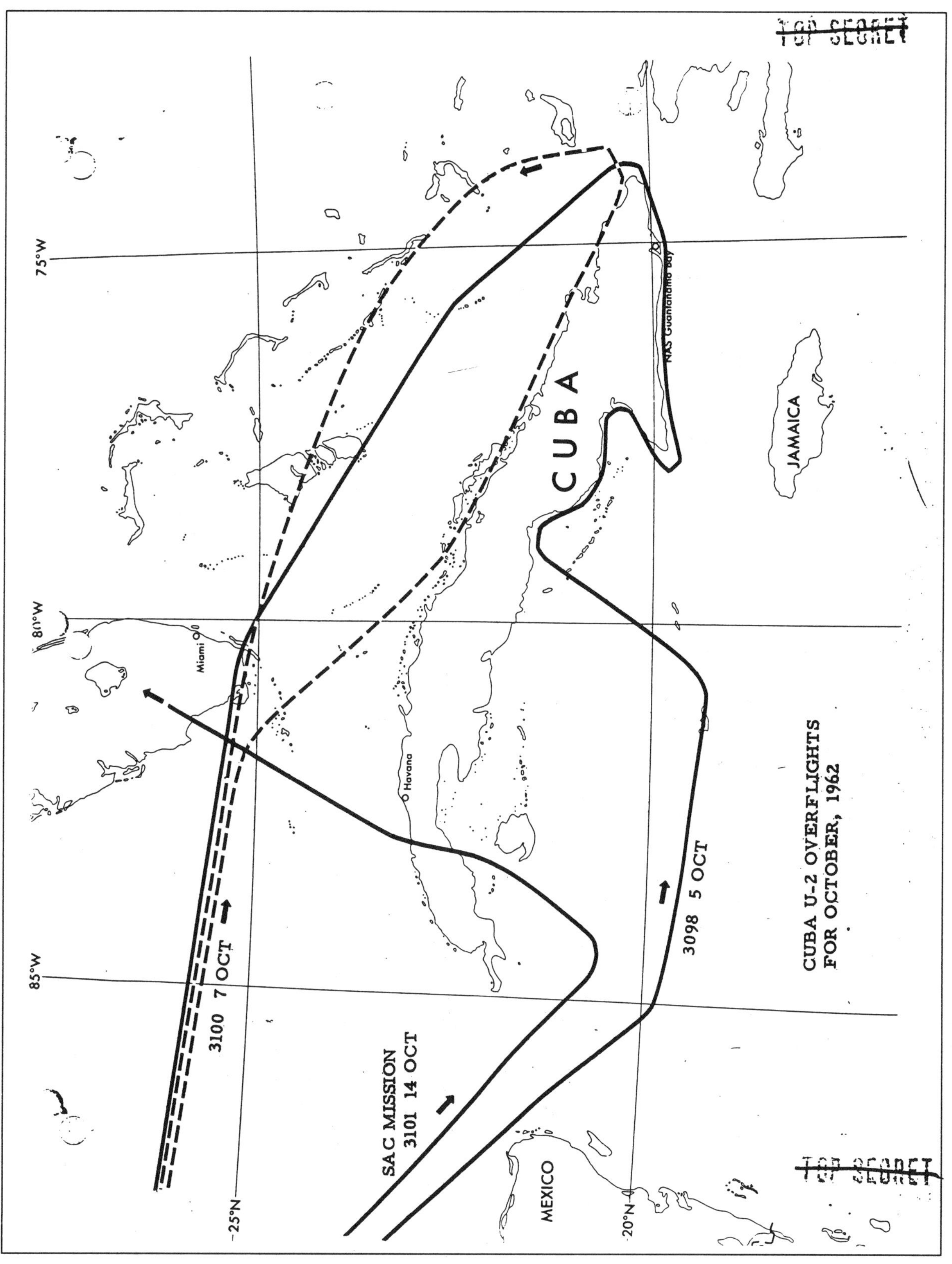

TOP SECRET
75°W
80°W
85°W
25°N
20°N
Miami
Havana
CUBA
NAS Guantanamo Bay
JAMAICA
MEXICO
3100 7 OCT
SAC MISSION
3101 14 OCT
3098 5 OCT
CUBA U-2 OVERFLIGHTS
FOR OCTOBER, 1962
TOP SECRET

1. *(Continued)*

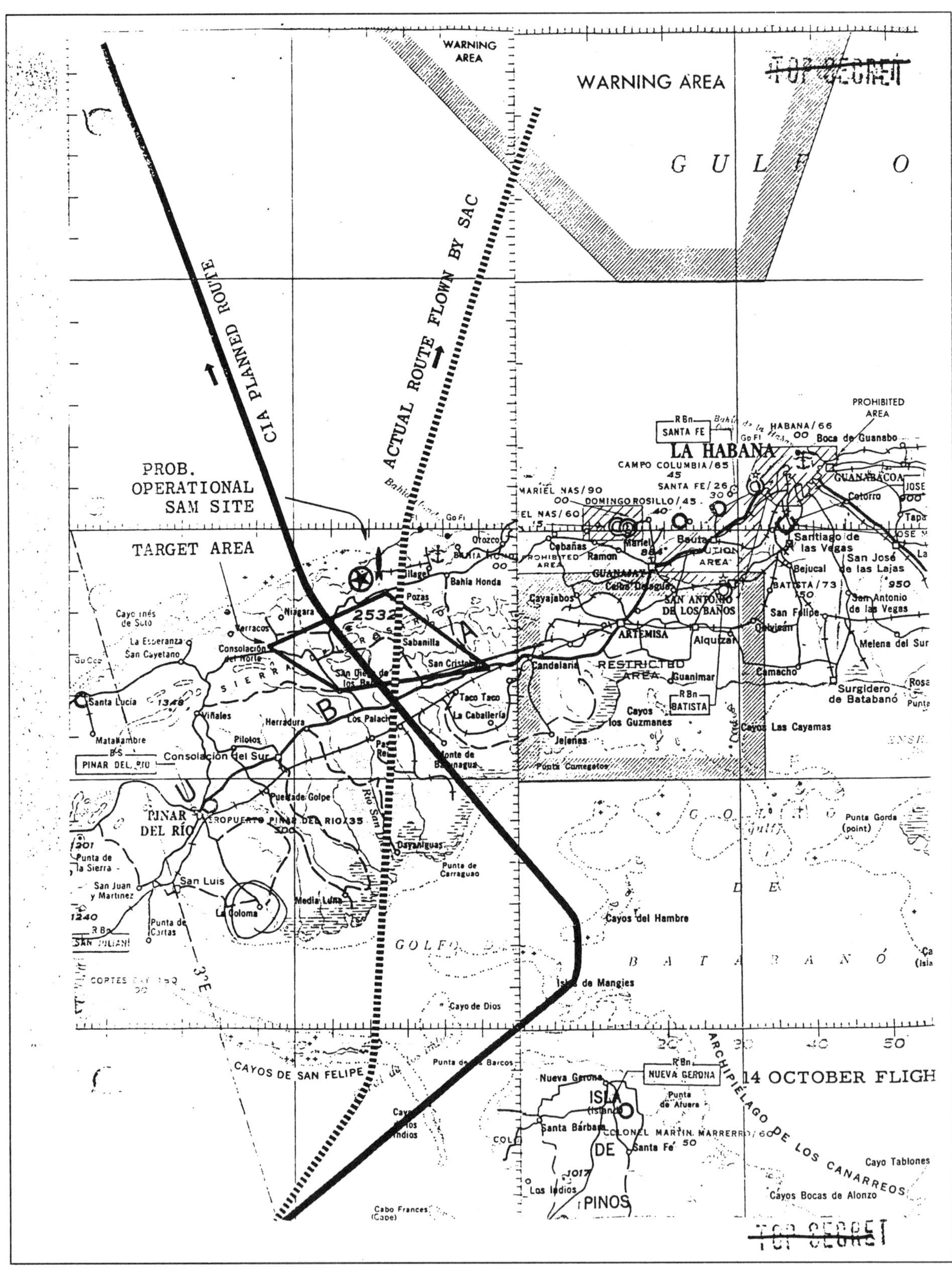
WARNING AREA
WARNING AREA
TOP SECRET
G U L F O
CIA PLANNED ROUTE
ACTUAL ROUTE FLOWN BY SAC
PROB. OPERATIONAL SAM SITE
TARGET AREA
PROHIBITED AREA
LA HABANA
HABANA/66
CAMPO COLUMBIA/65
SANTA FE/26
MARIEL NAS/90
DOMINGO ROSILLO/45
SANTA FE
GUANABACOA
RESTRICTED AREA
ARTEMISA
PINAR DEL RIO
BATISTA
2532
NUEVA GERONA
14 OCTOBER FLIGH
ARCHIPIÉLAGO DE LOS CANARREOS
TOP SECRET

1. *(Continued)*

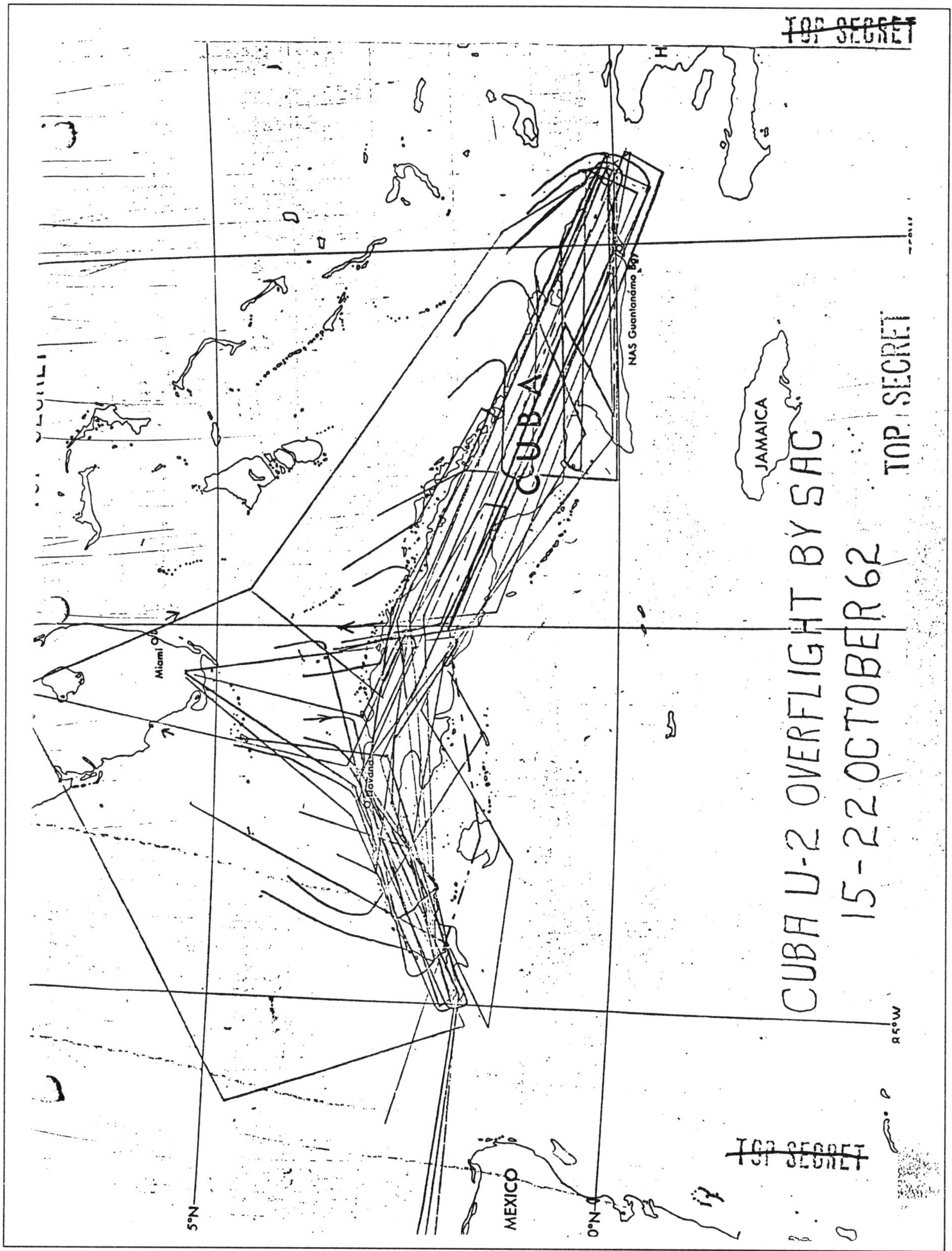
TOP SECRET
CUBA U-2 OVERFLIGHT BY SAC
15-22 OCTOBER 62
TOP SECRET
CUBA
JAMAICA
NAS Guantanamo Bay
Miami
Havana
MEXICO
TOP SECRET

2. *Timetable of Soviet Military Buildup in Cuba, July-October 1962*

~~SECRET~~

TAB A
SECTION II

TIMETABLE OF SOVIET MILITARY BUILD-UP IN CUBA

(July - October 1962)
(All dates approximate)

Date	Western Cuba	Central Cuba	Eastern Cuba
25-31 July	Upsurge of Soviet arms shipments begins arriving in western Cuban ports.		
1-5 August	Construction begins on SAM sites at Matanzas, Havana, Mariel, Bahia Honda, Santa Lucia, San Julian, & La Coloma.		
5-10 August			
10-15 August			
15-20 August	Soviet armored groups arrive at Santiago de las Vegas and Artemisa.	Upsurge of Soviet arms shipments begins arriving in central Cuban ports.	
20-25 August		Construction begins on SAM site at Cienfuegos.	
25-31 August			
1-5 September	Construction begins on Guanajay IRBM sites.	Construction begins on SAM sites at Saguá la Grande, Caibarien, & Sancti Spiritus.	

~~SECRET~~

2. *(Continued)*

~~SECRET~~

Date	Western Cuba	Central Cuba	Eastern Cuba
5-10 September		Soviet armored group arrives at Remedios.	
10-15 September			
15-20 September	Construction begins at San Cristobal MRBM sites.	Construction begins at Remedios IRBM site.	Upsurge of Soviet arms shipments begins arriving in eastern Cuban ports. Soviet armored group arrives at Holguin.
20-25 September			Construction begins on SAM sites at Los Angeles, Chaparra and Jiguani.
25-30 September		Construction begins at Sagua la Grande MRBM sites.	Construction begins on SAM sites at Manati, Senado, and Manzanillo.

NOTE: Construction of the remaining SAM sites, which apparently were considered less vital than those listed above to the protection of offensive missile bases in Cuba, began in late September or early October. Work probably began on the SAM site at Siguanea on the Isle of Pines in the last week of September and on the sites at Esmeralda, Chambas, Maldonado, Santiago de Cuba, Ciego de Avila, and Deleite during the first half of October.

~~SECRET~~

3. *National Intelligence Estimate 85-2-62, "The Situation and Prospects in Cuba," 1 August 1962 (Excerpt)*

~~SECRET~~

NATIONAL INTELLIGENCE ESTIMATE

NUMBER 85–2–62

The Situation and Prospects in Cuba

1 August 1962

~~SECRET~~

3. *(Continued)*

SECRET

THE SITUATION AND PROSPECTS IN CUBA[1]

THE PROBLEM

To analyze the situation in Cuba and to estimate the prospects over the next year or so, with particular reference to Castro's relations with the Communists and to the potential for resistance to his regime.

CONCLUSIONS

A. Fidel Castro has asserted his primacy in Cuban communism; the "old" Communists have had to accommodate themselves to this fact, as has the USSR. Further strains may develop in these relationships, but they are unlikely to break the ties of mutual interest between Castro and the "old" Communists and between Cuba and the USSR. *(Paras. 1–10)*

B. By force of circumstances, the USSR is becoming ever more deeply committed to preserve and strengthen the Castro regime. The USSR, however, has avoided any formal commitment to protect and defend the regime in all contingencies. *(Para. 11)*

C. The Cuban armed forces are loyal to the personal leadership of the Castro brothers. Their capabilities have been and are being greatly enhanced by the Soviet Bloc's provision of military equipment and instruction. Cuban military capabilities, however, are essentially defensive. We believe it unlikely that the Bloc will provide Cuba with the capability to undertake major independent military operations

[1] This estimate is designed to bring up-to-date NIE 85–62, "The Situation and Prospects in Cuba," dated 21 March 1962. The background information contained in that document remains generally valid.

SECRET

3. *(Continued)*

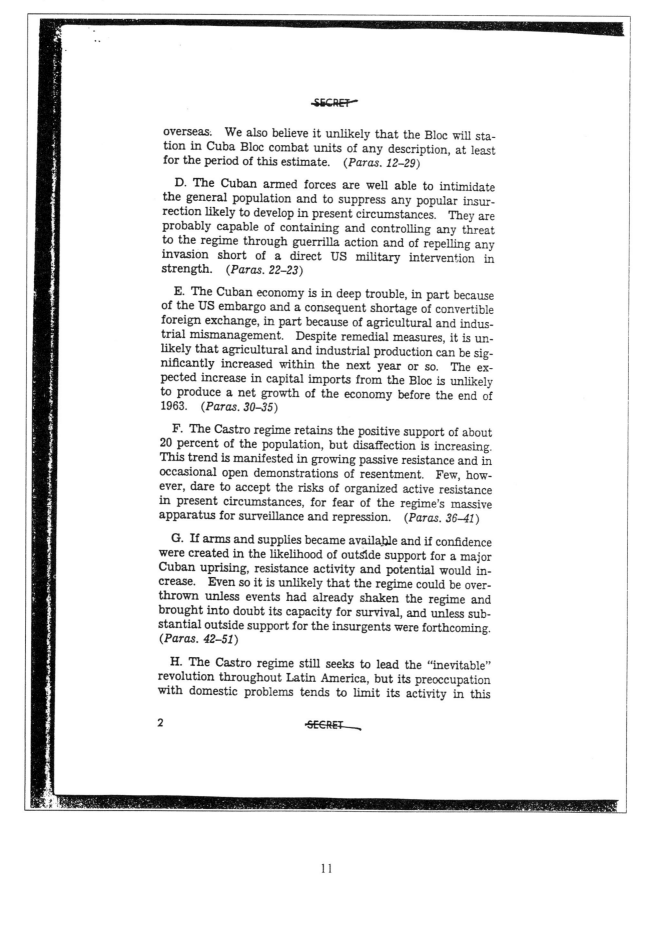

overseas. We also believe it unlikely that the Bloc will station in Cuba Bloc combat units of any description, at least for the period of this estimate. (*Paras. 12–29*)

D. The Cuban armed forces are well able to intimidate the general population and to suppress any popular insurrection likely to develop in present circumstances. They are probably capable of containing and controlling any threat to the regime through guerrilla action and of repelling any invasion short of a direct US military intervention in strength. (*Paras. 22–23*)

E. The Cuban economy is in deep trouble, in part because of the US embargo and a consequent shortage of convertible foreign exchange, in part because of agricultural and industrial mismanagement. Despite remedial measures, it is unlikely that agricultural and industrial production can be significantly increased within the next year or so. The expected increase in capital imports from the Bloc is unlikely to produce a net growth of the economy before the end of 1963. (*Paras. 30–35*)

F. The Castro regime retains the positive support of about 20 percent of the population, but disaffection is increasing. This trend is manifested in growing passive resistance and in occasional open demonstrations of resentment. Few, however, dare to accept the risks of organized active resistance in present circumstances, for fear of the regime's massive apparatus for surveillance and repression. (*Paras. 36–41*)

G. If arms and supplies became available and if confidence were created in the likelihood of outside support for a major Cuban uprising, resistance activity and potential would increase. Even so it is unlikely that the regime could be overthrown unless events had already shaken the regime and brought into doubt its capacity for survival, and unless substantial outside support for the insurgents were forthcoming. (*Paras. 42–51*)

H. The Castro regime still seeks to lead the "inevitable" revolution throughout Latin America, but its preoccupation with domestic problems tends to limit its activity in this

3. *(Continued)*

~~SECRET~~

respect. In Latin America there is widespread disillusionment regarding the Cuban revolution. Nevertheless, militant pro-Castro groups exist in several countries, and Cuban subversive activity could prove effective in certain unstable situations: e.g., in Guatemala or Venezuela. The appeal of the Cuban example will increase in Latin America if reform lags there and hopes and promises remain unfulfilled. (*Paras. 52–59*)

~~SECRET~~ 3

4. *John A. McCone, Memorandum, "Soviet MRBMs in Cuba," 31 October 1962*

~~TOP SECRET~~

#107

31 October 1962

MEMORANDUM

SUBJECT: Soviet MRBMs in Cuba

1. On August 10th at a meeting in Secretary Rusk's Conference Room attended by Rusk, Johnson, McNamara, Gilpatric, Bundy, Gen. Taylor and a number of others for the purpose of discussing General Lansdale's Phase II activities, McCone reported on the sudden importation of materiel -- at that time the characteristics of which was unidentified -- and Soviet personnel, and at that meeting speculated that this could be electronic equipment for use against Canavarel and/or military equipment including medium range ballistic missiles.

2. On August 21st at a meeting in Secretary Rusk's office attended by the same group, McCone again reviewed the situation as it developed since August 10th, reported definite information on surface to air missiles and again speculated on the probability of medium range ballistic missiles.

3. On August 22nd McCone gave the same information to the President, adding certain details concerning the number of Soviet and Chinese personnel who had recently entered Cuba as reported by [redacted] who had just returned from Havana.

4. On August 23rd in a meeting with the President, Rusk, McNamara, Gilpatric, General Taylor, Bundy and others, McCone again reviewed the situation and questioned the need for the extensive SAM installations unless they were to make possible the concealment of MRBMs.

5. The same reasoning was applied in discussions with Senator Russell's Subcommittees, Chairman Vinson's Subcommittee and in private talk with Chairman Cannon prior to McCone's departure on August 23rd.

6. On Saturday, August 25th, McCone urged General Carter, Acting DCI, to propose low level R 101 flights over certain Soviet-Cuban installations in order to obtain detailed technical information.

~~TOP SECRET~~

TOP SECRET

7. On September 7th, McCone wired General Carter as follows:

> "Question very much if C-package will be helpful Cuba and urge frequent repeat missions of recent reconnaissance operations which Gilpatric advises informative. Also I support use of R-101 if necessary. My hunch is we might face prospect of Soviet short-range surface-to-surface missiles of portable type in Cuba which could command important targets of southeast United States and possibly Latin American Caribbean areas. You might suggest to Rusk that we develop joint policies for action in Cuba with selected Caribbean, South-American states as an alternative to seeking unanimous OAS action which most certainly will be an ineffective compromise solution if past history is any indicator."

8. On September 10th McCone wired Carter [redacted] as follows:

> "Difficult for me to rationalize extensive costly defenses being established in Cuba as such extreme costly measures to accomplish security and secrecy not consistent with other policies such as refugees, legal travel, etc. Appears to me quite possible measures now being taken are for purpose of insuring secrecy of some offensive capability such as MRBMs to be installed by Soviets after present phase completed and country secured from overflights. Suggest BNE study motives behind these defensive measures which even seem to exceed those provided most satellites."

9. On September 13th McCone received communication from Carter stating that the BNE continued to feel that the installation of SA 2s is most reasonably explained by other than a desire to hide MRBM build-up. To this McCone responded on September 13th as follows:

> "Also I continue to be concerned that the establishment of defensive equipment and installations is merely a prelude to the location of an offensive weapon capability and once this is done the implementation of

- 2 -

TOP SECRET

~~TOP SECRET~~

our policy as reported in the press might be extremely difficult and involve unacceptable dangers. I would like to talk with you on [redacted] from Norstad's headquarters to the White House or Pentagon situation room tonight (13 Sept.) between 1700 and 1800 your time. Unless I hear to the contrary from you by twelve noon today your time I will proceed Paris this evening and make arrangements for this call."

10. On September 16th McCone cabled Carter as follows:

"Also believe we must carefully study the prospect of secret importation and placement of several Soviet MRBMs which could not be detected by us if Cuban defenses deny overflight. In reflecting on my observations of Thor installation in Britain and Jupiters in Italy I can envisage a Soviet plan to package missile, control and operating equipment in such a way that a unit could be made operational a few hours after a site cleared and a modest concrete pad poured. Do not wish to be overly alarming this matter but believe CIA and community must keep government informed of danger of a surprise and also that detection of preparatory steps possibly beyond our capbbility once Cuban defense system operative. Thrust of press reports reaching me is that there exists a clear demarcation between defensive and offensive preparations and I question if we can be sure of this. I recognize Cuban policy decisions most delicate and beyond Agency or my competence. However believe we must give those making decision our best estimate of possible developments and alternative situations which might evolve and unexpectedly confront us.

11. On 19 September Carter communicated the summary of the conclusions of Cuban SNIE of that date, paragraph D stating that in the opinion of the BNE, establishment of MRBMs in Cuba would be

- 3 -

~~TOP SECRET~~

incompatible with Soviet policy -- and indicate a greater willingness to increase risk in US/Soviet relations than the Soviet Union has displayed so far--.

12. On September 20th McCone responded as follows:

> "Ref DIR 37228: Suggest most careful consideration to conclusion last sentence paragraph d. As an alternative I can see that an offensive Soviet Cuban base will provide Soviets with most important and effective trading position in connection with all other critical areas and hence they might take an unexpected risk in order to establish such a position."

13. It is reported that during McCone's absence, Acting DCI, at a meeting held in Mr. Bundy's office on 10 September, proposed an overflight which would cover the entire north and south perimeter of Cuba east of Havana and out to the eastern tip of Oriente Province except for an area in the immediate vicinity of Santa Clara where four SAM sites were known to exist and had been photographed. The purpose of this flight was to make a final determination as to how many SAM sites existed or were under construction. It is reported that because of Rusk's concern for the safety of the U-2 in view of the Sakolin violation on 7 September and the ChiNat loss on 10 September, the sense of the meeting (particularly that of Secretary Rusk) that CIA be permitted to make 4 flights against Cuba, two peripheral and two overflights of limited penetration, including the Isle of Pines. These flights were executed between 26 September and 7 October. On the 14th of September the meeting of the Special Group, JCS representative outlined capabilities for low level coverage. Secretary of Defense indicated he did not wish this operation considered until the results were obtained from CIA reconnaissance as approved on September 11th.

14. On October 4th McCone noted to the Special Group that there had been no coverage of the center of Cuba and more particularly the entire western end of the Island for over a month, and all flights since 5 September had been either peripheral or limited and therefore CIA did not know, nor could advise, whether an offensive capability was being created. DCI objected strenuously to the limitations which had been placed on overflights and there arose a considerable discussion (with some heat) as to whether limitations had or had not been placed on CIA by the Special Group. [redacted] were requested

- 4 -

4. *(Continued)*

TOP SECRET

to prepare a comprehensive plan for aerial survey of Cuba and to submit the plan at a meeting scheduled for Tuesday, October 9th.

15. On 9 October Special Group (Augmented) met. Reviewed [redacted] JCS proposals and it was agreed that a U-2 flight flying from south to north across the western part of Cuba where at least two SAM sites were known to exist should be undertaken promptly and that a number of similar sorties might be mounted if this flight did not activate ground-air fire. (Higher authority approved this one mission and left consideration of further missions until the results of the approved mission were determined.)

16. This mission was flown on October 14th. It was successful and encountered no resistance. On October 15th at a Special Meeting (and prior to receipt of the results of the October 14th flight), two additional U-2 missions to cover all of Cuba were approved and this was concurred in by higher authority.

JOHN A. McCONE
Director

- 5 -

TOP SECRET

5. *[McCone], "Memorandum on Cuba," 20 August 1962*

84

SECRET

August 20, 1962

MEMORANDUM ON CUBA

The Soviet -- and probably bloc -- support of Cuba was stepped up in July and August. 21 ships docked in July and 17 have docked, or are en route, in August, 5 of which are passenger ships.

CIA has received approximately 60 reports on this increased activity; 40 out of Opa Locka, and the balance from controlled sources considered dependable.

It appears that between 4000 and 6000 Soviet/Bloc personnel have arrived in Cuba since 1 July. Many are known to be technicians, some are suspected to be military personnel; there is no evidence of organized Soviet military units, as such, being included. A great many of the arriving Soviet/Bloc personnel are isolated from the Cuban population.

The unloading of most ships takes place under maximum security, with the Cuban population excluded from the port areas. Large equipment is noticeable; large crates have been observed which could contain airplane fuselages or missile components.

SECRET

5. *(Continued)*

~~SECRET~~

Sophisticated electronic and radar gear has been identified. In some instances trucks or trailers have been lowered into ships holds, loaded, covered with tarpaulins and removed bodily.

The implications are:

(a) Increased technical assistance to Cuban industry and agriculture and/or the Cuban Armed Forces.

(b) Possible establishment of surface to air (SAM) missile sites.

(c) Possible establishment of Soviet COMINT-ELINT facilities targetted against Canaveral and other important U. S. installations.

The timing of this buildup coincides with Raoul Castro's trip to Moscow and this may in itself be significant.

JAM/at:ji

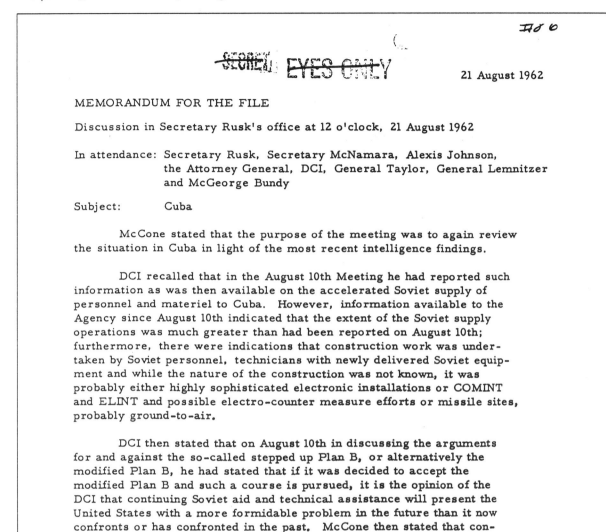

6. McCone, Memorandum for the File, "Discussion in Secretary Rusk's Office at 12 o'clock, 21 August 1962"

~~HS~~ 6

21 August 1962

MEMORANDUM FOR THE FILE

Discussion in Secretary Rusk's office at 12 o'clock, 21 August 1962

In attendance: Secretary Rusk, Secretary McNamara, Alexis Johnson, the Attorney General, DCI, General Taylor, General Lemnitzer and McGeorge Bundy

Subject: Cuba

McCone stated that the purpose of the meeting was to again review the situation in Cuba in light of the most recent intelligence findings.

DCI recalled that in the August 10th Meeting he had reported such information as was then available on the accelerated Soviet supply of personnel and materiel to Cuba. However, information available to the Agency since August 10th indicated that the extent of the Soviet supply operations was much greater than had been reported on August 10th; furthermore, there were indications that construction work was undertaken by Soviet personnel, technicians with newly delivered Soviet equipment and while the nature of the construction was not known, it was probably either highly sophisticated electronic installations or COMINT and ELINT and possible electro-counter measure efforts or missile sites, probably ground-to-air.

DCI then stated that on August 10th in discussing the arguments for and against the so-called stepped up Plan B, or alternatively the modified Plan B, he had stated that if it was decided to accept the modified Plan B and such a course is pursued, it is the opinion of the DCI that continuing Soviet aid and technical assistance will present the United States with a more formidable problem in the future than it now confronts or has confronted in the past. McCone then stated that conclusive evidence indicated such a stepped-up Soviet effort.

DCI then read 21 August paper entitled, "Recent Soviet Military Aid to Cuba" as prepared by DD/I. He then referred to 21 August paper of the office of National Estimates, subject, "Soviet View of the Cuban Economy" emphasizing the conclusion that under energetic Soviet direction, the potential of the Cuban agricultural, industrial and natural resources could be so developed that the economy would be reasonably viable and over a decade might even earn sufficiently from export surpluses to repay credits and advances already made to Cuba by the Soviet Union. Therefore, the CIA's conclusion that Soviet economists in analyzing Cuba

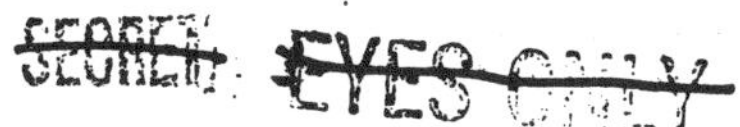

6. *(Continued)*

~~SECRET~~ ~~EYES ONLY~~

would conclude that in supporting Cuba the Soviets were not involving themselves with a permanent liability; furthermore, there was an opportunity of creating a viable and reasonably prosperous economy which, while not a showcase, would always be an annoyance to the United States and a model for all dissident groups in Latin America.

DCI then referred to the 15th August paper of the Board of National Estimates, subject, "The Soviet Stake in Cuba" and read the summary of this paper which is in numbered paragraph 7, page 3.

In support of the above DCI then briefly reviewed a chronology of unevaluated reports on recent Soviet military aid to Cuba, 21 August, and noted my reference to maps; location of the reported activities.

There was general agreement that the situation was critical and that the most dynamic action was indicated.

There was discussion of various courses of action open to us in case the Soviets place MRBM missiles on Cuban territory. There was also discussion of blockades of Soviet and Bloc shipping into Cuba or alternatively a total blockade of Cuba.

Throughout these discussions, it was abundantly clear that in the minds of State, and Mr. Bundy, speaking for the White House, there is a very definite inter-relationship between Cuba and other trouble spots, such as Berlin. It was felt that a blockade of Cuba would automatically bring about a blockade of Berlin; that drastic action on a missile site or other military installation of the Soviets in Cuba would bring about similar action by the Soviets with respect to our bases and numerous missile sites, particularly Turkey and southern Italy. Also, there is a reluctance, as previously, to the commitment of military forces because of the task involved and also because of retaliatory actions of the Soviets elsewhere throughout the world.

McNamara expressed strong feelings that we should take every possible aggressive action in the fields of intelligence, sabotage and guerrilla warfare, utilizing Cubans and do such other things as might be indicated to divide the Castro regime. McCone pointed out that all of these things could be done. Efforts to date with agent teams had been disappointing. Sabotage activities were planned on a priority basis and in all probability, we would witness more failures than successes. To date we had experienced a very tight internal security situation and probably this would become more so in the future.

- 2 -

6. *(Continued)*

~~SECRET~~ ~~EYES ONLY~~

The Attorney General queried the meeting as to what other aggressive steps could be taken, questioning the feasibility of provoking an action against Guantanamo which would permit us to retaliate, or involving a third country in some way.

It was Mr. Bundy's opinion that all overt actions would involve serious consequences throughout the world and therefore our operations must be covert at this time, although we should expect a high degree of attribution.

The meeting was inconclusive with respect to any particular course of action. It was felt that the President should be informed on the evolving situation and the DCI agreed to brief him at the Meeting on Wednesday, August 22nd at 6 o'clock.

We further agreed that the entire matter should be reviewed with the President by Rusk, McNamara, Bundy and McCone. Mr. Bundy undertook to arrange for this meeting following the Special Meeting scheduled for ten o'clock on Thursday, August 23rd.

Following this discussion, there was a brief discussion of the Donovan matter as covered in DCI's memorandum to Rusk and the Attorney General, copy of which is attached. It was agreed that Mr. Hurwitz would meet with Mr. Donovan on Thursday, together with the Attorney General, and determine the extent of the commitment we would make for the government which would permit Mr. Donovan to engage in the prisoner release negotiations. DCI made it abundantly clear that the existing commitments to Committees of the Congress prevented CIA from using covert resources for this purpose.

McCone stated that in view of these commitments to the Congress he did not feel that he should meet with Mr. Donovan. Furthermore, that McCone stated that he felt that if a reasonable deal could be made for the release of the prisoners, the Committees of Congress would change the view expressed a year ago at the time of the tractor negotiation.

John A. McCone
Director

JAM:ji

~~SECRET~~ ~~EYES ONLY~~

7. *McCone, "Memorandum of the Meeting with the President at 6:00 p.m., on August 22, 1962"*

~~SECRET~~, ~~EYES ONLY~~

#35

22 August 1962

MEMORANDUM OF THE MEETING WITH THE PRESIDENT
at 6:00 p. m., on August 22, 1962

Attendance: General Taylor

The following points were covered:

~~SECRET~~, ~~EYES ONLY~~

7. *(Continued)*

SECRET, ~~EYES ONLY~~

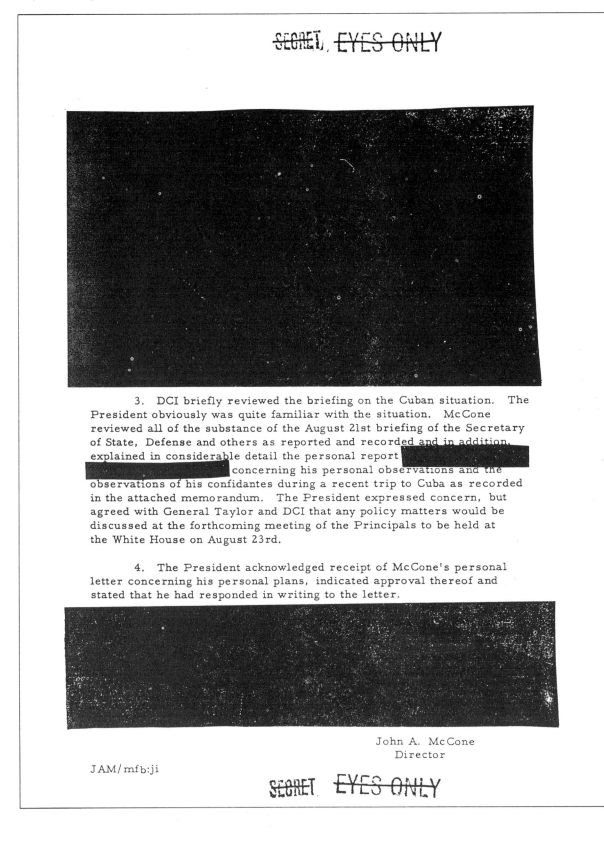

3. DCI briefly reviewed the briefing on the Cuban situation. The President obviously was quite familiar with the situation. McCone reviewed all of the substance of the August 21st briefing of the Secretary of State, Defense and others as reported and recorded and in addition, explained in considerable detail the personal report [redacted] concerning his personal observations and the observations of his confidantes during a recent trip to Cuba as recorded in the attached memorandum. The President expressed concern, but agreed with General Taylor and DCI that any policy matters would be discussed at the forthcoming meeting of the Principals to be held at the White House on August 23rd.

4. The President acknowledged receipt of McCone's personal letter concerning his personal plans, indicated approval thereof and stated that he had responded in writing to the letter.

John A. McCone
Director

JAM/mfb:ji

SECRET ~~EYES ONLY~~

8. *McCone, "Memorandum of Meeting with the President," 23 August 1962*

23 August 1962

Memorandum of Meeting with the President

Attended by Secretaries Rusk, McNamara, Gilpatric, General Taylor, Mr. Bundy, McCone

Subject: Cuba

1. McCone advised that President had been briefed on the Cuban situation but added the information given [redacted]

Rusk advocated informing Canadians and all NATO allies of growing seriousness of situation; also advocated removal of restrictions on use of Guantanamo by the Lansdale group.

ACTION: This point not cleared and should be pursued as strongly opposed by Chiefs.

2. The President requested a continuing analysis of the number and type of Soviet and Oriental personnel imported into Cuba; quantity and type of equipment and its probable use; all construction - particularly anxious to know whether construction involved SAM sites might differ from the ground sites. McCone stated we probably could not differentiate between surface-to-air and 350 mile ground-to-ground offensive missile. McNamara observed portable ground missiles could not be located under any circumstances.

ACTION: DDCI should have Board of National Estimates working continuously on this analysis.

8. *(Continued)*

SECRET EYES ONLY

3. President requested analysis of the danger to the United States and the effect on Latin America of missile installations.

ACTION: DDCI should arrange for preparation of such estimates.

4. President raised the question of whether we should make a statement in advance of our position, should the Soviets install missiles and the alternative actions open to us in such event. In the course of the discussion, apparent many in the room related action in Cuba to Soviet actions in Turkey, Greece, Berlin, Far East and elsewhere. McCone questioned value of Jupiter missiles in Turkey and Italy. McNamara agreed they were useless but difficult politically to remove them.

5. ACTION: He agreed to study this possibility.

President raised question of what we could do against Soviet missile sites in Cuba. Could we take them out by air or would a ground offensive be necessary or alternatively could they be destroyed by a substantial guerrilla effort.

6. President raised question of what we should do in Cuba if Soviets precipated a Berlin crisis. This is the alternative to the proposition of what Soviets would do in Berlin if we moved in Cuba.

7. During the conversation I raised substance of my plan of action as outlined in the attached paper. There was no disagreement that we must solve the ~~Berlin~~ Cuba problem. However, we should not start the political action and propaganda effort now until we had decided on the policy of following through to the complete solution of the Cuban problem.

- 2 -

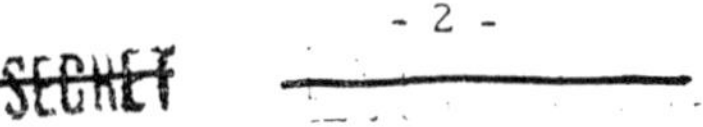
SECRET

8. *(Continued)*

~~SECRET~~ ~~EYES ONLY~~

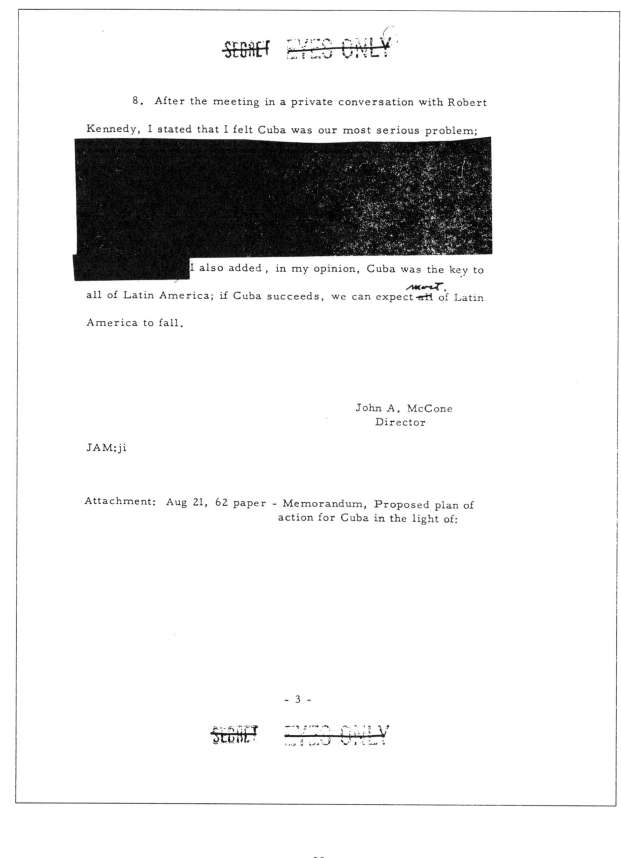

8. After the meeting in a private conversation with Robert Kennedy, I stated that I felt Cuba was our most serious problem; I also added, in my opinion, Cuba was the key to all of Latin America; if Cuba succeeds, we can expect ~~all~~ most of Latin America to fall.

John A. McCone
Director

JAM:ji

Attachment: Aug 21, 62 paper - Memorandum, Proposed plan of action for Cuba in the light of:

- 3 -

~~SECRET~~ ~~EYES ONLY~~

9. *J.A.M. [McCone], Memorandum, "Proposed Plan of Action for Cuba," 21 August 1962 (originally attached to Document 8)*

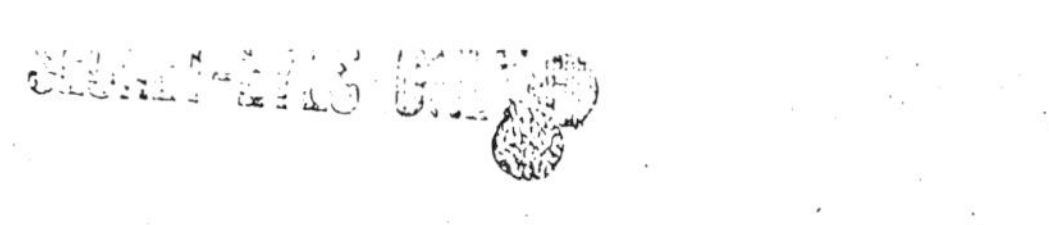

August 21, 1962

MEMORANDUM:

Proposed plan of action for Cuba in the light of:

(a) The arrival of four to five thousand Soviet/Bloc technicians and possibly military personnel during July-August.

(b) Arrival of many ship loads of equipment and materiel during July and August.

(c) The conclusion that stepped up plan (b) will not, in the opinion of the National Board of Estimates, accomplish the stated purpose of overthrowing Castro from within, and moreover will be attributable to the United States and cause loss of face by the United States, and

(d) Modified plan (b) will contribute importantly to our intelligence gathering and will impede Castro regime's economic progress but will not be sufficient to frustrate the regime's progress in view of the evidences of substantial Soviet technical assistance.

The above all lead to the conclusion that with the passage of time, it is possible there will evolve in Cuba a stronger rather than a weaker Castro dominated communist state, fully oriented to Moscow, to serve on the one hand as a model for similar actions by disciplined groups throughout Latin America, and on the other as a bridgehead for Soviet subversive activities in Central and South America. Being dominated by Moscow, such a Cuba would also serve as a possible location for MRBMs, for COMINT and ELINT facilities targetted against United States activities, most particularly Canaveral, and finally as an ECM station which might adversely affect our space and missile work.

Therefore it seems to me a more aggressive action is indicated than any heretofore considered, and should be patterned along the following lines:

9. *(Continued)*

(1) An immediate continuing aggressive political action designed to awaken and alarm all of Latin America and all of the free world as to the extreme dangers inherent in the present Cuban situation.

Appropriate actions should be taken through domestic and foreign press media to inform and alarm the people, through the United Nations, through the Organization of American States and its subcommittees, by contact with each free world country at the level of head of state, foreign minister and ambassador, and through semi-public or private organizations such as labor, church, farm cooperatives, youth groups, et cetera.

(3) The instanteous commitment of sufficient armed forces to occupy the country, destroy the regime, free the people, and establish in Cuba a peaceful country which will be a member of the community of American states.

It is possible, though in my opinion improbable, that actions taken under (1) above would in themselves be sufficient to cause destruction of the Castro regime from dissension and disaffections within the regime itself which would obviate steps (2) or (3).

Alternatively, actions under (1) above might cause internal strife of sufficient proportion to prompt the action outlined under (3) above with no further provocation.

Concurrently with this plan, we should go forward with all possible activities called for under plan (b).

J.A.M.

JAM:at

- 2 -

10. *William A. Tidwell, Memorandum for the Record, "Instructions Concerning the Handling of Certain Information Concerning Cuba," 1 September 1962*

~~SECRET~~ Cy#1

1 September 1962

MEMORANDUM FOR THE RECORD

SUBJECT: Instructions Concerning the Handling of Certain Information Concerning Cuba

General Carter called Mr. Cline to say that he had just completed a telephone conversation with the President and that according to the President's instructions the clamps were to remain on the release of certain information concerning Cuba except for the barest minimum access on a need-to-know basis for the purpose of preparing a comprehensive briefing for the President Tuesday morning, 4 September. This instruction was interpreted to permit the release of a single copy of the report concerning Cuba [redacted] to OCI for them to use in preparing the briefing with a deadline of 7:30 a.m. 4 September, and a single copy to State, Army, Navy, Air and DIA. All recipients of these copies to be advised that there is to be no further dissemination except on a minimum need-to-know basis to those people who might need to become involved in the preparation of the briefing for the President. They were also to be advised that no actions were to be taken on the basis of the information.

WILLIAM A. TIDWELL
Assistant to DD/I (Planning)

~~SECRET~~

11. *Ray S. Cline, Memorandum for Acting Director of Central Intelligence, "Recent Soviet Military Activities in Cuba," 3 September 1962*

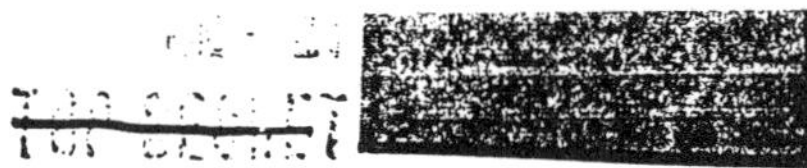

SC-08458-62
3 September 1962

Copy 2 of 3

MEMORANDUM FOR: Acting Director of Central Intelligence

SUBJECT : Recent Soviet Military Activities in Cuba

1. U-2 photography of 29 August confirms extensive Soviet military deliveries to Cuba in recent weeks. Surface-to-air missile (SAM) sites, guided missile boats, and additional land armaments were observed.

2. The photography shows eight SAM sites being set up. One probable assembly area has been identified and SAM equipment has been located at one additional site.

A. The small amount of permanent construction at these sites and the speed of the work indicate the program is proceeding on a crash basis.

B. Some of these sites could be operational within a week or two.

C. A minimum of 125 technically trained personnel will be required to operate each site.

1. This figure excludes security and support personnel.

2. No indications that Cubans are trained for SAMs. Soviet personnel doubtless will man the sites for at least the 9 to 12 months while Cubans are being trained.

3. Additional SAM sites probably will be set up in the near future.

A. All sites now confirmed are in the Western one-third of the island.

1. The one area of SAM activity in Oriente province probably will be followed by several others in the vicinity.

2. Defector and clandestine reports from Las Villas province indicate that at least two sites will be located there, but no confirmation or definite locations thus far.

GROUP 1
Excluded from automatic downgrading and declassification

11. *(Continued)*

SC-084-58-62
Page 2

B. The pattern now emerging suggests as many as 24 sites may eventually be set up -- enough to blanket the entire island.

4. At least 8 Komar-class missile boats have been delivered to Cuba in recent weeks.

A. These PT-like boats carry two missile launchers each, with the radar guided missile effective against surface targets to ranges of between 15 and 17 miles. The missile carries a 2,000 lb. HE warhead.

B. Some Cuban naval personnel have received training in the USSR, but it is not known if this included Komar training.

C. These boats are in addition to 13 or more torpedo boats and 6 submarine chasers delivered by the USSR earlier this year.

5. The photography shows that current deliveries to Cuba also contain land armaments, including tanks and possibly self-propelled guns.

A. Reports indicate other shipments have contained artillery, tanks, and possibly combat aircraft, but these are not confirmed.

B. The photography of 29 August turned up the highest number of MIG aircraft yet noted, some 37.

1. We believe Cuba's aircraft inventory includes approximately 60 MIG jet fighters, including at least a dozen MIG-19s.

2. No MIG-21s or any type of bomber have been noted.

6. Soviet shipments of military equipment and personnel to Cuba show no sign of letting up.

A. About 16 Soviet dry-cargo ships are now en route to Cuba, of which at least 10 probably are carrying military equipment.

11. *(Continued)*

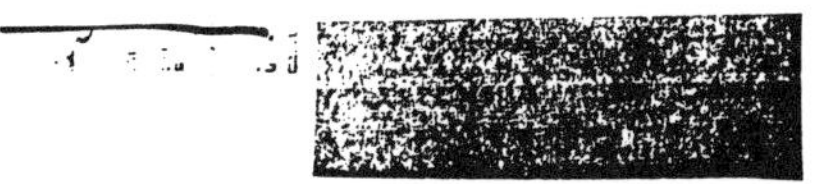

SC-08458-62
Page 3

1. Total number of military or military-related shipments to Cuba since the current deliveries began in mid-July may be as high as 65.

2. Routine Soviet deliveries of economic aid and trade goods are being made largely on Western ships.

B. At least 1,700 Soviet military technicians arrived in Cuba in late July and early August in connection with these military activities.

1. Most of these Soviets appear to be involved in setting up SAM facilities but thus far we cannot conclude that this is their only objective.

C. At least 1,300 more Soviets are arriving unannounced this week; no reports on their activities so far.

1. Still additional bloc personnel probably have arrived on some of the cargo ships.

RAY S. CLINE
Deputy Director (Intelligence)

Annex A Surface-to-Air Missile Deployment in Cuba
Annex B Description of Komar-Class Missile Boat
Annex C Cuba's Air Defense Capabilities
Annex D Sigint Collection
Annex E USSR-Cuban Communique of 2 September

12. *Lyman B. Kirkpatrick, Memorandum for the Director, "Action Generated by DCI Cables Concerning Cuban Low-Level Photography and Offensive Weapons" (n. d.)*

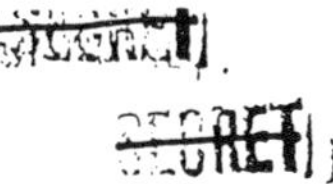

MEMORANDUM FOR THE DIRECTOR

SUBJECT: Action Generated by DCI Cables [redacted] Concerning Cuban Low-Level Photography and Offensive Weapons

1. Based upon your proposal of Saturday, 25 August, that RF-101's be used over Cuba, General Carter asked General Lemnitzer on 27 August about the possibility of low-level photography using RF-101 or F8U aircraft. At that time General Lemnitzer indicated that something probably could be dug up. General Carter informed USIB at the 29 August meeting of his conversation with General Lemnitzer. At the Special Group Meeting the following day, General Lemnitzer raised the issue and said that use of RF -101 or F8U aircraft flown by US pilots would be feasible from the military point of view. General Carter pressed the point by indicating that other types of photography did not give sufficient detail and precise identification of certain types of equipment. After some discussion, the Group agreed to take cognizance of this matter and requested it be reopened at an appropriate time when specific targets and information needs could be identified.

2. On 31 August, after General Carter informed Mr. McGeorge Bundy and General Lemnitzer of the readout of U-2 flights showing SA-2 sites, the President called General Carter at 1300, asked how many people had this information, and told General Carter that he wished it put back in the box and nailed tight. This freeze continued until Saturday, 1 September, when the information was extended slightly further to the working analysts. General Carter informed Secretary Gilpatric on 1 September that the General and Karl Kaysen agreed a full readout was necessary and that some low-altitude flights were needed to pinpoint the sites.

3. Not until Tuesday, 4 September, did the President announce the presence of a missile defense system in Cuba. That day General Carter approved COMOR recommendations: in view of SAM sites on the western end of the island, it was particularly important that the next authorized mission should cover those areas of the island which were not photographed because weather or range did not permit, and that the complex eastern end of the island should be photographed again.

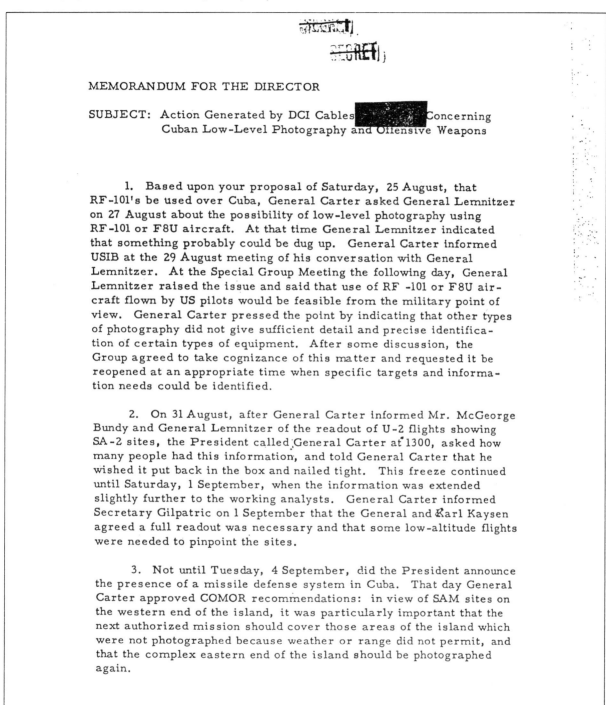

12. *(Continued)*

4. General Carter asked DD/R on 5 September to initiate steps for fixing [redacted] to cover Cuba.

5. The President and Secretaries of State and Defense were briefed by General Carter late 6 September of a more detailed readout of the 29 August mission which led our analysts to suspect the presence of another kind of missile site--possibly surface-to-surface--at Banes. The White House put a complete freeze on this information; however, Bundy gave an OK to put the analysts to work on providing information to the policymakers on a need-to-know basis but without normal distribution.

6. USIB was brought up to date in executive session at its 7 September meeting on information concerning the SA-2 sites, the new unknown site at Banes, and also the freezing atmosphere of the White House. General Carter requested all members to advise their principals and asked also to be alerted immediately if NSA came up with further information.

7. This was the climate in the Community in early September when a U-2 had just violated the Soviet Far East; when another U-2 was lost on 8 September over the Chinese mainland; and when your first cable of 7 September arrived:

> "Question very much if C-package will be helpful Cuba and urge frequent repeat missions of recent reconnaissance operations which Gilpatric advises informative. Also I support use of RF-101's if necessary. My hunch is we might face prospect of Soviet short-range surface-to-surface missiles of portable types in Cuba which could command important targets in Southeast U. S. and possibly Latin America and the Caribbean areas."

8. General Carter, as related above and follows, had already urged use of RF-101's relative to your "hunch" about missiles. General Carter recollects showing your cable to Mr. Bundy the following day, Saturday afternoon. There is no evidence that the information was passed outside of the Agency, presumably because it was a reaffirmation of a position you had already taken before Secretaries Rusk and McNamara, General Taylor and Messrs. Johnson, Gilpatric and Bundy on 10, 21 and 23 August.

-2-

12. *(Continued)*

SECRET

9. On 8 September, upon learning COMOR made Cuba targets available to JRC for possible RF-101 coverage, General Carter instructed Mr. Reber to check with Colonel Steakley to determine when JRC would seek Special Group approval.

10. On 10 September you cabled following 

"Difficult for me to rationalize extensive costly defenses being established in Cuba as such extreme costly measures to accomplish security and secrecy not consistent with other policies such as refugees, legal travel, etc. Appears to me quite possible measures now being taken are for purpose of ensuring secrecy of some offensive capability such as MRBM's to be installed by Soviets after present phase completed and country secured from over-flights. Suggest BNE study motives behind these defensive measures which even seem to exceed those provided most satellites."

General Carter sent an action memorandum on 10 September to the DD/I quoting this passage and asked the BNE to undertake the necessary analysis. BNE's response was sent to you in an 11 September cable. The response said that BNE "still persuaded that costly crash operation to install SA-2's is reasonably explained by other than desire to hide later build-up and the Soviets likely to regard advantage of major offensive build-up not equal to dangers of U. S. intervention."

11. The events of 10 September have already been chronicled in my separate memorandum. However, it was also this date that General Carter sent a memorandum to the Secretary of Defense calling further need to conduct tactical reconnaissance of Cuba, particularly the facility near Banes, indicating that the site would require in the near future photography of a larger scale than acquired by a U-2, and recommending that SecDef initiate necessary action to provide for employment of this tactical-type reconnaissance.

-3-

SECRET

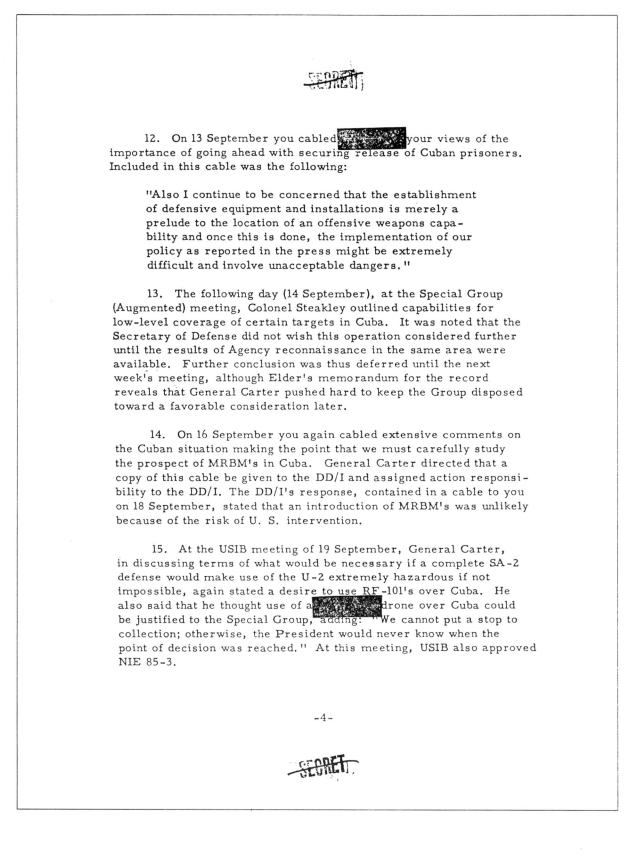

12. On 13 September you cabled [redacted] your views of the importance of going ahead with securing release of Cuban prisoners. Included in this cable was the following:

> "Also I continue to be concerned that the establishment of defensive equipment and installations is merely a prelude to the location of an offensive weapons capability and once this is done, the implementation of our policy as reported in the press might be extremely difficult and involve unacceptable dangers."

13. The following day (14 September), at the Special Group (Augmented) meeting, Colonel Steakley outlined capabilities for low-level coverage of certain targets in Cuba. It was noted that the Secretary of Defense did not wish this operation considered further until the results of Agency reconnaissance in the same area were available. Further conclusion was thus deferred until the next week's meeting, although Elder's memorandum for the record reveals that General Carter pushed hard to keep the Group disposed toward a favorable consideration later.

14. On 16 September you again cabled extensive comments on the Cuban situation making the point that we must carefully study the prospect of MRBM's in Cuba. General Carter directed that a copy of this cable be given to the DD/I and assigned action responsibility to the DD/I. The DD/I's response, contained in a cable to you on 18 September, stated that an introduction of MRBM's was unlikely because of the risk of U. S. intervention.

15. At the USIB meeting of 19 September, General Carter, in discussing terms of what would be necessary if a complete SA-2 defense would make use of the U-2 extremely hazardous if not impossible, again stated a desire to use RF-101's over Cuba. He also said that he thought use of a [redacted] drone over Cuba could be justified to the Special Group, adding: "We cannot put a stop to collection; otherwise, the President would never know when the point of decision was reached." At this meeting, USIB also approved NIE 85-3.

-4-

SECRET

16. At the Special Group Meeting on 20 September, [redacted] was discussed. After its use over Kamchatka was disapproved, General Carter urged its possible use against Cuba and State appeared enthusiastic. Based upon this, General Carter dispatched an action memorandum to the DD/R assigning them responsibility "within CIA [redacted] also CIA responsibility for planning other aerial reconnaissance operations against Cuban targets and for presentation of these CIA operations to the Special Group (Augmented) after appropriate Agency and Community coordination."

17. During this period, poor weather resulted in no exploitable take from U-2 operations. The Agency had made an operational determination that none of the four flights which evolved from the 10 September meeting would be made unless weather along the flight routes was less than 25% overcast. The first of the four flights was made on 26 September; the last on 7 October. The peripheral flights turned up additional SAM sites and coastal defense cruise-missile sites, but that is about all.

18. Conclusions of the Cuban SNIE, approved by USIB on 19 September, were cabled to you that day. While the SNIE stated that the Soviets might be tempted to establish other weapons of a more "offensive" character, such as additional types of short-range surface-to-surface missiles, and that the Soviet Union could derive considerable advantage from the establishment of medium and intermediate range ballistic missiles in Cuba, the estimate concluded:

> ". . . It would indicate a far greater willingness to increase the level of risk in US-Soviet relations than the Soviet Union has displayed thus far, and consequently would have important policy implications with respect to other areas and other problems in East-West relations."

-5-

SECRET

12. *(Continued)*

19. The following day, 20 September, you cabled [redacted] suggesting a most careful consideration of the conclusion that introduction of offensive missiles was unlikely. This paragraph, paragraph one of your cable, was immediately passed to the DD/I. However, no change was made to the estimate. It had already been endorsed by the Intelligence Community and released.

Lyman B. Kirkpatrick
Executive Director

-6-

13. *Lt. Gen. Marshall S. Carter to McCone, Cable, 4 September 1962 (Excerpt)*

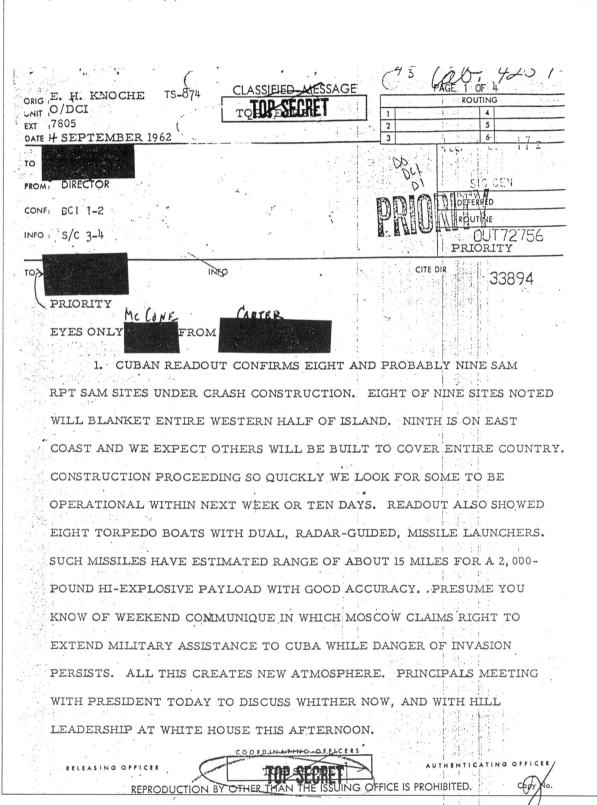

ORIG: E. H. KNOCHE TS-874

UNIT: O/DCI

EXT: 7805

DATE: 4 SEPTEMBER 1962

CLASSIFIED MESSAGE

TOP SECRET

PAGE 1 OF 4

ROUTING

TO: [redacted]

FROM: DIRECTOR

CONF: DCI 1-2

INFO: S/C 3-4

PRIORITY

DEFERRED

ROUTINE

OUT72756

PRIORITY

TO [redacted] INFO CITE DIR 33894

PRIORITY

EYES ONLY McCONE [redacted] FROM CARTER [redacted]

1. CUBAN READOUT CONFIRMS EIGHT AND PROBABLY NINE SAM RPT SAM SITES UNDER CRASH CONSTRUCTION. EIGHT OF NINE SITES NOTED WILL BLANKET ENTIRE WESTERN HALF OF ISLAND. NINTH IS ON EAST COAST AND WE EXPECT OTHERS WILL BE BUILT TO COVER ENTIRE COUNTRY. CONSTRUCTION PROCEEDING SO QUICKLY WE LOOK FOR SOME TO BE OPERATIONAL WITHIN NEXT WEEK OR TEN DAYS. READOUT ALSO SHOWED EIGHT TORPEDO BOATS WITH DUAL, RADAR-GUIDED, MISSILE LAUNCHERS. SUCH MISSILES HAVE ESTIMATED RANGE OF ABOUT 15 MILES FOR A 2,000-POUND HI-EXPLOSIVE PAYLOAD WITH GOOD ACCURACY. PRESUME YOU KNOW OF WEEKEND COMMUNIQUE IN WHICH MOSCOW CLAIMS RIGHT TO EXTEND MILITARY ASSISTANCE TO CUBA WHILE DANGER OF INVASION PERSISTS. ALL THIS CREATES NEW ATMOSPHERE. PRINCIPALS MEETING WITH PRESIDENT TODAY TO DISCUSS WHITHER NOW, AND WITH HILL LEADERSHIP AT WHITE HOUSE THIS AFTERNOON.

RELEASING OFFICER · COORDINATING OFFICERS · AUTHENTICATING OFFICER

TOP SECRET

Copy No.

13. *(Continued)*

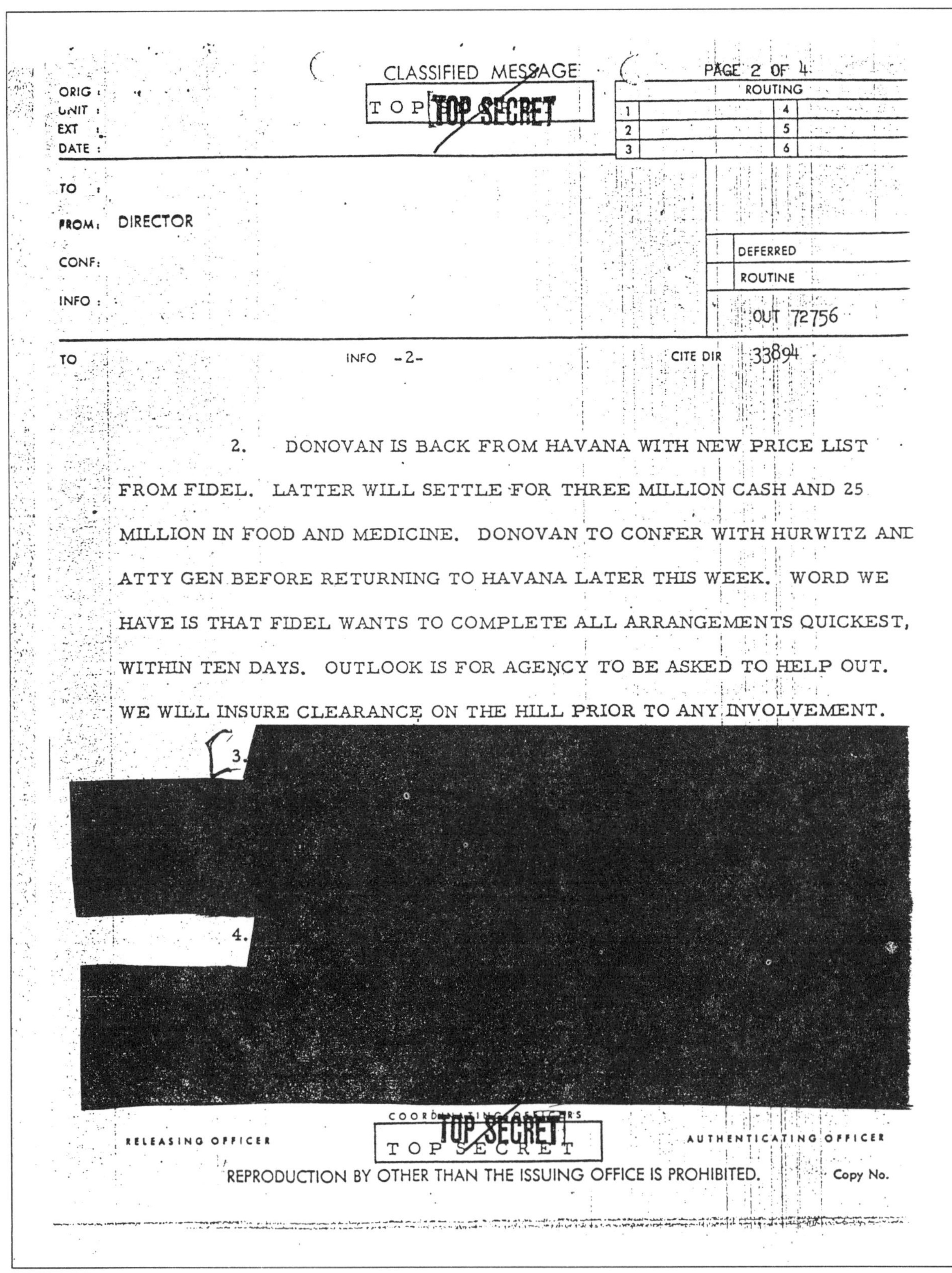

CLASSIFIED MESSAGE

TOP SECRET

PAGE 2 OF 4

ROUTING

1		4	
2		5	
3		6	

ORIG :
UNIT :
EXT :
DATE :

TO :

FROM: DIRECTOR

CONF:

INFO :

DEFERRED

ROUTINE

OUT 72756

TO INFO -2- CITE DIR 33894

2. DONOVAN IS BACK FROM HAVANA WITH NEW PRICE LIST FROM FIDEL. LATTER WILL SETTLE FOR THREE MILLION CASH AND 25 MILLION IN FOOD AND MEDICINE. DONOVAN TO CONFER WITH HURWITZ AND ATTY GEN BEFORE RETURNING TO HAVANA LATER THIS WEEK. WORD WE HAVE IS THAT FIDEL WANTS TO COMPLETE ALL ARRANGEMENTS QUICKEST, WITHIN TEN DAYS. OUTLOOK IS FOR AGENCY TO BE ASKED TO HELP OUT. WE WILL INSURE CLEARANCE ON THE HILL PRIOR TO ANY INVOLVEMENT.

3.

4.

RELEASING OFFICER — COORDINATING OFFICERS — AUTHENTICATING OFFICER

TOP SECRET

REPRODUCTION BY OTHER THAN THE ISSUING OFFICE IS PROHIBITED. Copy No.

14. *Carter to McCone, Cable, 5 September 1962 (Excerpt)*

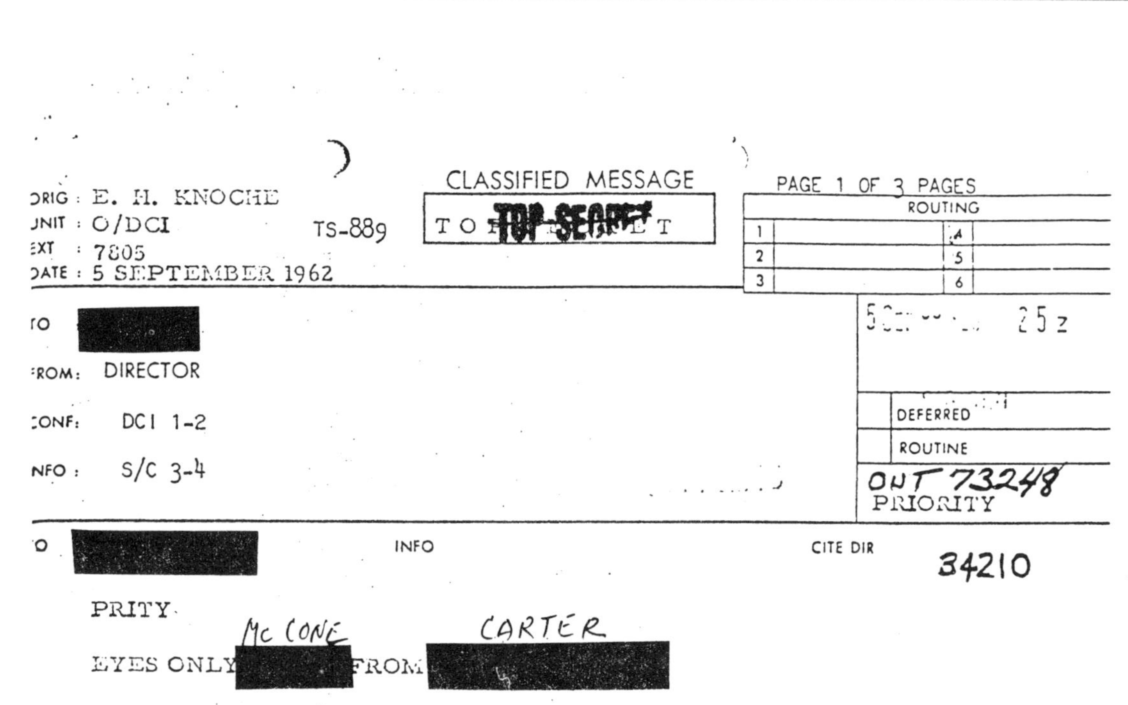

ORIG : E. H. KNOCHE
UNIT : O/DCI TS-889
EXT : 7805
DATE : 5 SEPTEMBER 1962

CLASSIFIED MESSAGE
TOP SECRET

PAGE 1 OF 3 PAGES
ROUTING

TO [redacted]
FROM: DIRECTOR
CONF: DCI 1-2
INFO: S/C 3-4

DEFERRED
ROUTINE
OUT 73248
PRIORITY

TO [redacted] INFO CITE DIR 34210

PRITY

EYES ONLY McCONE FROM CARTER

1. IN INITIAL REACTION TO OFFICIAL US STATEMENT 4 SEPT RE SAM SITES AND PT BOATS, CUBAN SPOKESMEN EMPHASIZING CLAIM THAT ARMS BUILDUP IS EXERCISE OF RIGHT OF SELF-DEFENSE. MOSCOW IS SILENT SO FAR. CUBAN MILITARY FORCES FOR PAST WEEK OR SO IN HIGH STATE OF ALERT. IT MAY BE THAT REGIME DELIBERATELY ALARMING POPULACE TO JUSTIFY MASSIVE SOVIET ASSISTANCE AND TO DIVERT MINDS FROM ECONOMIC PLIGHT.

2. PETE SCOVILLE IS FIXING THE C-PACKAGE TO PERMIT COVERAGE OF CUBA. THIS WILL TAKE ABOUT THREE WEEKS. IN BACKS OF OUR MINDS IS GROWING DANGER TO THE BIRDS.

3. [redacted]

COORDINATING OFFICERS

RELEASING OFFICER TOP SECRET AUTHENTICATING OFFICER

REPRODUCTION BY OTHER THAN THE ISSUING OFFICE IS PROHIBITED. Copy No.

15. *Carter to McCone, Cable, 6 September 1962 (Excerpt)*

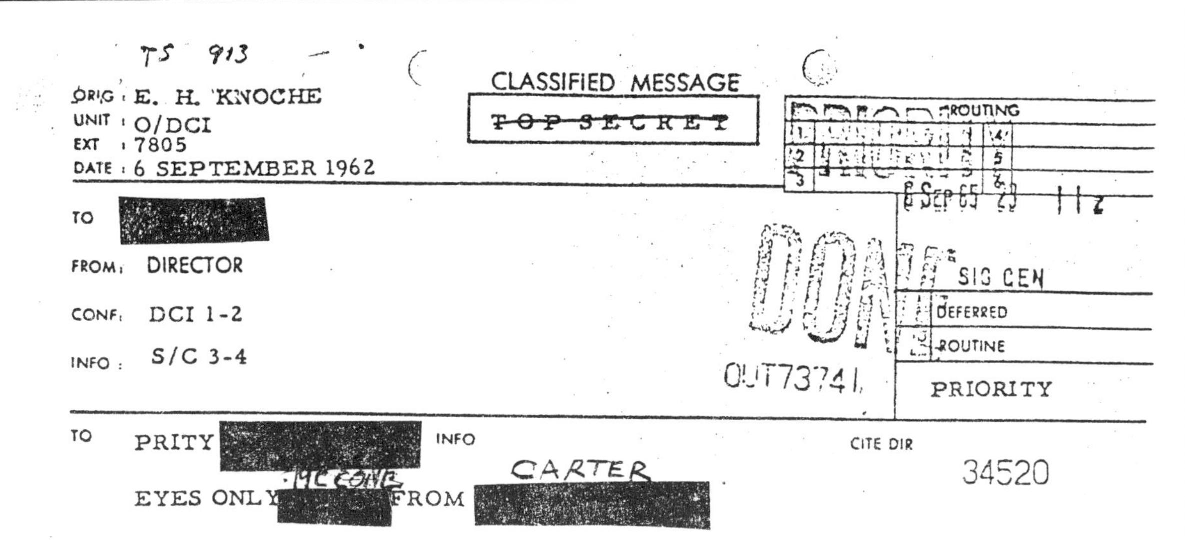

TS 913

ORIG: E. H. KNOCHE
UNIT: O/DCI
EXT: 7805
DATE: 6 SEPTEMBER 1962

CLASSIFIED MESSAGE
~~TOP SECRET~~

ROUTING

6 SEP 62 23 11z

SIG CEN
DEFERRED
ROUTINE
PRIORITY

TO [redacted]
FROM: DIRECTOR
CONF: DCI 1-2
INFO: S/C 3-4

OUT73741

TO PRITY [redacted] INFO CITE DIR 34520

EYES ONLY MCCONE FROM CARTER

1. CONTINUED READOUT NOW SHOWS TOTAL OF NINE, PROBABLY TEN, SAM SITES. OTHER INFO, FROM GROUND REPORTS, POINTS STRONGLY TO AT LEAST TWO OTHERS. IN MEETING WITH LATIN AMERICAN AMBASSADORS HERE 5 SEPT RE CUBA, SEC STATE ASKED THEM TO TOUCH BASE WITH HOME GOVTS AND REACH EARLY AGREEMENT TO GONVENE MEETING OF OAS FOREIGN MINISTERS TO DISCUSS CUBAN DEVELOPMENTS. SEC STATE IN RESPONSE TO QUERY FROM MEXICAN AMB SAID WE HAVE IMPRESSION MOSCOW DOES NOT RPT NOT DESIRE DEVELOP CUBA AS SOVIET BASE THIS HEMISPHERE. HE SAID SOVIETS UNDER CUBAN PRESSURE GIVE ECON AND MILITARY HELP BUT ARE THUS FAR CAREFUL NOT TO MAKE UNLIMITED SECURITY COMMITMENT.

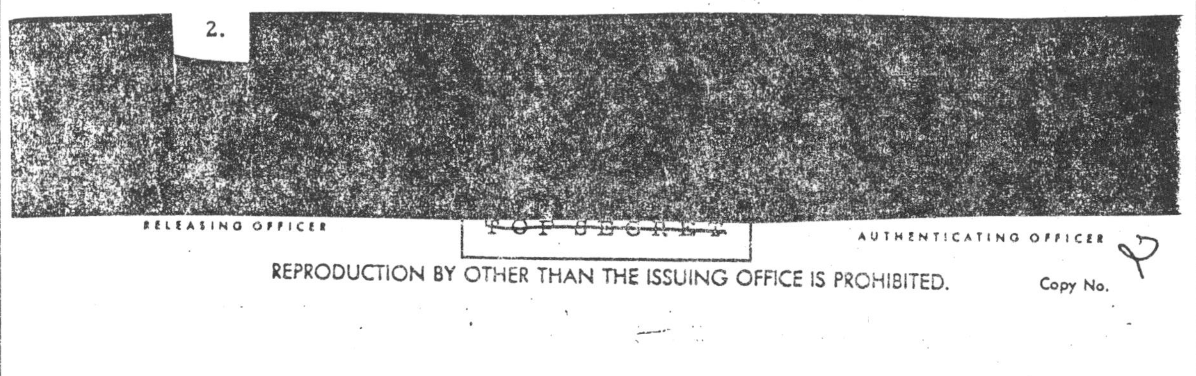

2. [redacted]

RELEASING OFFICER ~~TOP SECRET~~ AUTHENTICATING OFFICER

REPRODUCTION BY OTHER THAN THE ISSUING OFFICE IS PROHIBITED. Copy No.

16. *McCone to Carter, Cable, 7 September 1962*

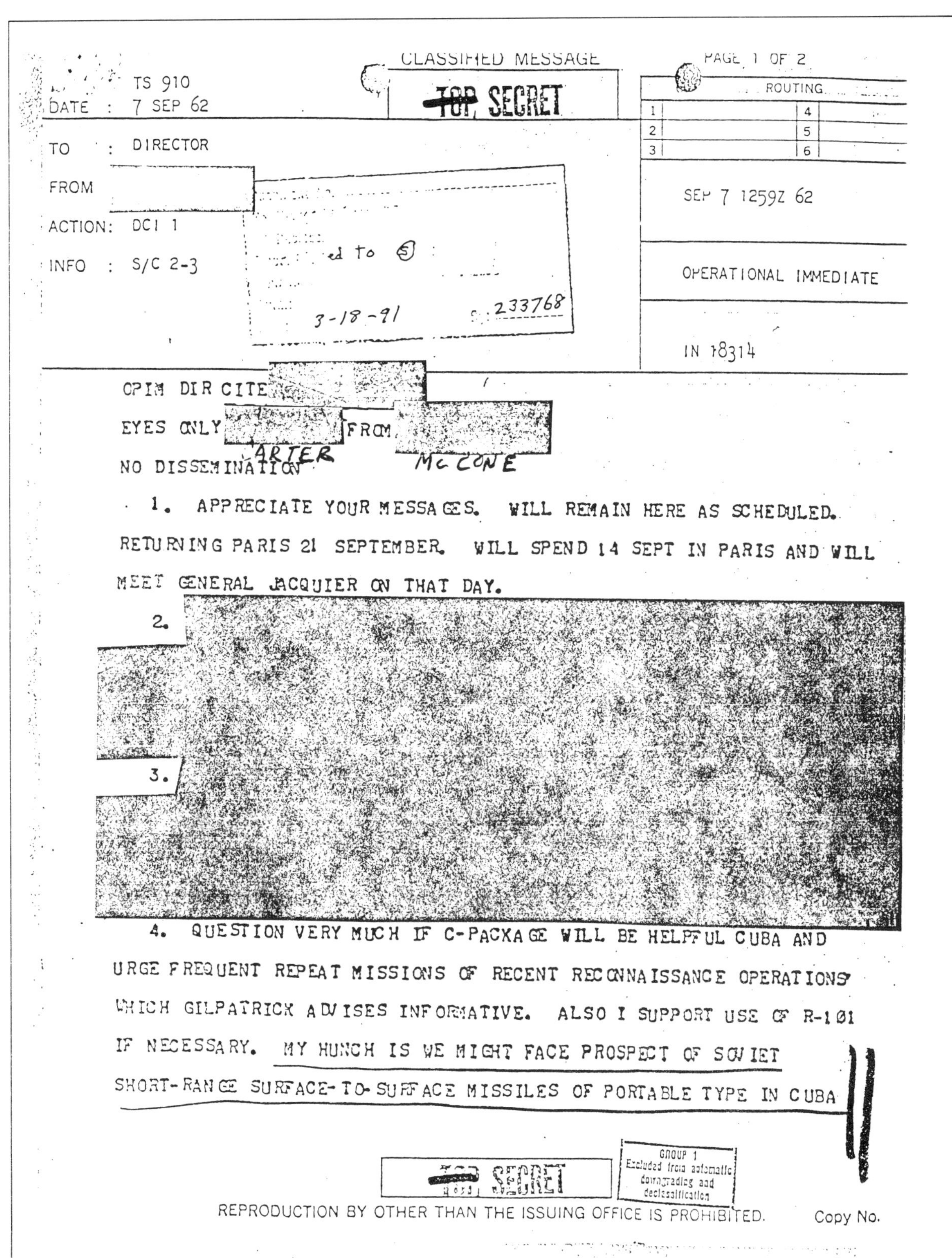

CLASSIFIED MESSAGE

PAGE 1 OF 2

TS 910

DATE : 7 SEP 62

TOP SECRET

ROUTING

1	4
2	5
3	6

TO : DIRECTOR

FROM

ACTION: DCI 1

INFO : S/C 2-3

...ed to ⑤

3-18-91 ...233768

SEP 7 1259Z 62

OPERATIONAL IMMEDIATE

IN 18314

OPIM DIR CITE [redacted]

EYES ONLY [redacted] CARTER FROM [redacted] McCONE

NO DISSEMINATION

1. APPRECIATE YOUR MESSAGES. WILL REMAIN HERE AS SCHEDULED. RETURNING PARIS 21 SEPTEMBER. WILL SPEND 14 SEPT IN PARIS AND WILL MEET GENERAL JACQUIER ON THAT DAY.

2. [redacted]

3. [redacted]

4. QUESTION VERY MUCH IF C-PACKAGE WILL BE HELPFUL CUBA AND URGE FREQUENT REPEAT MISSIONS OF RECENT RECONNAISSANCE OPERATIONS WHICH GILPATRICK ADVISES INFORMATIVE. ALSO I SUPPORT USE OF R-101 IF NECESSARY. MY HUNCH IS WE MIGHT FACE PROSPECT OF SOVIET SHORT-RANGE SURFACE-TO-SURFACE MISSILES OF PORTABLE TYPE IN CUBA

TOP SECRET

GROUP 1
Excluded from automatic downgrading and declassification

REPRODUCTION BY OTHER THAN THE ISSUING OFFICE IS PROHIBITED. Copy No.

16. *(Continued)*

CLASSIFIED MESSAGE

~~TOP SECRET~~

DATE :

TO :

FROM :

ACTION:

INFO :

ROUTING			
1		4	
2		5	
3		6	

PAGE 2 OF 2

IN 18314

WHICH COULD COMMAND IMPORTANT TARGETS OF SOUTHEAST UNITED STATES AND POSSIBLY LATIN AMERICAN CARIBBEAN AREAS.

5. YOU MIGHT SUGGEST TO RUSK THAT WE DEVELOP JOINT POLICIES FOR ACTION IN CUBA WITH SELECTED CARIBBEAN, SOUTH-AMERICAN STATES AS AN ALTERNATIVE TO SEEKING UNANIMOUS OAS ACTION WHICH MOST CERTAINLY WILL BE AN INEFFECTIVE COMPROMISE SOLUTION IF PAST HISTORY IS ANY INDICATOR.

END OF MESSAGE

I did this

He was most appreciative -

JAM

8 Sept 6[illegible]

~~TOP SECRET~~

GROUP 1
Excluded from automatic downgrading and declassification

REPRODUCTION BY OTHER THAN THE ISSUING OFFICE IS PROHIBITED.

Copy No.

17. *Carter to McCone, Cable, 7 September 1962 (Excerpt)*

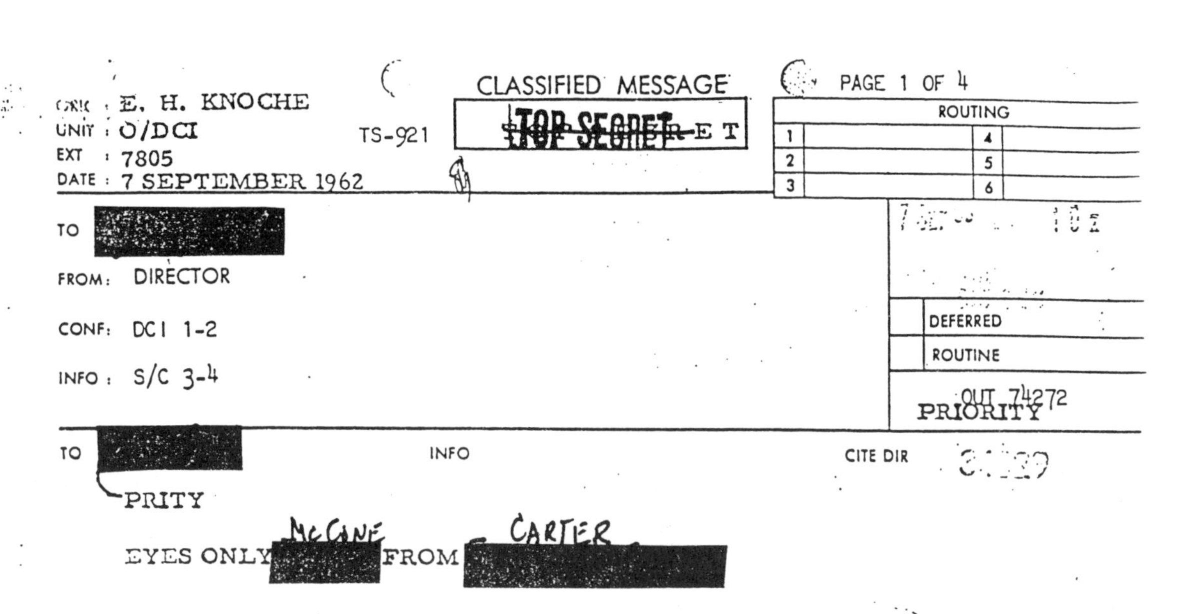

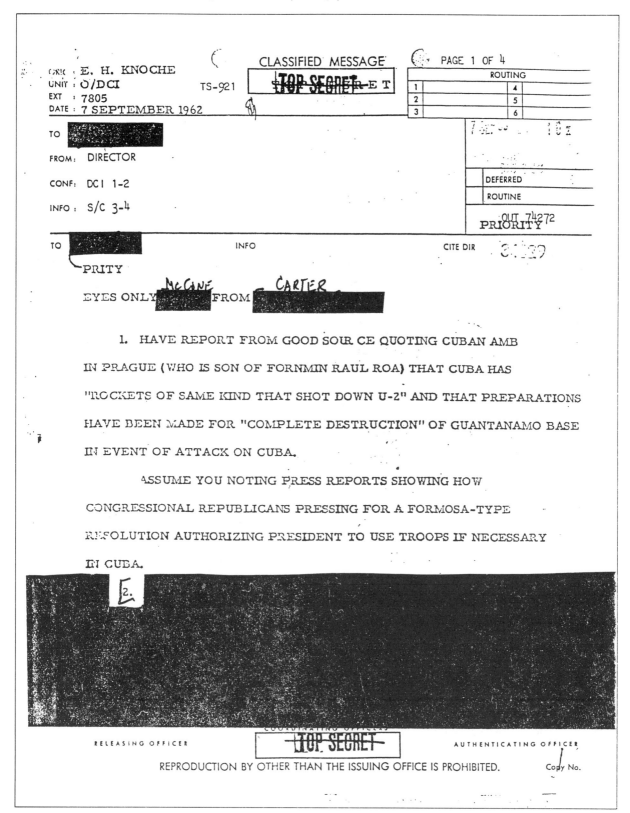

ORIG : E. H. KNOCHE
UNIT : O/DCI
EXT : 7805
DATE : 7 SEPTEMBER 1962

TS-921

CLASSIFIED MESSAGE

TOP SECRET

PAGE 1 OF 4

ROUTING

TO [redacted]

FROM: DIRECTOR

CONF: DCI 1-2

INFO : S/C 3-4

DEFERRED

ROUTINE

OUT 74272

PRIORITY

TO [redacted] INFO CITE DIR

PRITY

EYES ONLY McCONE FROM CARTER

1. HAVE REPORT FROM GOOD SOUR CE QUOTING CUBAN AMB IN PRAGUE (WHO IS SON OF FORNMIN RAUL ROA) THAT CUBA HAS "ROCKETS OF SAME KIND THAT SHOT DOWN U-2" AND THAT PREPARATIONS HAVE BEEN MADE FOR "COMPLETE DESTRUCTION" OF GUANTANAMO BASE IN EVENT OF ATTACK ON CUBA.

ASSUME YOU NOTING PRESS REPORTS SHOWING HOW CONGRESSIONAL REPUBLICANS PRESSING FOR A FORMOSA-TYPE RESOLUTION AUTHORIZING PRESIDENT TO USE TROOPS IF NECESSARY IN CUBA.

2.

RELEASING OFFICER

COORDINATING OFFICERS

TOP SECRET

AUTHENTICATING OFFICER

REPRODUCTION BY OTHER THAN THE ISSUING OFFICE IS PROHIBITED.

Copy No.

17. *(Continued)*

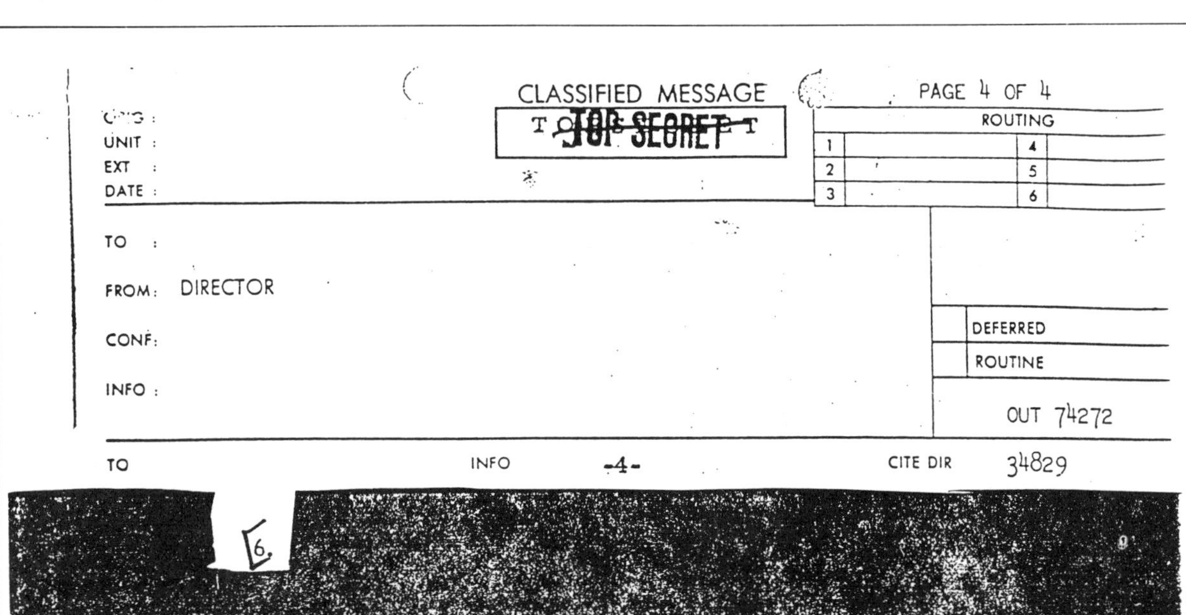

CLASSIFIED MESSAGE

TOP SECRET

PAGE 4 OF 4

ORIG :
UNIT :
EXT :
DATE :

ROUTING			
1		4	
2		5	
3		6	

TO :

FROM: DIRECTOR

CONF:

INFO :

DEFERRED

ROUTINE

OUT 74272

TO INFO -4- CITE DIR 34829

[6.

7. WE HAVE YOUR MESSAGE AND ARE LOOKING INTO ALL MATTERS YOU RAISE. WILL ADVISE. TERRY LEE TAKING NECESSARY ACTION RE YOUR HOUSE PLANS.

8. WE HAVE THE MESSAGE ASKING FOR DAILY BULLETIN TO BE SENT TO YOU EVERY DAY. PLEASE BE ASSURED THAT ALL SIGNIFICANT DEVELOPMENTS, INCLUDING THOSE COVERED IN BULLETIN, ARE INCLUDED IN THIS DAILY CABLE SERIES.

END OF MESSAGE

LT. GEN. MARSHALL S. CARTER
A/DCI

RELEASING OFFICER

COORDINATING OFFICERS

TOP SECRET

AUTHENTICATING OFFICER

REPRODUCTION BY OTHER THAN THE ISSUING OFFICE IS PROHIBITED.

Copy No.

18. *Carter to McCone, Cable, 8 September 1962 (Excerpt)*

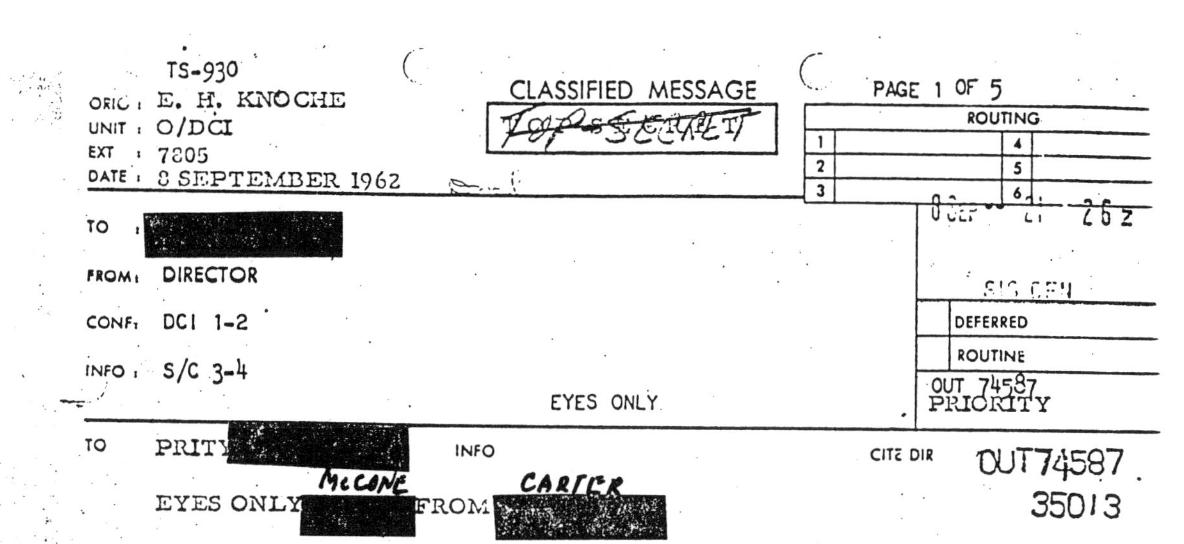

TS-930

ORIG: E. H. KNOCHE
UNIT: O/DCI
EXT: 7805
DATE: 8 SEPTEMBER 1962

CLASSIFIED MESSAGE
~~TOP SECRET~~

PAGE 1 OF 5

ROUTING

TO: [redacted]
FROM: DIRECTOR
CONF: DCI 1-2
INFO: S/C 3-4

EYES ONLY

DEFERRED
ROUTINE
OUT 74587
PRIORITY

TO PRITY [redacted] INFO CITE DIR OUT74587 35013

EYES ONLY [redacted] McCONE FROM [redacted] CARTER

1. READOUT OF LATEST (5 SEPTEMBER) TAKE SHOWS THREE MORE SAMS, THESE IN LAS VILLAS PROVINCE IN CENTRAL CUBA. TOTAL SAMS NOW TWELVE, PROBABLY THIRTEEN. TO BLANKET ISLAND, WE LOOK FOR EVENTUAL TOTAL OF ABOUT 25. ALSO SPOTTED ONE MIG-21 AT SANTA CLARA AIRFIELD. NINETEEN CRATES SEEN PROBABLY HOUSE MIG-21 WHICH WOULD TOTAL 20. (TOTAL NUMBER MIG-15, 17 AND 19 IS CARRIED AT ABOUT 60.) MIG-21 IS 1,000 MPH JET, WITH ALTITUDE CAPABILITY 60,000 FEET, EQUIPPED WITH TWO AIR-AIR INFRARED MISSILES AS WELL AS STANDARD ROCKETS AND CANNONS.

I HAVE TALKED WITH RUSK WHO WAS MOST APPRECIATIVE FOR YOUR SUGGESTION RE JOINT ACTION PLANNING WITH SELECTED LATINO STATES.

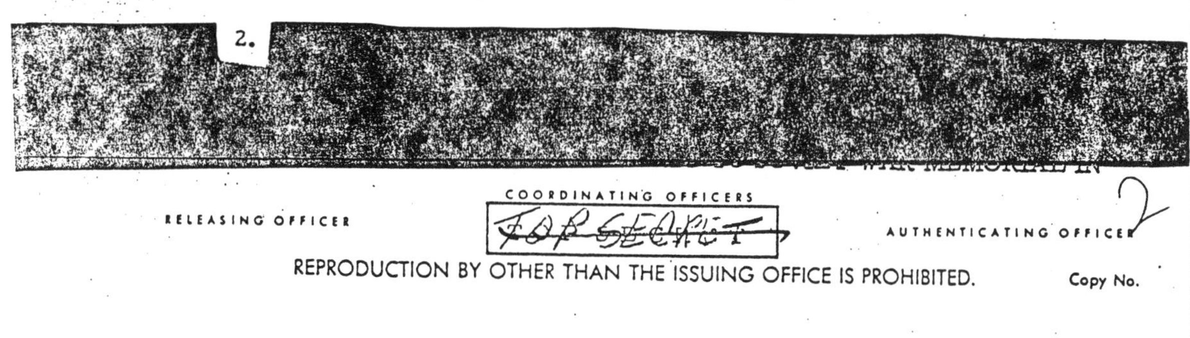

2. [redacted]

RELEASING OFFICER

COORDINATING OFFICERS

~~TOP SECRET~~

AUTHENTICATING OFFICER

REPRODUCTION BY OTHER THAN THE ISSUING OFFICE IS PROHIBITED.

Copy No.

18. *(Continued)*

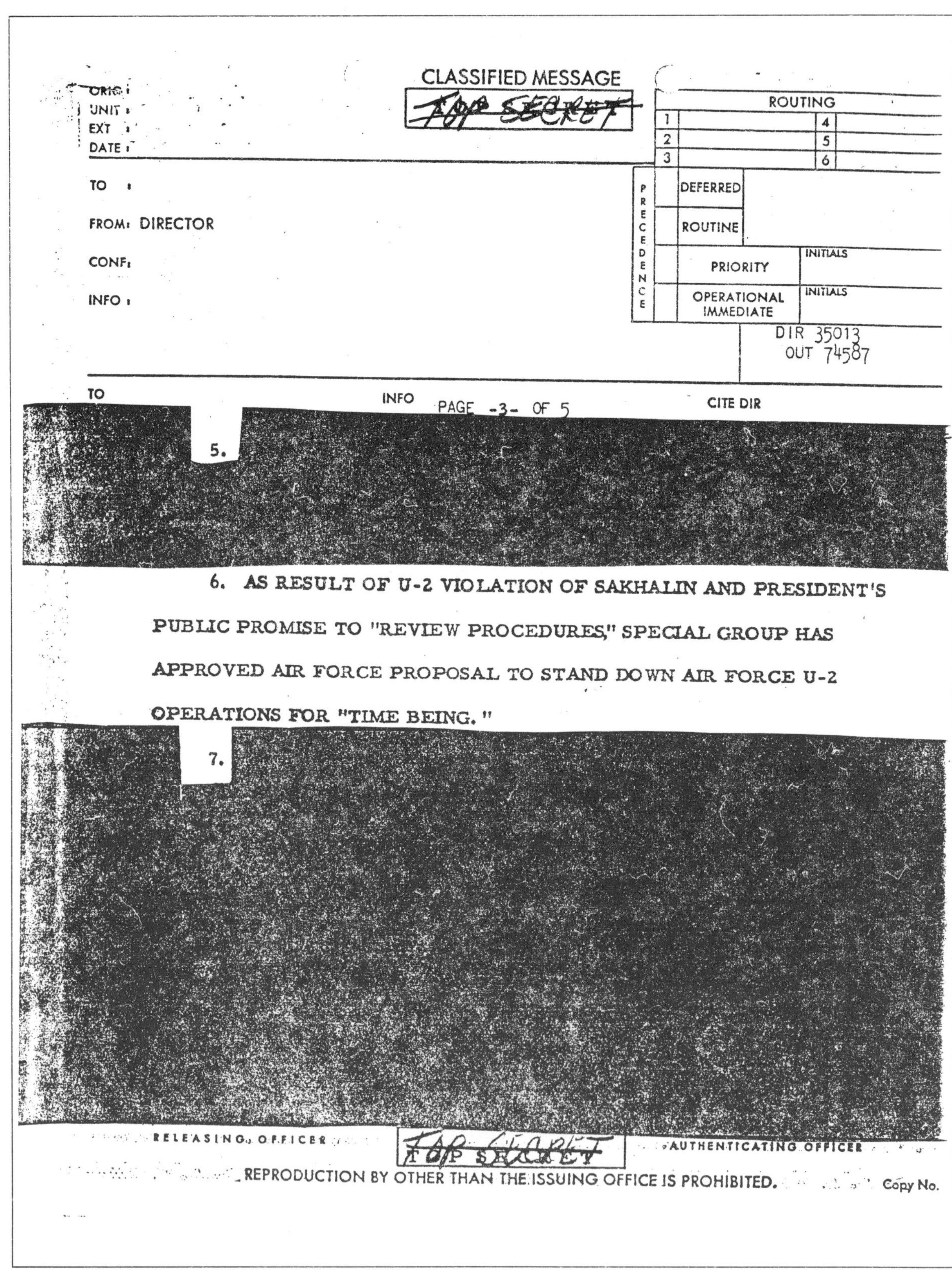

CLASSIFIED MESSAGE

~~TOP SECRET~~

ORIG :
UNIT :
EXT :
DATE :

ROUTING

1		4
2		5
3		6

TO :

FROM: DIRECTOR

CONF:

INFO :

PRECEDENCE: DEFERRED / ROUTINE / PRIORITY (INITIALS) / OPERATIONAL IMMEDIATE (INITIALS)

DIR 35013
OUT 74587

TO INFO PAGE -3- OF 5 CITE DIR

5.

6. AS RESULT OF U-2 VIOLATION OF SAKHALIN AND PRESIDENT'S PUBLIC PROMISE TO "REVIEW PROCEDURES," SPECIAL GROUP HAS APPROVED AIR FORCE PROPOSAL TO STAND DOWN AIR FORCE U-2 OPERATIONS FOR "TIME BEING."

7.

RELEASING OFFICER ~~TOP SECRET~~ AUTHENTICATING OFFICER

REPRODUCTION BY OTHER THAN THE ISSUING OFFICE IS PROHIBITED. Copy No.

19. *Carter to McCone, Cable, 10 September 1962 (Excerpt)*

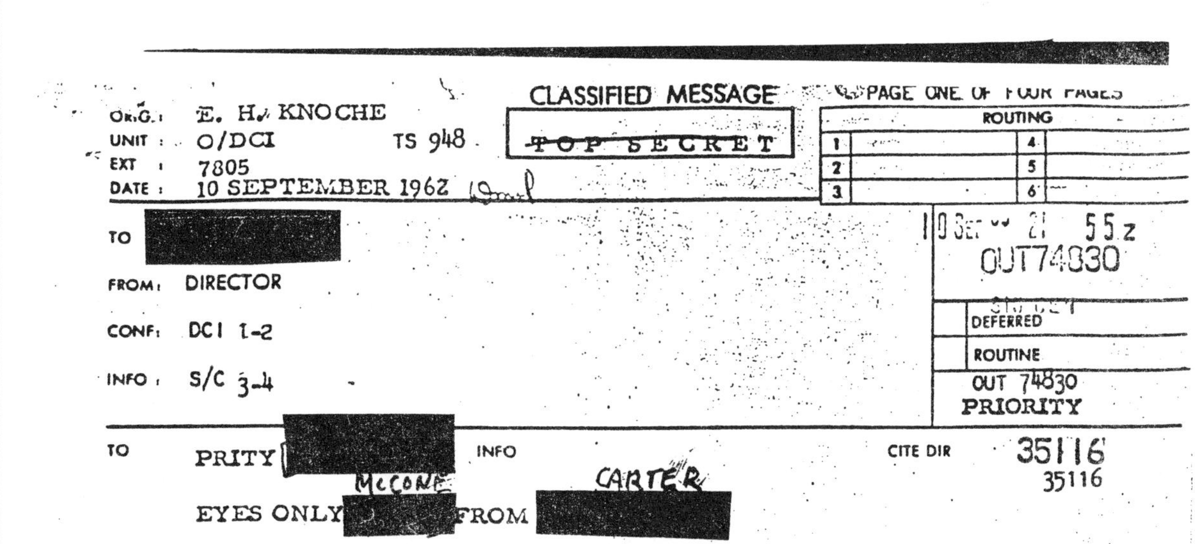

CLASSIFIED MESSAGE — PAGE ONE OF FOUR PAGES

ORIG.: E. H. KNOCHE
UNIT: O/DCI TS 948
EXT: 7805
DATE: 10 SEPTEMBER 1962

TOP SECRET

ROUTING 1 2 3 4 5 6

TO: [redacted]
FROM: DIRECTOR
CONF: DCI 1-2
INFO: S/C 3-4

10 Sep 62 21 55z
OUT74830
DEFERRED
ROUTINE
OUT 74830
PRIORITY

TO PRITY [redacted] INFO CITE DIR 35116
EYES ONLY McCONE FROM CARTER 35116

1. STILL UNABLE TO CONCLUDE ON FATE OF LOST U-2. THERE IS NOTHING TO ~~XXXXXXX~~ CONFIRM MECHANICAL MALFUNCTION AND GRADUAL OR SUDDEN LOSS OF ALTITUDE. THERE WERE CHICOM MIGS IN THE AREA BUT NOT AT U-2 ALTITUDE SO FAR AS WE CAN TELL. NO KNOWLEDGE RE FATE OF PILOT.

SOVIETS PLAYING INCIDENT IN LOW KEY THUS FAR. CHICOMS ACCUSING UNITED STATES OF BEING INSTIGATOR AND LINKING MAXWELL TAYLOR PRESENCE IN TAIPEI WITH DISPATCH OF SPY PLANE.

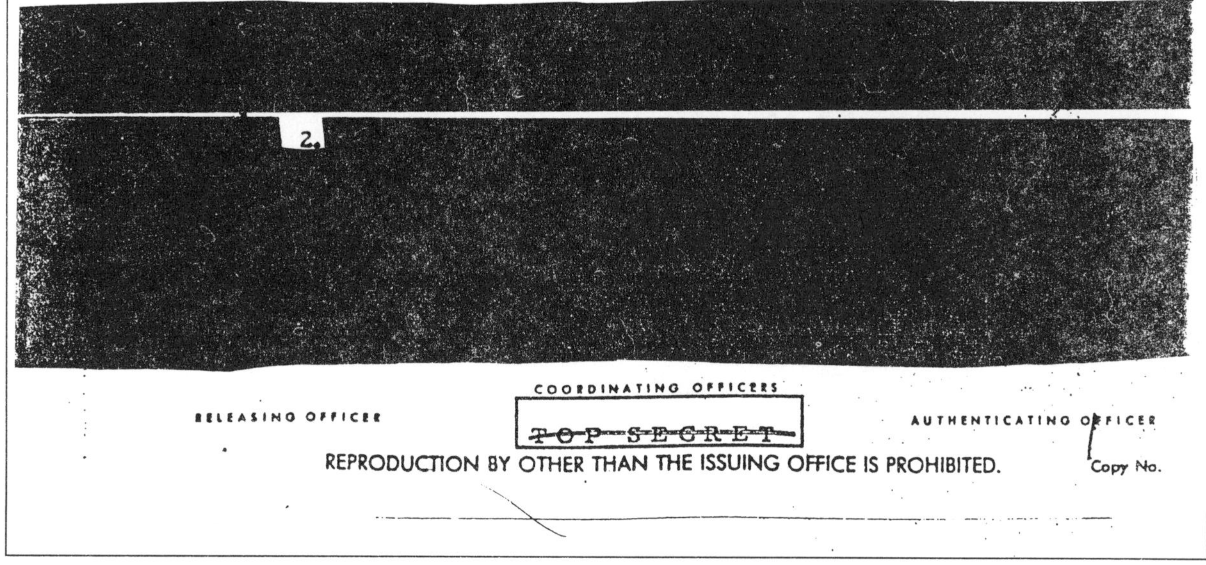

2. [redacted]

COORDINATING OFFICERS
RELEASING OFFICER
TOP SECRET
AUTHENTICATING OFFICER
REPRODUCTION BY OTHER THAN THE ISSUING OFFICE IS PROHIBITED. Copy No.

19. *(Continued)*

CLASSIFIED MESSAGE

~~TOP SECR~~ET

PAGE TWO OF FOUR PAGES

ROUTING

1	4
2	5
3	6

ORIG :
UNIT :
EXT :
DATE :

TO :

FROM : DIRECTOR

CONF :

INFO :

DEFERRED
ROUTINE

OUT 74830

TO INFO -2- CITE DIR 35116

3. OUR EMBASSY IN MEXICO CITY HAS RELIABLE INFO THAT MEXICO AND BRAZIL (WHO HAVE BEEN IN VANGUARD OF THOSE OPPOSING TOUGH POLICY RE CASTRO) NOW JOINTLY DISCUSSING POSSIBILITY OF MAKING DIPLOMATIC BREAK WITH CUBA. REASON IS NOT RPT NOT NEW SOVIET INROADS BUT THAT MEXICAN AND BRAZILIAN GOVTS NOW THINK WE WILL INVADE AND ERASE CASTRO AND WANT TO BE SPARED DOMESTIC EMBARRASSMENT BY BREAKING BEFOREHAND.

4. THANKS FOR YOUR THOUGHTS RE CUBA. BNE HAS THEM AND IS CONSIDERING. ENVY THE "BEAUTIFUL ENVIRONMENT" YOU DESCRIBE. HAVEN'T SEEN ANY HERE FOR A WHILE. SPECIAL PROJECT SHOULD BE READY IN APRIL. EVEN WITH CRASH PROGRAM, IT COULD NOT BE READY BEFORE JANUARY OR FEBRUARY.

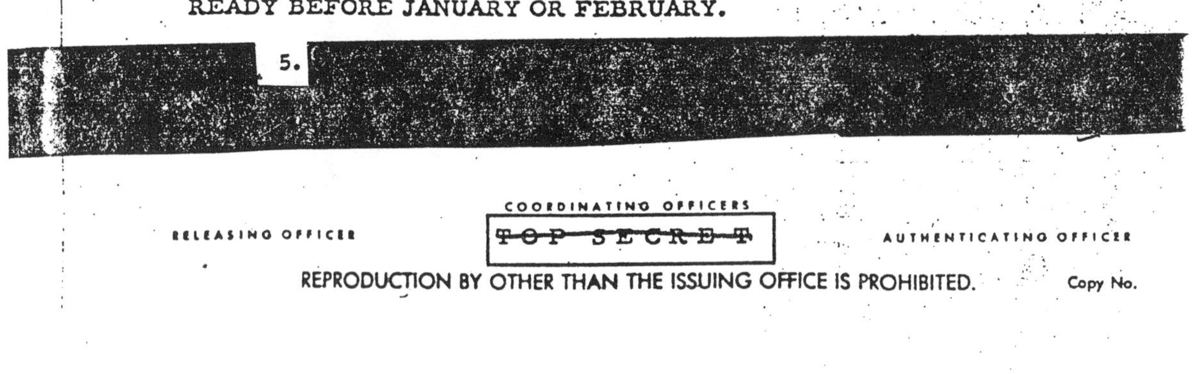

5.

COORDINATING OFFICERS

RELEASING OFFICER ~~TOP SECRET~~ AUTHENTICATING OFFICER

REPRODUCTION BY OTHER THAN THE ISSUING OFFICE IS PROHIBITED. Copy No.

20. *McCone to Carter and Elder, 10 September 1962*

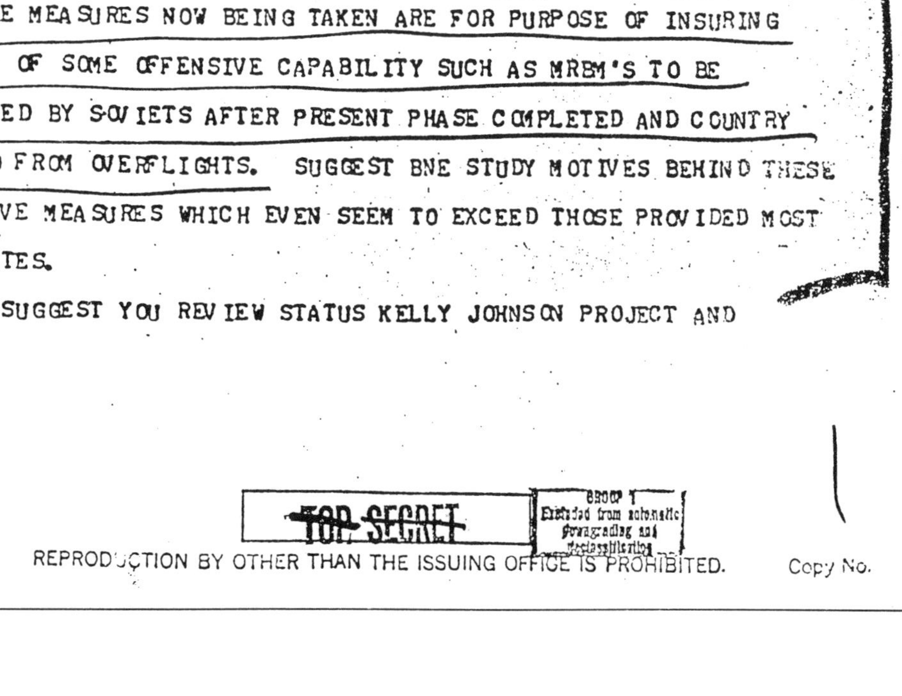

CLASSIFIED MESSAGE

~~TOP SECRET~~

TS 940
DATE : 10 SEP 62

TO : DIRECTOR

FROM : [redacted]

ACTION: DCI 1 (COPY ISSUED TO DCI 0725 10 SEP 62)

INFO : S/C 2-3

ROUTING: 1, 2, 3, 4, 5, 6

SEP 10 1104Z 62

PRIORITY

IN 19372

Document No.
No Change In Class. ☐
☐ Declassified
Class. Changed to: TS (S) C
Next Review Date:
Auth: HR 70-3
Date: 3-18-91 By: 233768

DIR CITE [redacted]

EYES ONLY [CARTER] AND ELDER FROM [McCONE]

1. VERY APPRECIATIVE YOUR DETAILED DAILY REPORTS. CHINA INCIDENT MOST DISTRESSING BUT NOT SURPRISING AND RECALL THAT ON SEVERAL OCCASIONS I POINTED OUT TO SPECIAL GROUP PACFI AND HIGHER AUTHORITY THAT AN INCIDENT WAS INEVITABLE.

2. DIFFICULT FOR ME TO RATIONALIZE EXTENSIVE COSTLY DEFENSES BEING ESTABLISHED IN CUBA AS SUCH EXTREME COSTLY MEASURES TO ACCOMPLISH SECURITY AND SECRECY NOT CONSISTENT WITH OTHER POLICIES SUCH AS REFUGEES, LEGAL TRAVEL, ETC. APPEARS TO ME QUITE POSSIBLE MEASURES NOW BEING TAKEN ARE FOR PURPOSE OF INSURING SECRECY OF SOME OFFENSIVE CAPABILITY SUCH AS MRBM'S TO BE INSTALLED BY SOVIETS AFTER PRESENT PHASE COMPLETED AND COUNTRY SECURED FROM OVERFLIGHTS. SUGGEST BNE STUDY MOTIVES BEHIND THESE DEFENSIVE MEASURES WHICH EVEN SEEM TO EXCEED THOSE PROVIDED MOST SATELLITES.

3. SUGGEST YOU REVIEW STATUS KELLY JOHNSON PROJECT AND

~~TOP SECRET~~

GROUP 1
Excluded from automatic downgrading and declassification

REPRODUCTION BY OTHER THAN THE ISSUING OFFICE IS PROHIBITED. Copy No.

20. *(Continued)*

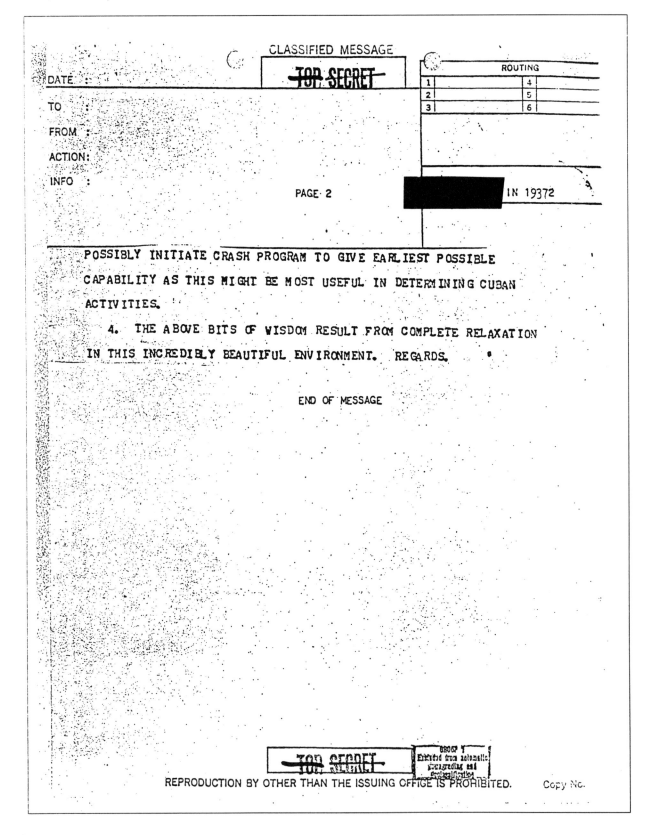

CLASSIFIED MESSAGE

~~TOP SECRET~~

DATE :

TO :

FROM :

ACTION:

INFO :

ROUTING	
1	4
2	5
3	6

PAGE 2 [redacted] IN 19372

POSSIBLY INITIATE CRASH PROGRAM TO GIVE EARLIEST POSSIBLE CAPABILITY AS THIS MIGHT BE MOST USEFUL IN DETERMINING CUBAN ACTIVITIES.

4. THE ABOVE BITS OF WISDOM RESULT FROM COMPLETE RELAXATION IN THIS INCREDIBLY BEAUTIFUL ENVIRONMENT. REGARDS.

END OF MESSAGE

~~TOP SECRET~~

GROUP 1 Excluded from automatic downgrading and declassification

REPRODUCTION BY OTHER THAN THE ISSUING OFFICE IS PROHIBITED. Copy No.

21. *Kirkpatrick, Memorandum for the Director, "White House Meeting on 10 September 1962 on Cuban Overflights," 1 March 1963*

SECRET

1 March 1963

MEMORANDUM FOR THE DIRECTOR

SUBJECT: White House Meeting on 10 September 1962 on Cuban Overflights

1. The following is a reconstruction of the reasons for the meeting at the White House in Mr. McGeorge Bundy's office on 10 September 1962 at approximately 5:45 p.m., and a report on what transpired at that meeting. This memorandum is based upon discussions with Mr. Parrott of the White House, General Carter, Dr. Herbert Scoville, and Messrs. [redacted] and Reber of Dr. Scoville's office who also attended the meeting.

2. A memorandum for the record prepared by Mr. McMahon [redacted] records that at approximately 10:00 on the morning of 10 September he received a telephone call from Mr. Parrott passing on a request made by Mr. Bundy on behalf of the Secretary of State. According to Mr. Parrott, the Secretary of State had expressed the hope that there wouldn't be any incidents this week, and Mr. Bundy asked that the following questions posed by the Secretary of State be answered.

a. How important is it to our intelligence objectives that we overfly Cuban soil?

b. How much would our intelligence suffer if we limited our reconnaissance to peripheral activities utilizing oblique photography?

c. Is there anyone in the planning of these missions who might wish to provoke an incident?

3. Mr. Parrott indicated that Mr. Bundy desired an answer within a half hour. Mr. McMahon immediately contacted the Chairman of COMOR which was in session at that moment, and they agreed to provide a response as quickly as possible. Mr. Parrott called a second time to advise Mr. McMahon that Mr. Roger Hilsman had advised that he

SECRET

21. *(Continued)*

SECRET

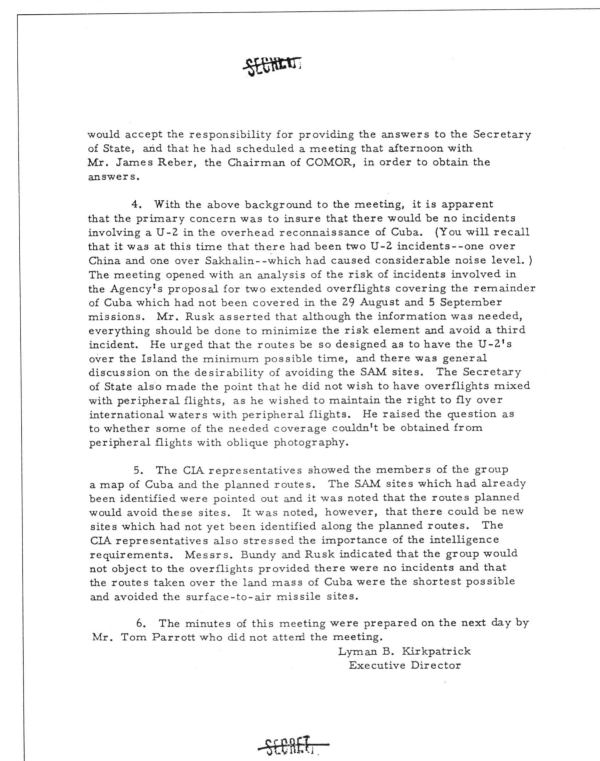

would accept the responsibility for providing the answers to the Secretary of State, and that he had scheduled a meeting that afternoon with Mr. James Reber, the Chairman of COMOR, in order to obtain the answers.

4. With the above background to the meeting, it is apparent that the primary concern was to insure that there would be no incidents involving a U-2 in the overhead reconnaissance of Cuba. (You will recall that it was at this time that there had been two U-2 incidents--one over China and one over Sakhalin--which had caused considerable noise level.) The meeting opened with an analysis of the risk of incidents involved in the Agency's proposal for two extended overflights covering the remainder of Cuba which had not been covered in the 29 August and 5 September missions. Mr. Rusk asserted that although the information was needed, everything should be done to minimize the risk element and avoid a third incident. He urged that the routes be so designed as to have the U-2's over the Island the minimum possible time, and there was general discussion on the desirability of avoiding the SAM sites. The Secretary of State also made the point that he did not wish to have overflights mixed with peripheral flights, as he wished to maintain the right to fly over international waters with peripheral flights. He raised the question as to whether some of the needed coverage couldn't be obtained from peripheral flights with oblique photography.

5. The CIA representatives showed the members of the group a map of Cuba and the planned routes. The SAM sites which had already been identified were pointed out and it was noted that the routes planned would avoid these sites. It was noted, however, that there could be new sites which had not yet been identified along the planned routes. The CIA representatives also stressed the importance of the intelligence requirements. Messrs. Bundy and Rusk indicated that the group would not object to the overflights provided there were no incidents and that the routes taken over the land mass of Cuba were the shortest possible and avoided the surface-to-air missile sites.

6. The minutes of this meeting were prepared on the next day by Mr. Tom Parrott who did not attend the meeting.

Lyman B. Kirkpatrick
Executive Director

22. *Carter to McCone, Cable, 11 September 1962 (Excerpt)*

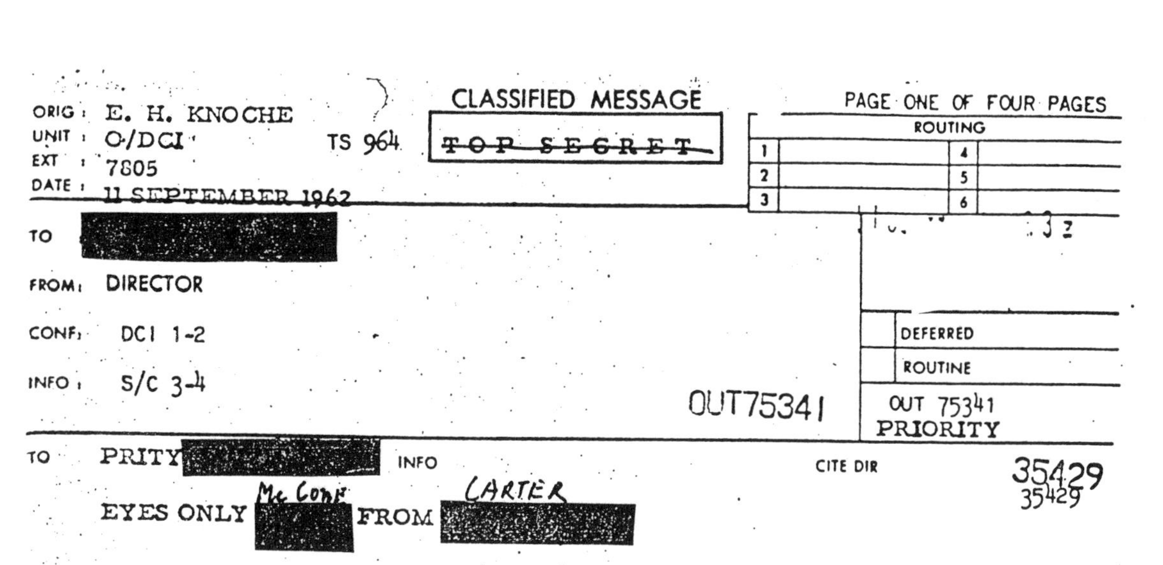

ORIG: E. H. KNOCHE
UNIT: O/DCI
EXT: 7805
DATE: 11 SEPTEMBER 1962

TS 964

CLASSIFIED MESSAGE

~~TOP SECRET~~

PAGE ONE OF FOUR PAGES

ROUTING

1	4
2	5
3	6

TO [redacted]

FROM: DIRECTOR

CONF: DCI 1-2

INFO: S/C 3-4

OUT75341

DEFERRED

ROUTINE

OUT 75341
PRIORITY

TO PRITY [redacted] INFO CITE DIR 35429

EYES ONLY McCone [redacted] FROM Carter [redacted]

1. HAVANA RADIO CHARGES THAT TWO CARGO SHIPS, OUTWARD BOUND FROM CUBA, ONE CUBAN AND THE OTHER BRITISH, WERE ATTACKED 11 SEPT OFF NORTHERN COAST OF CUBA. WE HAVE INFO THAT AN EXILE GROUP CALLED ALPHA-66 (BASED IN PUERTO RICO) PROBABLY DID THE JOB. STUDENT EXILE GROUP IN MIAMI LAST WEEKEND PUBLICLY ANNOUNCED INTENTION TO ATTACK BLOC SHIPS MOVING IN AND OUT OF CUBA. THERE IS GROWING MOOD OF FRUSTRATION AMONG REFUGEES AND DANGER OF UNILATERAL OPERATIONS AND INCIDENTS IS LIKEWISE GROWING.

ASSUME YOU NOTING IN PRESS THE SOVIET STATEMENT ISSUED 11 SEPT MAKING SWEEPING CHARGES THAT US PREPARING CUBA INVASION AND WARNING THAT "IF THIS ATTACK IS MADE, THIS WILL BE BEGINNING OF UNLEASHING OF WAR." IMPLICATIONS OF THE 4,000-WORD STATEMENT UNDER STUDY. WILL ADVISE YOU FURTHER.

RELEASING OFFICER

COORDINATING OFFICERS

AUTHENTICATING OFFICER

~~TOP SECRET~~

REPRODUCTION BY OTHER THAN THE ISSUING OFFICE IS PROHIBITED.

Copy No.

22. *(Continued)*

CLASSIFIED MESSAGE

~~TOP SECRET~~

PAGE TWO OF FOUR PAGE

ROUTING

1	4
2	5
3	6

ORIG :
UNIT :
EXT :
DATE :

TO :

FROM : DIRECTOR

CONF :

INFO :

DEFERRED
ROUTINE

OUT 75341 DIR 35429

TO INFO -2- CITE DIR

2. REF YOUR REQUEST THAT BNE EXAMINE IMPLICATIONS OF DEFENSIVE EQUIPMENT. FOLLOWING IS PRELIM BNE STATEMENT:

"WHOLE QUESTION SOV MOTIVATIONS, INCLUDING POSSIBLE REASONS WHY SOVS MIGHT CONSIDER INSTALLATION MRBMS, BEING EXAMINED IN SNIE BEING DRAFTED FOR USIB NEXT WEEK. BNE STILL PERSUADED THAT COSTLY CRASH OPERATION TO INSTALL SA-2S IS MORE REASONABLY EXPLAINED BY OTHER THAN DESIRE TO HIDE LATER BUILDUP AND THAT SOVS LIKELY TO REGARD ADVANTAGES OF MAJOR OFFENSIVE BUILDUP NOT EQUAL TO DANGERS OF US INTERVENTION. CUBA LEAKING LIKE SIEVE FROM GROUND OBSERVATION ALONE. THUS SUDDEN CRACKDOWN ON REFUGEE FLOW AND LEGAL TRAFFIC WOULD BE STRONG INDICATOR OF POSSIBLE DESIRE TO UNDERTAKE FURTHER MILITARY BUILDUP IN SECRET."

3. [redacted]

RELEASING OFFICER ~~TOP SECRET~~ AUTHENTICATING OFFICER

23. *Carter to McCone, Cable, 12 September 1962 (Excerpt)*

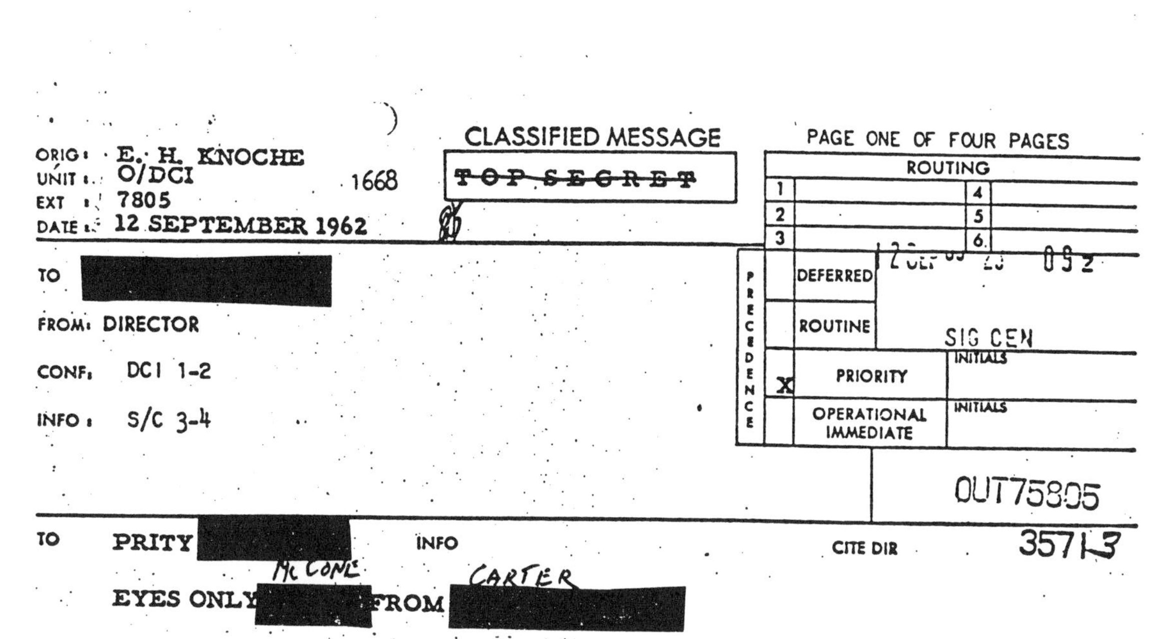

ORIG: E. H. KNOCHE
UNIT: O/DCI 1668
EXT: 7805
DATE: 12 SEPTEMBER 1962

CLASSIFIED MESSAGE
~~TOP SECRET~~

PAGE ONE OF FOUR PAGES

ROUTING

TO [redacted]

FROM: DIRECTOR

CONF: DCI 1-2

INFO: S/C 3-4

PRECEDENCE: DEFERRED / ROUTINE / X PRIORITY / OPERATIONAL IMMEDIATE

SIG CEN

OUT75805

TO PRITY [redacted] INFO CITE DIR 35713

EYES ONLY [redacted] McCONE FROM [redacted] CARTER

1. CASTRO HAS LAID DOWN STRICT CENSORSHIP FROM CUBA. WESTERN PRESS AND RADIO SERVICES HAVE BEEN OUT OF TOUCH WITH CORRESPONDENTS SINCE ABOUT MID-DAY 11 SEPTEMBER. REUTERS MAN ARRESTED. OTHERS MISSING AND MAY BE IN CUSTODY.

2. HEREWITH EXTRACTS FROM AGENCY ASSESSMENT OF MOSCOW STATEMENT 11 SEPTEMBER RE CUBA:

STATEMENT DESIGNED TO FURTHER VARIETY OF SOVIET OBJECTIVES, FOREMOST BEING TO DETER US FROM ACTIVE INTERVENTION. STATEMENT DOES NOT SIGNIFICANTLY ALTER NATURE OF SOVIET COMMITMENT TO DEFEND CASTRO. MOSCOW HAS ONCE AGAIN USED VAGUE AND AMBIGUOUS LANGUAGE TO AVOID CLEAR-CUT OBLIGATION OF MILITARY SUPPORT IN EVENT OF ATTACK.

STATEMENT ALSO CALCULATED TO ENABLE MOSCOW TO CLAIM FULL CREDIT FOR PROTECTING CUBA IF NO INVASION OCCURS.

COORDINATING OFFICERS

RELEASING OFFICER ~~TOP SECRET~~ AUTHENTICATING OFFICER

REPRODUCTION BY OTHER THAN THE ISSUING OFFICE IS PROHIBITED. Copy No 2

23. *(Continued)*

CLASSIFIED MESSAGE

~~TOP SECRET~~

PAGE TWO OF FOUR PAGES

ROUTING

1		4	
2		5	
3		6	

ORIG :
UNIT :
EXT :
DATE :

TO :

FROM: DIRECTOR

CONF:

INFO :

DEFERRED
ROUTINE

OUT 75805 DIR 35713
OUT 75805

TO INFO -2- CITE DIR 35713

IN ADDITION TO DETERRENT EFFECT, STATEMENT SEEMS INTENDED TO CHECK GROWING ALARM RE SOVIET INTENTIONS. IT STRESSES DEFENSIVE NATURE OF SOVIET MILITARY EQUIPMENT AND DENIES INTENTION TO ESTABLISH SOVIET BASE IN CUBA. AT SAME TIME MOSCOW EMPHASIZES RIGHT TO PROVIDE HELP TO CUBA, CITING EXISTENCE OF US ALLIANCES AND BASES ALL ALONG PERIPHERY OF SINO-SOVIET BLOC.

STATEMENT BRUSQUE AND STRONG RE CUBA, BUT MODERATE ON BERLIN. IT NOTES "PAUSE NOW HAS BEEN REACHED" IN BERLIN TALKS AND SAYS IT IS "DIFFICULT" FOR THE US TO NEGOTIATE DURING ELECTION CAMPAIGNS.

3.

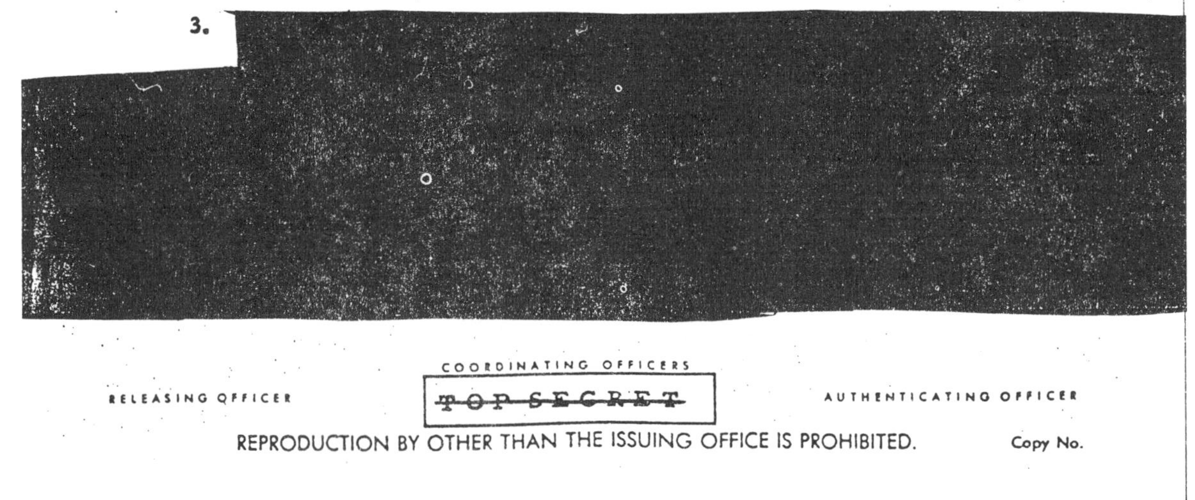

COORDINATING OFFICERS

RELEASING OFFICER ~~TOP SECRET~~ AUTHENTICATING OFFICER

REPRODUCTION BY OTHER THAN THE ISSUING OFFICE IS PROHIBITED. Copy No.

24. *McCone to Carter, Cable, 13 September 1962*

TS-003 CLASSIFIED MESSAGE PAGE 1 OF 2

TOP SECRET

ROUTING

1	4
2	5
3	6

DATE : 13 SEP 62

TO : DIRECTOR

FROM : [redacted]

SEP 13 1248Z 62

ACTION: DCI 1-2 (Tempo copy issued DCI at 0855 13 Sept.)

INFO : S/C 3-4

Document No.
No Change In Class.
Declassified
Class. Changed to: TS (S) C
Next Review Date:
HR 70-3

OPERATIONAL IMMEDIATE

IN 21493

OPIM DIR CITE [redacted]

EYES ONLY [redacted] CARTER FROM [redacted] MC CONE

REF DIR 35650 (OUT 75733) *

1. I BELIEVE SECURING PRISONER RELEASE A SERIOUS OBLIGATION OF UNITED STATES, IMPORTANT FROM A HUMANITARIAN STANDPOINT AND AN ESSENTIAL STEP IN OUR ULTIMATE OBJECTIVES FOR CUBA. THEREFORE PERFECTLY AGREEABLE TO ALTER MY PLANS TO ASSIST WITH CONGRESSIONAL LEADERSHIP AND COMMITTEE CHAIRMEN. DO NOT BELIEVE MY IDENTIFICATION AS REPUBLICAN PARTICULARLY IMPORTANT BUT RECOGNIZE A BI-PARTISAN APPROACH BY THE EXECUTIVE BRANCH OF THE GOVERNMENT ON THIS DELICATE MATTER IMPORTANT, AS ARE MY PERSONAL CONNECTIONS ON THE HILL.

2. DO NOT UNDERSTAND APPARENT READINESS TO APPROVE MEDICINE AND DRUGS TO THE EXTENT INDICATED BUT NO FOOD, AS I BELIEVE BOTH HAVE THEIR HUMANITARIAN CONSIDERATIONS AND PERSONALLY SUPPORT BOTH. ALSO I CONTINUE TO BE CONCERNED THAT THE ESTABLISHMENT OF DEFENSIVE EQUIPMENT AND INSTALLATIONS IS MERELY A PRELUDE TO THE LOCATION OF AN OFFENSIVE WEAPON CAPABILITY AND ONCE THIS IS DONE THE IMPLEMENTATION OF OUR POLICY AS REPORTED IN THE PRESS MIGHT BE EXTREMELY DIFFICULT AND INVOLVE

TOP SECRET

GROUP 1
Excluded from automatic downgrading and declassification

REPRODUCTION BY OTHER THAN THE ISSUING OFFICE IS PROHIBITED. Copy No.

CLASSIFIED MESSAGE

~~TOP SECRET~~

PAGE 2 OF 2

ROUTING

1	4
2	5
3	6

DATE :

TO :

FROM :

ACTION:

INFO :

IN 21493

UNACCEPTABLE DANGERS.

3. I WOULD LIKE TO TALK WITH YOU [redacted] FROM NORSTAD'S HEADQUARTERS TO THE WHITE HOUSE OR PENTAGON SITUATION ROOM TONIGHT (13 SEPT) BETWEEN 1700 AND 1800 YOUR TIME. UNLESS I HEAR TO THE CONTRARY FROM YOU BY TWELVE NOON TODAY YOUR TIME, I WILL PROCEED PARIS THIS EVENING AND MAKE ARRANGEMENTS FOR THIS CALL.

~~TOP SECRET~~

END OF MESSAGE

C/S Comment: [redacted] CARTER'S message to [redacted] MC CONE re procedures to effect release of the Cuban prisoners.

~~TOP SECRET~~

GROUP 1
Excluded from automatic downgrading and declassification

REPRODUCTION BY OTHER THAN THE ISSUING OFFICE IS PROHIBITED.

Copy No.

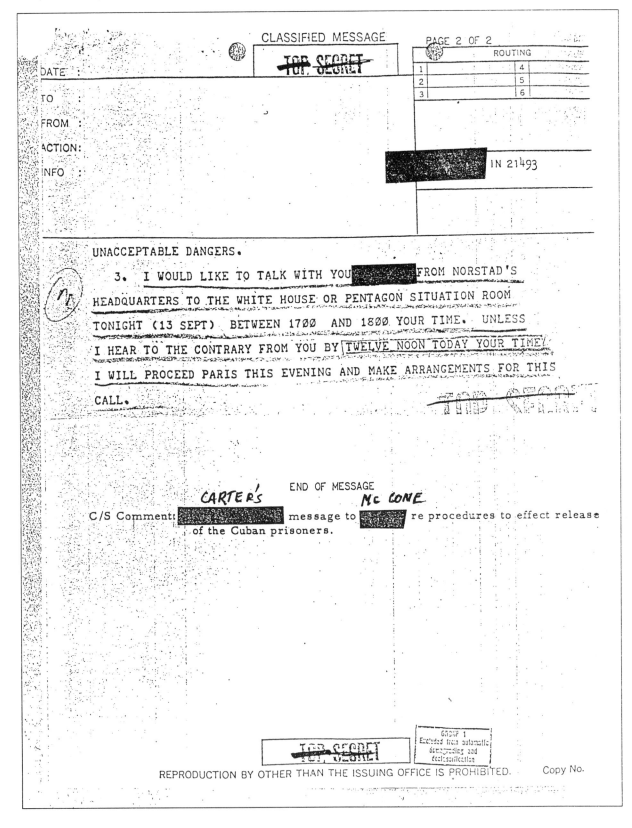

25. *Carter to McCone, Cable, 13 September 1962 (Excerpt)*

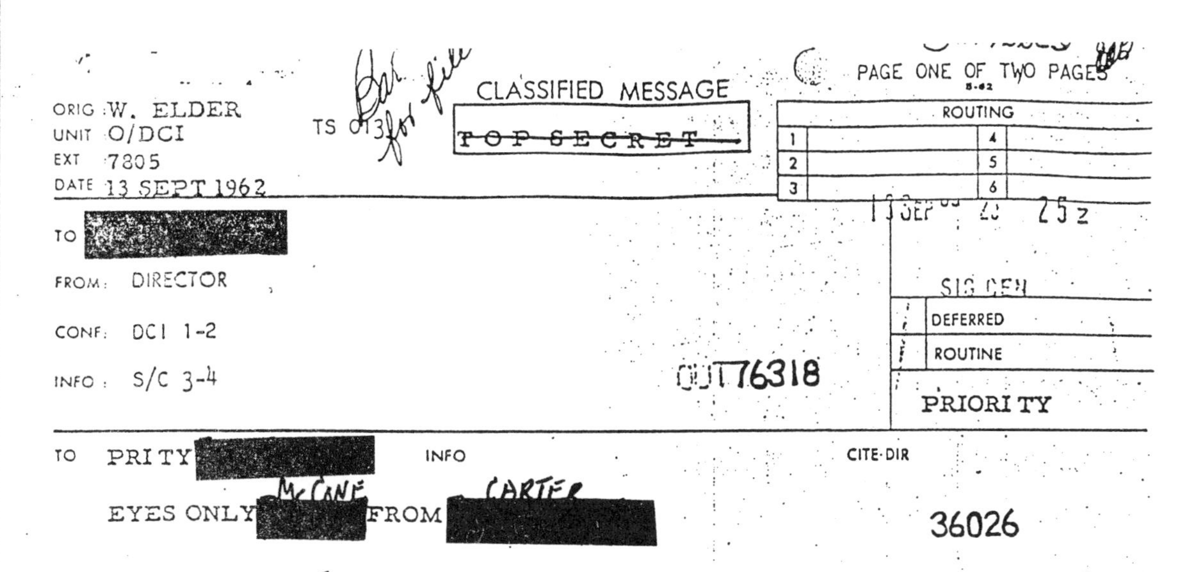

PAGE ONE OF TWO PAGES

CLASSIFIED MESSAGE

~~TOP SECRET~~

ORIG: W. ELDER
UNIT: O/DCI
EXT: 7805
DATE: 13 SEPT 1962

TS

ROUTING: 1 2 3 4 5 6

13 SEP 62 25 Z

TO: [redacted]

FROM: DIRECTOR

CONF: DCI 1-2

INFO: S/C 3-4

OUT76318

SIG CEN

DEFERRED

ROUTINE

PRIORITY

TO PRITY [redacted] INFO CITE DIR

EYES ONLY McCONE FROM CARTER

36026

1. AT LEAST TWENTY SIX MORE SOVIET SHIPS CURRENTLY EN ROUTE TO CUBA. REFUGEE SOURCE REPORTS EQUIPMENT FOR SAM SITE PROBABLY MOVED TO ISLE OF PINES IN LATE AUGUST. ANOTHER SOURCE WITH CUBAN NAVY CONTACTS REPORTS MORE TORPEDO BOATS AND TWO TYPES ANTI-SUB SHIPS EXPECTED TO ARRIVE IN CUBA FROM SOVIET UNION LATE 1962 AND EARLY 1963.

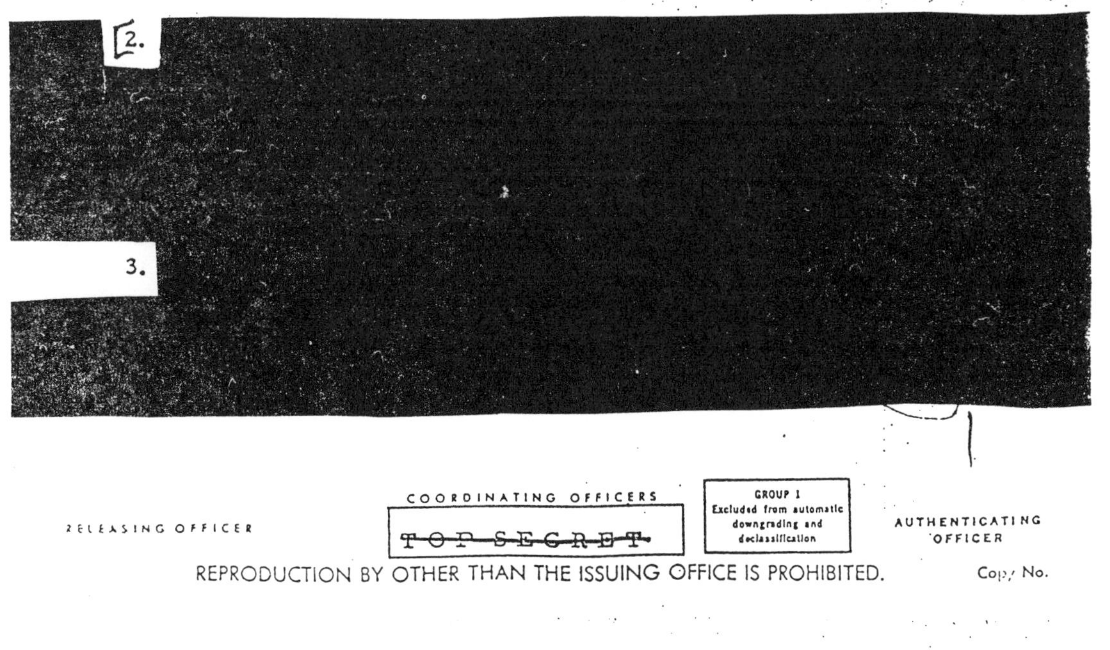

2.

3.

RELEASING OFFICER

COORDINATING OFFICERS

~~TOP SECRET~~

GROUP 1
Excluded from automatic downgrading and declassification

AUTHENTICATING OFFICER

REPRODUCTION BY OTHER THAN THE ISSUING OFFICE IS PROHIBITED.

Copy No.

26. *Central Intelligence Agency, Office of Current Intelligence, Current Intelligence Memorandum, "Analysis of the Suspect Missile Site at Banes, Cuba," 13 September 1962*

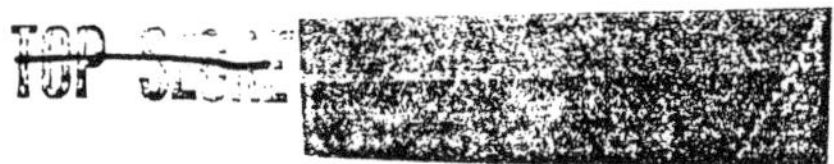

CENTRAL INTELLIGENCE AGENCY
OFFICE OF CURRENT INTELLIGENCE
13 September 1962

CURRENT INTELLIGENCE MEMORANDUM

SUBJECT: Analysis of the Suspect Missile Site at Banes, Cuba

1. A review of all available evidence leads us to conclude it is highly likely that the suspect missile site near Banes, Cuba is a facility for launching cruise missiles against ship targets at fairly close ranges.

2. The site, which is located about 300 feet above sea level and 3.5 nm from the sea is oriented in a general easterly (seaward) direction. It consists of two 30 foot rail launchers in revetments, each connected by cable to a Soviet Whiff tracking radar. Ground support equipment consists of eight canvas-covered, missile-type trailers, two probable generators and electronic vans, and other general purpose vehicles. The area is being fenced, and the personnel are housed in tents. The site configuration and the equipment observed are compatible with a cruise missile system and not compatible with surface-to-air or ballistic systems.

3. Although our knowledge of Soviet cruise missiles is incomplete, we know of three systems which could fit those facilities observed at Banes. We have eliminated other operational Soviet cruise missile systems, with ranges from 1000 to 4000 nm, because their missiles probably would be too large for the Banes facility. A 600 nm cruise missile has had a test range firing in the USSR, but it too would be too large for the Banes site.

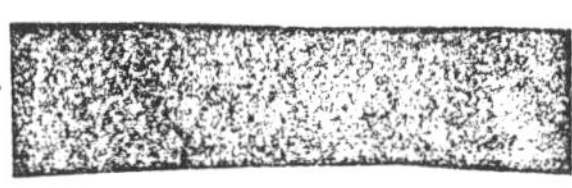

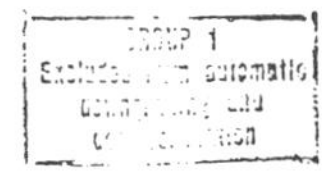

26. *(Continued)*

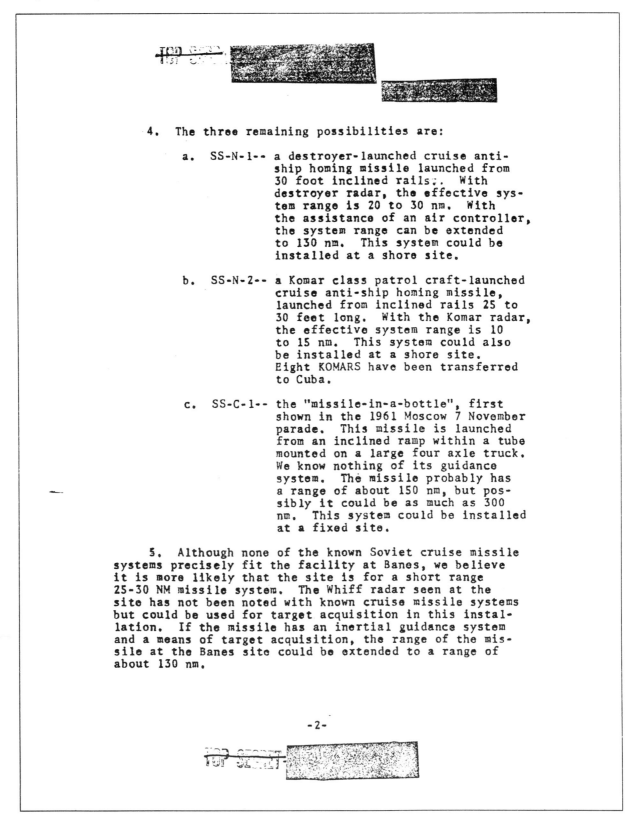

4. The three remaining possibilities are:

   a. SS-N-1-- a destroyer-launched cruise anti-ship homing missile launched from 30 foot inclined rails. With destroyer radar, the effective system range is 20 to 30 nm. With the assistance of an air controller, the system range can be extended to 130 nm. This system could be installed at a shore site.

   b. SS-N-2-- a Komar class patrol craft-launched cruise anti-ship homing missile, launched from inclined rails 25 to 30 feet long. With the Komar radar, the effective system range is 10 to 15 nm. This system could also be installed at a shore site. Eight KOMARS have been transferred to Cuba.

   c. SS-C-1-- the "missile-in-a-bottle", first shown in the 1961 Moscow 7 November parade. This missile is launched from an inclined ramp within a tube mounted on a large four axle truck. We know nothing of its guidance system. The missile probably has a range of about 150 nm, but possibly it could be as much as 300 nm. This system could be installed at a fixed site.

5. Although none of the known Soviet cruise missile systems precisely fit the facility at Banes, we believe it is more likely that the site is for a short range 25-30 NM missile system. The Whiff radar seen at the site has not been noted with known cruise missile systems but could be used for target acquisition in this installation. If the missile has an inertial guidance system and a means of target acquisition, the range of the missile at the Banes site could be extended to a range of about 130 nm.

-2-

26. *(Continued)*

6. There are several items of circumstantial evidence which tend to support the conclusion that the Banes site is for relatively short range coastal defense cruise missiles. The fact that the site is near the coast suggests that the range of its missile is short; otherwise it could be located inland in a less vulnerable area. It is located where short-range missiles could defend against seaborne assault on deep water ports in Nipe Bay south of Banes.* Thus far, the Soviets apparently have not given Cuba any weapons which provide them a long range striking capability, suggesting that their policy is to provide for Cuba's defense only. Because neither the SS-N-1 nor the SS-C-1 has sufficient range to hit any target in the United States, such missiles would fit this policy pattern.

7. If the analysis that the Banes missile site is a coastal defense installation is correct, it would follow that similar facilities may be set up at a number of other locations favorable for protecting beaches against amphibious attack.

8. We doubt that Cubans have been given sufficient training in the use of such missiles to allow them to have operational control over the sites. It seems likely that Soviet technical training personnel would be needed for some time to come and would be available for operating the installation in time of crisis.

---

* Cuba's two nickel plants are in this general area. Their output is being sent to the Soviet Bloc and is equivalent to 20 percent of Soviet production. The more important of these two plants is on the bay protected by the Banes site.

-3

TOP SECRET

27. *Carter to McCone, Cable, 14 September 1962 (Excerpt)*

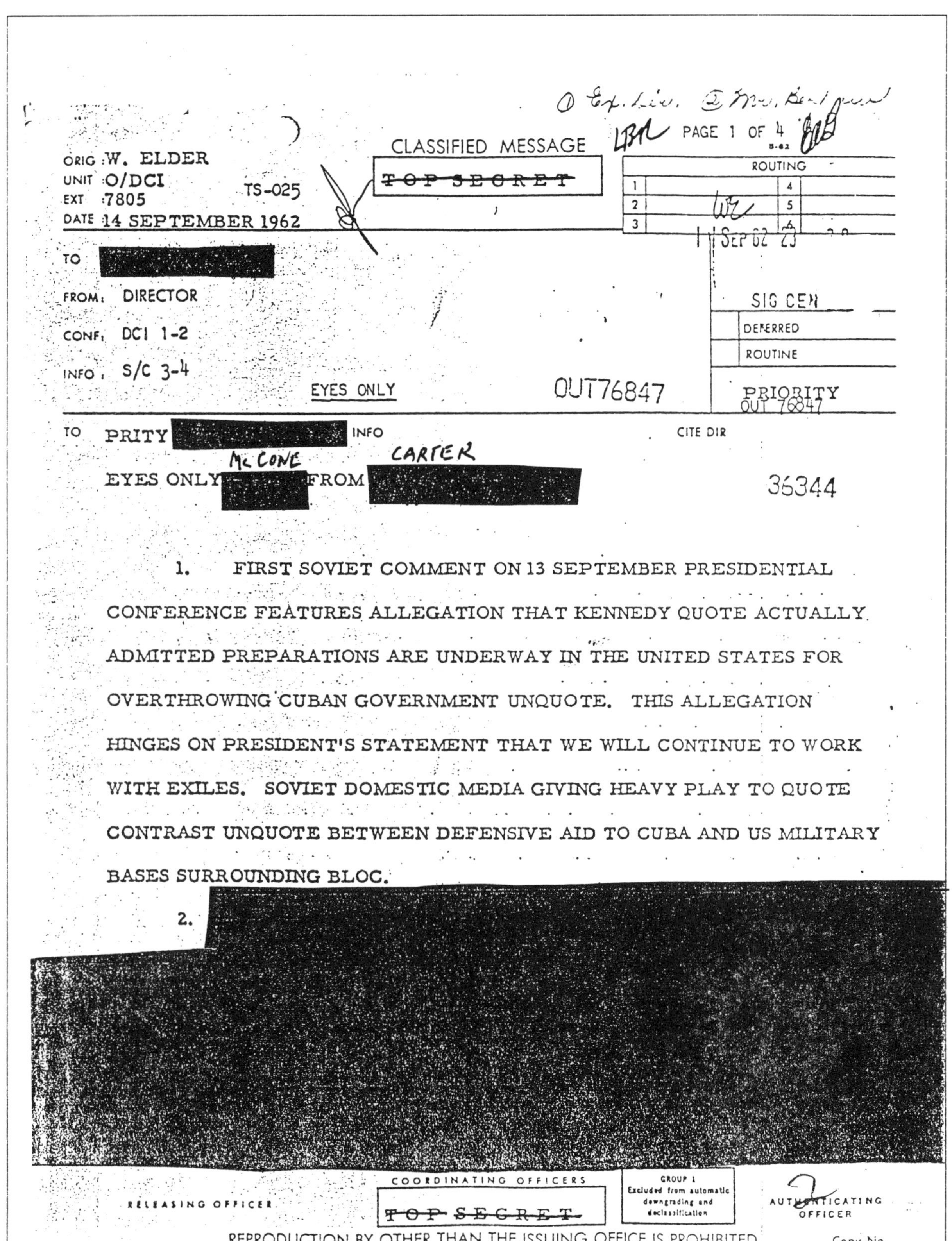

PAGE 1 OF 4

CLASSIFIED MESSAGE

~~TOP SECRET~~

ORIG: W. ELDER
UNIT: O/DCI
EXT: 7805
DATE: 14 SEPTEMBER 1962

TS-025

ROUTING

TO [redacted]

FROM: DIRECTOR

CONF: DCI 1-2

INFO: S/C 3-4

EYES ONLY

OUT76847

SIG CEN

DEFERRED

ROUTINE

PRIORITY

OUT 76847

TO PRITY [redacted] INFO CITE DIR

EYES ONLY [redacted] McCONE FROM [redacted] CARTER

36344

1. FIRST SOVIET COMMENT ON 13 SEPTEMBER PRESIDENTIAL CONFERENCE FEATURES ALLEGATION THAT KENNEDY QUOTE ACTUALLY ADMITTED PREPARATIONS ARE UNDERWAY IN THE UNITED STATES FOR OVERTHROWING CUBAN GOVERNMENT UNQUOTE. THIS ALLEGATION HINGES ON PRESIDENT'S STATEMENT THAT WE WILL CONTINUE TO WORK WITH EXILES. SOVIET DOMESTIC MEDIA GIVING HEAVY PLAY TO QUOTE CONTRAST UNQUOTE BETWEEN DEFENSIVE AID TO CUBA AND US MILITARY BASES SURROUNDING BLOC.

2. [redacted]

RELEASING OFFICER

COORDINATING OFFICERS

~~TOP SECRET~~

GROUP 1
Excluded from automatic downgrading and declassification

AUTHENTICATING OFFICER

REPRODUCTION BY OTHER THAN THE ISSUING OFFICE IS PROHIBITED.

Copy No.

28. *McCone to Carter, Cable, with attached note from MSC [Carter], 16 September 1962*

CENTRAL INTELLIGENCE AGENCY

OFFICE OF THE DEPUTY DIRECTOR

Get a copy to Cline + Kent and Helms and have ~~[illegible]~~ Cline advise as to action —

DONE
17 Sep 62

17 Sep 62

28. *(Continued)*

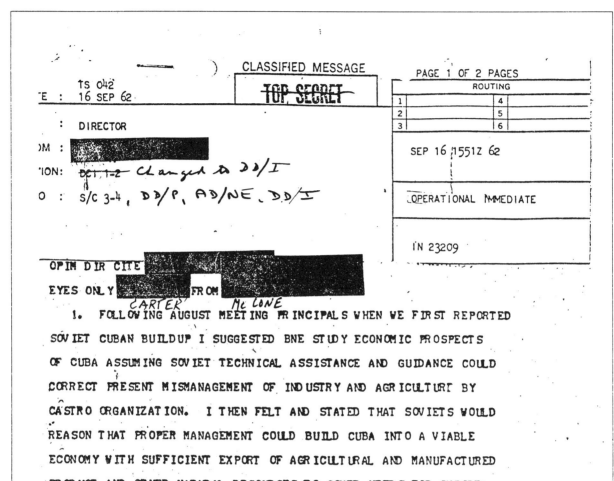

CLASSIFIED MESSAGE

TOP SECRET

PAGE 1 OF 2 PAGES

ROUTING

1		4	
2		5	
3		6	

TS 042
E : 16 SEP 62

: DIRECTOR

OM : [redacted]

ION: ~~DCI 1-2~~ Changed to DD/I

O : S/C 3-4, DD/P, AD/NE, DD/I

SEP 16 1551Z 62

OPERATIONAL IMMEDIATE

IN 23209

OPIM DIR CITE [redacted]

EYES ONLY [redacted] CARTER FROM [redacted] McCONE

1. FOLLOWING AUGUST MEETING PRINCIPALS WHEN WE FIRST REPORTED SOVIET CUBAN BUILDUP I SUGGESTED BNE STUDY ECONOMIC PROSPECTS OF CUBA ASSUMING SOVIET TECHNICAL ASSISTANCE AND GUIDANCE COULD CORRECT PRESENT MISMANAGEMENT OF INDUSTRY AND AGRICULTURE BY CASTRO ORGANIZATION. I THEN FELT AND STATED THAT SOVIETS WOULD REASON THAT PROPER MANAGEMENT COULD BUILD CUBA INTO A VIABLE ECONOMY WITH SUFFICIENT EXPORT OF AGRICULTURAL AND MANUFACTURED PRODUCT AND OTHER NATURAL RESOURCES TO COVER NEEDS FOR IMPORT AND PROVIDE SOME EXCESS FOR SOCIAL BETTERMENT. IN VIEW OF VERY EXTENSIVE PRESS COMMENT ON DETERIORATION OF CUBAN ECONOMY LEAVING IMPRESSION SITUATION CAN NEVER BE REVERSED AND POSSIBILITY OF SUCH REASONING INFLUENCING U. S. POLICY IMPORTANTLY I BELIEVE THE STUDY PROPOSED WILL BE REVEALING AND USEFUL.

2. ALSO BELIEVE WE MUST CAREFULLY STUDY THE PROSPECT OF SECRET IMPORTATION AND PLACEMENT OF SEVERAL SOVIET MRBMS WHICH COULD NOT BE DETECTED BY US IF CUBAN DEFENSES DENY OVERFLIGHT. IN REFLECTING ON MY OBSERVATIONS OF THOR INSTALLATION IN BRITAIN AND JUPITERS

TOP SECRET

GROUP 1 Excluded from automatic downgrading and declassification

REPRODUCTION BY OTHER THAN THE ISSUING OFFICE IS PROHIBITED Copy No.

28. *(Continued)*

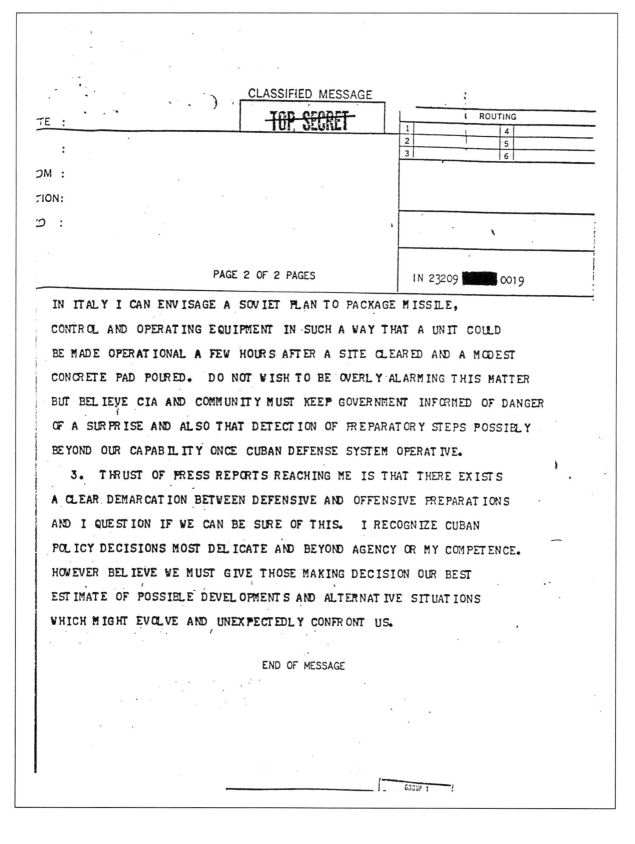

CLASSIFIED MESSAGE

~~TOP SECRET~~

TE :

:

OM :

TION:

D :

ROUTING

1		4
2		5
3		6

PAGE 2 OF 2 PAGES

IN 23209 [redacted] 0019

IN ITALY I CAN ENVISAGE A SOVIET PLAN TO PACKAGE MISSILE, CONTROL AND OPERATING EQUIPMENT IN SUCH A WAY THAT A UNIT COULD BE MADE OPERATIONAL A FEW HOURS AFTER A SITE CLEARED AND A MODEST CONCRETE PAD POURED. DO NOT WISH TO BE OVERLY ALARMING THIS MATTER BUT BELIEVE CIA AND COMMUNITY MUST KEEP GOVERNMENT INFORMED OF DANGER OF A SURPRISE AND ALSO THAT DETECTION OF PREPARATORY STEPS POSSIBLY BEYOND OUR CAPABILITY ONCE CUBAN DEFENSE SYSTEM OPERATIVE.

3. THRUST OF PRESS REPORTS REACHING ME IS THAT THERE EXISTS A CLEAR DEMARCATION BETWEEN DEFENSIVE AND OFFENSIVE PREPARATIONS AND I QUESTION IF WE CAN BE SURE OF THIS. I RECOGNIZE CUBAN POLICY DECISIONS MOST DELICATE AND BEYOND AGENCY OR MY COMPETENCE. HOWEVER BELIEVE WE MUST GIVE THOSE MAKING DECISION OUR BEST ESTIMATE OF POSSIBLE DEVELOPMENTS AND ALTERNATIVE SITUATIONS WHICH MIGHT EVOLVE AND UNEXPECTEDLY CONFRONT US.

END OF MESSAGE

GROUP 1

29. *Carter to McCone, Cable, 17 September 1962 (Excerpt)*

① Ex. Dir. ② Mr. Berkow

CLASSIFIED MESSAGE **TOP SECRET**

PAGE ONE OF FIVE PAGES

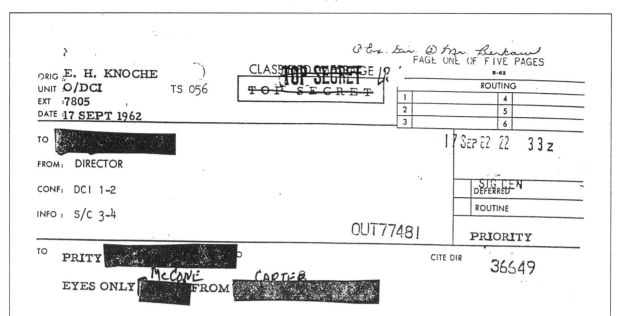

ORIG E. H. KNOCHE
UNIT O/DCI TS 056
EXT 7805
DATE 17 SEPT 1962

ROUTING 1 2 3 4 5 6

TO [redacted]

FROM: DIRECTOR

CONF: DCI 1-2

INFO: S/C 3-4

17 SEP 62 22 33z

SIG CEN

DEFERRED

ROUTINE

OUT77481

PRIORITY

TO PRITY [redacted]

CITE DIR 36649

EYES ONLY McCONE FROM CARTER

1. SOVIET PASSENGER SHIPS HAVE MADE NINE UNPUBLICIZED TRIPS TO CUBA SINCE LATE JULY; TWO MORE BELIEVED EN ROUTE NOW. THE TWO WILL BRING ESTIMATED TOTAL MILITARY TECHNICIANS ARRIVING SINCE MID-JULY TO ABOUT FORTY-TWO HUNDRED.

UNDER AGREEMENT NEGOTIATED RECENTLY BY BRITISH GUIANA TRADE MINISTER ON VISIT TO HAVANA, BRITISH GUIANA WILL SEND UP TO ONE THOUSAND EXPERIENCED CANE CUTTERS TO HELP WITH NEXT YEARS HARVEST.

2. CHICOMS HAVE ASKED FOR EMERGENCY MEETING OF WANG AND CABOT IN WARSAW. DATE SET IS 21 SEPT. NO HINT OF SUBJECT, BUT WE SUSPEC T IT WILL BE CHICOM CHARGE OF "AGGRESSIVE INTENT" IN WAKE OF U-2 INCIDENT. CHICOM PRESS BENDING EVERY EFFORT TO TAG US WITH RESPONSIBILITY FOR THE U-2 OPERATIONS OVER MAINLAND, AND WE ARE ALSO GETTING COMPLAINTS FROM PEIPING ABOUT US

RELEASING OFFICER

COORDINATING OFFICERS

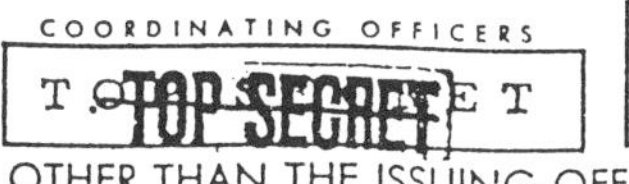

GROUP 1 Excluded from automatic downgrading and declassification

AUTHENTICATING OFFICER

REPRODUCTION BY OTHER THAN THE ISSUING OFFICE IS PROHIBITED.

Copy No.

30. *Carter to McCone, Cable, 18 September 1962*

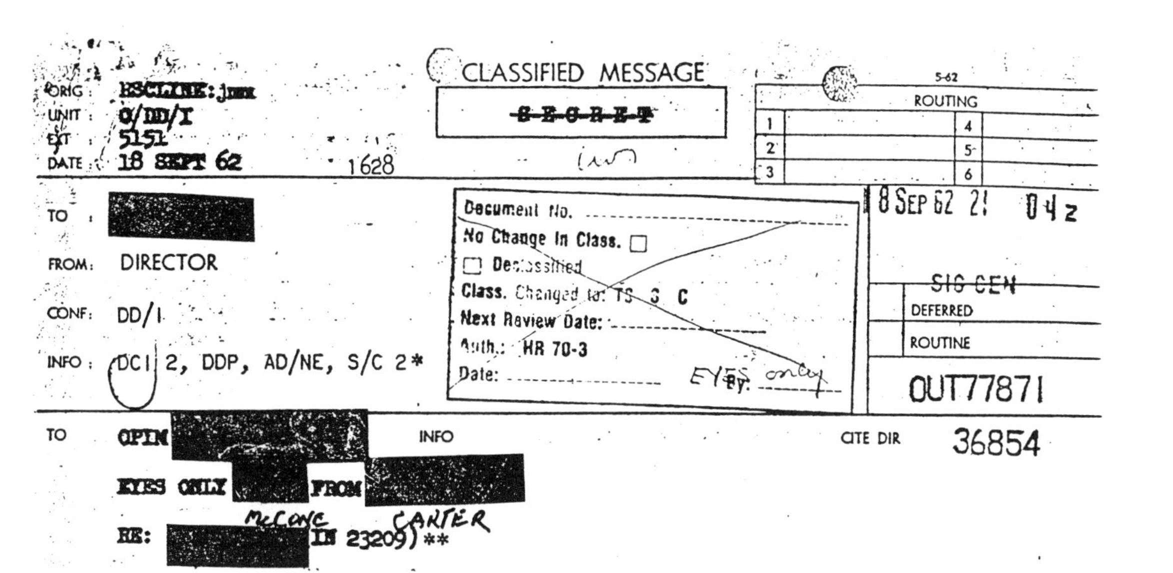

CLASSIFIED MESSAGE

~~SECRET~~

ORIG: RSCLINE:jmm
UNIT: O/DD/I
EXT: 5151
DATE: 18 SEPT 62 1628

ROUTING

1		4	
2		5	
3		6	

TO: [redacted]

FROM: DIRECTOR

CONF: DD/I

INFO: DCI 2, DDP, AD/NE, S/C 2*

Document No.
No Change In Class. ☐
☐ Declassified
Class. Changed to: TS S C
Next Review Date:
Auth.: HR 70-3
Date: By:
EYES only

18 SEP 62 21 04z

SIG CEN
DEFERRED
ROUTINE

OUT77871

TO OPIM [redacted] INFO CITE DIR 36854

EYES ONLY [redacted] FROM [redacted]

McCONE CARTER

RE: [redacted] IN 23209)**

1. NO DOUBT THAT CUBAN ECONOMIC RESOURCES CAPABLE OF SUBSTANTIAL DEVELOPMENT GIVEN BETTER MANAGEMENT AND SUFFICIENT CAPITAL INVESTMENT. SNIE 85-3, BEFORE USIB TOMORROW, RECOGNIZES THIS AS A PROBABLE SOVIET INTENTION AND THAT THE OBJECTIVE IS TO STIMULATE COMMUNIST POLITICAL ACTION ELSEWHERE IN LATIN AMERICA. AS NOTED IN 85-2 (1 AUG), HOWEVER, PRESENT STATE OF CUBAN ECONOMY IS VERY BAD AND SUBSTANTIAL UPTURN WILL BE DELAYED UNTIL AFTER 1963.

2. SNIE 85-3 DISCUSSES IN DETAIL POSSIBILITY OF INTRODUCTION OF MRBMs INTO CUBA, BUT JUDGES THIS TO BE UNLIKELY BECAUSE OF RISK OF U.S. INTERVENTION INVOLVED UNLESS THERE IS A RADICAL CHANGE IN SOVIET POLICY NOT PRESENTLY INDICATED. SUCH A CHANGE WOULD HAVE IMPLICATIONS EXTENDING FAR BEYOND CUBA. WE KNOW FROM OUR BRIEFINGS THAT GOVERNMENT TOP LEVEL REALIZES POSSIBILITY OF DEVELOPMENTS SHIELDED FROM OUR DETECTION ONCE SA-2's OPERATIVE. SNIE 85-3 STRESSES THAT THERE IS A MIDDLE GROUND IN WHICH DEFENSIVE OR OFFENSIVE CHARACTER OF BUILDUP IS A MATTER OF INTERPRETATION. VARIOUS ALTERNATIVES

RELEASING OFFICER

COORDINATING OFFICERS

~~SECRET~~

GROUP 1
Excluded from automatic downgrading and declassification

AUTHENTICATING OFFICER

REPRODUCTION BY OTHER THAN THE ISSUING OFFICE IS PROHIBITED. Copy No.

30. *(Continued)*

CLASSIFIED MESSAGE

SECRET

ROUTING

ORIG :
UNIT :
EXT :
DATE :

TO :
FROM: DIRECTOR
CONF:
INFO :

PAGE 2

DEFERRED
ROUTINE

OUT77871

TO INFO CITE DIR 36854

EXPLORED. AGAIN WE KNOW AMBIGUITIES OF OFFENSIVE-DEFENSIVE DISTINCTION BROUGHT TO TOP LEVEL ATTENTION BEFORE PUBLIC STATEMENTS FORMULATED.

END OF MESSAGE

C/S COMMENT: *DISSEMINATION SAME AS REFERENCED CABLE.

McCONE CARTER

**Cable from [redacted] to [redacted] concerning the Soviet buildup of Cuba.

MARSHALL S. CARTER, A/DCI
RELEASING OFFICER

COORDINATING OFFICERS

S-E-C-R-E-T

GROUP 1
Excluded from automatic downgrading and declassification

RAY S. CLINE, DDI
AUTHENTICATING OFFICER

REPRODUCTION BY OTHER THAN THE ISSUING OFFICE IS PROHIBITED. Copy No.

31. *Carter to McCone, Cable, 18 September 1962 (Excerpt)*

CLASSIFIED MESSAGE

~~TOP SECRET~~

TOP SECRET

PAGE 1 OF 2

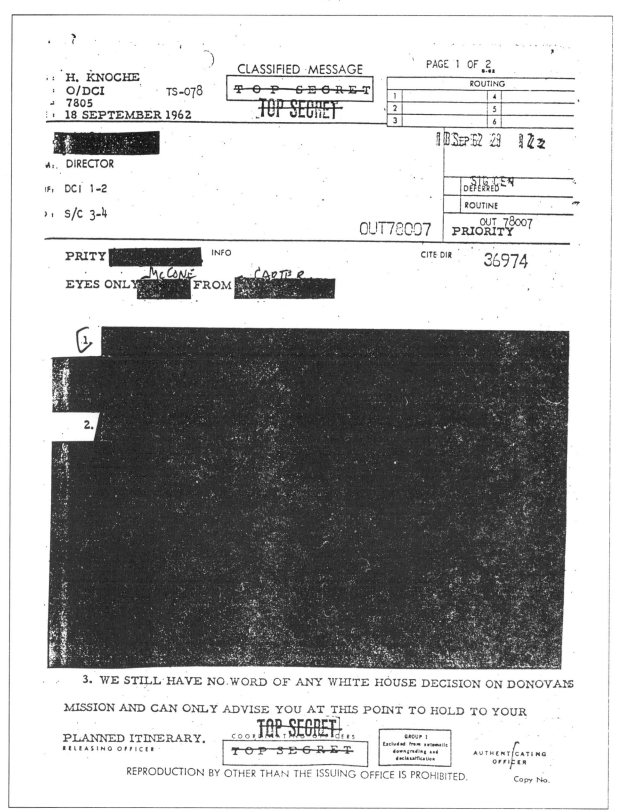

H. KNOCHE
O/DCI TS-078
7805
18 SEPTEMBER 1962

ROUTING	
1	4
2	5
3	6

18 SEP 62 23 12z

DIRECTOR

DCI 1-2

S/C 3-4

SIG CEN

DEFERRED

ROUTINE

OUT78007

OUT 78007 PRIORITY

PRITY [redacted] INFO CITE DIR 36974

EYES ONLY McCONE FROM CARTER

1. [redacted]

2. [redacted]

3. WE STILL HAVE NO WORD OF ANY WHITE HOUSE DECISION ON DONOVANS MISSION AND CAN ONLY ADVISE YOU AT THIS POINT TO HOLD TO YOUR PLANNED ITINERARY.

RELEASING OFFICER

COORDINATING OFFICERS

TOP SECRET

~~TOP SECRET~~

GROUP 1
Excluded from automatic downgrading and declassification

AUTHENTICATING OFFICER

REPRODUCTION BY OTHER THAN THE ISSUING OFFICE IS PROHIBITED.

Copy No.

32. *Carter to McCone, Cable, 19 September 1962 (Excerpt)*

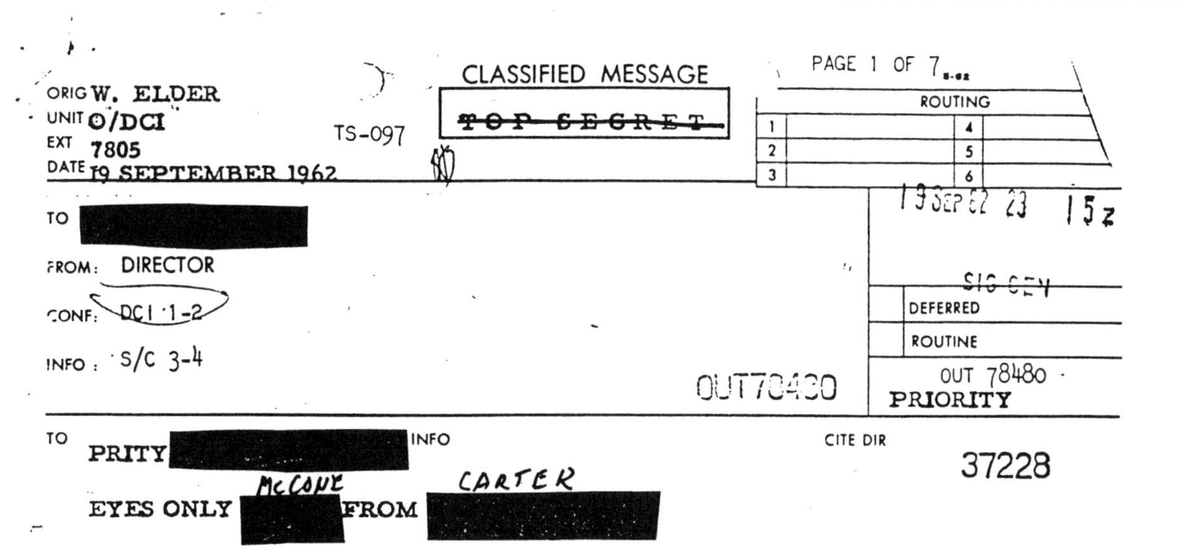

ORIG W. ELDER
UNIT O/DCI
EXT 7805
DATE 19 SEPTEMBER 1962

TS-097

CLASSIFIED MESSAGE

~~TOP SECRET~~

PAGE 1 OF 7

ROUTING

1		4	
2		5	
3		6	

19 SEP 62 23 15z

TO [redacted]

FROM: DIRECTOR

CONF: DCI 1-2

INFO: S/C 3-4

OUT78480

SIG CEN

DEFERRED

ROUTINE

OUT 78480

PRIORITY

TO PRITY [redacted] INFO

CITE DIR 37228

EYES ONLY McCONE [redacted] FROM CARTER [redacted]

1. HEREWITH CONCLUSIONS OF SPECIAL NATIONAL INTELLIGENCE ESTIMATE APPROVED BY USIB ON 19 SEPTEMBER.

A. WE BELIEVE THAT SOVIET UNION VALUES ITS POSITION IN CUBA PRIMARILY FOR THE POLITICAL ADVANTAGES TO BE DERIVED FROM IT, AND CONSEQUENTLY THAT THE MAIN PURPOSE OF THE PRESENT MILITARY BUILDUP IN CUBA IS TO STRENGTHEN THE COMMUNIST REGIME THERE AGAINST WHAT THE CUBANS AND THE SOVIETS CONCEIVE TO BE A DANGER THAT THE US MAY ATTEMPT BY ONE MEANS OR ANOTHER TO OVERTHROW IT. THE SOVIETS EVIDENTLY HOPE TO DETER ANY SUCH ATTEMPT BY ENHANCING CASTRO'S DEFENSIVE CAPABILITIES AND BY THREATENING SOVIET MILITARY RETALIATION. AT THE SAME TIME, THEY EVIDENTLY RECOGNIZE THAT THE DEVELOPMENT OF AN OFFENSIVE MILITARY BASE IN CUBA MIGHT PROVOKE US MILITARY INTERVENTION AND THUS DEFEAT THEIR PRESENT PURPOSE.

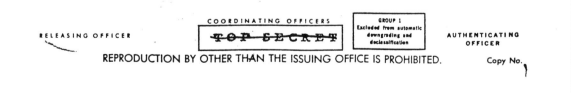

RELEASING OFFICER

COORDINATING OFFICERS

~~TOP SECRET~~

GROUP 1
Excluded from automatic downgrading and declassification

AUTHENTICATING OFFICER

REPRODUCTION BY OTHER THAN THE ISSUING OFFICE IS PROHIBITED.

Copy No. 1

32. *(Continued)*

CLASSIFIED MESSAGE

~~TOP SECRET~~

PAGE 2 OF 7

ORIG :
UNIT :
EXT :
DATE :

ROUTING	
1	4
2	5
3	6

TO :

FROM: DIRECTOR

CONF:

INFO :

DEFERRED

ROUTINE

OUT 78480

TO INFO CITE DIR 37228

-2-

B. IN TERMS OF MILITARY SIGNIFICANCE, THE CURRENT SOVIET DELIVERIES ARE SUBSTANTIALLY IMPROVING AIR DEFENSE AND COASTAL DEFENSE CAPABILITIES IN CUBA. THEIR POLITICAL SIGNIFICANCE IS THAT, IN CONJUNCTION WITH THE SOVIET STATEMENT OF 11 SEPTEMBER, THEY ARE LIKELY TO BE REGARDED AS ENSURING THE CONTINUATION OF THE CASTRO REGIME IN POWER, WITH CONSEQUENT DISCOURAGEMENT TO THE OPPOSITION AT HOME AND IN EXILE. THE THREAT INHERENT IN THESE DEVELOPMENTS IS THAT, TO THE EXTENT THAT THE CASTRO REGIME THEREBY GAINS A SENSE OF SECURITY AT HOME, IT WILL BE EMBOLDENED TO BECOME MORE AGGRESSIVE IN FOMENTING REVOLUTIONARY ACTIVITY IN LATIN AMERICA.

C. AS THE BUILDUP CONTINUES, THE SOVIET UNION MAY BE TEMPTED TO ESTABLISH IN CUBA, OTHER WEAPONS REPRESENTED TO BE DEFENSIVE IN PURPOSE, BUT OF A MORE "OFFENSIVE" CHARACTER: E.G., LIGHT BOMBERS, SUBMARINES, AND ADDITIONAL TYPES OF SHORT-RANGE SURFACE-TO-SURFACE MISSILES. A DECISION TO PROVIDE SUCH WEAPONS

COORDINATING OFFICERS

RELEASING OFFICER

~~TOP SECRET~~

GROUP 1
Excluded from automatic downgrading and declassification

AUTHENTICATING OFFICER

REPRODUCTION BY OTHER THAN THE ISSUING OFFICE IS PROHIBITED. Copy No.

CLASSIFIED MESSAGE

~~TOP SECRET~~

PAGE 3 OF 7

ROUTING

1		4	
2		5	
3		6	

ORIG :
UNIT :
EXT :
DATE :

TO :

FROM: DIRECTOR

CONF:

INFO :

DEFERRED

ROUTINE

OUT 78480

TO INFO CITE DIR 37228

-3-

WILL CONTINUE TO DEPEND HEAVILY ON THE SOVIET ESTIMATE AS TO WHETHER THEY COULD BE INTRODUCED WITHOUT PROVOKING A US MILITARY REACTION.

D. THE SOVIET UNION COULD DERIVE CONSIDERABLE MILITARY ADVANTAGE FROM THE ESTABLISHMENT OF SOVIET MEDIUM AND INTERMEDIATE RANGE BALLISTIC MISSILES IN CUBA, OR FROM THE ESTABLISHMENT OF A SOVIET SUBMARINE BASE THERE. AS BETWEEN THESE TWO, THE ESTABLISHMENT OF SUB BASE COULD BE MORE LIKELY. EITHER DEVELOPMENT, HOWEVER, WOULD BE INCOMPATIBLE WITH SOVIET PRACTICE TO DATE AND WITH SOVIET POLICY AS WE PRESENTLY ESTIMATE IT. IT WOULD INDICATE A FAR GREATER WILLINGNESS TO INCREASE THE LEVEL OF RISK IN US-SOVIET RELATIONS THAN THE SOVIET UNION HAS DISPLAYED THUS FAR, AND CONSEQUENTLY WOULD HAVE IMPORTANT POLICY IMPLICATIONS WITH RESPECT TO OTHER AREAS AND OTHER PROBLEMS IN EAST-WEST RELATIONS.

RELEASING OFFICER

COORDINATING OFFICERS

~~TOP SECRET~~

GROUP 1
Excluded from automatic downgrading and declassification

AUTHENTICATING OFFICER

Copy No.

32. *(Continued)*

CLASSIFIED MESSAGE

~~TOP SECRET~~

PAGE 4 OF 7

ORIG :
UNIT :
EXT :
DATE :

ROUTING

1		4	
2		5	
3		6	

TO :

FROM: DIRECTOR

CONF:

INFO :

DEFERRED

ROUTINE

OUT 78480

TO INFO -4- CITE DIR 37228

E. THE LATIN AMERICAN REACTION WILL BE TO THE EVIDENCE OF AN INCREASED SOVIET COMMITMENT TO CUBA, RATHER THAN TO THE TECHNICAL IMPLICATIONS OF THE MILITARY BUILDUP. MANY LATIN AMERICANS WILL FEAR AND RESENT A SOVIET MILITARY INTRUSION INTO THE HEMISPHERE, BUT WILL REGARD THE PROBLEM AS ONE TO BE MET BY THE US AND NOT THEIR RESPONSIBILITY. WE ESTIMATE THE CHANCES ARE BETTER NOW THAN THEY WERE AT PUNTA DEL ESTE TO OBTAIN 2/3 OAS MAJORITY FOR SANCTIONS AND OTHER STEPS SHORT OF MILITARY ACTION AIMED AT CUBA. IT BECAME CLEAR THAT THE SOVIET UNION WAS ESTABLISHING AN "OFFENSIVE" BASE IN CUBA, MOST LATIN AMERICAN GOVERNMENTS WOULD EXPECT THE US TO ELIMINATE IT, BY WHATEVER MEANS WERE NECESSARY, BUT MANY OF THEM WOULD STILL SEEK TO AVOID DIRECT INVOLVEMENT.

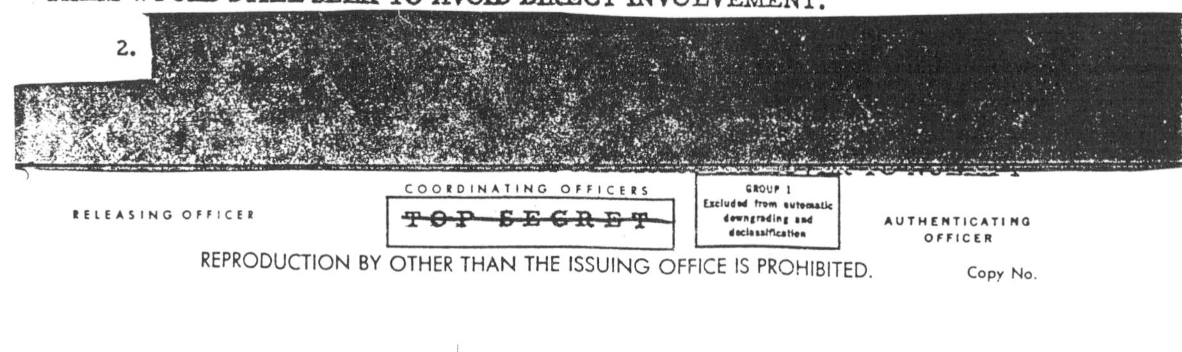

2.

RELEASING OFFICER

COORDINATING OFFICERS

~~TOP SECRET~~

GROUP 1
Excluded from automatic downgrading and declassification

AUTHENTICATING OFFICER

REPRODUCTION BY OTHER THAN THE ISSUING OFFICE IS PROHIBITED.

Copy No.

33. *Special National Intelligence Estimate 85-3-62 "The Military Buildup in Cuba," 19 September 1962 (Excerpt)*

SECRET

SPECIAL

NATIONAL INTELLIGENCE ESTIMATE

NUMBER 85-3-62

The Military Buildup in Cuba

19 September 1962

SECRET

~~SECRET~~

THE MILITARY BUILDUP IN CUBA

THE PROBLEM

To assess the strategic and political significance of the recent military buildup in Cuba and of the possible future development of additional military capabilities there.

CONCLUSIONS

A. We believe that the USSR values its position in Cuba primarily for the political advantages to be derived from it, and consequently that the main purpose of the present military buildup in Cuba is to strengthen the Communist regime there against what the Cubans and the Soviets conceive to be a danger that the US may attempt by one means or another to overthrow it. The Soviets evidently hope to deter any such attempt by enhancing Castro's defensive capabilities and by threatening Soviet military retaliation. At the same time, they evidently recognize that the development of an offensive military base in Cuba might provoke US military intervention and thus defeat their present purpose. (*Paras. 1–11*)

B. In terms of military significance, the current Soviet deliveries are substantially improving air defense and coastal defense capabilities in Cuba. Their political significance is that, in conjunction with the Soviet statement of 11 September, they are likely to be regarded as ensuring the continuation of the Castro regime in power, with consequent discouragement to the opposition at home and in exile. The threat inherent in these developments is that, to the extent that the Castro regime thereby gains a sense of security at home,

~~SECRET~~ 1

it will be emboldened to become more aggressive in fomenting revolutionary activity in Latin America. *(Paras. 18–21)*

C. As the buildup continues, the USSR may be tempted to establish in Cuba other weapons represented to be defensive in purpose, but of a more "offensive" character: e.g., light bombers, submarines, and additional types of short-range surface-to-surface missiles (SSMs). A decision to provide such weapons will continue to depend heavily on the Soviet estimate as to whether they could be introduced without provoking a US military reaction. *(Paras. 22–28)*

D. The USSR could derive considerable military advantage from the establishment of Soviet medium and intermediate range ballistic missiles in Cuba, or from the establishment of a Soviet submarine base there. As between these two, the establishment of a submarine base would be the more likely. Either development, however, would be incompatible with Soviet practice to date and with Soviet policy as we presently estimate it. It would indicate a far greater willingness to increase the level of risk in US-Soviet relations than the USSR has displayed thus far, and consequently would have important policy implications with respect to other areas and other problems in East-West relations. *(Paras. 29–33)*

E. The Latin American reaction will be to the evidence of an increased Soviet commitment to Cuba, rather than to the technical implications of the military buildup. Many Latin Americans will fear and resent a Soviet military intrusion into the Hemisphere, but will regard the problem as one to be met by the US and not their responsibility. We estimate the chances are better now than they were at Punta del Este to obtain the necessary two-thirds OAS majority for sanctions and other steps short of direct military action aimed at Cuba. If it became clear that the USSR was establishing an "offensive" base in Cuba, most Latin American governments would expect the US to eliminate it, by whatever means were necessary, but many of them would still seek to avoid direct involvement. *(Paras. 34–37)*

34. *McCone to Carter, Cable, 20 September 1962*

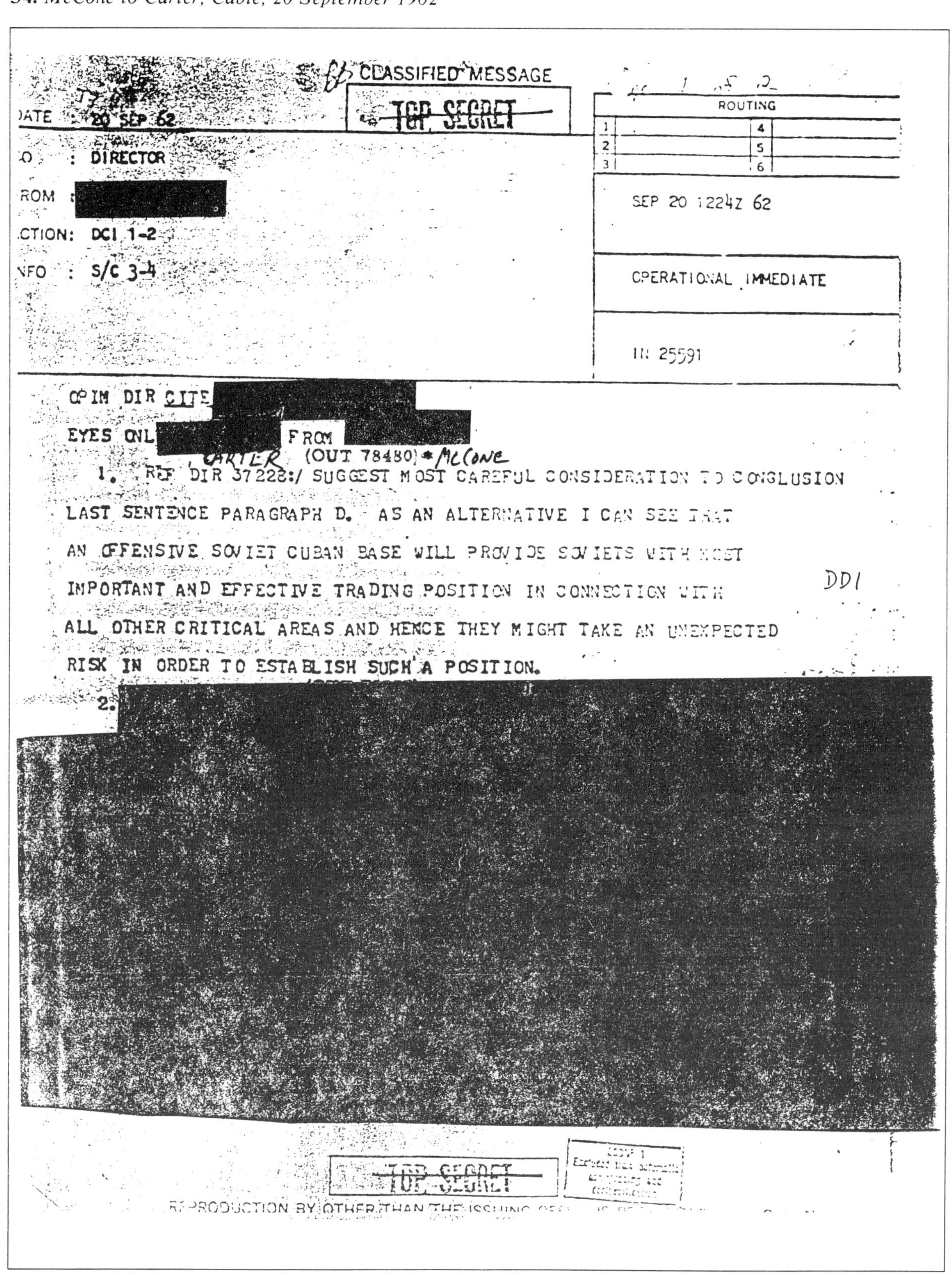

CLASSIFIED MESSAGE

TOP SECRET

DATE : 20 SEP 62

TO : DIRECTOR

FROM : [redacted]

ACTION: DCI 1-2

INFO : S/C 3-4

ROUTING

SEP 20 1224Z 62

OPERATIONAL IMMEDIATE

IN 25591

OPIM DIR CITE [redacted]

EYES ONLY [redacted] FROM [redacted]

CARTER (OUT 78480) * McCone

1\. REF DIR 37223:/ SUGGEST MOST CAREFUL CONSIDERATION TO CONCLUSION LAST SENTENCE PARAGRAPH D. AS AN ALTERNATIVE I CAN SEE THAT AN OFFENSIVE SOVIET CUBAN BASE WILL PROVIDE SOVIETS WITH MOST IMPORTANT AND EFFECTIVE TRADING POSITION IN CONNECTION WITH ALL OTHER CRITICAL AREAS AND HENCE THEY MIGHT TAKE AN UNEXPECTED RISK IN ORDER TO ESTABLISH SUCH A POSITION.

DDI

2\. [redacted]

TOP SECRET

REPRODUCTION BY OTHER THAN THE ISSUING OFFICE IS PROHIBITED

34. *(Continued)*

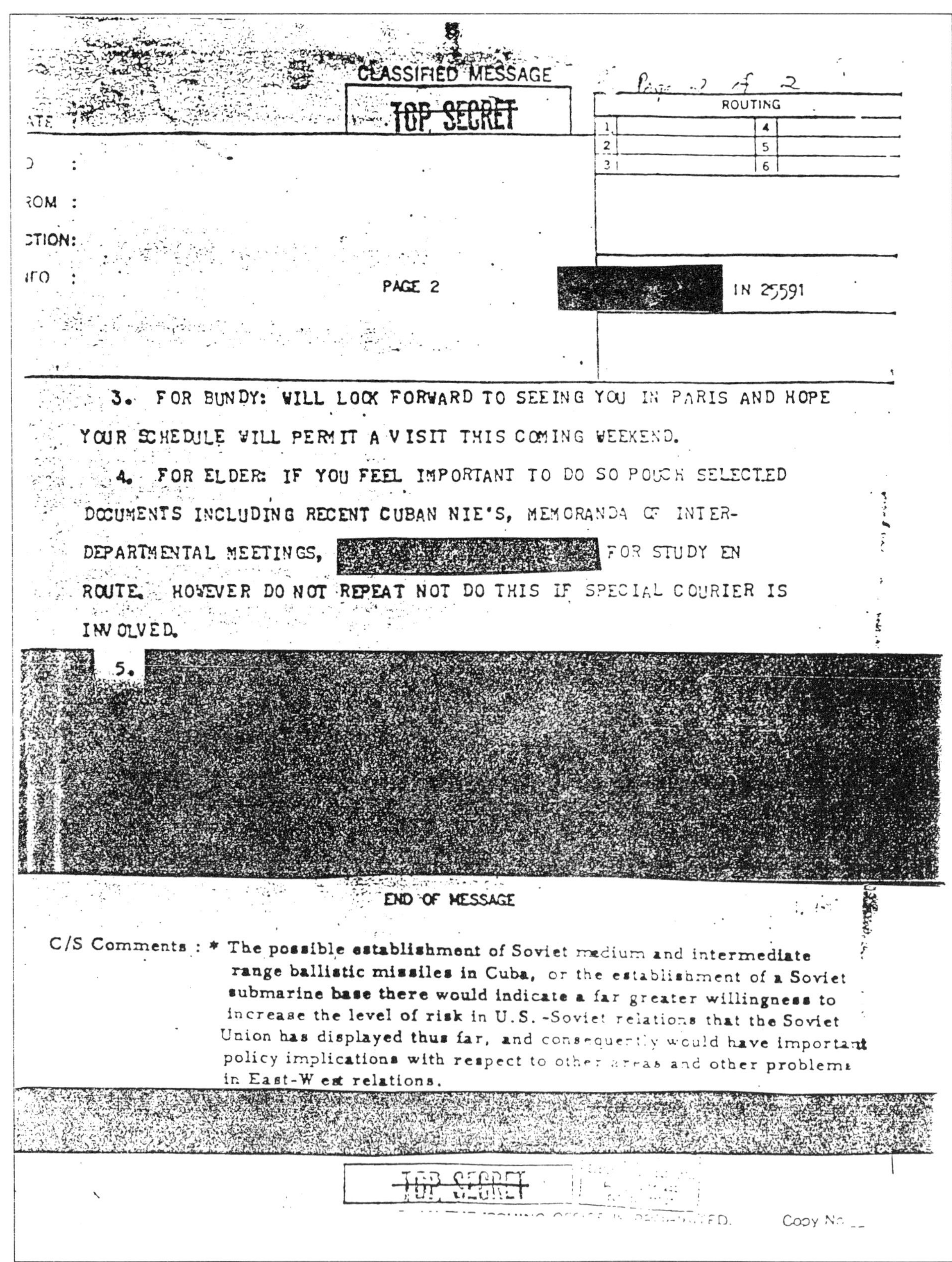

CLASSIFIED MESSAGE

TOP SECRET

Page 2 of 2

ROUTING

1	4
2	5
3	6

TO :

FROM :

ACTION:

INFO :

PAGE 2 [redacted] IN 25591

3. FOR BUNDY: WILL LOOK FORWARD TO SEEING YOU IN PARIS AND HOPE YOUR SCHEDULE WILL PERMIT A VISIT THIS COMING WEEKEND.

4. FOR ELDER: IF YOU FEEL IMPORTANT TO DO SO POUCH SELECTED DOCUMENTS INCLUDING RECENT CUBAN NIE'S, MEMORANDA OF INTER-DEPARTMENTAL MEETINGS, [redacted] FOR STUDY EN ROUTE. HOWEVER DO NOT REPEAT NOT DO THIS IF SPECIAL COURIER IS INVOLVED.

5. [redacted]

END OF MESSAGE

C/S Comments : * The possible establishment of Soviet medium and intermediate range ballistic missiles in Cuba, or the establishment of a Soviet submarine base there would indicate a far greater willingness to increase the level of risk in U.S.-Soviet relations that the Soviet Union has displayed thus far, and consequently would have important policy implications with respect to other areas and other problems in East-West relations.

TOP SECRET

Copy No. __

35. *Carter to McCone, Cable, 21 September 1962 (Excerpt)*

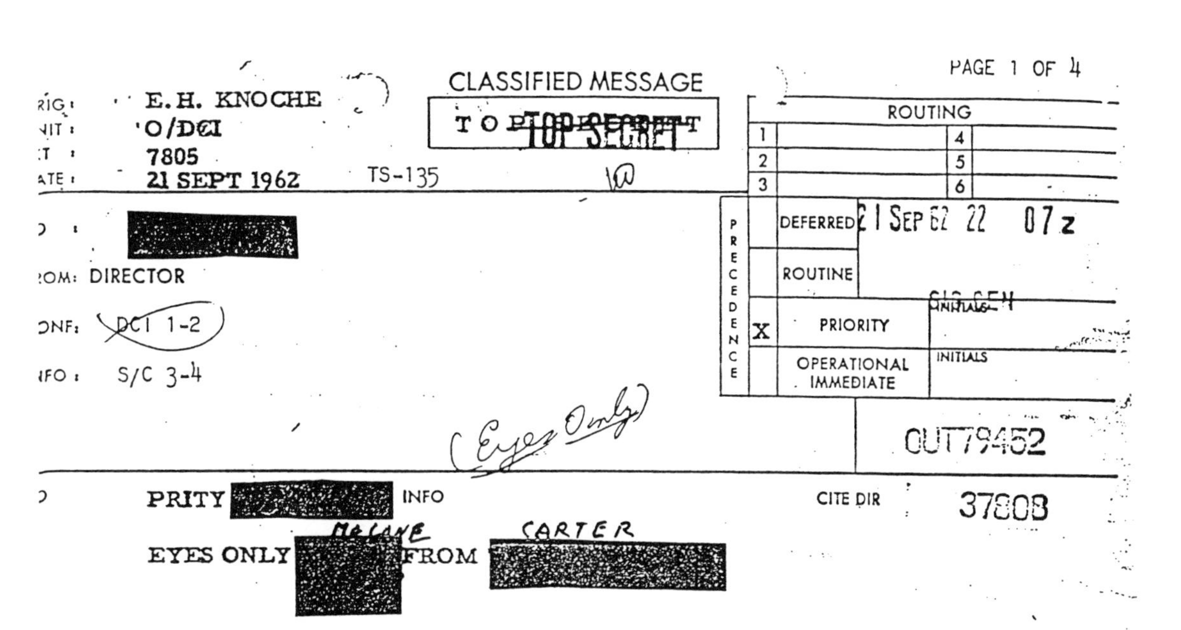

PAGE 1 OF 4

CLASSIFIED MESSAGE

TOP SECRET

ORIG: E.H. KNOCHE
UNIT: O/DCI
EXT: 7805
DATE: 21 SEPT 1962 TS-135

TO: [redacted]
FROM: DIRECTOR
CONF: DCI 1-2
INFO: S/C 3-4

(Eyes Only)

ROUTING: 1 2 3 4 5 6

PRECEDENCE: DEFERRED 21 SEP 62 22 07z; ROUTINE; X PRIORITY; OPERATIONAL IMMEDIATE

OUT79452

TO PRITY [redacted] INFO CITE DIR 37808

EYES ONLY [redacted] McCONE FROM [redacted] CARTER

1. ONE OF OUR BEST SOURCES (A DIPLOMAT IN HAVANA) REPORTS A RESURGENCE SINCE MID-AUGUST OF OLD-LINE COMMUNISTS, ESPECIALLY BLAS ROCA. CASTRO SAID TO BE UNHAPPY OVER DOMINANT ROLE, WITH SOVIET BACKING, THE OLD COMMUNISTS PLAYING ONCE AGAIN. SOURCE REPORTS:

A. IN ECON FIELD (THIS IS THE PRIMARY PRESERVE OF THE CZECHS), BLOC TECHNICIANS WORKING CLOSELY WITH CUBANS AT PLANT AND PRODUCTION LEVELS.

B. AT MINISTRY, POLIT, AND POLICY LEVELS, SOVIETS EXERTING INFLUENCE THRU OLD AND TRUSTED COMRADES (ROCA, RODRIGUEZ, AND PENA).

C. IN MILITARY FIELD, SOVIETS PROVIDING ADVISERS AND CONVENTIONAL EQUIPMENT TO CUBAN ARMY BUT ARE KEEPING

COORDINATING OFFICERS

RELEASING OFFICER TOP SECRET AUTHENTICATING OFFICER

REPRODUCTION BY OTHER THAN THE ISSUING OFFICE IS PROHIBITED. Copy No.

35. *(Continued)*

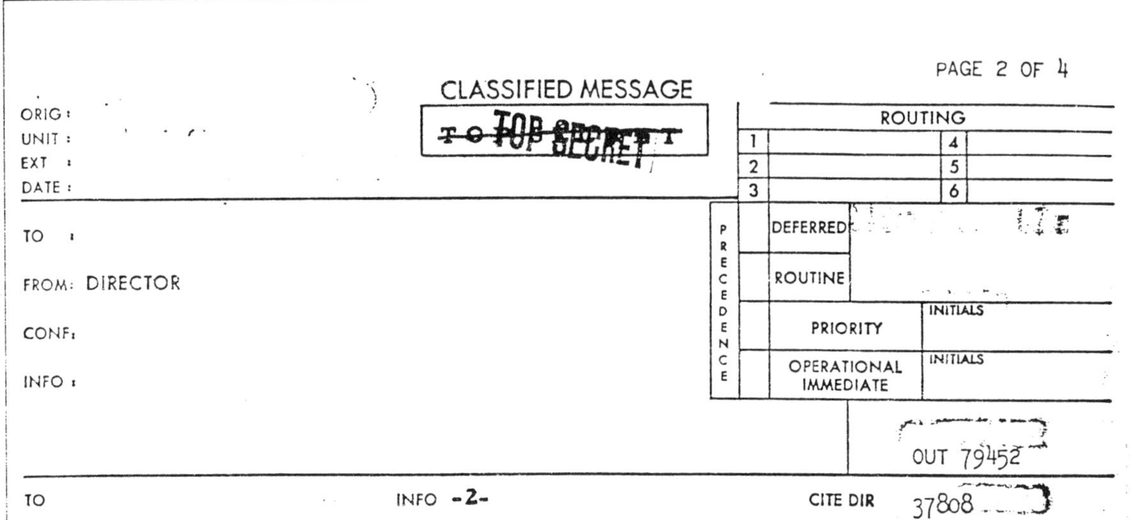

PAGE 2 OF 4

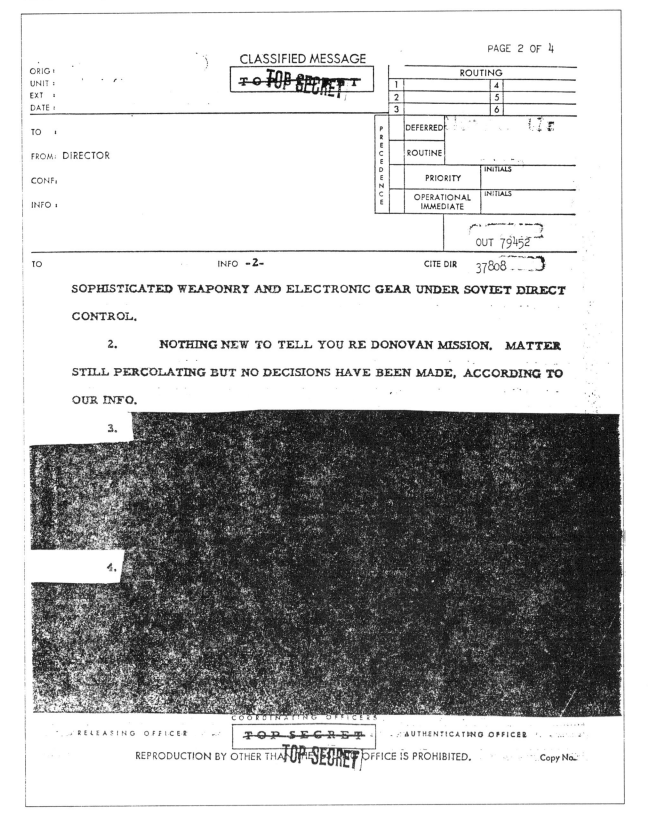

CLASSIFIED MESSAGE

TOP SECRET

ORIG:
UNIT:
EXT:
DATE:

ROUTING

1		4	
2		5	
3		6	

TO:

FROM: DIRECTOR

CONF:

INFO:

PRECEDENCE: DEFERRED / ROUTINE / PRIORITY (INITIALS) / OPERATIONAL IMMEDIATE (INITIALS)

OUT 79452

TO INFO -2- CITE DIR 37808

SOPHISTICATED WEAPONRY AND ELECTRONIC GEAR UNDER SOVIET DIRECT CONTROL.

2. NOTHING NEW TO TELL YOU RE DONOVAN MISSION. MATTER STILL PERCOLATING BUT NO DECISIONS HAVE BEEN MADE, ACCORDING TO OUR INFO.

3.

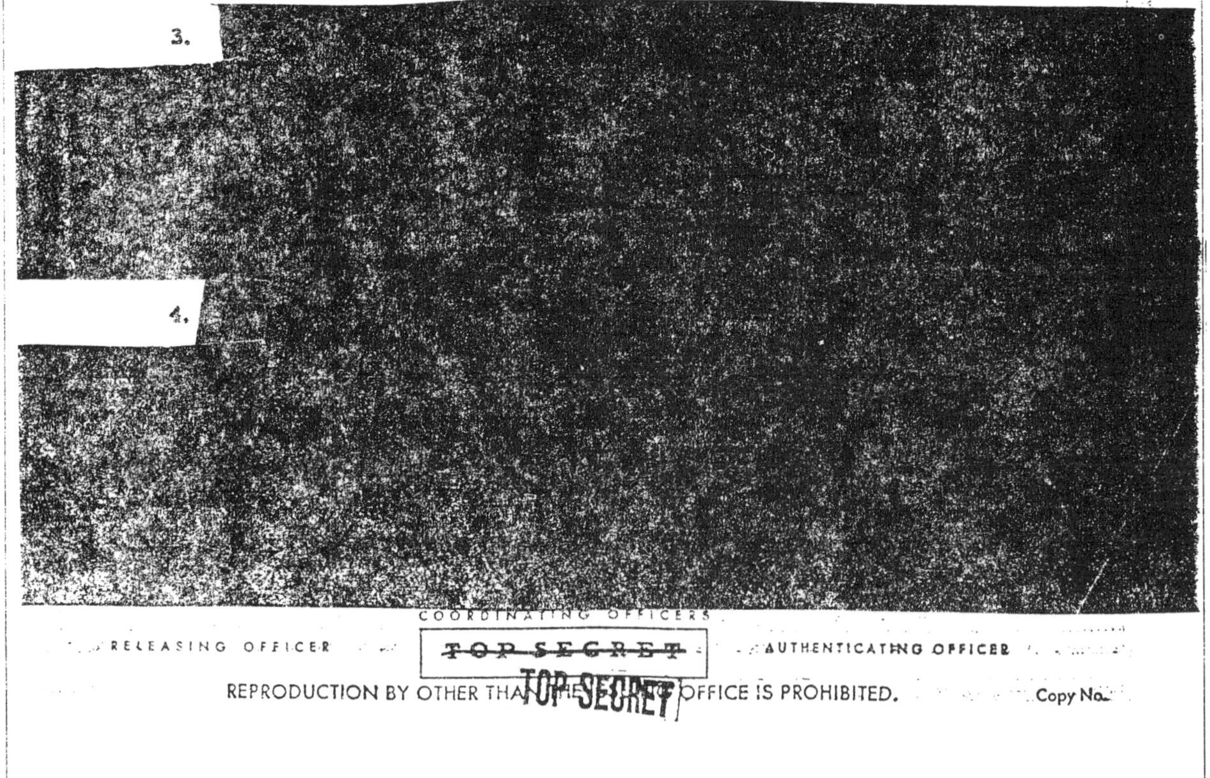

4.

COORDINATING OFFICERS

RELEASING OFFICER TOP SECRET AUTHENTICATING OFFICER

REPRODUCTION BY OTHER THAN THE ISSUING OFFICE IS PROHIBITED. Copy No.

36. *[Richard Lehman], Excerpt from Memorandum for Director of Central Intelligence, "CIA Handling of the Soviet Buildup in Cuba," 14 November 1962 (Excerpt)*

~~TOP SECRET~~

K. The Targeting of San Cristobal

40. Although the sites themselves were closed to ground observation, the movement of equipment to them from the ports was in fact seen by CIA agents and by a number of individuals who later fled to the US. The agents reported this information as soon as they were able, but in most cases had to depend on secret writing for communication. Hence, there was a lag of several days at least before their information became available. Refugee reports were delayed considerably longer for other, and uncontrollable, reasons--the time of the individual's decision to leave Cuba, his discovery of means for doing so, and his delivery to an interrogation center. Many of the reports so received dealt with unidentifiable construction activity. Many of them, because of the time-lags noted above, did not arrive in Washington until after 14 October, and some are still coming in.

41. Nevertheless, by about 1 October, the San Cristobal area had been pinpointed as a suspect MRBM site and photographic confirmation had been requested. This represents a considerable technical achievement. To understand why, it is again necessary to back-track in time. Since the moment of Castro's triumphal march into Havana, the Intelligence Community had been flooded with reports of Soviet weapons shipments and missile installations in Cuba. There were several hundred such reports, claiming the presence of everything from small arms to ICBMs, before August 1960, i.e., before the USSR had supplied Cuba with any weapons at all. More specifically, CIA's files contain 211 intelligence reports (this does not include press items) on missile and missile-associated activity in Cuba before 1 Jan 1962. All of these were either totally false or misinterpretations by the observer of other kinds of activity. CIA analysts had naturally come to view all such reports with a high degree of suspicion.

42. On 15 February 1962 an interagency interrogation center was established by CIA at Opa Locka, near Miami, to handle Cuban refugees and improve the quality of intelligence collected from them. It was manned by trained bilingual interrogators from the armed services and CIA. The establishment of Opa Locka coincided with a sharp drop in reports of missile activity received in Washington. When the defensive phase of the Soviet buildup began, the volume of Opa Locka reporting rose very rapidly, and provided good information on the types of equipment coming in, on the use of Soviet personnel and on the security precautions imposed by the Soviets on this operation. (Such reports were the basis for the Checklist item cited in para 9).

-23-

~~TOP SECRET~~

43. For the better part of two years, CIA had been checking information obtained from refugee, defector, and agent sources with NPIC whenever it was apparent that the information was of a kind that could be verified or negated by aerial reconnaissance. In May 1962, NPIC began publishing a series of formal listings (Photographic Evaluation of Information on Cuba) in which these reports were evaluated in the light of photographic coverage. In the 7 issues of this publication between 31 May and 5 October NPIC examined 138 raw reports referred to it for comment. Of this total, only three cited missile activity which could not be linked directly to the SA-2 and cruise missile deployments. NPIC's evidence negated those three.

44. When the first indications of build-up began to come in in August, these procedures were further tightened. CIA current intelligence was ordered orally by the DD/I's office on about 14 August not to publish any information on the construction of missile bases in Cuba until they had been checked out with NPIC. (This instruction was in the field of intelligence technique rather than of policy; it had no relation to later restrictions; (see para 50). Between 14 August and mid-October this office sent NPIC 13 memoranda asking for a check on 25 separate reports containing information which was thought to raise the possibility of Soviet offensive weapons in Cuba. A great many more such reports were checked with NPIC informally by telephone. In all cases, NPIC either lacked the necessary coverage or made a negative finding.

45. On 20 August, the COMOR Targeting Working Group (chaired and staffed largely by CIA) set up the first comprehensive card file system for Cuban targets. An example of its procedures is the handling of targets in the Sagua La Grande area. Based on refugee reporting, the COMOR Targeting Working Group on 27 August pinpointed four farms in this area as suspect missile sites. Readout of the 29 August coverage showed an SA-2 site near Sagua La Grande which apparently was the basis for the reported activity there, and the target card was changed to show a confirmed SA-2 site. It should be noted that knowledge that this site was in the area could have led analysts to misinterpret any subsequent reports of MRBM activity as part of the SAM development,but in fact no such reports were received.

46. By September, the volume of agent and refugee reporting had become very large indeed. During the month 882 reports on internal activities in Cuba were disseminated, exclusive of telegraphic dissemination. (The CIA clandestine collectors report that their output represented only the small publishable fraction of the raw material collected.) A substantial

-24-

~~TOP SECRET~~ 

~~TOP SECRET~~ 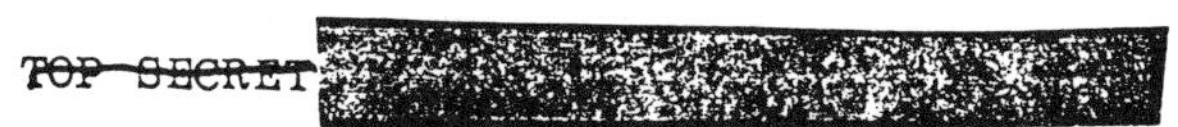

proportion of these dealt with the deployment of defensive missiles and related activities. Knowledge on the part of the analysts that such a deployment was in fact going on, plus the normal difficulties encountered by untrained observers in telling an offensive missile from a defensive one, tended to throw a sort of smoke-screen around the Soviet offensive deployment when it finally began. The CIA analytic apparatus, however, recognized and correlated the first authentic reports of MRBM equipment ever to be received in Washington, and took action upon them. It targeted the San Cristobal area, not as another location where alleged missile activity should be negated by photography, but as a suspect SS-4 site.

47. This process took about three weeks, from the date when the first observation was made on the ground in Cuba to the preparation of the target card. The two reports from Opa Locka which triggered it were:

a. An observation in Havana on 12 September of a convoy carrying long canvas-covered objects which the source identified under interrogation as resembling SS-4s. This report, which was disseminated by CIA on 21 September, contained sufficient accurate detail to alert intelligence analysts.

b. An observation on 17 September of a convoy moving toward the San Cristobal area. This information, received on 27 September, dovetailed in many respects with the earlier report.

48. The arrival of the second report led CIA analysts to a tentative conclusion that the two observers had in fact seen the same convoy, and that there was a possibility of the SS-4 identification being genuine. A day or so earlier, a target card on San Cristobal had been prepared on the basis of a vague report of "Russians building a rocket base." Now this card was removed and, with the two reports cited above and other less specific information on activity in this area which was beginning to trickle in, a new card was prepared between 1 and 3 October which was in effect a priority requirement for photographic coverage. This card was used in the targeting of the 14 October flight (see para 63). It read as follows: "Collateral reports indicate the existence of a restricted area in Pinar del Rio Province which is suspected of including an SSM site under construction, particularly SS-4 Shyster. The area is bounded by a line connecting the following four town: Consolacion del Norte (8332N/2244W); San Diego del Los Banos (8325N/2235W); San Cristobal (8301N/2243W); and Las Pozos (8317N/2250W). Requirement: Search the area delineated for possible surface missile construction, with particular attention to SS-4 Shyster."

-25-

~~TOP SECRET~~ 

TOP SECRET

49. Another report, too general to be used in the process described above, is nevertheless of interest as the first good information distributed on the Soviet offensive build-up. On 20 September, CIA disseminated a [redacted] report that Castro's personal pilot, Claudio Morinas, had said on 9 September "We have 40-mile range guided missiles, both surface-to-surface and surface-to-air, and we have a radar system which covers, sector by sector, all of the Cuban air space and (beyond) as far as Florida. There are also many mobile ramps for intermediate range rockets."

-26-

TOP SECRET

37. *CIA Information Report, 18 September 1962*

TELEGRAM INFORM TION REPORT TELEGRA

CENTRAL INTELLIGENCE AGENCY

This material contains information affecting the National Defense of the United States within the meaning of the Espionage Laws, Title 18, U.S.C. 793 and 794, the transmission or revelation of which in any manner to an unauthorized person is prohibited by law

CLASSIFICATION — DISSEMINATION CONTROLS

~~SECRET~~

COUNTRY CUBA

REPORT NO. TDCS -3/522,702

SUBJECT RESTRICTED MILITARY AREA IN PINAR DEL RIO PROVINCE AND POSSIBLE MISSILE INSTALLATION AT LA GUIRA

DATE DISTR. 18 SEPTEMBER 1962

PRECEDENCE ROUTINE

DATE OF INFO. 7 SEPTEMBER 1962

REFERENCES IN 23874 RD-ACQ-01258

PLACE & DATE ACQ. CUBA (15 SEPTEMBER 1962)

APPRAISAL PARA. 1: 4; PARA. 2: 3.

FIELD REPORT NO.

THIS IS UNEVALUATED INFORMATION. SOURCE GRADINGS ARE DEFINITIVE. APPRAISAL OF CONTENT IS TENTATIVE.

SOURCE RESIDENT OF HABANA

1. A LARGE ZONE IN PINAR DEL RIO PROVINCE WITHIN A PERIMETER BOUNDED BY THE CITIES OF SAN CRISTOBAL, SAN DIEGO (DE LOS BANOS), CONSOLACION DEL NORTE, AND LAS POZAS IS HEAVILY GUARDED BY SOVIETS WITH THE ASSISTANCE OF PERUVIAN AND COLOMBIAN NATIONALS. (HEADQUARTERS COMMENT: IT IS DOUBTFUL THAT GROUND FORCES COULD EFFECTIVELY CONTROL AS ONE COMPLETE AREA A ZONE AS LARGE AS THE ONE CITED ABOVE. THE GRIDS FOR THE ABOVE AREAS ARE AS FOLLOWS:

A. SAN CRISTOBAL (N 22-43.00, W 83-02.50; AMS E 723, SHEET 3584 II, UTM GRID 17QKR89?134).

B. SAN DIEGO DE LOS BANOS (N 22-38.45, W 83-22.15; AMS E 723, SHEET 3583 IV, UTM GRID 17QKR563061).

CLASSIFICATION — DISSEMINATION CONTROLS

~~SECRET~~

GROUP 1 Excluded from automatic downgrading and declassification

STATE/INR	DIA	ARMY/ACSI	NAVY	AIR	JCS	SECDEF	NSA	NIC	XXX	USIA	OCI	ONE	OCR	ORR	OO	OO
STATE/DIR																

REPCINCLANT FBI INS

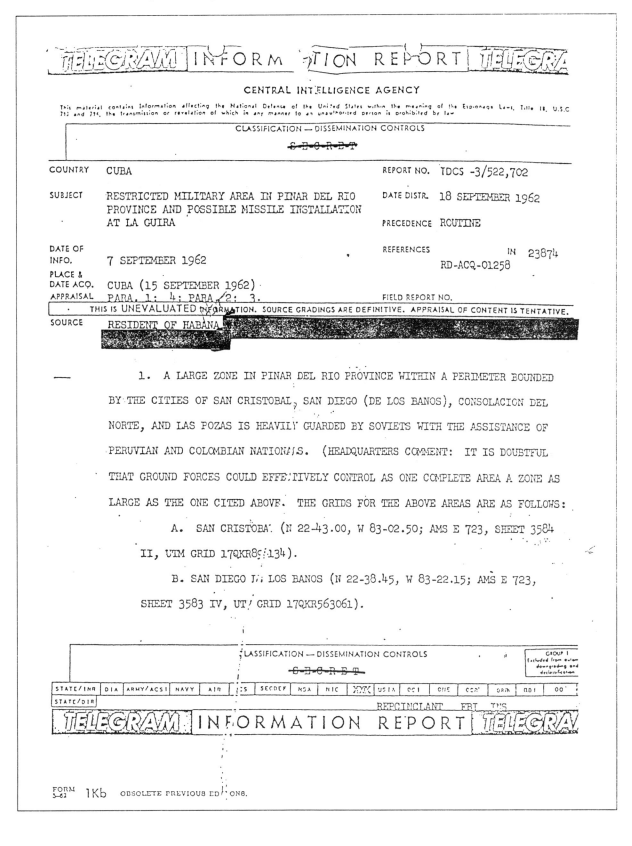

TELEGRAM INFORMATION REPORT TELEGRA

FORM 5-62 1Kb OBSOLETE PREVIOUS EDITIONS.

37. *(Continued)*

CLASSIFICATION — DISSEMINATION CONTROLS

~~S-E-C-R-E-T~~ | TDCS -3/522,702 | IN 238 | PAGE 2

C. CONSOLACION DEL NORTE (N 22-44.55, W 83-33.15; AMS E 723, SHEET 3484 II, UTM 17QKR377177).

D. LAS POZAS (N 22-52.02, W 83-17.58; AMS E 723, SHEET 3584 IV, UTM GRID 17QKR642305).

2. SECURITY IS ENFORCED TO PREVENT ACCESS TO THE FINCA OF DR. CORTINA, AT LA GUIRA, WHERE VERY SECRET AND IMPORTANT WORK IS IN PROGRESS, BELIEVED TO BE CONCERNED WITH MISSILES. (HEADQUARTERS COMMENT: THE FINCA BELONGING TO DR. CORTINA AT LA GUIRA IS PROBABLY THE CORTINA FINCA AT N 22-37.05, W 83-24.20; AMS E 723, SHEET 3583 IV, UTM GRID 17QKR527049. LA GUIRA IS AT N 22-37.56, W 83-24.00; AMS E 723, SHEET 3583 IV, UTM GRID 17QKR533046.)

3. FIELD DISSEM: CINCLANT, CINCARIB.

END OF MESSAGE

CLASSIFICATION — DISSEMINATION CONTROLS

~~S-E-C-R-E-T~~

38. *CIA Information Report, 20 September 1962*

TELEGRAM INFORMATION REPORT TELEGRAM

CENTRAL INTELLIGENCE AGENCY

This material contains information affecting the National Defense of the United States within the meaning of the Espionage Laws, Title 18, U.S.C Secs 793 and 794, the transmission or revelation of which in any manner to an unauthorized person is prohibited by law

CLASSIFICATION — DISSEMINATION CONTROLS

~~S-E-C-R-E-T~~

COUNTRY CUBA

REPORT NO. TDCS -3/522,948

SUBJECT COMMENTS OF CUBAN PILOT CONCERNING PRESENCE OF GUIDED MISSILES IN CUBA

DATE DISTR. 20 SEPTEMBER 1962

PRECEDENCE ROUTINE

DATE OF INFO. 9 SEPTEMBER 1962

REFERENCES RD-ACQ-01258 IN 25363

PLACE & DATE ACQ. CUBA (15 SEPTEMBER 1962)

APPRAISAL SEE BELOW

FIELD REPORT NO.

THIS IS UNEVALUATED INFORMATION. SOURCE GRADINGS ARE DEFINITIVE. APPRAISAL OF CONTENT IS TENTATIVE.

SOURCE

1. IN A CONVERSATION BETWEEN CLAUDIO MORINAS, PERSONAL PILOT OF FIDEL CASTRO, AND WHO HAD INQUIRED IF THERE WERE ROCKETS IN CUBA, MORINAS REPLIED: "WE HAVE 40-MILE RANGE GUIDED MISSILES, BOTH SURFACE-TO-SURFACE AND SURFACE-TO-AIR, AND WE HAVE A RADAR SYSTEM WHICH COVERS, SECTOR BY SECTOR, ALL OF THE CUBAN AIR SPACE AND (BEYOND) AS FAR AS FLORIDA. THERE ARE ALSO MANY MOBILE RAMPS FOR INTERMEDIATE RANGE ROCKETS. THEY DON'T KNOW WHAT IS AWAITING THEM."

2. FIELD DISSEM: CINCLANT, CINCARIB.

END OF MESSAGE

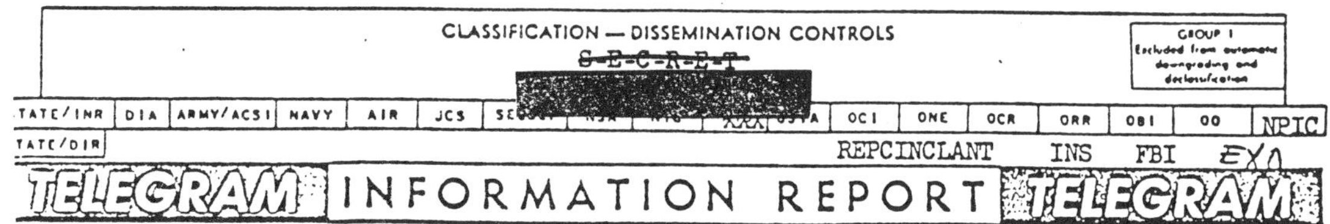

CLASSIFICATION — DISSEMINATION CONTROLS

~~S-E-C-R-E-T~~

GROUP 1 Excluded from automatic downgrading and declassification

STATE/INR	DIA	ARMY/ACSI	NAVY	AIR	JCS	SECDEF	NSA	NIC	XXX	USIA	OCI	ONE	OCR	ORR	OBI	OO	NPIC

STATE/DIR REPCINCLANT INS FBI EXO

TELEGRAM INFORMATION REPORT TELEGRAM

FORM 1Kb OBSOLETE PREVIOUS EDITIONS. (15-20)

39. *CIA Information Report, 27 September 1962*

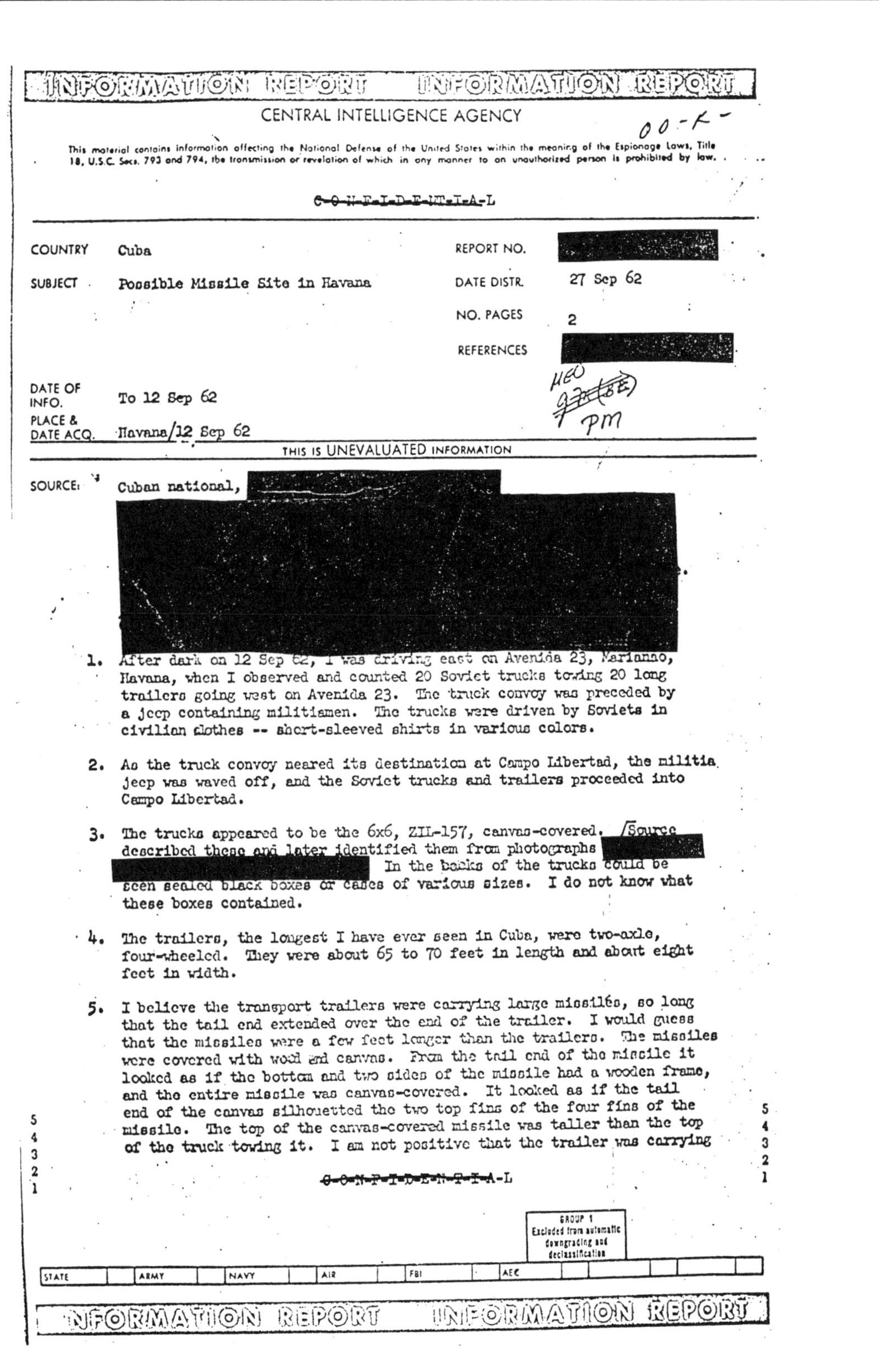

INFORMATION REPORT INFORMATION REPORT

CENTRAL INTELLIGENCE AGENCY

This material contains information affecting the National Defense of the United States within the meaning of the Espionage Laws, Title 18, U.S.C. Secs. 793 and 794, the transmission or revelation of which in any manner to an unauthorized person is prohibited by law.

~~C-O-N-F-I-D-E-N-T-I-A-L~~

COUNTRY	Cuba	REPORT NO.	[redacted]
SUBJECT	Possible Missile Site in Havana	DATE DISTR.	27 Sep 62
		NO. PAGES	2
		REFERENCES	[redacted]
DATE OF INFO.	To 12 Sep 62		
PLACE & DATE ACQ.	Havana/12 Sep 62		

THIS IS UNEVALUATED INFORMATION

SOURCE: Cuban national, [redacted]

1. After dark on 12 Sep 62, I was driving east on Avenida 23, Marianao, Havana, when I observed and counted 20 Soviet trucks towing 20 long trailers going west on Avenida 23. The truck convoy was preceded by a jeep containing militiamen. The trucks were driven by Soviets in civilian clothes -- short-sleeved shirts in various colors.

2. As the truck convoy neared its destination at Campo Libertad, the militia jeep was waved off, and the Soviet trucks and trailers proceeded into Campo Libertad.

3. The trucks appeared to be the 6x6, ZIL-157, canvas-covered. /Source [redacted] described these and later identified them from photographs [redacted] [redacted] In the backs of the trucks could be seen sealed black boxes or cases of various sizes. I do not know what these boxes contained.

4. The trailers, the longest I have ever seen in Cuba, were two-axle, four-wheeled. They were about 65 to 70 feet in length and about eight feet in width.

5. I believe the transport trailers were carrying large missiles, so long that the tail end extended over the end of the trailer. I would guess that the missiles were a few feet longer than the trailers. The missiles were covered with wood and canvas. From the tail end of the missile it looked as if the bottom and two sides of the missile had a wooden frame, and the entire missile was canvas-covered. It looked as if the tail end of the canvas silhouetted the two top fins of the four fins of the missile. The top of the canvas-covered missile was taller than the top of the truck towing it. I am not positive that the trailer was carrying

~~C-O-N-F-I-D-E-N-T-I-A-L~~

GROUP 1
Excluded from automatic downgrading and declassification

STATE		ARMY		NAVY		AIR		FBI		AEC						

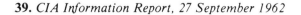

INFORMATION REPORT INFORMATION REPORT

C-O-N-F-I-D-E-N-T-I-A-L 00-K-3,219,040

-2-

a missile, but it surely looked that way. [Source described, then drew rough sketches of, the missile silhouette and tail fin silhouette; later, from photographs, he identified Guided Missile, Surface-to-Surface, SS-4 "Shyster,"

6. I do not know where the truck convoy originated. told me that Soviet cargo ships, names unknown, had docked at the Flota Blanca piers around 10 or 11 Sep 62. He told me that all Cuban dock-workers and other Cubans who worked in that area were forbidden to be in the area during the unloading of the ships and that the unloading was handled only by Sovbloc personnel. He said the cargo unloaded at the Flota Blanca docks consisted of missiles. I do not know where he got his information, but he is usually pretty reliable.

- end -

C-O-N-F-I-D-E-N-T-I-A-L

40. *CIA Information Report, 1 October 1962*

INFORMATION REPORT INFORMATION REPORT

CENTRAL INTELLIGENCE AGENCY

This material contains information affecting the National Defense of the United States within the meaning of the Espionage Laws, Title 18, U.S.C. Secs. 793 and 794, the transmission or revelation of which in any manner to an unauthorized person is prohibited by law.

C-O-N-F-I-D-E-N-T-I-A-L

COUNTRY	Cuba	REPORT NO.	
SUBJECT	Soviet and Rebel Army Convoy	DATE DISTR.	1 Oct 62
		NO. PAGES	1
		REFERENCES	
DATE OF INFO.	17 Sep 62		
PLACE & DATE ACQ.			

THIS IS UNEVALUATED INFORMATION

SOURCE: Cuban national, A 12 853 974, 47 years old.

Source [ ] Traveled on business throughout the island a great deal. Four years of schooling, average intelligence.

1. On 17 Sep 62, about 2100 hours, while traveling by automobile from Havana toward my home in [ ] Pinar del Rio, I observed a convoy of 10 motorcycles, 16 trucks, and eight trailers proceeding southwest on the Central Highway toward Pinar del Rio. Since I was traveling in the same direction as the convoy, I passed what were the last units of the convoy at the entrance to Guanajay, Havana [Grid coord 270360, Sheet 3684 I, Series E723], and then passed the leading element of the convoy immediately after Artemisa, Pinar del Rio [Grid coord 190235, Sheet 3684 III, Series E723]. Although the vehicles were scattered over a distance, I am of the opinion they were all part of the same convoy.

2. The leading element of the convoy was five motorcycles driven by unarmed Rebel Army soldiers whose function appeared to be clearing the civilian traffic ahead. The motorcycles were followed by six MAZ-502 trucks, each carrying about 30 Rebel Army soldiers armed with 9 mm submachine guns M-25 and rifles. Since it was dark, I could not see who the drivers of the trucks were.

3. The trucks were followed by eight Soviet-built flatbed-type trailers approximately 32 feet long, seven of which were carrying what looked like huge tubes extending over the entire length of the flatbed and completely covered with canvas. I could not distinguish what the eighth trailer was carrying since it was completely covered with canvas. However, I did notice what looked like large metal prongs sticking out from under the canvas at the rear of the trailer. Although I don't know too much about it, it looked like a piece of radar equipment.

4. The trailers were followed by six MAZ-502 trucks, each carrying about 30 Rebel Army soldiers, also armed with rifles and 9 mm submachine guns M-25. The trucks were in turn followed by five motorcycles driven by unarmed Rebel Army soldiers. Because of darkness and rain I could not distinguish who the drivers of any of the vehicles in the convoy were.

[Collector's Note: [ ]

-end-

C-O-N-F-I-D-E-N-T-I-A-L

GROUP 1
Excluded from automatic downgrading and declassification

STATE		ARMY		NAVY		AIR		FBI		AEC					

INFORMATION REPORT INFORMATION REPORT

41. *McCone, "Memorandum of MONGOOSE Meeting Held on Thursday, October 4, 1962"*

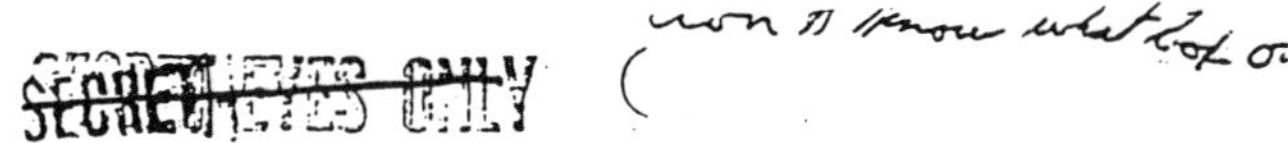

October 4, 1962

MEMORANDUM OF MONGOOSE MEETING HELD ON THURSDAY, OCTOBER 4, 1962.

Chaired by the Attorney General.

Attended by: Gilpatric, Johnson, General Taylor, General Carter, McCone, Scoville, General Lansdale and Colonel Steakley (part of the time).

The Attorney General reported on discussions with the President on Cuba; dissatisfied with lack of action in the sabotage field, went on to stress that nothing was moving forward, commented that one effort attempted had failed, expressed general concern over developing situation.

General Lansdale reviewed operations, pointing out that no sabotage had been attempted and gave general impression that things were all right.

McCone then stated that phase one was principally intelligence gathering, organizing and training, that no sabotage was authorized, that one operation against a powerhouse had been contemplated but was discouraged by group, that he had called a meeting to review matters this morning and that he had observed a lack of forward motion due principally to "hesitancy" in government circles to engage in any activities which would involve attribution to the United States.

AG took sharp exception stating the Special Group had not withheld approval on any specified actions to his knowledge, but to the contrary had urged and insisted upon action by the Lansdale operating organization.

There followed a sharp exchange which finally was clarifying inasmuch as it resulted in a reaffirmation of a determination to move forward. In effect it seemed to be the consensus that phase two

SECRET

SECRET—EYES ONLY

as approved on September 6, was now outmoded, that more dynamic action was indicated, that hesitancy about overflights must be reconsidered (this to be commented on later in this memorandum), that actions which could be attributed to indigenous Cubans would not be important or very effective, and that a very considerable amount of attribution and "noise" must be expected.

As a result, General Lansdale was instructed to give consideration to new and more dynamic approaches, the specific items of sabotage should be brought forward immediately and new ones conceived, that a plan for mining harbors should be developed and presented, and the possibility of capturing Castro forces for interrogation should be studied.

With respect to overflights, [redacted] were instructed to prepare and present to the Special Group on next Tuesday at a special meeting alternate recommendations for overflights. These to include the use of U-2s on complete sweeps (as contrasted with peripheral or limited missions), the use of firefly drones, the use of 101s or other reconnaissance planes on x low level, intermediate level, and high level missions, and other possible reconnaissance operations.

Consideration was given to stating publicly that we propose to overfly Cuba in the interest of our own security and the security of the Western Hemisphere, and then to proceed even though doing so involved risk.

It was the consensus that we could not accept restrictions which would foreclose gaining all reasonable knowledge of military installations in Cuba.

During the meeting McCone reviewed the earlier meeting with General Lansdale, and pointed out to the group that this meeting clarified General Lansdale's authority over the entire MONGOOSE operation and that the CIA organization was responsive to his policy and operational guidance, and this was thoroughly understood.

- 2 -

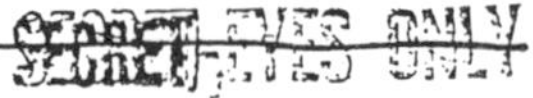

41. *(Continued)*

SECRET EYES ONLY

Consideration was given to the existing guidelines and it was the consensus that the August 1st guidelines for phase two were inadequate and new guidelines must be considered.

John A. McCone
Director

- 3 -

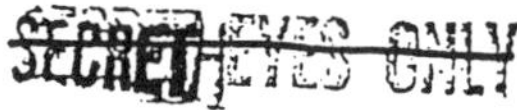

42. *McCone, "Memorandum of Discussion with Mr. McGeorge Bundy, Friday, October 5, 1962, 5:15 p.m."*

MR #97

~~SECRET~~

Memorandum of Discussion with Mr. McGeorge Bundy Friday, October 5, 1962, 5:15 p. m.

1. McCone reviewed details of the Donovan negotiations, discussions with the President, Attorney General, Eisenhower, the decisions not to approach Congressional leadership, the discussion with Senator Javits, and the final report from Donovan. Bundy expressed general agreement.

2. At the October 4th meeting of the Special Group Mongoose was discussed in some detail as was the meeting with Carter, Lansdale, et al in DCI's office on that day. McCone stated there was a feeling in CIA and Defense that the "activist policy" which founded the Mongoose operation was gone and that while no specific operational activities had been (refused) the amount of "noise" from minor incidents such as the sugar, the students firing on the Havana Hotel and other matters and the extreme caution expressed by State had led to this conclusion. More importantly, however, the decisions to restrict U-2 flights had placed the United States Intelligence Community in a position where it could not report with assurance the development of offensive capabilities in Cuba. McCone stated he felt it most probable that Soviet-Castro operations would end up with an established offensive capability in Cuba including MRBMs. McCone stated he thought this a probability rather than a mere possibility. Bundy took issue stating that he felt the Soviets would not go that far, that he was satisfied that no offensive capability would be installed in Cuba because of its world-wide effects and therefore seemed relaxed over the fact that the Intelligence Community cannot produce hard information onthis important subject. McCone said that Bundy's viewpoint was reflected by many in the Intelligence Community, perhaps a majority, but he just did not agree and furthermore did not think the United States could afford to take such a risk.

3. Bundy then philosophized on Cuba stating that he felt that our policy was not clear, our objectives not determined and therefore our efforts were not productive. He discussed both the Mongoose operations and the Rostow "Track Two". Bundy was not critical of either or of the Lansdale operations. It was obvious that he was not in sympathy with a more active role such as those discussed at 5412 on Thursday as he felt none of them would bring Castro down nor would they particularly enhance U. S. position of world leadership. Bundy seemed inclined to support the Track Two idea and also inclined (though he was not specific) to play down the more active Lansdale

42. *(Continued)*

operation. Bundy had not talked to Lansdale but obviously had received some of the "static" that is being passed around in Washington. (Before) McCone in reporting on the discussions at Thursday's 5412 meeting repeated the views of the President and expressed by the Attorney General it was agreed that the whole Government policy with reference to Cuba must be resolved promptly as basic to further actions on our part. In general, Bundy's views were that we should either make a judgment that we would have to go in militarily (which seemed to him intolerable) or alternatively we would have to learn to live with Castro, and his Cuba and adjust our policies accordingly.

4. McCone then elaborated on his views of the evolution of Soviet-Castro military capability stating he felt defense was just phase one, phase two would be followed by various offensive capabilities and indeed the existing defensive capabilities such as the (MIG) 21s a very definite offensive capability against nearby American cities and installations. McCone stated that he thought that the establishment of a very expensive offensive mechanism could not be the ultimate objective of the Soviets or Castro and therefore the objective was (a) to establish an offensive base or (b) to insert sufficient Soviet specialists and military leaders to take Cuba away from Castro and establish it as a true Soviet controlled satellite. McCone stated that he felt there were only two courses open -- one was to take military action at the appropriate time or secondly to pursue an effort to split Castro off from the Communists and for this reason he, McCone, had vigorously supported the Donovan mission as it is the only link that we have to the Castro hierarchy at the present time. Note in this connection it might be well to study the evolution of the Toure experience in Guinea when the Communists moved in and captured all elements of the Government and economy and forced Toure to expel the Ambassador and try to rectify the situation. There may be a parallel here.

5. McCone reviewed the Eisenhower discussions. Bundy read the memorandum covering these discussions. Bundy stated that Adenauer did not express the concern of the U. S. policy reflected by Eisenhower and reported in the memorandum.

6. Bundy rejected the idea of regular NSC meetings stating that every President has to organize his Government as he desires and that the Eisenhower pattern was not necessarily adaptable to the Kennedy type of administration. McCone stated that if this is the case he intended to request

2

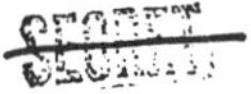

~~SECRET~~

occasional NSC meetings to review specific estimates or other intelligence situations and the next one would be a report and discussion of the estimate of Soviet air defense capabilities. Bundy agreed.

7. Bundy rejected the idea (calling) the several Special Groups 5412, CIA, Mongoose, and North Vietnam together feeling it was better to keep them separated. He also rejected the idea that the visiting commissions such as the Byroade Team and the Draper Team should report back to the Special Group (CI) feeling it was appropriate that they report to the President, (through) the Secretary of State, with consultation with the Special Group (CI). It was agreed that we would have a further discussion over the weekend.

JOHN A. McCONE
Director

JAM/lucy W

3

~~SECRET~~

43. *Sherman Kent, Memorandum for the Director, "Implications of an Announcement by the President that the US would Conduct Overhead Reconnaissance of Cuba . . . ," 8 October 1962*

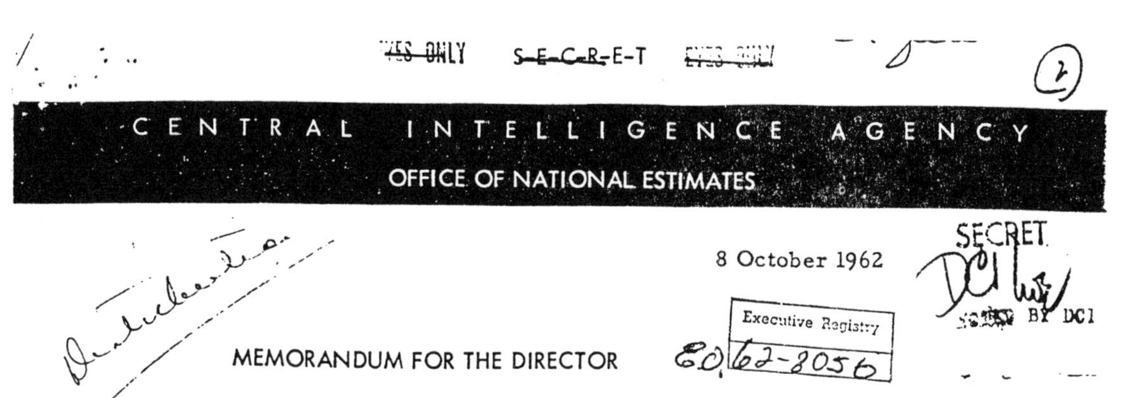

SECRET

8 October 1962

Executive Registry
62-8056

SIGNED BY DCI

MEMORANDUM FOR THE DIRECTOR

SUBJECT: Implications of an Announcement by the President that the US would Conduct Overhead Reconnaissance of Cuba, and of the Actual Reconnaissance Thereafter

NOTE: The following are the conclusions reached by a panel of members of the Board of National Estimates and of the ONE Staff

1. The President's announcement would be vigorously condemned by the Soviets and the Cubans as evincing an intention to commit acts of international aggression.

2. The weight of publicly expressed opinion in the free world would probably condemn the announcement as threatening a marked increase in international tensions. Many Latin Americans would probably look upon it as incompatible with the principle of non-intervention. On the other hand,

S-E-C-R-E-T

GROUP I
Excluded from automatic downgrading and declassification

SECRET

those few which desire the US to take decisive action against Cuba would probably consider the announcement as a disappointingly weak manifestation.

3. The Cubans, or some other country, would probably bring the matter before the UN shortly after the announcement. (They would be virtually certain to do so if a reconnaissance vehicle were shot down.) Having international law on their side, they would hope to achieve a UN condemnation of the US for acts threatening peace. The UN situation would be complicated, and it is possible that in one way or another the US could avert a formal resolution. Nevertheless, it is highly unlikely that the US would find much support among the assembled nations. It might find itself, for the first time, in virtual isolation.

4. The Soviets and the Cubans would probably be impressed by the evident willingness of the US government to raise still further the level of tension over Cuba, and to commit itself to further risks. We do not believe, however,

- 2 -

SECRET

that this would lead to any change in Soviet policy toward Cuba. The USSR would not consider that the US announcement created such a dangerous situation as to require it to reduce its support of Castro. Moreover, it would judge that, in political terms, it could ill afford to make any reduction at such a time. On the other hand, we do not believe that the announcement, or succeeding overflights, would cause the USSR to alter its Cuban policy in a direction which increased the provocation offered to the US, e.g., the provision of medium-range missile bases. In reacting publicly, the Soviets would probably reaffirm their commitment to Cuba's defense, though they would probably not make the commitment more specific or binding.

5. We think it unlikely that the Soviets would retaliate directly with any major moves against the Western position in Berlin. In confronting the Allies with local crises which raise the level of risk in Berlin, they generally prefer to choose a time when US opinion is not highly agitated over other East-West issues. While the announcement would

- 3 -

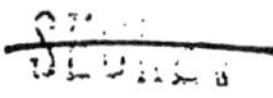

SECRET

create new strains in Soviet-American relations, this effect would not be so strong or so long-lasting as to influence basic Soviet choices with respect to Berlin.

6. The Soviets and Cubans would make every effort to shoot down any reconnaissance vehicle that came over Cuba. If they succeeded in doing so, the tensions would be somewhat increased, though the international political effects of the shootdown would not in themselves be as great as if it had occurred without the prior Presidential announcement. The demonstration of military capability which such an incident would provide would almost certainly impress many Latin Americans.

Sherman Kent

SHERMAN KENT
Chairman
Board of National Estimates

- 4 -

SECRET

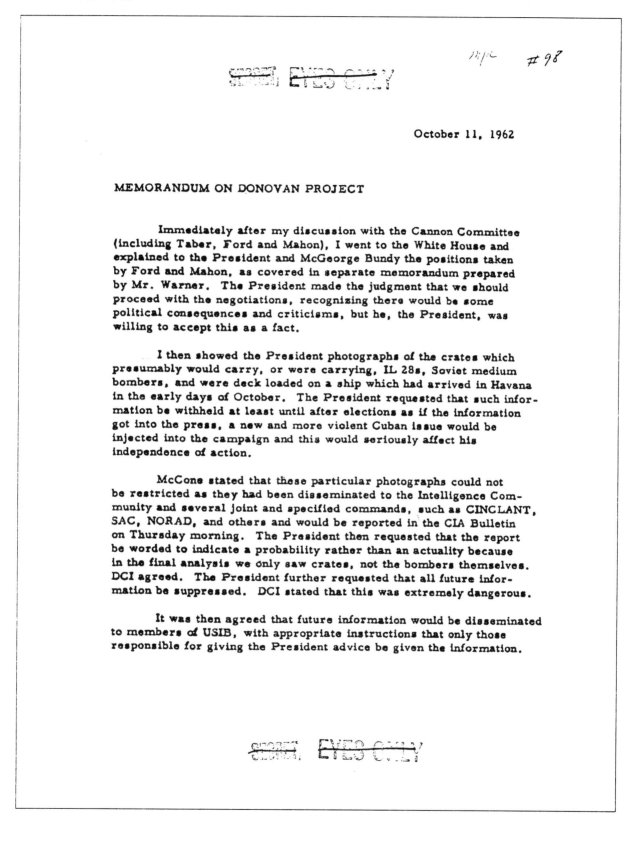

44. *McCone, "Memorandum on Donovan Project," 11 October 1962*

mpc #98

~~SECRET~~ EYES ONLY

October 11, 1962

MEMORANDUM ON DONOVAN PROJECT

Immediately after my discussion with the Cannon Committee (including Taber, Ford and Mahon), I went to the White House and explained to the President and McGeorge Bundy the positions taken by Ford and Mahon, as covered in separate memorandum prepared by Mr. Warner. The President made the judgment that we should proceed with the negotiations, recognizing there would be some political consequences and criticisms, but he, the President, was willing to accept this as a fact.

I then showed the President photographs of the crates which presumably would carry, or were carrying, IL 28s, Soviet medium bombers, and were deck loaded on a ship which had arrived in Havana in the early days of October. The President requested that such information be withheld at least until after elections as if the information got into the press, a new and more violent Cuban issue would be injected into the campaign and this would seriously affect his independence of action.

McCone stated that these particular photographs could not be restricted as they had been disseminated to the Intelligence Community and several joint and specified commands, such as CINCLANT, SAC, NORAD, and others and would be reported in the CIA Bulletin on Thursday morning. The President then requested that the report be worded to indicate a probability rather than an actuality because in the final analysis we only saw crates, not the bombers themselves. DCI agreed. The President further requested that all future information be suppressed. DCI stated that this was extremely dangerous.

It was then agreed that future information would be disseminated to members of USIB, with appropriate instructions that only those responsible for giving the President advice be given the information.

~~SECRET~~ EYES ONLY

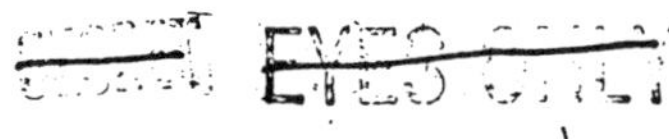

Furthermore, that within CIA circles a minimum number of experts be informed. McCone stated there was no problem in CIA, that it was secure. It was therefore agreed that the USIB members would be instructed to restrict the information to their personal offices and fully and currently inform the Chiefs of Staff, the Chairman, the Service Secretaries and the Secretary of Defense. Similar restrictive action would be taken in State. Therefore all those involved in "giving advice to the President" would be fully informed. However operational divisions and the joint and specified commands would not be informed at this time, except at the direction of the above people who are receiving the information.

At this point the President mentioned that "we'll have to do something drastic about Cuba" and I am anxiously looking forward to the JCS operational plan which is to be presented to me next week.

McCone effected the above instructions by calling Mr. Cline, who was unavailable, and then Mr. Sheldon who agreed to prepare a procedure for review on Thursday morning.

McCone then called the Attorney General and advised him of his talk with the Cannon Committee. The Attorney General had no particular comment.

At six o'clock McCone received a report from Houston that Donovan had gone into a meeting at five o'clock. At eleven o'clock Houston reported the meeting was still in progress. At seven o'clock on Thursday morning Donovan still had no report.

At 11:15 General Eisenhower called McCone stating he was sorry a meeting could not be arranged, he was leaving very early the following morning for Gettysburg. McCone reported that negotiations were in progress and he also reported objections stated by several members of Congress. Eisenhower advised that the negotiations be pursued, indicating his support of it and furthermore stated that if the negotiations were satisfactorily concluded the complaints and objections would, in his words, disappear.

- 2 -

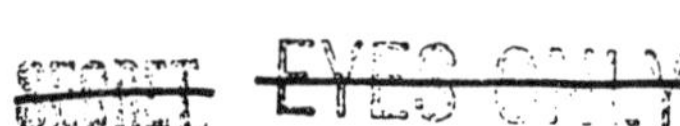

44. *(Continued)*

~~SECRET~~ ~~EYES ONLY~~

McCone told General Eisenhower there were some defendable evidences of shipments of twin-engined light jet bombers. Eisenhower responded the situation must be watched very carefully. Positive action might be indicated and then he said there had been two instances where action was warranted but had not been taken. Eisenhower did not elaborate; however, I know from previous discussions he feels that when Castro embraced Communism publicly and announced publicly his allegiance to Moscow, we had then a reason to act militarily and if we had chosen to so act, such action would have been defendable.

On Thursday morning McCone reported by telephone to Mr. Kennedy, reviewing the Eisenhower discussion and stating that he, McCone, was concerned over Donovan's safety in view of the rash of publicity, most particularly the Herald Tribune article, and that he had instructed that contact be made with Donovan and that if things were not proceeding satisfactorily and a conclusion to the negotiations along the lines agreed in sight, then Donovan should come out. The Attorney General stated that he had no concern over Donovan's personal safety, that "they will not do anything to him". McCone stated he was not so sure and that he therefore concluded to bring Donovan out unless things were going well.

With reference to the political implications, McCone recalled that he had told the President and the AG that he would take all, or his full share of responsibility, that he wished the AG to bear this in mind as the position taken in this respect by Mr. McCone in the first conversation after his return from Europe still stood. AG expressed appreciation for this statement.

John A. McCone
Director

JAM:at

- 3 -

~~SECRET~~ ~~EYES ONLY~~

45. *Memorandum, "U-2 Overflights of Cuba, 29 August through 14 October 1962," 27 February 1963*

~~SECRE~~T

27 February 1963

MEMORANDUM

SUBJECT: U-2 Overflights of Cuba, 29 August through 14 October 1962

The August 29th flight flew over most of the island and photographed much of it. The photography revealed that eight SAM sites were under construction in the western half of the island. The flight also discovered an installation at Banes in the eastern end of the island that was not familiar to the photo interpreters. Subsequent research by the interpreters, comparing the August 29th photography with that of two similar installations recently noted elsewhere, had by September 14th enabled them to identify the installation as a cruise missile site.

The finding of SA-2's in Cuba on the August 29th flight presented us with a new problem in planning U-2 flights over Cuba.

Today, there is general acceptance of the fact that we are carrying out overhead reconnaissance of Cuba and that we will continue to do so as long as our national security requires it. This almost universal approval of U-2 flights over Cuba is an attitude that has existed only since the middle of last October. Prior to the finding of offensive ballistic missiles in Cuba, quite a different public attitude existed.

~~SECRE~~T

45. *(Continued)*

~~SECRET~~

In planning for any U-2 operations over well-defended, denied territory we were always aware of criticism that attended the U-2 incident over the USSR in May of 1960. The two incidents involving the straying of a U-2 over Sakhalin on August 30th and the loss of a Chinese Nationalist U-2 over the China mainland on September 8th served to sharpen the already existing apprehensions.

Within the intelligence community there was always at the backs of our minds the knowledge that in the event of a mishap we would have to be able to explain, convincingly and in detail, the justification--in terms of the highest priority intelligence needs--for having undertaken the mission.

Elsewhere in Government and among persons whose stated views strongly influence public opinion there were serious reservations regarding the use of the U-2. There were expressions of extreme concern from some public leaders over the increase in tension that might result from overflights, and others voiced the opinion that such flights were illegal or immoral. Although many public figures conceded the necessity of the United States securing intelligence by whatever means required, they were quick to caution that the use of the U-2 was quite a different matter from the classical use of spies and agents.

- 2 -

~~SECRET~~

SECRET

The vulnerability of the U-2 to Soviet SA-2 systems and the discovery of those systems in Cuba contributed further complicating factors in weighing risks against the need for hard intelligence.

The situation as of September 1962 must be viewed against this background of universal repugnance, or, at the very least, extreme uneasiness regarding overflights.

Because of the widespread apprehension over use of the U-2, we took particular care to ensure that each flight produced the maximum of information of value to the entire intelligence community. Each track was drawn to cover high priority targets agreed upon by an inter-agency group known as the Committee on Overhead Reconnaissance, a committee of the United States Intelligence Board.

We were also concerned with the conservation of the asset. The U-2 is not a sturdily-built aircraft. It is designed for one purpose--long flights at very high altitudes and at relatively low speeds. We had very few of these planes. Therefore, before we committed one to a mission we wanted to be absolutely certain that the intelligence need was great enough to justify the risk of loss of the pilot and aircraft. The Committee on Overhead Reconnaissance was the intelligence community's vehicle for making the target studies.

All CIA overflights were programmed through the medium of the CIA Monthly Forecast. At the time the Soviet arms build-up

- 3 -

SECRET

~~SECRET~~

began in Cuba, flights over Cuba were being forecast and flown at the rate of two per month.

Because of the need to husband our resources and to ensure that highest quality photography was obtained from each U-2 flight, it was the practice not to launch a mission unless weather over most of the critical targets was predicted to be less than 25 per cent overcast.

After reviewing the result of the August 29th mission, the Committee on Overhead Reconnaissance, in undeniably good judgment, recommended that the next mission should cover those areas of the island which were not photographed on the August 29th flight and that particular attention should be paid to the then unidentified site at Banes. It was important to learn whether the Soviets had made a limited deployment of SA-2's to Cuba or whether an island-wide defense was being built.

The next mission was successfully flown on schedule on September 5th over the eastern and central portions of the island. Three additional SAM sites were detected in the central portion of the island. Unfortunately, the flight encountered heavy cloud cover over eastern Cuba.

Late in August, Mr. McCone suggested to General Carter, who was acting as DCI during Mr. McCone's absence, that low-level

- 4 -

~~SECRET~~

SECRET

reconnaissance of Cuba be proposed. General Carter requested the Committee on Overhead Reconnaissance to consider the kind of information that could be obtained thus. The Committee met on September first and third and reported its views on what might be accomplished through low-level flights.

As a result of the Committee's deliberations and because of the heavy cloud cover encountered over eastern Cuba on the September 5th mission, General Carter, on September 10th, 1962, addressed a memorandum to the Secretary of Defense recommending that the Secretary initiate the necessary action to provide for employment of tactical-type reconnaissance against Banes, which was still unidentified, or other targets identified by the Committee on Overhead Reconnaissance as being suitable for low-level reconnaissance. The Secretary of Defense felt it preferable not to mount a low-level reconnaissance of Banes until the results of CIA high-level reconnaissance became available. As noted in the first paragraph, continuing research had by September 14th identified the Banes installation as a cruise missile site.

Now, let us return to the matter of the September U-2 flights. One mission had already been flown on September 5th. One flight remained yet to be flown in September. A special meeting was held on September 10th to consider the specific track for that second flight.

- 5 -

SECRET

~~S E C R E~~ T

General Carter presented a CIA proposal for a single high-level flight designed specifically to photograph the Banes area, where earlier photography had not been conclusive, and generally to search for SAM sites in those areas of central and eastern Cuba that had not been covered since the September 5th flight.

This meeting followed closely on the heels of the two U-2 incidents previously mentioned: the straying of a U-2 over Sakhalin on August 30th and the loss of a Chinese Nationalist U-2 over the China mainland on September 8th.

The Secretary of State expressed concern at CIA's planned coverage of Cuba, involving extensive peripheral coverage as well as two legs directly over Cuban air space, all in one flight. He said that he had no objection to the peripheral parts and, in fact, thought it useful to continue to establish our right to fly over international waters. On the other hand, he recognized the necessity of obtaining vertical coverage of the Isle of Pines and the eastern portion of Cuba. He felt, however, that it was unwise to combine extensive overflying of international waters with actual overflights. He pointed out that the long peripheral flight would draw undue attention to the mission and further that should the aircraft fall into enemy hands after an overflight had occurred, this would put the United States in a very poor position for standing on its rights to overfly international waters.

- 6 -

~~S E C R E T~~

~~SECRE~~T

Taking these views into account the plan was changed and four flights were substituted for the one. Two flights were to be wholly peripheral, involving no land overflight. One was to cover the Isle of Pines, and the other was to overfly the eastern end of the island targeted against Banes and Guantanamo.

There was a three-week period from the 5th to the 26th of September during which only one flight was flown (on September 17th), and it yielded no useable photography. We finally acquired a moderately complete mosaic of the SA-2 defense of Cuba by piece-meal photography search carried out in late September and early October. The delay in completing the photographic coverage was due solely to the unfavorable weather predicted during this period.

- 7 -

~~SECRE~~T

45. *(Continued)*

~~SECRE~~T

Much of Cuba was under heavy cloud cover throughout most of September, and the cloud patterns were rapidly and continually changing. The few periods of acceptable weather were so fleeting that they had passed before flights could be mounted.

The weather was checked for a possible mission every day beginning on September 6th. There was a one- or two- day period around the middle of the month when the forecasts were moderately favorable. A flight to the northeast was scheduled for the 16th. It went to the final briefing on the 15th, but was delayed for 24 hours because of weather and was cancelled when the weather continued unfavorable. Planning for a flight over the Isle of Pines was under way on September 15th. At the final briefing on the 16th, the forecast remained favorable. The mission was flown on September 17th, but by then the weather had turned sour and no useable photography was acquired.

Another mission was under consideration between September 18th and 21st, but the weather was bad and the mission was cancelled.

The mission to cover the Guantanamo and Banes areas was under consideration beginning 22 September. It went to alert daily, but weather was not acceptable until the 26th. On that date the mission was successfully flown and three SAM sites were discovered. This was the first of the four flights agreed upon on September 10th, and

- 8 -

~~SECRE~~T

~~SECRE~~T

it was the first day on which weather permitted a successful flight.

One of the four tracks was originally approved to cover only the Isle of Pines. Mr. McCone called Mr. U. Alexis Johnson on September 28th and got approval to include coverage of the Bay of Pigs area. The flight was successfully flown on September 29th. The SAM and the cruise missile sites at Siguanea on the Isle of Pines were discovered.

Two of the three remaining missions for September were considered during the period September 29th through October 2nd. Both were cancelled because of bad weather.

The next flight under consideration was that along the periphery of the southeastern coast. It was delayed because of weather on October 3rd. It was briefed on October 4th and successfully flew the mission on the 5th. One additional SAM site was discovered.

There was good weather along the northeastern coast on October 6th. A flight was launched but it aborted because of aircraft fuel problems.

The flight along the northeastern coast was successfully flown the next day, October 7th. Four more SAM sites were discovered.

The mission of October 7th completed the September flight program.

- 9 -

~~SECRE~~T

~~SECRE~~T

As the September overflight program progressed, identifying additional SAM sites, it became apparent that an island-wide SA-2 defense was being constructed. The next step was to discover how far advanced the earlier SAM sites were. This information could be obtained only by taking the risk of overflying an SA-2 site that might be operational.

At an interdepartmental group meeting on October 4th, the DCI made a strong representation for extensive overflights of Cuba. The group requested [redacted] JCS, and CIA to examine all alternative means of conducting aerial reconnaissance and to report back as soon as possible. A meeting was called on October 9th to hear this report, and at this meeting the flight was planned which was actually flown on the 14th of October.

Additionally, from September 18th through October 2nd, agent and refugee reports dovetailed sufficiently to create a suspicion that there was something of unusual importance going on in a definite area west of Havana and that this unusual activity might be concerned with MRBM's. These reports, however, were not of sufficient credibility to warrant their being used in intelligence publications. Accordingly, the track of the flight planned at the October 9th meeting to test the operational readiness of the known SAM sites was drawn to cover the area in which MRBM's were suspected.

- 10 -

~~SECRET~~

SECRET

The weather was checked daily on October 10th, 11th and 12th, but the forecasts were unfavorable. On October 12th, operational control of U-2 overflights of Cuba was transferred to the Strategic Air Command of the U.S. Air Force. The weather forecast continued unfavorable on October 13th. The mission was successfully flown by SAC on October 14th over the suspect area west of Havana and near the SAM site thought most likely to be operational. The flight was the first to discover the presence of MRBM's.

As of October 16th, blanket authority was given for unrestricted overflights of Cuba.

Attached at Tab A is a summary of weather forecasts and the status of missions, 5 September through 14 October 1962.

- 11 -

SECRET

PART II

CRISIS OCTOBER 16-28 1962

Notification of high US officials . . . Formation of National Security Council Executive Committee (Ex Comm) . . . Policy debate over appropriate US response to missile threat . . . Continuation of Operation MONGOOSE . . . Discovery of intermediate-range ballistic missile sites in Cuba . . . Notification of Allied heads of government . . . The President's speech . . .Quarantine . . . Construction of missile bases continues at rapid pace . . . U-2 shootdown . . . Resolution of Crisis . . .

46. *CIA Memorandum, "Probable Soviet MRBM Sites in Cuba,"*
16 October 1962

~~TOP SECRET~~

CONTROL NO. [redacted]

x ~~xerox of~~ copy #5

REFERRED TO OFFICE	RECEIVED			RELEASED		SEEN BY	
	SIGNATURE	DATE	TIME	DATE	TIME	NAME & OFFICE SYMBOL	DATE

(OVER)

Handle Via Indicated Controls

[redacted]

First memo on the Missile Sites in Cuba

....

....

....

....

WARNING

This document contains information affecting the national security of the United States within the meaning of the espionage laws U. S. Code Title 18, Sections 793 and 794. The law prohibits its transmission or the revelation of its contents in any manner to an unauthorized person, as well as its use in any manner prejudicial to the safety or interest of the United States or for the benefit of any foreign government to the detriment of the United States. It is to be seen only by personnel especially indoctrinated and authorized to receive information in the designated control channels. Its security must be maintained in accordance with regulations pertaining to TALENT Control System.

~~TOP SECRET~~

GROUP 1
Excluded from automatic downgrading and declassification

46. *(Continued)*

16 October 1962

CENTRAL INTELLIGENCE AGENCY

MEMORANDUM: Probable Soviet MRBM Sites in Cuba

1. Photography of 14 October 1962 has disclosed two areas in the Sierra del Rosario mountains about 50 n.m. west southwest of Havana which appear to contain Soviet MRBMs in the early stages of deployment. A third area, about five and ten miles east of the first two, respectively, appears to be a military encampment. The first site includes 14 large tents, 15 smaller tents and 75 vehicles of a number of different types. The most significant vehicles at this site are six canvas-covered trailers of 80 feet in overall length which are of the general size and configuration of those used to transport the Soviet SS-3 (700 n.m. ballistic missile) and SS-4 (1100 n.m. ballistic missile). These trailers, of which eight more are located at the second site, are believed to be larger than those required to transport the Soviet SS-2 (350 n.m. ballistic missile).

2. The second site is 5 n.m. east of the first, and in addition to the eight trailers, contains four specially configured vehicles or pieces of equipment which could be used for missile erection in a field environment. At the time of photography, one of the trailers was in juxtaposition with one of these possible erectors. This site also contains 17 large tents, 20 small tents, 10 large trucks, 16 small trucks and 12 unidentified pieces of large equipment. No other missile associated equipment, such as instrumentation or propellant storage, have been detected. No facility to store nuclear warheads can be identified at any of these three installations.

PSALM

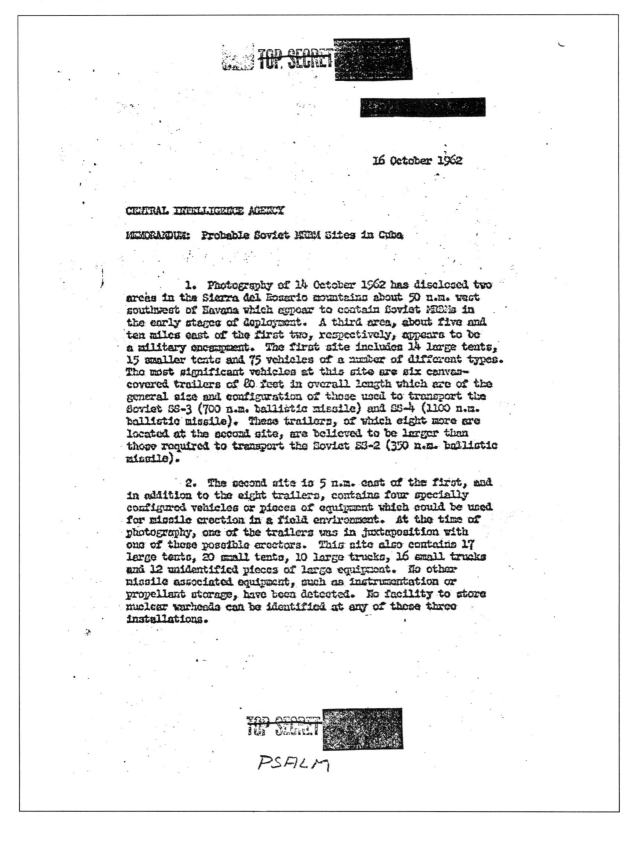

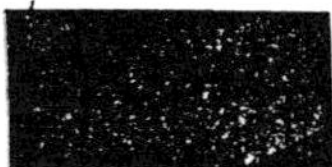

TOP SECRET

3. The dimensions of the trailers indicate that either the SS-3 or SS-4 ballistic missile systems are involved. Both of these systems are road-mobile and can be deployed with no heavy construction work for launch pads, etc. Both the SS-3 and SS-4 are single stage vehicles which will carry a 3,000 lb. warhead to a maximum range of 700 n.m. and 1100 n.m. respectively. The SS-3 system requires liquid oxygen as an oxidant, while the SS-4 employs storable propellants. From a logistic and operational standpoint it would be more advantageous to deploy the SS-4 system to Cuba.

4. We do not have evidence from shipping coverage or other sources to indicate definitely when the missile units arrived in Cuba. From the extensiveness of the present activity, we judge that equipment may have begun to arrive during September. At the time of the 14 October photography, a column of trucks and equipment was visible on a road within one of the installations. Although we cannot be sure, it seems likely that the bulk of the personnel and equipment were shipped from the USSR as an integrated road mobile unit, suitable for field deployment. The time required to reach operational readiness could thus be quite short. Assuming that the necessary fueling and handling equipment is available, that communications are being installed, and that warheads are in Cuba or en route, an operational MRBM capability could probably exist in Cuba within the next few weeks.

5. The Soviet leaders' decision to deploy ballistic missiles to Cuba testifies to their determination to deter any active US intervention to weaken or overthrow the Castro regime, which they apparently regard as likely and imminent. This estimate of US intentions prompted Moscow's statement of 11 September which warned that an attack on Cuba would lead to a general nuclear conflict. The Soviets presumably believe that the presence of these missiles, which they expect would quickly become known to the US government, will significantly increase the costs and risks of any US action against the Cuban regime. They also probably believe that the missiles will reinforce the deterrent link between Cuba and Berlin which was implicit in the 11 September Soviet statement and in subsequent private conversations. Moscow clearly is seeking to portray Berlin as a hostage for Cuba.

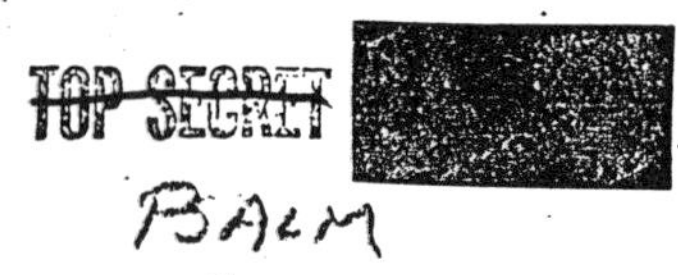

TOP SECRET

BALM

-2-

46. *(Continued)*

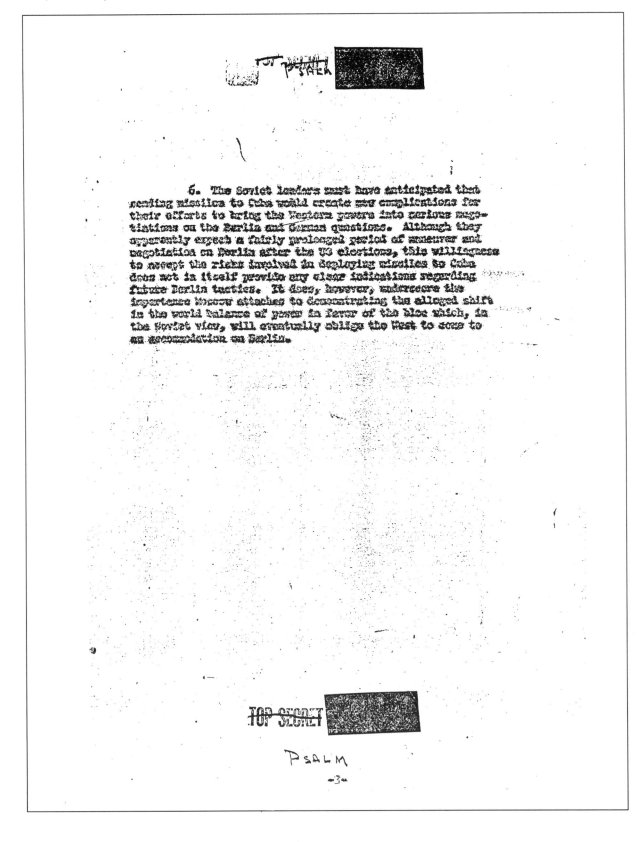

6. The Soviet leaders must have anticipated that sending missiles to Cuba would create new complications for their efforts to bring the Western powers into serious negotiations on the Berlin and German questions. Although they apparently expect a fairly prolonged period of maneuver and negotiation on Berlin after the US elections, this willingness to accept the risks involved in deploying missiles to Cuba does not in itself provide any clear indications regarding future Berlin tactics. It does, however, underscore the importance Moscow attaches to demonstrating the alleged shift in the world balance of power in favor of the bloc which, in the Soviet view, will eventually oblige the West to come to an accommodation on Berlin.

PSALM

-3-

PSALM ~~TOP SECRET~~ [redacted]

ANNEX: Strategic Considerations

1. In weighing their decision to install ballistic missiles in Cuba, the Soviet leaders must have considered the military utility of these weapons with and without nuclear warheads, the targets in the US and elsewhere which they could reach, and the strategic value of deploying missile forces of various sizes in Cuba.

2. Because of their type of guidance and relative inaccuracy, ballistic missiles have utility against fixed targets of known location, and not against such targets as convoys or naval forces at sea. The Soviet 700 and 1,100 n.m. missiles, whose CEP's are estimated to be in the 1 to 1.5 n.m. range, could conceivably be employed with HE warheads against large military centers and urban areas. It is highly unlikely that the Soviets would see any advantage in deployment for this purpose, but they might regard this threat as contribution to the deterrence of Latin American support for US or Cuban refugee operations against the Castro regime.

3. Deployed 700 and 1,100 n.m. missiles with nuclear warheads would augment Soviet strategic striking power by virtue of their ability to reach a number of American targets with warheads having yields which are not significantly smaller than those of current Soviet ICBMs. From the present base area in Cuba, 700 n.m. missiles with nuclear warheads could reach eastern US targets within an arc including Savannah and New Orleans, including 7 SAC bomber and tanker bases and at least one important naval base. (The 350 n.m missiles could reach bomber bases in Florida, of which there are only two.) The 1,100 n.m. missile would threaten a much more significant number of critical military targets, including 18 SAC bomber and tanker bases, an ICBM base, and three major naval bases. In addition, such targets as the Panama Canal and US bases as far east as Puerto Rico could be reached. Both of these missiles have ranges sufficient to reach many US population, industrial and administrative center--including, in the case of the 1,100 n.m. missile, Washington, D.C. Installations of importance to the US atomic energy and space programs also would be within range of Cuban-based 700 and 1,100 n.m. missiles.

PSALM ~~TOP SECRET~~ [redacted]

46. *(Continued)*

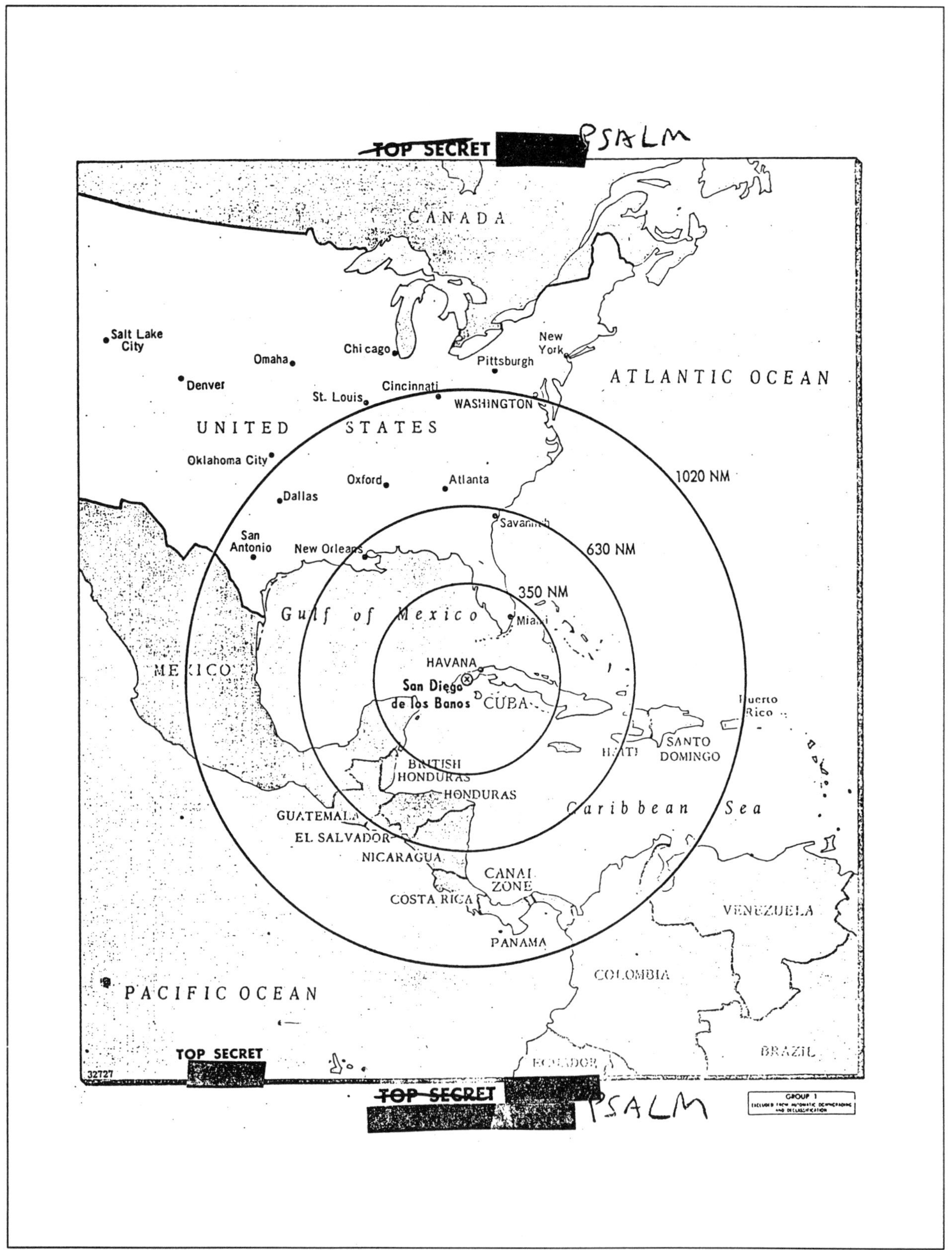

47. *Carter, Memorandum for the Record, 17 October 1962*

SECRET

17 October 1962

MEMORANDUM FOR THE RECORD

1. On Monday evening, 15 October late, I was informed that the latest readout from Cuban U-2 photography indicated initial deployment of Medium Range Ballistic Missiles. I immediately authorized the dissemination of this information on a very limited need-to-know basis to USIB members and their immediate commanders. On Tuesday morning at 11:45 I attended an NSC Meeting at the White House which included the President, Secretary Rusk, Secretary Ball, Secretary Martin, Secretary McNamara, Secretary Gilpatric, General Taylor, the Vice President, Secretary Dillon, the Attorney General, Mr. McGeorge Bundy, and myself. I made a preliminary briefing to the group as to what we thought we saw and Mr. Lundahl and Mr. Graybeal expanded thereon. At the end of the intelligence portion of the briefing, the group went into general discussion.

2. Secretary Rusk was greatly disturbed about this new development but pointed out that Mr. McCone had predicted such a possibility back in mid-August. He said that he had been thinking about courses of action and that he had a number of comments to make, along the following lines:

a. A quick-strike surprise attack by air to wipe out these bases;

b. Consideration to expand this into a total invasion to take over the island;

c. We must not operate in a vacuum but must of course pre-inform our allies, at least in part;

d. We should consider making an announcement very shortly and to determine whether or not to call up the Reserves;

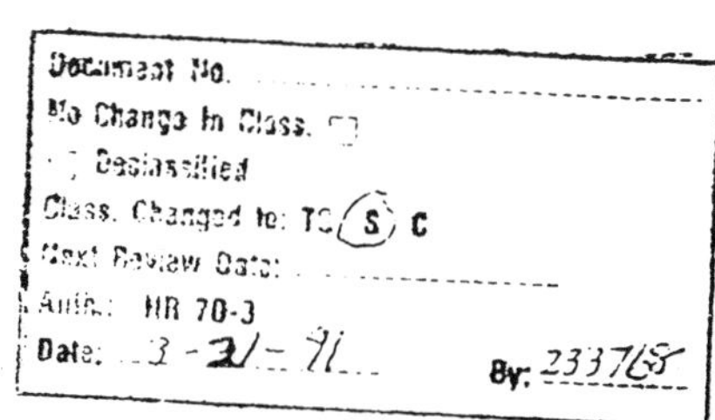

- 2 -

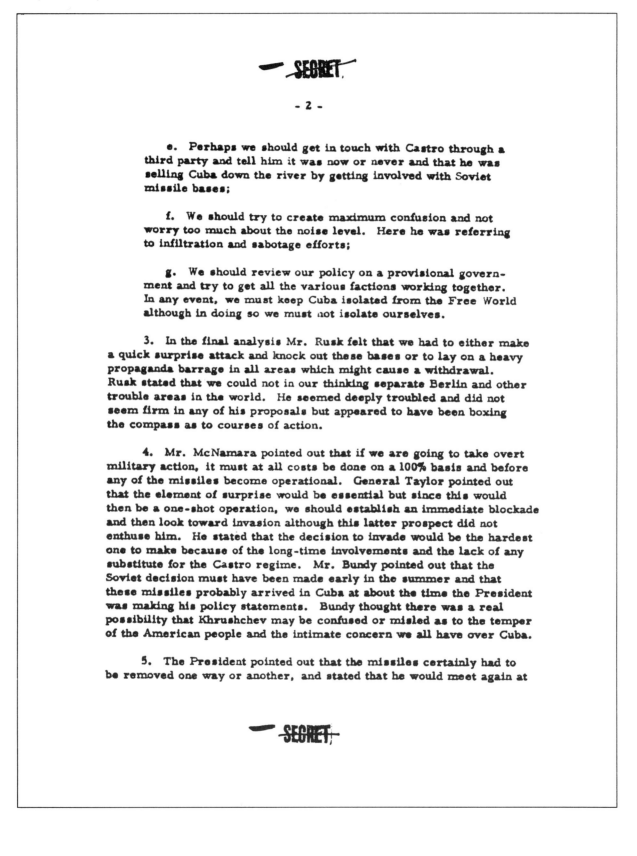

e. Perhaps we should get in touch with Castro through a third party and tell him it was now or never and that he was selling Cuba down the river by getting involved with Soviet missile bases;

f. We should try to create maximum confusion and not worry too much about the noise level. Here he was referring to infiltration and sabotage efforts;

g. We should review our policy on a provisional government and try to get all the various factions working together. In any event, we must keep Cuba isolated from the Free World although in doing so we must not isolate ourselves.

3. In the final analysis Mr. Rusk felt that we had to either make a quick surprise attack and knock out these bases or to lay on a heavy propaganda barrage in all areas which might cause a withdrawal. Rusk stated that we could not in our thinking separate Berlin and other trouble areas in the world. He seemed deeply troubled and did not seem firm in any of his proposals but appeared to have been boxing the compass as to courses of action.

4. Mr. McNamara pointed out that if we are going to take overt military action, it must at all costs be done on a 100% basis and before any of the missiles become operational. General Taylor pointed out that the element of surprise would be essential but since this would then be a one-shot operation, we should establish an immediate blockade and then look toward invasion although this latter prospect did not enthuse him. He stated that the decision to invade would be the hardest one to make because of the long-time involvements and the lack of any substitute for the Castro regime. Mr. Bundy pointed out that the Soviet decision must have been made early in the summer and that these missiles probably arrived in Cuba at about the time the President was making his policy statements. Bundy thought there was a real possibility that Khrushchev may be confused or misled as to the temper of the American people and the intimate concern we all have over Cuba.

5. The President pointed out that the missiles certainly had to be removed one way or another, and stated that he would meet again at

47. *(Continued)*

- 3 -

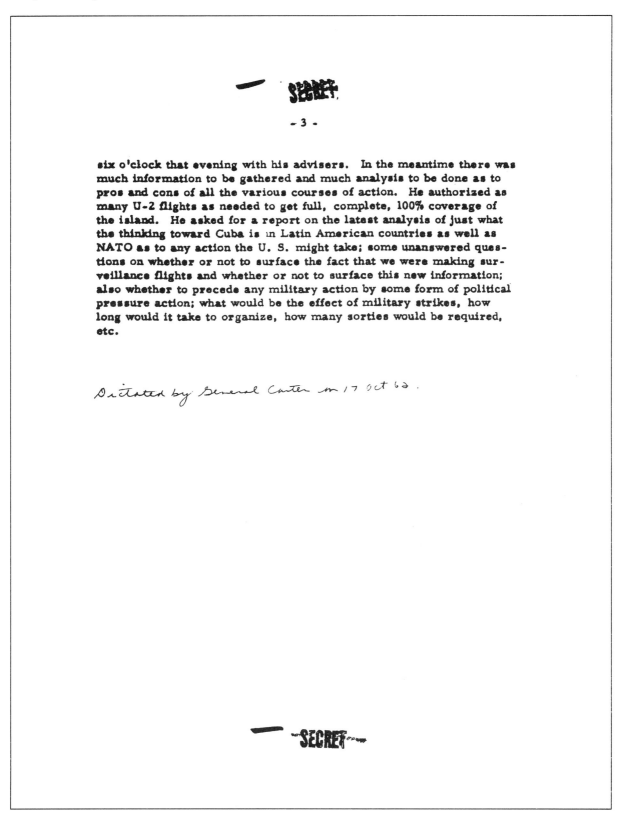

six o'clock that evening with his advisers. In the meantime there was much information to be gathered and much analysis to be done as to pros and cons of all the various courses of action. He authorized as many U-2 flights as needed to get full, complete, 100% coverage of the island. He asked for a report on the latest analysis of just what the thinking toward Cuba is in Latin American countries as well as NATO as to any action the U. S. might take; some unanswered questions on whether or not to surface the fact that we were making surveillance flights and whether or not to surface this new information; also whether to precede any military action by some form of political pressure action; what would be the effect of military strikes, how long would it take to organize, how many sorties would be required, etc.

Dictated by General Carter on 17 Oct 62.

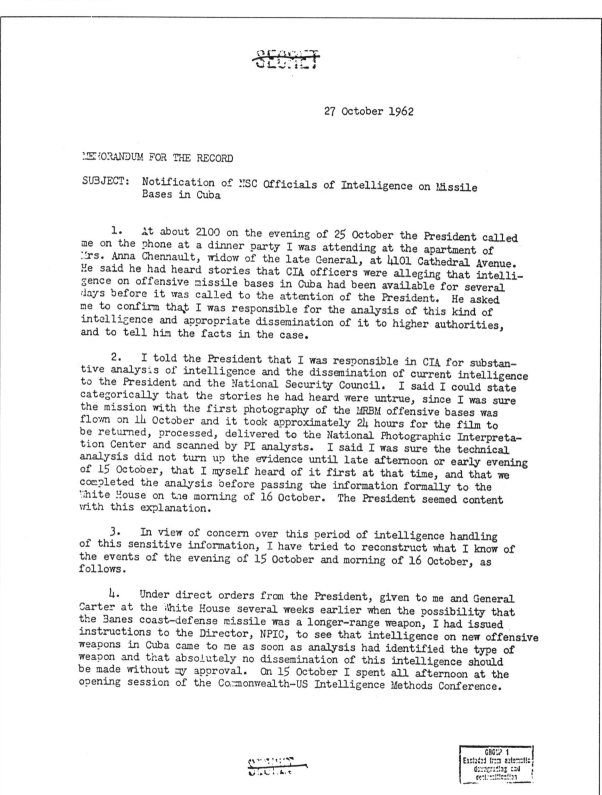

48. *Cline, Memorandum for the Record, "Notification of NSC Officials of Intelligence on Missile Bases in Cuba," 27 October 1962*

SECRET

27 October 1962

MEMORANDUM FOR THE RECORD

SUBJECT: Notification of NSC Officials of Intelligence on Missile Bases in Cuba

1. At about 2100 on the evening of 25 October the President called me on the phone at a dinner party I was attending at the apartment of Mrs. Anna Chennault, widow of the late General, at 4101 Cathedral Avenue. He said he had heard stories that CIA officers were alleging that intelligence on offensive missile bases in Cuba had been available for several days before it was called to the attention of the President. He asked me to confirm that I was responsible for the analysis of this kind of intelligence and appropriate dissemination of it to higher authorities, and to tell him the facts in the case.

2. I told the President that I was responsible in CIA for substantive analysis of intelligence and the dissemination of current intelligence to the President and the National Security Council. I said I could state categorically that the stories he had heard were untrue, since I was sure the mission with the first photography of the MRBM offensive bases was flown on 14 October and it took approximately 24 hours for the film to be returned, processed, delivered to the National Photographic Interpretation Center and scanned by PI analysts. I said I was sure the technical analysis did not turn up the evidence until late afternoon or early evening of 15 October, that I myself heard of it first at that time, and that we completed the analysis before passing the information formally to the White House on the morning of 16 October. The President seemed content with this explanation.

3. In view of concern over this period of intelligence handling of this sensitive information, I have tried to reconstruct what I know of the events of the evening of 15 October and morning of 16 October, as follows.

4. Under direct orders from the President, given to me and General Carter at the White House several weeks earlier when the possibility that the Banes coast-defense missile was a longer-range weapon, I had issued instructions to the Director, NPIC, to see that intelligence on new offensive weapons in Cuba came to me as soon as analysis had identified the type of weapon and that absolutely no dissemination of this intelligence should be made without my approval. On 15 October I spent all afternoon at the opening session of the Commonwealth-US Intelligence Methods Conference.

SECRET

GROUP 1
Excluded from automatic downgrading and declassification

SECRET

When I returned to my office at 1730 I found a delegation of PI and military intelligence analysts awaiting me. I do not know how long they had been waiting to see me but it could not have been many minutes or they would have passed a message to me at the Conference Room. They were all agreed that they had just identified a missile base for missiles of a range upwards of 350 miles. I reviewed their evidence and was obliged to concur.

5. The DCI had gone to the West Coast and General Carter was then at an informal reception for the Commonwealth conferees in the Executive Dining Room at the Headquarters building in McLean. I was the host but delayed my arrival until 1815 to study this intelligence. Upon arrival I called General Carter aside and advised him in broad terms of the intelligence. I said it would take several hours to wrap up a definitive report with fully considered analysis. General Carter said he was going to dinner with General Taylor and General Carroll (DIA) and would let them know. I asked if he would notify Mr. McGeorge Bundy for the White House and he said he thought he might be at the dinner and would notify him there.

6. About 2130 that evening my intelligence officers checking out the evidence on the site reported somewhat cryptically by phone that they had agreed on a report identifying offensive missile systems probably in the 700-mile and possibly in the 1,000-mile range. I instructed them to complete a written report and stand by for action early the next morning.

7. A few minutes later I decided it was a mistake to wait until morning to alert the key officers at the White House and State Department, so they should insure early attention to the problem on the next day. I assumed General Carter would have alerted the Pentagon adequately via JCS and DIA but that he might have missed the White House. Accordingly I called Mr. McGeorge Bundy, found he had not seen General Carter, and double-talked the information to him in broad terms. He was very clear as to the import despite being short on facts due to the problem of security over the phone. This was about 2200. I then called Roger Hilsman of the State Department and conveyed the same information to him. I had more difficulty indicating securely to him that I really meant MRBM's rather than aircraft or other equipment we had anticipated, but the light finally dawned and he (as he later informed me) called the Secretary of State to pass on the word.

8. Early the next morning, 16 October, at about 0830, I talked again on the phone to Mr. Bundy. (I forget whether he called me or vice versa) I had by then reviewed a brief memorandum on the subject and calculated the ranges of possible missiles (by then we had settled on 700 to 1100 miles) and crudely indicated them on a map. At Mr. Bundy's invitation I went immediately to his office, having cleared this with General Carter, who had another engagement and instructed me to follow through on the White House formal notification. Sid Graybeal, my missiles expert from OSI, accompanied me. In Bundy's office I told him the story. He shortly

SECRET

SECRET

brought in the Attorney General, whom I also briefed. His initial comment was one four-letter word, off the record. If I remember correctly, Alex Johnson also came in to get the briefing. At any rate Mr. Bundy said that he had arranged an 1100 meeting with the President to fill him in and consider the US policy problems involved. At 0930 General Carter arrived. I showed him the memorandum we had prepared, discussed the evidence, and advised him Graybeal could support him fully with analytical back-up. I said I felt the Acting DCI should handle the briefing of the President, with which General Carter agreed; that he probably did not need me, with which he somewhat reluctantly agreed; and that somebody had better get back to see that the DCI on the West Coast got the word, and continue research and analysis on the Cuban missile problem — with all of which General Carter heartily agreed.

9. I presume General Carter did surface the information at 1100, the DCI returned later that afternoon, and a whirlwind of intelligence reporting and policy formulation on Cuba set in from which we have not yet recovered.

Ray S. Cline

RAY S. CLINE
Deputy Director (Intelligence)

SECRET

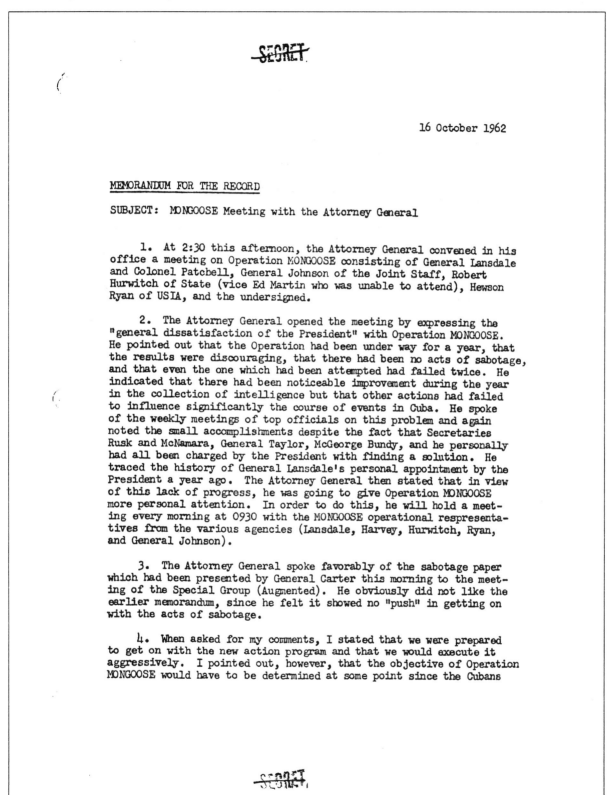

49. *Richard Helms, Memorandum for the Record, "MONGOOSE Meeting with the Attorney General," 16 October 1962*

SECRET

16 October 1962

MEMORANDUM FOR THE RECORD

SUBJECT: MONGOOSE Meeting with the Attorney General

1. At 2:30 this afternoon, the Attorney General convened in his office a meeting on Operation MONGOOSE consisting of General Lansdale and Colonel Patchell, General Johnson of the Joint Staff, Robert Hurwitch of State (vice Ed Martin who was unable to attend), Hewson Ryan of USIA, and the undersigned.

2. The Attorney General opened the meeting by expressing the "general dissatisfaction of the President" with Operation MONGOOSE. He pointed out that the Operation had been under way for a year, that the results were discouraging, that there had been no acts of sabotage, and that even the one which had been attempted had failed twice. He indicated that there had been noticeable improvement during the year in the collection of intelligence but that other actions had failed to influence significantly the course of events in Cuba. He spoke of the weekly meetings of top officials on this problem and again noted the small accomplishments despite the fact that Secretaries Rusk and McNamara, General Taylor, McGeorge Bundy, and he personally had all been charged by the President with finding a solution. He traced the history of General Lansdale's personal appointment by the President a year ago. The Attorney General then stated that in view of this lack of progress, he was going to give Operation MONGOOSE more personal attention. In order to do this, he will hold a meeting every morning at 0930 with the MONGOOSE operational respresentatives from the various agencies (Lansdale, Harvey, Hurwitch, Ryan, and General Johnson).

3. The Attorney General spoke favorably of the sabotage paper which had been presented by General Carter this morning to the meeting of the Special Group (Augmented). He obviously did not like the earlier memorandum, since he felt it showed no "push" in getting on with the acts of sabotage.

4. When asked for my comments, I stated that we were prepared to get on with the new action program and that we would execute it aggressively. I pointed out, however, that the objective of Operation MONGOOSE would have to be determined at some point since the Cubans

SECRET

SECRET

\- 2 -

with whom we have to work were seeking a reason for risking their lives in these operations. I retailed my conversation with the young Cuban from the DRE who pointed out that they were willing to commit their people only on operations which they regarded as sensible. I defined "sensible" in Cuban terminology these days as meaning an action which would contribute to the liberation of their country, another way of saying that the United States, perhaps in conjunction with other Latin countries, would bail them out militarily. My point was specifically echoed by Hewson Ryan. The Attorney General's rejoinder was a plea for new ideas of things that could be done against Cuba. In passing, he made reference to the change in atmosphere in the United States Government during the last twenty-four hours, and asked some questions about the percentage of Cubans whom we thought would fight for the regime if the country were invaded.

5\. The meeting concluded with the reaffirmation by the Attorney General of his desire to hold a meeting each day, beginning tomorrow. He said that these meetings might later be changed to every other day when and if he finds a daily get-together is not necessary. The meetings are to last no more than one-half hour.

RH

Richard Helms
Deputy Director (Plans)

Distribution:
Original - Mr. Elder for the DCI and DDCI
1 cc - Chief, TFW
1 cc - DD/P

SECRET

50. *Arthur C. Lundahl, Memorandum for Director of Central Intelligence and Director, Defense Intelligence Agency, "Additional Information—Mission 3101," 16 October 1962*

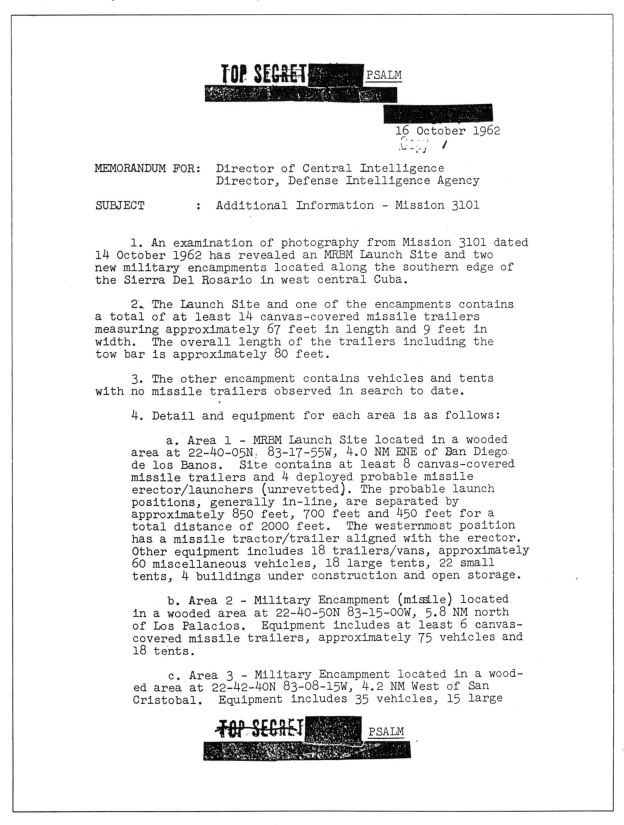

16 October 1962
Copy 1

MEMORANDUM FOR: Director of Central Intelligence
Director, Defense Intelligence Agency

SUBJECT : Additional Information - Mission 3101

1. An examination of photography from Mission 3101 dated 14 October 1962 has revealed an MRBM Launch Site and two new military encampments located along the southern edge of the Sierra Del Rosario in west central Cuba.

2. The Launch Site and one of the encampments contains a total of at least 14 canvas-covered missile trailers measuring approximately 67 feet in length and 9 feet in width. The overall length of the trailers including the tow bar is approximately 80 feet.

3. The other encampment contains vehicles and tents with no missile trailers observed in search to date.

4. Detail and equipment for each area is as follows:

a. Area 1 - MRBM Launch Site located in a wooded area at 22-40-05N, 83-17-55W, 4.0 NM ENE of San Diego de los Banos. Site contains at least 8 canvas-covered missile trailers and 4 deployed probable missile erector/launchers (unrevetted). The probable launch positions, generally in-line, are separated by approximately 850 feet, 700 feet and 450 feet for a total distance of 2000 feet. The westernmost position has a missile tractor/trailer aligned with the erector. Other equipment includes 18 trailers/vans, approximately 60 miscellaneous vehicles, 18 large tents, 22 small tents, 4 buildings under construction and open storage.

b. Area 2 - Military Encampment (missile) located in a wooded area at 22-40-50N 83-15-00W, 5.8 NM north of Los Palacios. Equipment includes at least 6 canvas-covered missile trailers, approximately 75 vehicles and 18 tents.

c. Area 3 - Military Encampment located in a wooded area at 22-42-40N 83-08-15W, 4.2 NM West of San Cristobal. Equipment includes 35 vehicles, 15 large

50. *(Continued)*

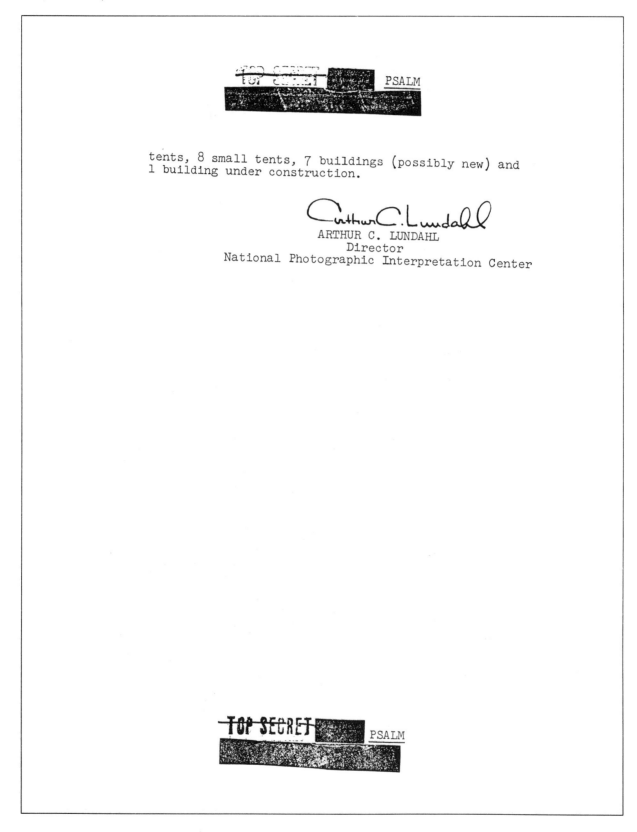

tents, 8 small tents, 7 buildings (possibly new) and 1 building under construction.

ARTHUR C. LUNDAHL
Director
National Photographic Interpretation Center

51. *McCone meeting schedule, 17-23 October 1962*

~~SECRET~~

17 October 1962 - Wednesday

8:30 a.m.	Meeting of study group: DCI, Secty. Rusk, Secty. McNamara, Gen. Taylor, Secty. Gilpatric Mr. McGeorge Bundy, Amb. Bohlen, Amb. Thompson, Amb. Acheson, Secty. Ball, Mr. Sorenson, Mr. Martin, Mr. Johnson
9:30 a.m.	DCI met with the President
11:30 a.m.	DCI went to Gettysburg - brief Gen. Eisenhower
4:00 p.m.	Meeting of study group
10:00 p.m.	Meeting of study group

18 October 1962 - Thursday

10:45 a.m.	Mr. McGeorge Bundy
11:00 a.m.	The President and others
4:00 p.m.	Meeting at State Department with study group
7:30 p.m.	Meeting at State Department with study group
9:00 p.m.	Meeting at State Department with study group

19 October 1962 - Friday

11:00 a.m.	Meeting at State Department with study group
4:00 p.m.	Meeting at State Department with study group

~~SECRET~~

51. *(Continued)*

~~SECRET~~

20 October 1962 - Saturday

8:30 a.m.	USIB Meeting
10:30 a.m.	Meeting of study group
1:30 p.m.	Meeting of study group
2:00 p.m.	Meeting at White House

21 October 1962 - Sunday

8:30 a.m.	USIB Meeting
9:00 a.m.	Meeting with Gen. Eisenhower
10:00 a.m.	Meeting at White House
2:30 p.m.	Special NSC Meeting
8:30 p.m.	Brief the Vice President

22 October 1962 - Monday

8:30 a.m.	USIB Meeting
10:30 a.m.	Meeting with The President
3:00 p.m.	NSC Meeting
5:00 p.m.	Meeting with Congressional Leaders

23 October 1962 - Tuesday

10:00 a.m.	Executive Committee of the NSC		
1:30 p.m.	Arthur Krock		
2:00 p.m.	Chairman Vinson	5:00 p.m.	David Lawrence
2:30 p.m.	Senator Hickenlooper	6:00 p.m.	Executive Com: of the NSC
3:30 p.m.	Senator Russell		

~~SECRET~~

52. *[McCone], "Memorandum of Meeting attended in Secretary Ball's Conference Room . . . at 0830, 17 October"*

M/K #101

Memorandum of Meeting attended in Secretary Ball's Conference Room by Secretary McNamara, Bundy, General Taylor, Robert Kennedy, Martin and McCone at 0830, 17 October.

1. Meeting involved an inclusive exploration of alternatives open to us in connection with the Cuban matter.

Ball seemed to feel military action would throw the NATO allies in disarray and permit Britain and France to separate from us on Berlin policy. Stated Kohler discussions with Khrushchev did not fit in with Soviet action in Cuba. Suggested Cuban situation might be by inadvertance . Suggested we might give Khrushchev an "out" on the grounds that he does not know what is going on in Cuba and discussed various types of action ranging from a limited military strike to minimize losses to xx the calling of a Summit conference.

2. During the discussion Taylor and Ball speculated as to whether this whole thing was not a "mock up" designed to draw out action by us. and that the war heads were not there. This view was not supported.

3. McNamara urged avoiding taking a position, considering all alternatives, with meetings this afternoon and this evening in preparation of final discussion with the President tomorrow.

4. Urged exploration of all facts and listed the following:

About 50 or 60 MIG 17s and 19s now in Cuba and these apparently have no offensive capability.

One MIG 21 has been seen and a number of suspicious crates also seen indicating some MIG 21 capability and we do not know whether the MIG 21 has an offensive capability.

IL 28's have been delivered

Three MRBM sites under construction and can be ready in two weeks

Warhead locations unknown; also unknown whether MRBM's are nuclear or conventional. Also feels that if nuclear warheads supplied them Soviet will also supply nuclear bombs for bombers with offensive capability

52. *(Continued)*

TOP SECRET EYES ONLY

Shiploads of boxes of unknown purpose reported by Lundahl to DCI on October 14th.

28 Soviet ships en route to Cuba at the present time.

Sited at Havana, mysterious excavations, revetments, covered buildings, railroad tracks through tunnels, etc., might be nuclear storage site.

Other facts should be developed today.

Note: McCone responded by reading numbered paragraphs 2, 3, and 4 of attached memorandum dated October 17th.

5. General Taylor and Thompson discussed political nature of problem including possibility of forcing settlement in Berlin and elsewhere - Khrushchev wished show down on Berlin and this gives a show down issue. Believes Khrushchev would be surprised to find we know about MRBMs. Thompson emphasized Khrushchev wants Berlih settlement but on his terms. And will probably deny knowledge of Cuban situation but at any event would justify actions because of our missiles in Italy and Turkey. Also Khrushchev recognizes that action by us would be devisive among our allies.

6. McCone emphasized his views on political objectives as stated in paragraph 5 of the attached memorandum, and also repeated paragraph 2-C. Also made the point in paragraph 6.

7. McNamara discussed many operational questions concerning the use of Soviet nuclear warheads in Cuba; how communications could be arranged; what authority was in the field. Thompson believes Soviet nuclear warheads was under very tight control. McCone reviewed recent Chicadee reports, indicated considerable automony in hands of field commanders much more so than we have.

8. Bundy and McCone left for meeting with the President.

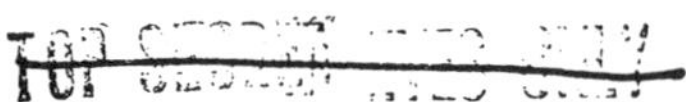

53. *McCone, Memorandum for Discussion Today, October 17, 1962, "The Cuban Situation"*

October 17, 1962

MEMORANDUM FOR DISCUSSION TODAY, OCTOBER 17, 1962.

SUBJECT: The Cuban Situation.

1. The establishment of medium range strike capability in Cuba by the Soviets was predicted by me in at least a dozen reports since the Soviet buildup was noted in early August.

2. Purposes are to:

(a) Provide Cuba with an offensive or retaliatory power for use if attacked.

(b) Enhance Soviet strike capability against the United States.

(c) Establish a "hall mark" of accomplishment by other Latin American countries, most particularly Mexico, and other Central American countries within strike range of the United States.

3. The MRBM capability we have witnessed will expand and the defensive establishments to protect this capability likewise will be expanded. There appears to me to be no other explanation for the extensive and elaborate air defense establishment.

4. In my opinion the missiles are Soviet, they will remain under Soviet operational control as do ours, they will be equipped with nuclear warheads under Soviet control (because conventional warheads would be absolutely ineffective), Cubans will supply most of the manpower needs with the Soviets permanently exercising operational command and control. Nevertheless, there will be a substantial number of Soviets on site at all times.

SECRET ~~EYES ONLY~~

~~SECRET~~ EYES ONLY

5. Soviet political objectives appear to me to be:

(a) The establishment of a "trading position" to force removal of U.S. overseas bases and Berlin.

(b) To satisfy their ambitions in Latin America by this show of determination and courage against the American Imperialist.

6. Consequences of action by the United States will be the inevitable "spilling of blood" of Soviet military personnel. This will increase tension everywhere and undoubtedly bring retaliation against U.S. foreign military installations, where substantial U.S. casualties would result, [redacted]

7. The situation cannot be tolerated. However, the United States should not act without warning and thus be forced to live with a "Pearl Harbor indictment" for the indefinite future. I would therefore:

(a) Notify Gromyko and Castro that we know all about this.

(b) Give them 24 hours to commence dismantling and removal of MRBMs, coastal defense missiles, surface to air missiles, IL 28s and all other aircraft which have a dual defensive-offensive capability, including MIG 21s.

(c) Notify the American public and the world of the situation created by the Soviets.

(d) If Khrushchev and Castro fail to act at once, we should make a massive surprise strike at air fields, MRBM sites and SAM sites concurrently.

John A. McCone
Director

- 2 -

SECRET ~~EYES ONLY~~

54. *McCone memorandum, 17 October 1962*

TOP SECRET EYES ONLY

October 17, 1962

Several alternatives indicated below were posed for consideration at the close of meeting covered by memorandum dated October 17th.

All dealt with the specific actions U.S. Government should take against Cuba at this time. The discussions centered around:

(a) Whether military action should be taken prior to a warning to, or discussions with, Khrushchev and Castro.

(b) Notification to or consultation with our allies, including NATO, OAS, and others.

(c) Referral to the United Nations.

(d) Effect on the "balance of nuclear power equation" of the MRBM installations in Cuba.

Three principal courses of action are open to us, and of course there are variations of each.

(1) Do nothing and live with the situation. It was pointed out clearly that Western Europe, Greece, Turkey, and other countries had lived under the Soviet MRBMs for years; therefore, why should the United States be so concerned.

(2) Resort to an all-out blockade which would probably require a declaration of war and to be effective would mean the interruption of all incoming shipping. This was discussed as a slow strangulation process, but it was stated that "intelligence reports" indicated that a blockade would bring Castro down in four months. (Note: I have seen no such estimate).

TOP SECRET EYES ONLY

54. *(Continued)*

TOP SECRET EYES ONLY

(3) Military action which was considered at several levels. The following alternatives are:

(a) Strafing identified MRBM installations.

(b) Strafing MRBM installations and air fields with MIGs.

(c) (a) and (b) plus all SAM sites and coastal missile sites.

(d) (a), (b), and (c) above plus all other significant military installations, none of which were identified.

Discussions of all of the above were inconclusive and it was asked that the group reassemble , and develop their views on the advantages and disadvantages and the effects of the following:

(1) Warning to Khrushchev and Castro.

(a) If the response is unsatisfactory, pursuing a course of military action.

(b) If the response is unsatisfactory, referring to the OAS and the United Nations prior to taking military action.

(2) Warning to Khrushchev and Castro and if the response is unsatisfactory, convening Congress, seeking a declaration of war, and proceeding with an all-out blockade.

(3) Strike militarily with no warning, the level of the military effort being dependent upon evolving circumstances. In all probability this type of action would escalate into invasion and occupation, although the meeting was not agreed on this point.

(4) Blockade with no warning and no advance notice such as a declaration of war, with the President depending upon existing Congressional resolutions for authority.

John A. McCone
Director

TOP SECRET - 2 - EYES ONLY

55. *McCone memorandum, "Brief Discussion with the President—9:30 a.m.—17 October 1962"*

#40

~~TOP SECRET~~ ~~EYES ONLY~~

Brief Discussion with the President - 9:30 a.m. - 17 October 1962

Confirmed the situation and explored possible actions. McCone referred to but did not recommend warnings as outlined in paragraph 7. (This paragraph was not discussed in the earlier meeting in Ball's office).

President seemed inclined to act promptly if at all, without warning, targetting on MRBM's and possibly airfields. Stated Congressional Resolution gave him all authority he needed and this was confirmed by Bundy, and therefore seemed inclined to act.

President asked McCone to see Eisenhower promptly.

JOHN A. McCONE
Director

JAM/ji

1 cc - DDCI

~~TOP SECRET~~ ~~EYES ONLY~~

56. *McCone, Memorandum for the File, "Conversation with General Eisenhower—Wednesday, 17 October 1962"*

~~SECRET~~, ~~EYES ONLY~~

17 October 1962

MEMORANDUM FOR THE FILE

SUBJECT: Conversation with General Eisenhower - Wednesday, 17 October 1962

At President Kennedy's request I called on General Eisenhower today at 12:00 o'clock. Reviewed the Cuban developments. President Kennedy had asked that I carefully avoid indicating any particular line of action as none had been agreed upon, and this was observed.

I briefed Eisenhower on all aspects of the recent Cuban-Soviet build-up and showed him the U-2 pictures of three MRBM missile sites under development. Eisenhower expressed no particular surprise indicating that he felt this offensive build-up would probably occur.

He then expressed criticism of the Bay of Pigs failure and also the fact that we did not respond more energetically when Castro publicly embraced Communism.

With respect to the current situation, Eisenhower felt that it would prove to be intolerable, that its purposes can not be clearly defined, and that discussions or adamant demands to either Khrushchev or Castro or both, would be of no avail.

In discussing blockades, he mentioned the difficulty of type of action we would take if and when a Soviet ship, laden with military hardware and personnel, is stopped on the high seas. The question he raised, as do I, is "What would we do with the ship then?"

Eisenhower questioned limited military action as being indecisive, irritating world opinion, creating fear in all areas where the Soviets could retaliate with limited action and therefore would be ~~indecisive~~. inadvisable. He recalled that when President Truman ordered limited air support in the first two or three days of the Korean war, he, Eisenhower, told the President that from a military standpoint this would not work and more decisive action was required.

~~SECRET~~, ~~EYES ONLY~~

~~SECRET~~ ~~EYES ONLY~~

Throughout the conversation Eisenhower seemed to lean toward (but did not specifically recommend) military action which would cut off Havana and therefore take over the heart of the government. He thought this might be done by airborne divisions but was not familiar with the size of the Cuban forces in the immediate area, nor the equipment. Eisenhower seemed to feel that such a plan would be more decisive, would mean less bloodshed, could be accomplished more quickly than a landing and a conventional type of slow invasion.

I told General Eisenhower that I did not expect an answer but both the President and I wished him to be fully informed and that I would like to consult with him from time to time. He agreed to be available personally or by telephone at any time.

JOHN A. McCONE
Director

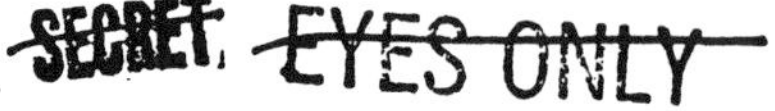

57. *McCone, Memorandum for the File, "Memorandum of Meeting, Wednesday, October 17th, at 8:30 a.m., and again at 4:00 p.m.," 19 October 1962*

October 19, 1962

MEMORANDUM FOR THE FILE

Memorandum of Meeting, Wednesday, October 17th, at 8:30 a.m., and again at 4:00 p.m., attended by Rusk, Ball (each part of the time) Martin, Johnson, McNamara, Gilpatric, Taylor, McCone, Bohlen, Thompson, Bundy, Sorenson, Dean Acheson (for a short time).

Note: The 4:00 o'clock meeting adjourned at about 7:00, and re-assembled at 10:00 p.m., in Secretary Ball's conference room, adjourning at 11:45 p.m.

Note: At 9:30 a.m. on 17 October DCI went to see the President, then went to Gettysburg to see General Eisenhower.

The purpose of the discussion was to develop a plan of action in connection with Cuba, and the alternatives are summarized in my memorandum of October 18th addressed to USIB, copy of which is attached.

This memorandum will record views as they were expressed and developed throughout the meetings.

Ambassador Bohlen warned against any action against Cuba, particularly an air strike without warning, stating such would be divisive with all Allies and subject us to criticism throughout the world. He advocated writing both Khrushchev and Castro; if their response was negative or unsatisfactory then we should plan action; advise our principal allies, seek a two-thirds vote from the OAS and then act. The Attorney General and Bohlen exchanged views as to just what type of an answer we could expect from Khrushchev and what he might do if we threatened an attack. During this discussion Secretary Rusk seemed to favor asking Congress for a declaration of a state of war against Cuba and then proceed with OAS, NATO, etc., but always preserve flexibility as to the type of action. Bohlen consistently warned that world opinion would be against us if we carried out a military strike. Secretary Ball emphasized the importance of time, stating that if action was over quickly, the repercussions would not be too serious.

No Change In Class. ☐
☐ Declassified
Class. Changed to: TS (S) C
Next Review Date: ----------------
Auth.: HR 70-3
Date: [illegible] By: [illegible]

SECRET

SECRET

The Attorney General raised the question of the attitude of Turkey, Italy, Western European countries , all of which have been "under the gun" for years, and would take the position that now that the U.S. has a few missiles in their backyard, they become hysterical. This point was discussed back and forth by various people throughout both days of discussion.

Secretary McNamara made the point that missiles in Cuba had no great military consequence because of the stalemate mentioned in my October 18th memorandum. General Taylor supported this view in the early parts of the discussion, but in the later meetings expressed increasing concern over the importance of the missile threat from Cuba. Gilpatric supported McNamars's position. McCone doubted it, stating that McNamara's facts were not new as they had appeared in estimates months ago (which McNamara questioned). Nevertheless, he and McCone felt that a complex of MRBMs and IRBMs in Cuba would have very important military significance. McNamara took issue claiming that the military equation would not be changed by the appearance of these missiles.

Bohlen and Thompson questioned the real purpose of the Soviet's actions in Cuba and seemed to feel that their acts may be in preparation for a confrontation with President Kennedy at which time they would seek to settle the entire subject of overseas bases as well as the Berlin question. McCone indicated this might be one of several objectives and undoubtedly would be the subject of discussion at the time of confrontation ; however, McCone doubted that this was the prime purpose of such an elaborate and expensive installation as the Soviets were going forward with in Cuba. Bohlen seemed to favor precipitating talks, and was supported by Thompson.

SecDef and Taylor both objected to political talks because it would give time for threatening missiles to become operational and also give the Soviets an opportunity to camouflage the missiles. McCone presented most recent photographs and indicated CIA opinion that the first missiles will be operational within one or two weeks.

Bohlen again raised the question of opening up discussions. McNamara agreed that ~~was should be~~ this would be desirable but emphasized the importance of developing sequence of events which would lead to military action.

- 2 -

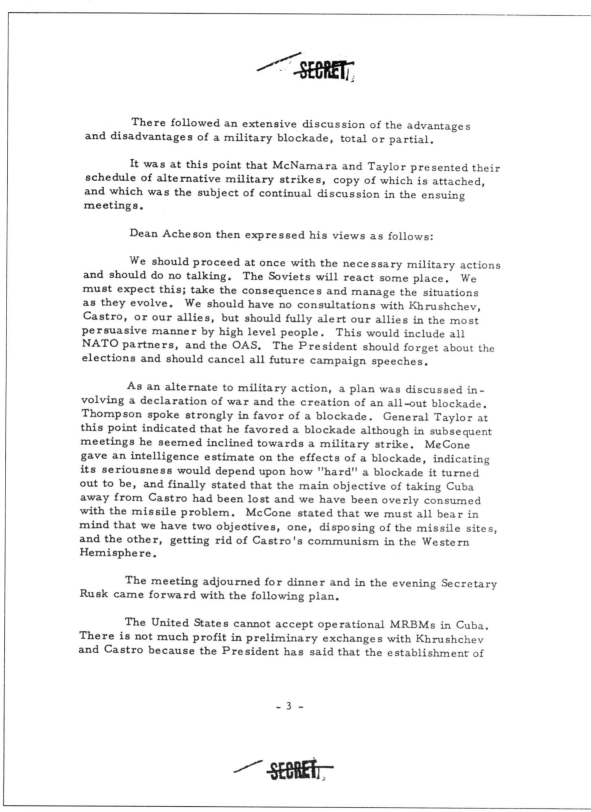

There followed an extensive discussion of the advantages and disadvantages of a military blockade, total or partial.

It was at this point that McNamara and Taylor presented their schedule of alternative military strikes, copy of which is attached, and which was the subject of continual discussion in the ensuing meetings.

Dean Acheson then expressed his views as follows:

We should proceed at once with the necessary military actions and should do no talking. The Soviets will react some place. We must expect this; take the consequences and manage the situations as they evolve. We should have no consultations with Khrushchev, Castro, or our allies, but should fully alert our allies in the most persuasive manner by high level people. This would include all NATO partners, and the OAS. The President should forget about the elections and should cancel all future campaign speeches.

As an alternate to military action, a plan was discussed involving a declaration of war and the creation of an all-out blockade. Thompson spoke strongly in favor of a blockade. General Taylor at this point indicated that he favored a blockade although in subsequent meetings he seemed inclined towards a military strike. McCone gave an intelligence estimate on the effects of a blockade, indicating its seriousness would depend upon how "hard" a blockade it turned out to be, and finally stated that the main objective of taking Cuba away from Castro had been lost and we have been overly consumed with the missile problem. McCone stated that we must all bear in mind that we have two objectives, one, disposing of the missile sites, and the other, getting rid of Castro's communism in the Western Hemisphere.

The meeting adjourned for dinner and in the evening Secretary Rusk came forward with the following plan.

The United States cannot accept operational MRBMs in Cuba. There is not much profit in preliminary exchanges with Khrushchev and Castro because the President has said that the establishment of

- 3 -

SECRET

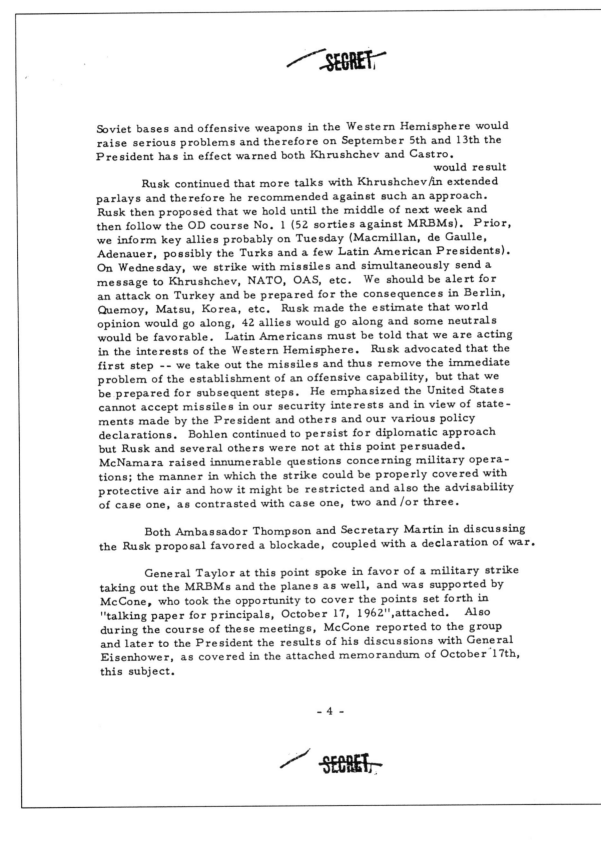

Soviet bases and offensive weapons in the Western Hemisphere would raise serious problems and therefore on September 5th and 13th the President has in effect warned both Khrushchev and Castro.

Rusk continued that more talks with Khrushchev would result in extended parlays and therefore he recommended against such an approach. Rusk then proposed that we hold until the middle of next week and then follow the OD course No. 1 (52 sorties against MRBMs). Prior, we inform key allies probably on Tuesday (Macmillan, de Gaulle, Adenauer, possibly the Turks and a few Latin American Presidents). On Wednesday, we strike with missiles and simultaneously send a message to Khrushchev, NATO, OAS, etc. We should be alert for an attack on Turkey and be prepared for the consequences in Berlin, Quemoy, Matsu, Korea, etc. Rusk made the estimate that world opinion would go along, 42 allies would go along and some neutrals would be favorable. Latin Americans must be told that we are acting in the interests of the Western Hemisphere. Rusk advocated that the first step -- we take out the missiles and thus remove the immediate problem of the establishment of an offensive capability, but that we be prepared for subsequent steps. He emphasized the United States cannot accept missiles in our security interests and in view of statements made by the President and others and our various policy declarations. Bohlen continued to persist for diplomatic approach but Rusk and several others were not at this point persuaded. McNamara raised innumerable questions concerning military operations; the manner in which the strike could be properly covered with protective air and how it might be restricted and also the advisability of case one, as contrasted with case one, two and /or three.

Both Ambassador Thompson and Secretary Martin in discussing the Rusk proposal favored a blockade, coupled with a declaration of war.

General Taylor at this point spoke in favor of a military strike taking out the MRBMs and the planes as well, and was supported by McCone, who took the opportunity to cover the points set forth in "talking paper for principals, October 17, 1962",attached. Also during the course of these meetings, McCone reported to the group and later to the President the results of his discussions with General Eisenhower, as covered in the attached memorandum of October 17th, this subject.

- 4 -

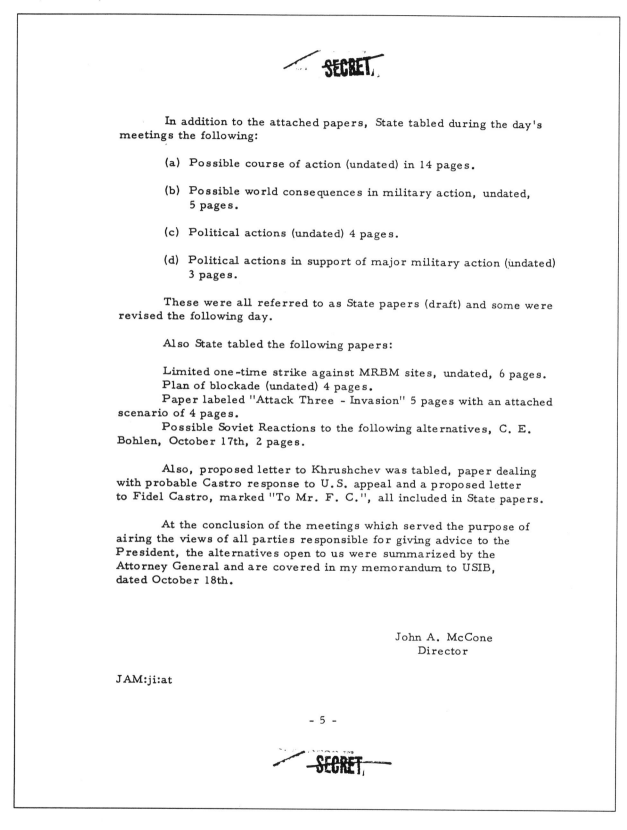

In addition to the attached papers, State tabled during the day's meetings the following:

(a) Possible course of action (undated) in 14 pages.

(b) Possible world consequences in military action, undated, 5 pages.

(c) Political actions (undated) 4 pages.

(d) Political actions in support of major military action (undated) 3 pages.

These were all referred to as State papers (draft) and some were revised the following day.

Also State tabled the following papers:

Limited one-time strike against MRBM sites, undated, 6 pages.
Plan of blockade (undated) 4 pages.
Paper labeled "Attack Three - Invasion" 5 pages with an attached scenario of 4 pages.
Possible Soviet Reactions to the following alternatives, C. E. Bohlen, October 17th, 2 pages.

Also, proposed letter to Khrushchev was tabled, paper dealing with probable Castro response to U.S. appeal and a proposed letter to Fidel Castro, marked "To Mr. F. C.", all included in State papers.

At the conclusion of the meetings which served the purpose of airing the views of all parties responsible for giving advice to the President, the alternatives open to us were summarized by the Attorney General and are covered in my memorandum to USIB, dated October 18th.

John A. McCone
Director

JAM:ji:at

- 5 -

58. *Albert D. Wheelon, Memorandum for Chairman, United States Intelligence Board, "Evaluation of Offensive Missile Threat in Cuba," 17 October 1962*

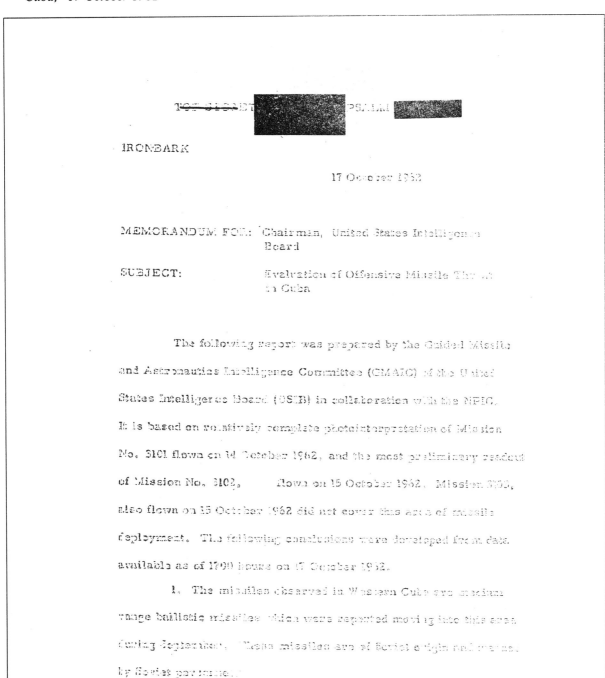

IRONBARK

17 October 1962

MEMORANDUM FOR: Chairman, United States Intelligence Board

SUBJECT: Evaluation of Offensive Missile Threat in Cuba

The following report was prepared by the Guided Missile and Astronautics Intelligence Committee (GMAIC) of the United States Intelligence Board (USIB) in collaboration with the NPIC. It is based on relatively complete photointerpretation of Mission No. 3101 flown on 14 October 1962, and the most preliminary readout of Mission No. 3102, flown on 15 October 1962. Mission 3103, also flown on 15 October 1962 did not cover this area of missile deployment. The following conclusions were developed from data available as of 1700 hours on 17 October 1962.

1. The missiles observed in Western Cuba are medium range ballistic missiles which were reported moving into this area during September. These missiles are of Soviet origin and manned by Soviet personnel.

IRONBARK

2. At least some of the missiles observed in photography are 1020 n.m. SS-4 missiles. Detailed photointerpretation shows that the missiles are canvas covered, have blunt noses, and are 66 feet, plus or minus two feet in length. This agrees well with the length of the SS-4 missile tankage (64 feet) without its nose cone, and is different from the tankage length (56 feet) of the 630 nm SS-3. However, there are less certain length measurements which range from 55 to 68 feet on missiles in another area, so that one cannot rule out the possibility of a mixed force including some 630 nm missiles. The general missile lengths provided in the clandestine reports are compatible with either the SS-3 or SS-4. The missile measurements, site configuration and ground support equipment mitigate against the SS-2 (350 nm), the SS-5 (2200 nm) and cruise type missiles.

3. Based on analysis of ████████ there is agreement that the last 630 nm missile was produced in early 1959 and that the present surplus of these missiles over those expended is between 70 and 80 missiles.

-2-

58. *(Continued)*

IRONBARK

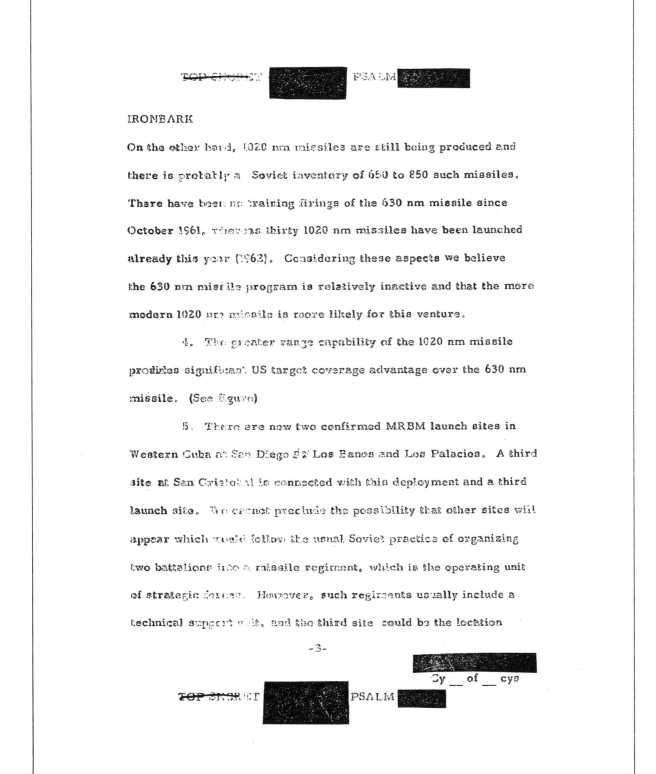

On the other hand, 1020 nm missiles are still being produced and there is probably a Soviet inventory of 650 to 850 such missiles. There have been no training firings of the 630 nm missile since October 1961, whereas thirty 1020 nm missiles have been launched already this year (1962). Considering these aspects we believe the 630 nm missile program is relatively inactive and that the more modern 1020 nm missile is more likely for this venture.

4. The greater range capability of the 1020 nm missile provides significant US target coverage advantage over the 630 nm missile. (See figure)

5. There are now two confirmed MRBM launch sites in Western Cuba at San Diego de Los Banos and Los Palacios. A third site at San Cristobal is connected with this deployment and a third launch site. We cannot preclude the possibility that other sites will appear which would follow the usual Soviet practice of organizing two battalions into a missile regiment, which is the operating unit of strategic forces. However, such regiments usually include a technical support unit, and the third site could be the location

-3-

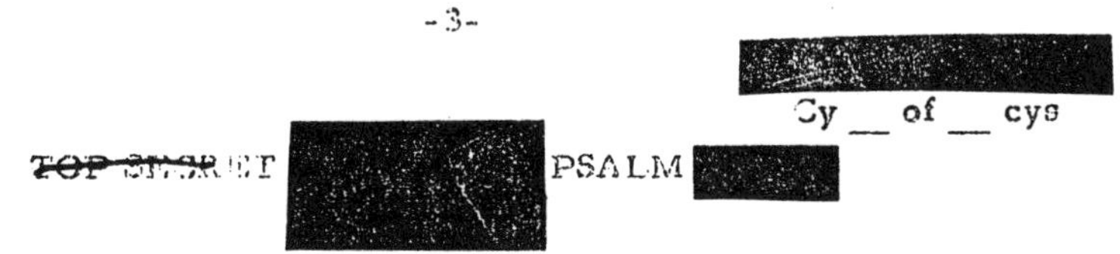

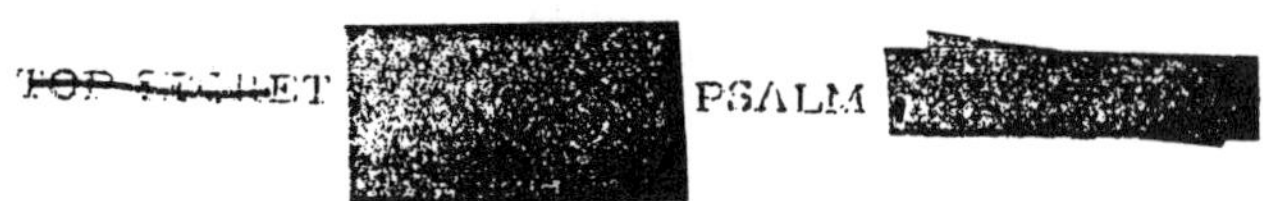
TOP SECRET PSALM

IRONBARK

of this unit.

6. There are eight missiles and four launchers visible at the most advanced site (San Diego de Los Banos). It is probable that eight missiles will be deployed to each such site, apparently for a refire capability. The total force structure depends upon the interpretation of the third site and possibilities of a fourth site. The best current estimate is that at least 16 and possibly as many as 32 missiles will be operational in Cuba in the next week or so.

7. The sites being deployed in Cuba are field type launchers which rely on mobile erection, checkout, and support equipment. The four-in-line deployment of launchers, at sites which are themselves five miles apart is representative of MRBM deployment in the Soviet Union. None of the sites are revetted, but this feature could be added at any time.

8. We are having difficulty in distinguishing between the 630 and 1020 nm systems on the basis of site characteristics, since neither can be ruled out on the basis of those physical measurements which have been made from the U-2 photography obtained to

-4-

TOP SECRET PSALM

58. *(Continued)*

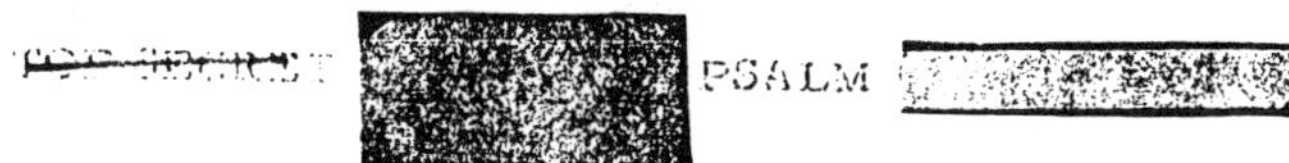

IRONBARK

date. The problem results from resolution limitations of satellite [redacted] photography and has precluded identification of similar field type launchers in the Soviet Union or European satellites. From valid clandestine sources, we gather that the 1020 nm missile can be readily deployed to presurveyed alternate sites in a matter of 6 hours plus transit time. The possibility that launch sites can be relocated must not be overlooked.

9. There is significant change detectable in the sites between the two overflights one day apart. Fencing of two areas is evident on the second day, and substantial progress is being made on erecting temporary buildings. Fifty vehicles (an increase of 15) and the possible appearance of erectors are noted at the third area.

10. The question of earliest operational capability with these sites depends critically on the type of missile being deployed. If we are correct in identifying these as 1020 nm missiles, with storable propellants and self-contained (inertial) guidance, the first site could be available almost immediately for emergency use. However, we do not see missile nose cones nor do we know of

-5-

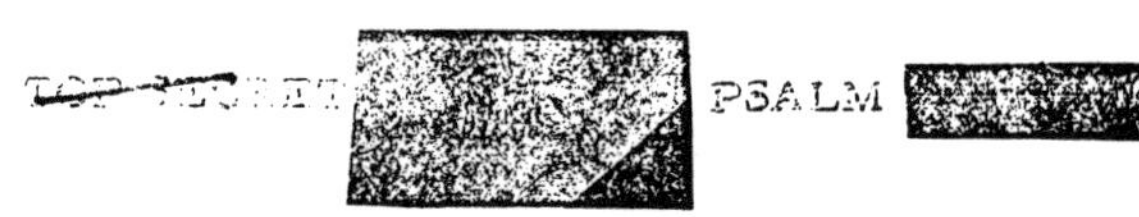

IRONBARK

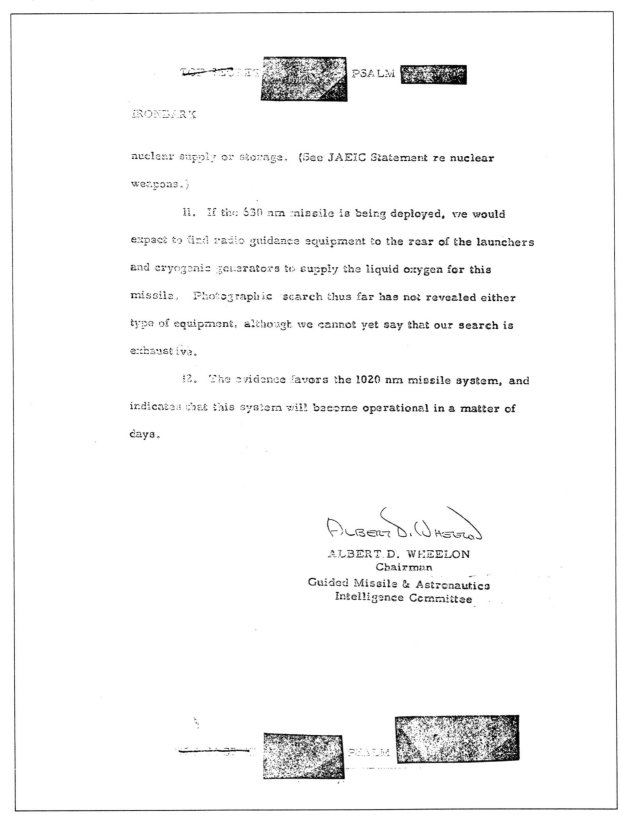

nuclear supply or storage. (See JAEIC Statement re nuclear weapons.)

11. If the 630 nm missile is being deployed, we would expect to find radio guidance equipment to the rear of the launchers and cryogenic generators to supply the liquid oxygen for this missile. Photographic search thus far has not revealed either type of equipment, although we cannot yet say that our search is exhaustive.

12. The evidence favors the 1020 nm missile system, and indicates that this system will become operational in a matter of days.

ALBERT D. WHEELON
Chairman
Guided Missile & Astronautics
Intelligence Committee

59. *Lundahl, Memorandum for Director of Central Intelligence and Director, Defense Intelligence Agency, "Additional Information—Mission 3102," 18 October 1962*

18 October 1962

MEMORANDUM FOR: Director of Central Intelligence
Director, Defense Intelligence Agency

SUBJECT : Additional Information - Mission 3102

1. An examination of photography from Mission 3102 dated 15 October 1962 has revealed a probable MRBM/IRBM Launch Complex, a confirmed MRBM site and a probable MRBM site. The latter two sites were previously reported as military encampments on Mission 3101.

2. A probable MRBM/IRBM Launch Complex consisting of two probable launch sites under construction, has been identified approximately 21 nm southwest of Havana. The launch sites are approximately 2.5 nm apart and are situated on a flat-topped ridge line.

Launch Site No 1 is located at 22-56-50N 82-39-20W and 2.4 nm northeast of Guanajay. It is of the offset inline configuration and consists of four elongated launch pad areas oriented at 315 degrees and separated by approximately 750 feet. A central bunker, 60 by 50 feet, is situated between the pads of each pair. This is connected by cable scar to a structure located inboard of each pad. The launch site is in an early stage of construction and is enclosed by fence.

Launch Site No 2 is located at 22-57-20N 82-37-05W and 4.3 nm northeast of Guanajay. This launch site also has an inline configuration, and consists of three launch pad areas, with indications of a fourth. The separation of the pad clearings of one pair and their orientation is the same as that at Site No 1. The launch site appears to be in a very early stage of construction and is secured by fence. Photography of 29 August 1962 indicates that initial construction had begun at Site No 1, and that Site No 2 did not exist.

3. Additional information from Mission 3102 on the previously reported MRBM area is as follows:

a. Site No 1 - MRBM Launch Site located 4 nm ENE of San Diego de los Banos at 22-40-05N 83-17-15W. Only the support area is visible through clouds and haze. Changes from Mission 3101 in area seen include 3 large tents and the completion of a building in early stages of construction on Mission 3101. A security fence under construction is present on the south side of the installation.

59. *(Continued)*

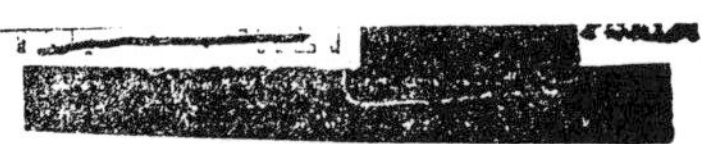

b. Site No 2 - A reanalysis of Site No 2 near Los Palacios, (previously identified as a military encampment) on photography of 15 October 1962, permits its upgrading to a confirmed MRBM launch site. Changes noted since Mission 3101 include the identification of an erector in the area where the 6 missiles are parked and the absence of a 60 foot unidentified object in the tent area.

c. Site No 3 - Previously identified as a military encampment is now considered to be a probable MRBM Launch Area and is located 5 nm west of San Cristobal at 22-42-50N 83-08-15W. The site is situated on the south side of and adjacent to the foothills of a mountain range. The area is under construction and contains the following elements: 2 missile erectors, 2 probable missile trailers, 2 structures, 100 by 18 feet, 1 building under construction, 70 by 35 feet with concrete arches lying nearby, 8 buildings, 70 by 30 feet under construction, at least 40 tents, and approximately 30 miscellaneous unidentified vehicles. Additional equipment may be parked beneath the trees, or hidden by shadows.

ARTHUR C. LUNDAHL
Director
National Photographic Interpretation Center

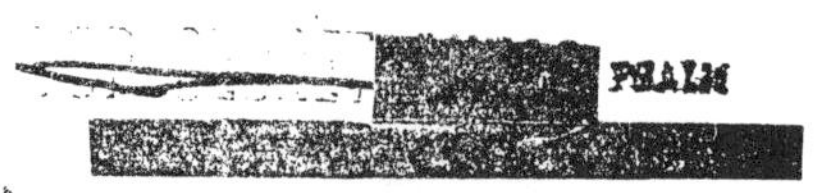

60. *McCone, Memorandum for File, 19 October 1962*

#41

~~TOP SECRET~~

19 October 1962

MEMORANDUM FOR FILE 11:00 AM - 10-18-62 w/The President, et al

Early in the morning of October 18th, Secretary McNamara called Mr. McCone at his residence expressing great concern over the reports from NPIC as a result of their examination of the two flights run on October 15th. Lundahl was at the house with the enlargements which indicated that, in addition to the three mobile MRBM sites detected on flight October 14th, there appeared to be now two IRBM sites with fixed launchers zeroed in on the Eastern United States. McNamara felt that this development demanded more prompt and decisive action.

The group which had been meeting on Tuesday met in the Cabinet Room at 11:00 a.m. on Wednesday with the President. State tabled revisions in their papers on covering a limited one-time strike and blockade, most of which are dated 10/18 - 11:00 a.m.

At the opening of the meeting, McCone gave a brief resume of current intelligence and Lundahl presented the most recent photography. President questioned Lundahl further if the uninitiated could be persuaded that the photographs presented offensive MRBM missiles. Lundahl stated probably not and that we must have low-level photography for public consumption.

Secretary Rusk then stated that developments in the last 24 hours had substantially changed his thinking. He first questioned whether, if it is necessary to move against Cuba, and then concluded that it was because Cuba can become a formidable military threat. He also referred to the President's recent public statements and indicated a feeling that if no action was taken, we would free the Soviets to act any place they wished and at their own will. Also, Rusk stated the failure on our part to act would make our situation unmanageable elsewhere in the world. He furthermore indicated that this would be an indication of weakness which would have serious effect on our Allies. Secretary pointed out to the President that action would involve risks. We could expect counter action and the cost may be heavy. The President must expect action in Berlin, Korea and possibly against the United States itself. Rusk felt a quick strike would minimize the risk of counter action. He raised the question of solidarity of the Alliance and seemed to dismiss this question, feeling that the Alliance would hold together. Rusk stated that if we enter upon positive action, we can not say for sure what the final Soviet response will be and therefore what the final outcome will be. However he felt that the American people will accept danger and suffering if they are convinced doing so is necessary and that they have a clear conscience. The Secretary reviewed the circumstances surrounding the outbreak of World War I, World War II, and the Korean war. These factors militated in favor of consulting with Khrushchev

~~TOP SECRET~~

and depending on the Rio pact. This, he indicated, might have the possibility of prevention of action and settlement by political means. The other course open was the declaration of war. Rusk expressed himself in favor of leaning upon the Rio pact, but does not dismiss the alternative of a unilateral declaration of war as the ultimate action we must take. The alternate is a quick strike.

Ambassador Bohlen was not present but his views were expressed in a message which was read in which he strongly advocated diplomatic effort and stated that military action prior to this would be wrong. He urged against action first and then decisive value of discussion. He also stated that limited quick military action was an illusion and that any military action would rapidly escalate into an invasion. McNamara at this point presented the alternatives referred to the previous day, stating that alternatives one and two were not conclusive and that we would have to resort to alternative 3 and in fact this would lead us ultimately into an invasion.

General Taylor generally reviewed the situation stating that the Chiefs looked upon Cuba as a forward base of serious proportions, that it cannot be taken out totally by air; that the military operation would be sizeable, nevertheless necessary.

Ambassador Thompson urged that any action be preceeded by a declaration of war; he strongly advocated that we institute a blockade and not resort to military action unless and until it is determined that Castro and Khrushchev refuse to reverse their activities and actually remove the missiles which are now in place.

Secretary Dillon questioned what would be accomplished by talking to Khrushchev. He pointed out that we would probably become engaged in discussions from which we could not extract ourselves and therefore our freedom of action would be frustrated. Dillon was very positive that whatever action we take should be done without consultation with Khrushchev. Rusk seemed to disagree indicating there was a possibility that Khrushchev might be persuaded to reduce his efforts but he admitted also that he might step them up as a result of discussions.

President Kennedy was non-committal, however he seemed to continually raise questions of reactions of our allies, NATO, South America, public opinion and others. Raised the question whether we should not move the missiles out of Turkey. All readily agreed they were not much use but a political question was involved. Bundy thought this a good idea either under conditions of a strike or during a preliminary talk.

2

TOP SECRET

McNamara discussed in some detail the effects of a strike indicating that we could expect several hundred Soviet citizens to be killed; he pointed out that all of the Sam sites were manned exclusively by Soviets and a great many Soviet technicians were working on the MRBMs and at the air fields. He agreed that we could move out of Turkey and Italy; pointed out the political complications. At this point McNamara seemed to be reconsidering his prior position of advocating military action and laid special emphasis on the fact that the price of Soviet retaliation, whether in Berlin or elsewhere, would be very high and we would not be able to control it.

Secretary Ball throughout the conversation maintained the position that strike without warning was not acceptable and that we should not proceed without discussion with Khrushchev. President Kennedy then said that he thought at some point Khrushchev would say that if we made a move against Cuba, he would take Berlin. McNamara surmised perhaps that was the price we must pay and perhaps we'd lose Berlin anyway. There followed an exchange of view on the possibility of the Soviets taking Berlin and our prospect of retaining it.

President Kennedy rather summed up the dilemma stating that action of a type contemplated would be opposed by the alliance - on the other hand, lack of action will create disunity, lack of confidence and disintegration of our several alliances and friendly relations with countries who have confidence in us.

As a result of discussions of the "price" of a strike, there followed a long discussion of the possibilities of a blockade, the advantages of it, and manner in which it would be carried out, etc. There seemed to be differences of opinion as to whether the blockade should be total, or should only involve military equipment which would mean blockading Soviet ships. Also there were continued references to blockading ships carrying offensive weapons and there seemed to be a differentiation in the minds of some in the policy of blockading offensive weapons as contrasted to blockading all weapons.

There followed discussion as to policies the President should follow with respect to calling Congress into session, asking for a declaration of war, advising the country and authorizing action. Thompson continued to insist that we must communicate with Khrushchev. There was a discussion concerning the President's meeting with Gromyko and the position he should take should the Cuban question come up. The President was advised to draw Gromyko out and it was indicated he probably would receive a flat denial that there were any offensive weapons in Cuba.

3 TOP SECRET

TOP SECRET 

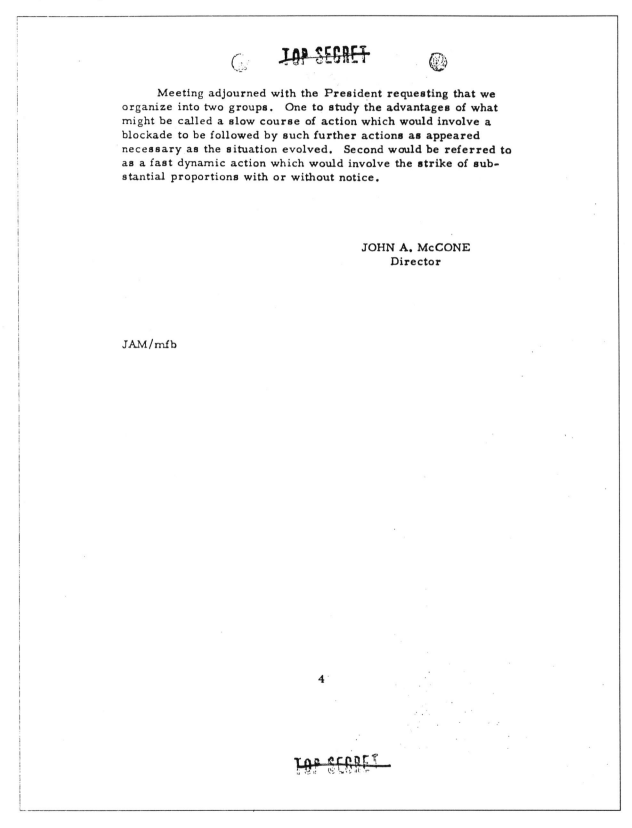

Meeting adjourned with the President requesting that we organize into two groups. One to study the advantages of what might be called a slow course of action which would involve a blockade to be followed by such further actions as appeared necessary as the situation evolved. Second would be referred to as a fast dynamic action which would involve the strike of substantial proportions with or without notice.

JOHN A. McCONE
Director

JAM/mfb

4

TOP SECRET

61. *Joint Evaluation of Soviet Missile Threat in Cuba, 18 October 1962 (Excerpt)*

JOINT EVALUATION

OF

SOVIET MISSILE THREAT IN CUBA

PREPARED BY

Guided Missile and Astronautics Intelligence Committee
Joint Atomic Energy Intelligence Committee
National Photographic Interpretation Center

2100 HOURS

18 OCTOBER 1962

This report is based on relatively complete photo interpretation of U-2 photography made on:

14 October 1962 Mission 3101
15 October 1962 Missions 3102 & 3103

Very preliminary and incomplete readout of coverage of the six U-2 Missions flown on 17 October 1962 are also reflected in this report.

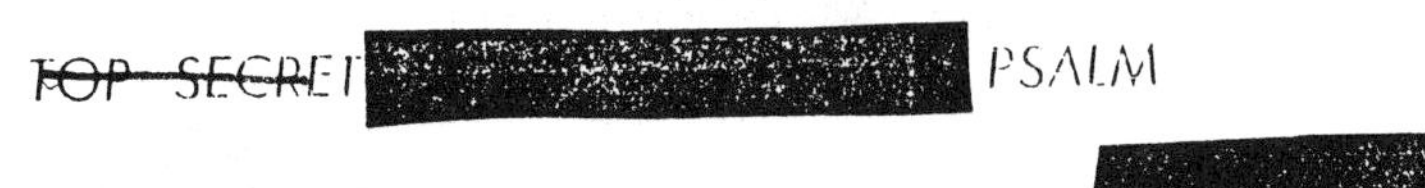

~~TOP SECRET~~ PSALM

IRONBARK

CONCLUSIONS IN BRIEF

Offensive Missiles

1. At least one Soviet regiment consisting of eight launchers and sixteen 1020-nm (SS-4) medium range ballistic missiles is now deployed in western Cuba at two launch sites. These sites presently contain unrevetted, field-type launchers which rely on mobile erection, checkout, and support equipment. These missiles are probably those reported moving into this area during September. Although there is continuing improvement of these sites, these mobile missiles must be considered operational now and could be launched within 18 hours after the decision to launch. A refire from each launcher could be accomplished within 5 hours after the initial firing.

2. Fixed, soft sites which could achieve initial operational capability during December 1962 are now being developed near Havana. We believe that the 2200-nm (SS-5) intermediate range ballistic missile is probably intended for these sites. Photography of these sites show eight, fixed launch pads under construction which probably equate to an additional missile regiment with eight ready missiles and eight for refire.

3. All of these offensive missile systems are Soviet manned and controlled. We believe that offensive action by these systems would be commanded from the Soviet Union but have not yet found the command and control communication links.

Nuclear Warheads for Offensive Missiles

4. There is no positive evidence of the presence of nuclear warheads in Cuba, nor have weapons storage facilities of the standard, highly secure Soviet type been identified. However, there are seven, large Cuban

- 1 -

~~TOP SECRET~~ PSALM

TOP SECRET  PSALM

IRONBARK

munitions' storage areas south of Havana which could be converted to Soviet needs in a relatively short time. Temporary storage could be provided in ships or field sites which might not be identified.

5. Nevertheless, one must assume that nuclear warheads could now be available in Cuba to support the offensive missile capability as it becomes operational. The warheads expected for these missiles weigh approximately 3,000 pounds and have yields in the low megaton range.

Coastal Defense Missiles

6. Three coastal defense missile sites have now been identified in Cuba, two of which must now be considered operational (Banes and Santa Cruz del Norte). In an alert status, these cruise missiles can be fired in about 10 minutes, with subsequent firings from each launcher at 5 minute intervals.

Air Defense Missiles

7. There are now 22 surface-to-air missiles (SA-2) sites located in Cuba, nine of which are believed to be individually operational at the present time. The remaining SA-2 sites could be operational in two to three weeks. Each site contains six missiles with six additional missiles in an adjacent hold area. The initial firing can take place anytime after an alert, providing the site has reached readiness. Refire from a single launcher will take approximately 3 to 5 minutes.

- 2 -

TOP SECRET  PSALM

Force Levels

9. There are now at least sixteen 1020-nm Soviet ballistic missiles in Cuba which are in such a state of readiness that they could be fired within 18 hours of a decision to launch. It is likely that other installations now being examined in photography will raise the number to 32, all of which could be ready in the next week. Furthermore, 8 launchers with sixteen 2200-nm missiles will probably be operational in Cuba during December 1962. We must emphasize that this is the visible threat, and that additional missiles may be discovered as additional photography is analyzed.

Support and Supply

10. Offensive missiles systems are being introduced into Cuba primarily through the Port of Mariel. Possible central missile checkout, storage and repair bases have been tentatively located at Soroa near the western deployment sites and at Managua south of Havana. It is significant that all three of the Soviet missiles now being deployed in Cuba (SS-4, SS-5, SA-2) probably use red fuming nitric acid as an oxidizer so that a common propellant supply and storage could be used.

Significance

11. The magnitude of the total Soviet missile force being deployed indicates that the USSR intends to develop Cuba into a prime strategic base, rather than as a token show of strength.

12. A mixed force of 1020- and 2200-nm missiles would give the USSR a significant strategic strike capability against almost all targets in the U.S. (see map). By deploying stockpiled shorter range ballistic missiles at overseas bases against which we have no BMEWS warning capability, the

- 3 -

~~TOP SECRET~~ [redacted] PSALM

IRONBARK

Soviet Union will supplement its ICBM home force in a significant way. This overseas strategic force is protected by an extensive SA-2 deployment in Cuba.

13. This same offensive force also poses a common threat to the U.S. and a large portion of Latin America for the first time.

14. The USSR is making a major military investment in Cuba with some of their most effective guided missile systems. The planning for this operation must have started at least one year ago and put into motion last spring.

ADDENDUM

Two additional launch sites have just been found north of Santa Clara (Mission 3107). Neither site was present on 5 September 1962. Analysis is still underway; only preliminary views can be expressed. One site is similar to the fixed soft site described in paragraph 2. This site is in a more advanced state of readiness and could have the essential features for an operational capability within one month. The other site is similar to the field-type installation described in paragraph 1. These new sites are not included in the numbers appearing elsewhere in this paper.

- 4 -

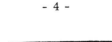

62. *McCone, Memorandum to USIB Members, 19 October 1962*

TOP SECRET

attch to #103A

October 19, 1962

MEMORANDUM TO USIB MEMBERS:

A discussion among the principals on October 18th indicated a probable decision, if any action is taken against Cuba, to initiate a limited blockade designed to prevent the importation into Cuba of additional arms. To do this the United States would make such statements concerning a condition of war as is necessary to meet the legal requirements of such a blockade, but a formal "declaration of war against Cuba" would be avoided if possible and resorted to only if absolutely necessary.

The blockade could be extended at our discretion to include POL and possibly a total blockade if Castro persisted in the offensive build-up.

Continued surveillance would go forward so that we would know of the siutation within Cuba as it evolved.

The blockade would start possibly on Monday, following a public announcement by the President which would include a display of photographic intelligence, persuasive notification to our Allies among the Soviets and the Cubans, but with no prior consultations with our Allies or any Latin Americans unless it proved necessary for legal reasons to assemble the OAS and secure the necessary approval to invoke the Rio Pact.

More extreme steps such as limited air strike, comprehensive air strike, or military invasion would be withheld awaiting developments. The possibility of more extreme actions has not been dismissed, however initiating such actions was considered unwise.

TOP SECRET

TOP SECRET

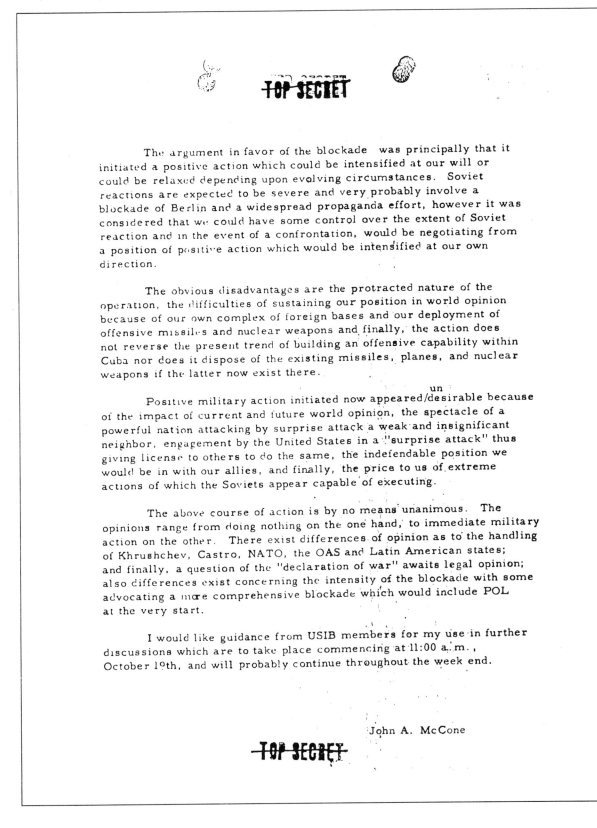

The argument in favor of the blockade was principally that it initiated a positive action which could be intensified at our will or could be relaxed depending upon evolving circumstances. Soviet reactions are expected to be severe and very probably involve a blockade of Berlin and a widespread propaganda effort, however it was considered that we could have some control over the extent of Soviet reaction and in the event of a confrontation, would be negotiating from a position of positive action which would be intensified at our own direction.

The obvious disadvantages are the protracted nature of the operation, the difficulties of sustaining our position in world opinion because of our own complex of foreign bases and our deployment of offensive missiles and nuclear weapons and finally, the action does not reverse the present trend of building an offensive capability within Cuba nor does it dispose of the existing missiles, planes, and nuclear weapons if the latter now exist there.

Positive military action initiated now appeared/undesirable because of the impact of current and future world opinion, the spectacle of a powerful nation attacking by surprise attack a weak and insignificant neighbor, engagement by the United States in a "surprise attack" thus giving license to others to do the same, the indefendable position we would be in with our allies, and finally, the price to us of extreme actions of which the Soviets appear capable of executing.

The above course of action is by no means unanimous. The opinions range from doing nothing on the one hand, to immediate military action on the other. There exist differences of opinion as to the handling of Khrushchev, Castro, NATO, the OAS and Latin American states; and finally, a question of the "declaration of war" awaits legal opinion; also differences exist concerning the intensity of the blockade with some advocating a more comprehensive blockade which would include POL at the very start.

I would like guidance from USIB members for my use in further discussions which are to take place commencing at 11:00 a.m., October 19th, and will probably continue throughout the week end.

John A. McCone

TOP SECRET

63. *LET [Llewellyn E. Thompson?] Memorandum, 19 October 1962*

~~TOP SECRET~~

October 19, 1962

Steps which would make air strike more acceptable to blockade group.

1. Prior notice to Khrushchev by message from the President giving Soviets possibility of backing down and strengthening our case with our Allies and world opinion in the event that Khrushchev takes such action as blockading Berlin.

2. Some effort to try to minimize number of Soviets killed, or at least show we wanted to avoid this. Message to Khrushchev might urge him to remove Soviet technicians immediately.

3. Prior notice to our principal Allies, and particularly Turkey and Italy (because of our missile bases there).

4. Prior ultimatum to Castro giving him chance to fold.

5. Prior notification to certain Latin American Governments to allow them to take steps to prevent their being overthrown.

(All these notifications could be short but should be maximum military considerations would allow. None of them need spell out our proposed actions, but should indicate it will be extremely serious.)

6. Some improvement in our position before world opinion. Example -- President might make reference to Soviet construction of "Fishing Port" in Cuba, saying that in view other Soviet actions we are convinced Soviets were constructing Naval base.

7. No attack on Havana to avoid killing foreign diplomats and thus arousing public opinion against us in those countries.

LET:mac

~~TOP SECRET~~

64. *Special National Intelligence Estimate 11-18-62, "Soviet Reactions to Certain US Courses of Action on Cuba," 19 October 1962 (Excerpt)*

PSALM T-O-P S-E-C-R-E-T

C E N T R A L   I N T E L L I G E N C E   A G E N C Y

19 October 1962

SUBJECT: SNIE 11-18-62: SOVIET REACTIONS TO CERTAIN US COURSES OF ACTION ON CUBA

THE PROBLEM

To estimate probable Soviet reactions to certain US courses of action with respect to Cuba.

THE ESTIMATE

1. A major Soviet objective in their military buildup in Cuba is to demonstrate that the world balance of forces has shifted so far in their favor that the US can no longer prevent the advance of Soviet offensive power even into its own hemisphere. In this connection they assume, of course, that these deployments sooner or later will become publicly known.

T-O-P S-E-C-R-E-T

GROUP 1
Excluded from automatic downgrading and declassification

PSALM

PSALM T-O-P S-E-C-R-E-T

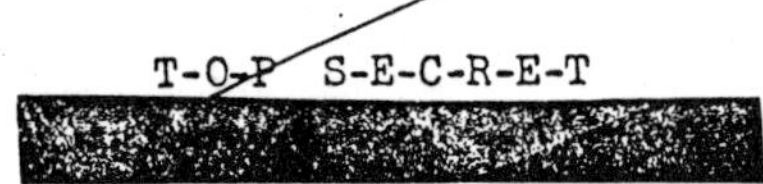

2. It is possible that the USSR is installing these missiles primarily in order to use them in bargaining for US concessions elsewhere. We think this unlikely, however. The public withdrawal of Soviet missiles from Cuba would create serious problems in the USSR's relations with Castro; it would cast doubt on the firmness of the Soviet intention to protect the Castro regime and perhaps on their commitments elsewhere.

3. If the US accepts the strategic missile buildup in Cuba, the Soviets would continue the buildup of strategic weapons in Cuba. We have no basis for estimating the force level which they would wish to reach, but it seems clear already that they intend to go beyond a token capability. They would probably expect their missile forces in Cuba to make some contribution to their total strategic capability vis-a-vis the US. We consider in Annex B the possible effects of a missile buildup in Cuba upon the overall relationship of strategic military power.

4. US acceptance of the strategic missile buildup would provide strong encouragement to Communists, pro-Communists, and the more anti-American sectors of opinion in Latin America and elsewhere. Conversely, anti-Communists and those who relate their own interests

- 2 -

T-O-P S-E-C-R-E-T PSALM

PSALM T-O-P S-E-C-R-E-T

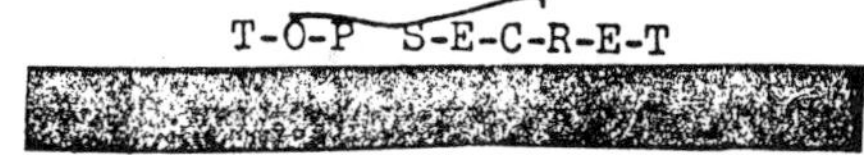

to those of the US would be strongly discouraged. It seems clear that, especially over the long run, there would be a loss of confidence in US power and determination and a serious decline of US influence generally.

EFFECT OF WARNING

5. If the US confronts Khrushchev with its knowledge of the MRBM deployment and presses for a withdrawal, we do not believe the Soviets would halt the deployment. Instead, they would propose negotiations on the general question of foreign bases, claiming equal right to establish Soviet bases and assuring the US of tight control over the missiles. They would probably link Cuba with the Berlin situation and emphasize their patience and preference for negotiations, implying that Berlin was held hostage to US actions in Cuba.

6. There is some slight chance that a warning to Castro might make a difference, since the Soviets could regard this as a chance to stand aside, but it also would give time for offers to negotiate, continued buildup, and counterpressures, and we think the result in the end would be the same.

- 3 -

T-O-P S-E-C-R-E-T

PSALM

PSALM T-O-P S-E-C-R-E-T

7. Any warning would of course degrade the element of surprise in a subsequent US attack.

EFFECT OF BLOCKADE

8. While the effectiveness of Castro's military machine might be impaired by a total US blockade, Castro would be certain to tighten internal security and would take ruthless action against any attempts at revolt. There is no reason to believe that a blockade of itself would bring down the Castro regime. The Soviets would almost certainly exert strong direct pressures elsewhere to end the blockade. The attitudes of other states toward a blockade action are not considered in this paper. It is obvious that the Soviets would heavily exploit all adverse reactions.

SOVIET REACTION TO USE OF MILITARY FORCE[1/]

9. If the US takes direct military action against Cuba, the Soviets would be placed automatically under great pressure to respond in ways which, if they could not save Cuba, would inflict

1/ For a further comment on differences between reaction to a blockade and to US measures of force against Cuba, see Annex A.

- 4 -

T-O-P S-E-C-R-E-T PSALM

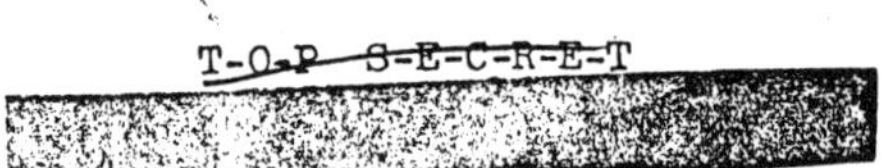

PSALM TOP SECRET

an offsetting injury to US interests. This would be true whether the action was limited to an effort to neutralize the strategic missiles, or these missiles plus airfields, surface-to-air missile sites, or cruise missile sites, or in fact an outright invasion designed to destroy the Castro regime.

10. In reaction to any of the various forms of US action, the Soviets would be alarmed and agitated, since they have to date estimated that the US would not take military action in the face of Soviet warnings of the danger of nuclear war. They would recognize that US military action posed a major challenge to the prestige of the USSR. We must of course recognize the possibility that the Soviets, under pressure to respond, would again miscalculate and respond in a way which, through a series of actions and reactions, could escalate to general war.

11. On the other hand, the Soviets have no public treaty with Cuba and have not acknowledged that Soviet bases are on the island. This situation provides them with a pretext for treating US military action against Cuba as an affair which does not directly involve them, and thereby avoiding the risks of a strong response. We do not believe that the USSR would attack the US, either from

- 5 -

TOP SECRET

PSALM

PSALM T-O-P S-E-C-R-E-T

Soviet bases or with its missiles in Cuba, even if the latter were operational and not put out of action before they could be readied for firing.

12. Since the USSR would not dare to resort to general war and could not hope to prevail locally, the Soviets would almost certainly consider retaliatory actions outside Cuba. The timing and selection of such moves would depend heavily upon the immediate context of events and the USSR's appreciation of US attitudes. The most likely location for broad retaliation outside Cuba appears to be Berlin. They might react here with major harassments, interruptions of access to the city or even a blockade, with or without the signing of a separate peace treaty.

13. We believe that whatever course of retaliation the USSR elected, the Soviet leaders would not deliberately initiate general war or take military measures, which in their calculation, would run the gravest risks of general war.

- 6 -

T-O-P S-E-C-R-E-T

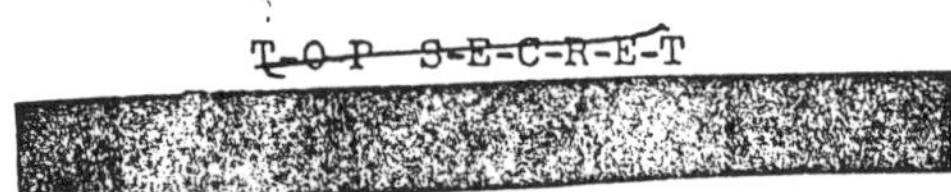

PSALM

65. *Joint Evaluation of Soviet Missile Threat in Cuba, 19 October 1962 (Excerpt)*

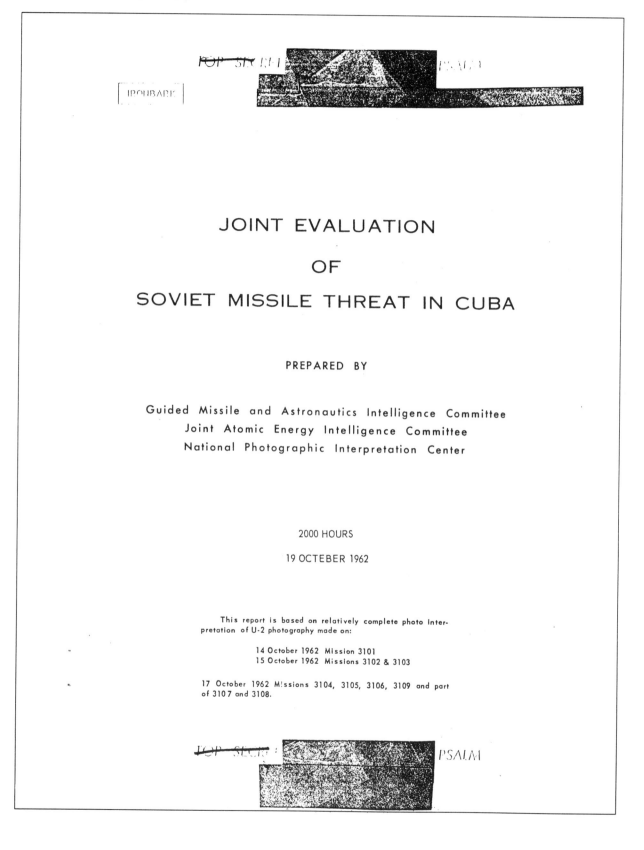

IRONBARK

JOINT EVALUATION
OF
SOVIET MISSILE THREAT IN CUBA

PREPARED BY

Guided Missile and Astronautics Intelligence Committee
Joint Atomic Energy Intelligence Committee
National Photographic Interpretation Center

2000 HOURS

19 OCTEBER 1962

This report is based on relatively complete photo interpretation of U-2 photography made on:

14 October 1962 Mission 3101
15 October 1962 Missions 3102 & 3103

17 October 1962 Missions 3104, 3105, 3106, 3109 and part of 3107 and 3108.

PSALM

65. *(Continued)*

IRONBARK

CONCLUSION

Offensive Missile Deployment*

1. At least one Soviet regiment of 1020-nm (SS-4) medium range ballistic missiles is now deployed in western Cuba at two launch sites near San Cristobal. Each of these sites presently contains eight missiles and four unrevetted, field-type launchers which rely on mobile erection, check-out, and support equipment. These missiles are probably those reported moving into this area during September. Although there is continuing improvement of these sites, this regiment must be considered operational now. The presence of eight missiles at each site indicates a refire capability from each of the four launchers. Refire could be accomplished in 4 to 6 hours after the initial firing. A third facility in this area, previously identified as Launch Site 3, could be either a technical support area for this regiment or a third launch site; however, the early stage of development precludes a positive identification of this activity.

2. An additional regiment of Soviet 1020-nm (SS-4) missiles is now deployed at two sites east of Havana in the Sagua La Grande area, nine miles apart. These sites closely resemble the sites at San Cristobal but appear to be more permanent in nature. Terrain features have dictated considerable clearing and grading for deployment of the system. Also, there are permanent structures at the launch pad areas which are not found at the San Cristobal sites. There are four launch positions at each site and we estimate an operational capability for each site within one week. The sizes of the missiles, associated equipment, and buildings found at the San Cristobal and Sagua La Grande sites are almost identical and are compatible with the 1020-nm MRBM system.

3. Two fixed sites are under construction in the Guanajay area near Havana. Four launchers, two blockhouses, and underground propellant storage are being built at each site. We believe that the 2200-nm (SS-5)

*See Figures 1-9.

- 1 -

PSALM

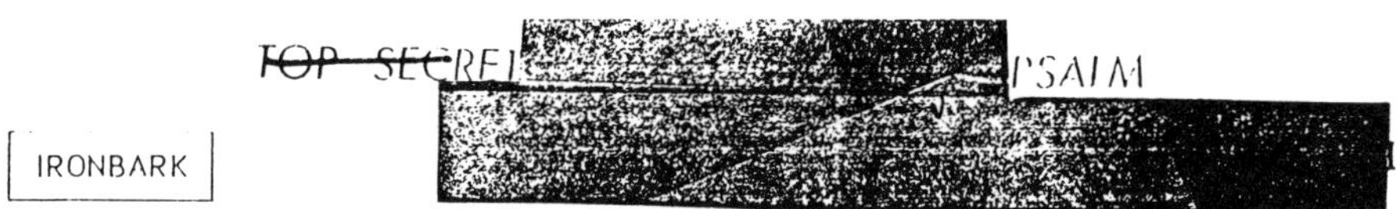

IRONBARK

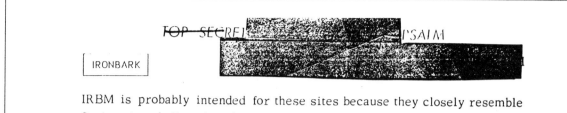

IRBM is probably intended for these sites because they closely resemble Soviet sites believed to be associated with testing and deployment of this missile system. Site 1 is considered to be in a mid- to late-stage of construction and should be operational within six weeks. Site 2 is in an earlier stage of construction and could be operational between 15 and 30 December 1962. There are no missiles or support equipment detectable within the Guanajay Area at the present time.

Command and Control

4. All of the offensive missile systems in Cuba are Soviet manned and controlled. We believe that offensive action by these systems would be commanded from the Soviet Union, but have not yet identified the communication link.

Nuclear Warheads for Offensive Missiles

5. We believe that a nuclear warhead storage site is under construction adjacent to the most complete of the fixed missile launch sites near Guanajay (see Figure 6). This site could become operational at about the same time as the associated Launch Site 1. Construction of similar facilities has not yet been identified at other sites.

6. An especially secure port facility located at Punta Gerardo may be used for nuclear weapons offloading (see Figure 10).

7. There is still no evidence of currently operational nuclear storage facilities in Cuba. Nevertheless, one must assume that nuclear weapons could now be in Cuba to support the operational missile capability as it becomes available.

8. The 1020-nm missiles would probably be equipped with nuclear warheads yielding 2 to 3 megatons. The 2200-nm IRBMs could have 3- to

- 2 -

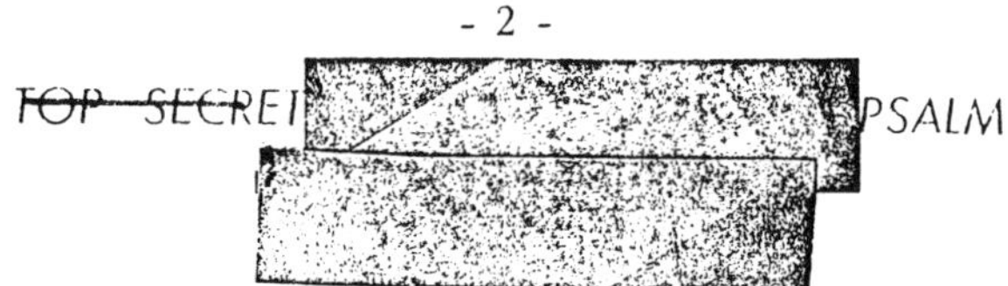

TOP SECRET 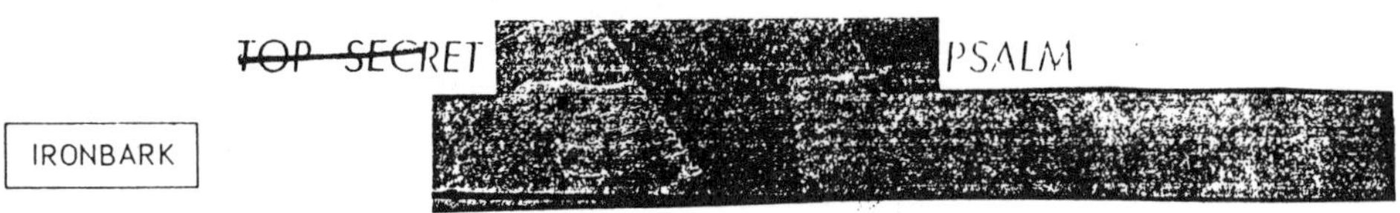 PSALM

IRONBARK

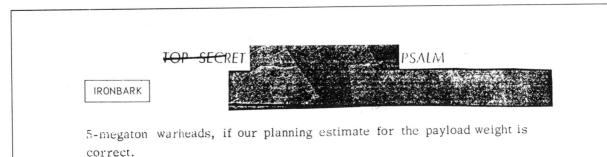

5-megaton warheads, if our planning estimate for the payload weight is correct.

Offensive Force Levels

9. We believe that there are now at least two regiments equipped with 1020-nm MRBM's in Cuba. One is located in the San Cristobal area and the other in the Sagua La Grande area. In addition, we believe a regiment equipped with 2200-nm IRBM's is being deployed to the Guanajay area. When operational, present MRBM and IRBM units will have an aggregate total of 24 launchers. An estimated schedule of site activation is presented in Table 1. Each launcher will have a refire capability. A summary of the MRBM and IRBM threat, including the projected number of operational ready missiles for each site, is presented in Table 2. The corresponding nuclear yield deliverable from each site is shown in Table 3. The technical characteristics of the two offensive missile weapons systems are summarized in Table 4.

Support and Supply

10. Offensive missile systems are being introduced into Cuba, probably through the Port of Mariel. A new Soviet ship, the Poltava, possibly designed as a ballistic missile transport, has been noted making frequent trips between the USSR and Cuba. This ship has made two trips to Cuba since 17 July, and is next estimated to arrive in Cuba on or about 2 November 1962. See Figures 11 and 12.

11. Possible central missile checkout, storage, and repair bases have been located at Soroa, between the two estern deployment areas, and at Managua, south of Havana.

- 3 -

TOP SECRET 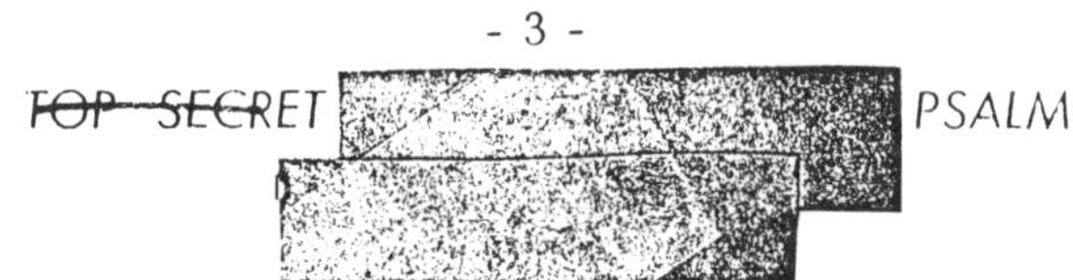 PSALM

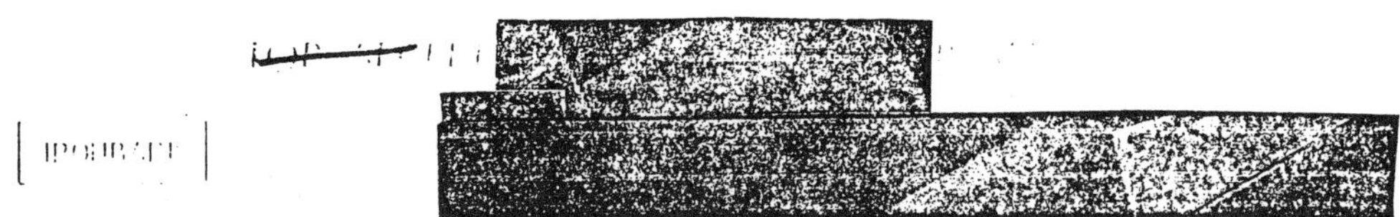

12. It is significant that three of the Soviet missiles now being deployed in Cuba (SS-4, SS-5, SA-2) probably use red fuming nitric acid as the oxidizer, permitting exploitation of a common system for propellant supply and storage.

Coastal Defense Missiles

13. Three coastal defense missile sites have now been identified in Cuba, two of which must now be considered operational (Banes and Santa Cruz del Norte). These cruise missiles have a range of 35 to 40 miles and are probably derived from the AS-1. They can be fired in about 10 minutes in an alert status, with subsequent firings from each launcher at 5 minute intervals.

Air Defense Missiles

14. There are now 26 surface-to-air missile (SA-2) sites located in Cuba, two of which appear to be alternate sites. See Figure 13. Of these, 16 are believed to be individually operational at the present time. The remaining SA-2 sites could be operational in two to three weeks. The list of sites considered to be operational is presented in Table 5.

15. Such SA-2 sites provide for six launchers with missiles, and an additional six missiles in an adjacent hold area. The initial firing can take place anytime after an alert, providing the site has reached readiness status. Reload and refire from a single launcher will take approximately 3 to 5 minutes.

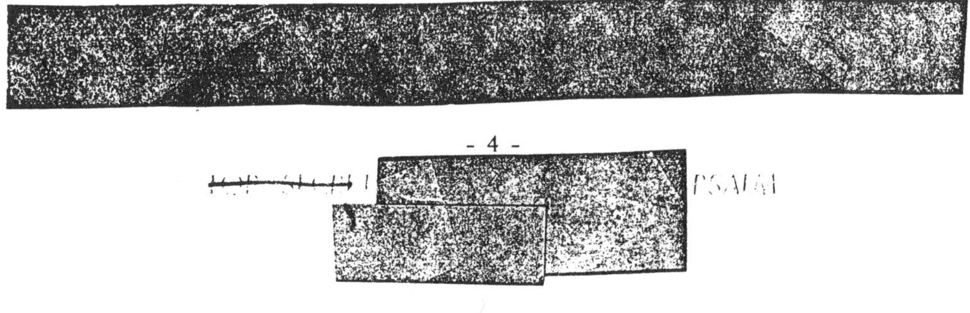

- 4 -

TOP SECRET PSALM

IRONBARK

Tactical Missiles

17. There are several refugee reports indicating the presence of tactical (FROG) missiles in Cuba, although there is no photographic confirmation thus far.

Significance

18. The magnitude of the total Soviet missile force being deployed indicates that the USSR intends to develop Cuba into a prime strategic base, rather than as a token show of strength. Some of the deployment characteristics include permanent elements which suggests that provision is being made for Soviet presence of long duration.

19. The rate of deployment to date, as well as the speed and variety of construction, indicates that the Soviet military build up in Cuba is being carried out on an urgent basis. This build-up has proceeded by deploying defensive weapons first, followed by deployment of offensive weapons. The pattern of missile deployment appears calculated to achieve quick operational status and then to complete site construction.

20. A mixed force of 1020- and 2200-nm missiles would give the USSR a significant strategic strike capability against almost all targets in the U.S. (see Figure 2). By deploying stockpiled MRBM/IRBMs at overseas bases, the Soviet Union will supplement its ICBM home force in a significant way.

21. This same offensive force also poses a common threat to the U.S. and a large portion of Latin America for the first time.

22. The USSR is making a major military investment in Cuba with some of their most effective guided missile systems. The planning for this operation must have started at least one year ago and the operation itself begun last spring.

- 5 -

TOP SECRET PSALM

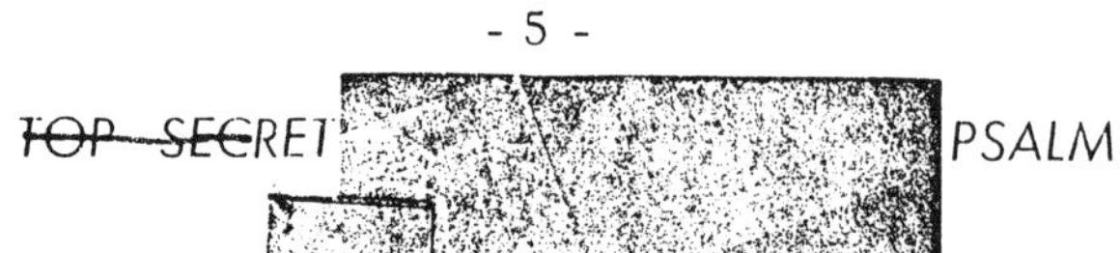

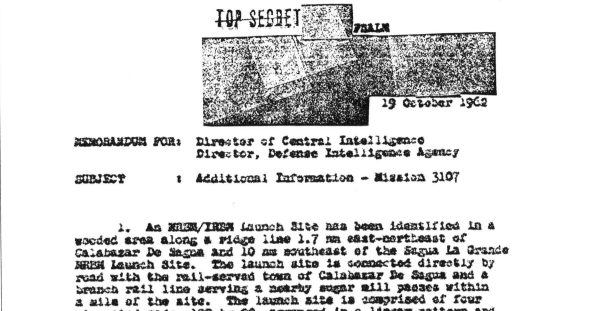

66. *Lundahl, Memorandum for Director of Central Intelligence and Director, Defense Intelligence Agency, "Additional Information—Mission 3107," 19 October 1962*

TOP SECRET

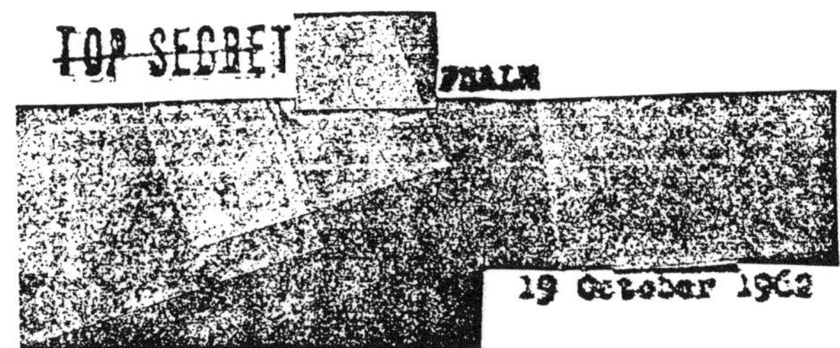

PSALM

19 October 1962

MEMORANDUM FOR: Director of Central Intelligence
Director, Defense Intelligence Agency

SUBJECT : Additional Information - Mission 3107

1. An MRBM/IRBM Launch Site has been identified in a wooded area along a ridge line 1.7 nm east-northeast of Calabazar De Sagua and 10 nm southeast of the Sagua La Grande MRBM Launch Site. The launch site is connected directly by road with the rail-served town of Calabazar De Sagua and a branch rail line serving a nearby sugar mill passes within a mile of the site. The launch site is comprised of four elongated pads, 190 by 90, arranged in a linear pattern and oriented on a 315 degree azimuth. The northern pair of pads are separated by approximately 750 feet and the southern pair by about 960 feet. A transporter/erector approximately 60 feet in length is in position on each of the two southern pads. A third transporter/erector is observed in a motor pool and a fourth is observed on the site service road. Additional facilities include at least 100 vehicles, 45 tents, 27 buildings and several open storage areas. The launch site appears to be in a late stage of completion or complete. No security fence is apparent. There was no evidence that site construction had begun on photography of 5 September 1962.

2. An MRBM Launch Site has been identified 5 nm southeast of Sagua La Grande at 22-43-45N 80-01-15W. It is situated in a level wooded area and contains the following elements: 4 launch positions, 2 missile erectors and 1 probable missile erector; 6 missile transporters with missiles, 1 building U/C with prefabricated arches, 3 buildings 100' x 18', numerous tents and vehicles. There was no evidence of this site on 5 September 1962 photography.

ARTHUR C. LUNDAHL
Director
National Photographic Interpretation Center

PSALM

TOP SECRET

67. *Special National Intelligence Estimate 11-19-62, "Major Consequences of Certain US Courses of Action on Cuba," 20 October 1962*

PSALM ~~T-O-P S-E-C-R-E-T~~ 

C E N T R A L   I N T E L L I G E N C E   A G E N C Y

20 October 1962

SUBJECT: SNIE 11-19-62: MAJOR CONSEQUENCES OF CERTAIN US COURSES OF ACTION ON CUBA

THE PROBLEM

To estimate the major consequences of certain US courses of action with respect to Cuba

THE ESTIMATE

STATUS OF SOVIET MILITARY BUILDUP IN CUBA

1. Firm evidence indicates the presence in Cuba of four MRBM and two IRBM launch sites in various stages of construction and organized into at least three regiments. Of these, two regiments of eight launchers each are mobile and designed to launch MRBMs with a range of about 1,100 n.m., while one regiment of eight fixed launchers may be designed for IRBMs with a range of about 2,200 n.m.

~~T-O-P S-E-C-R-E-T~~

GROUP 1
Excluded from automatic
downgrading and
declassification

PSALM

PSALM T-O-P S-E-C-R-E-T 

2. The 16 launchers for 1,100 n.m. MRBMs must be considered operational now. Four of the fixed launchers for the 2,200 n.m. IRBMs could probably become operational within the next six weeks. The other four would become operational in 8 to 10 weeks. We have no direct evidence that nuclear weapons are now present in Cuba, and it is unlikely that we would be able to obtain such evidence. However, the construction of at least one probable nuclear storage facility is a strong indication of the Soviet intent to provide nuclear warheads. In any case, it is prudent to assume that when the missiles are otherwise operational, nuclear warheads will be available. These could be brought in by air, submarine, or surface ship.

3. We estimate that operational MRBM missiles can be fired in eight hours or less after a decision to launch, depending on the condition of readiness. After the IRBM sites are completed and missiles are on launcher, a state of readiness of five hours may be maintained. Both systems are believed to be provided with two missiles per launcher, providing a refire capability from each launcher after about four to six additional hours for the MRBMs and six to eight hours for the IRBMs.

4. It is possible that further evidence will uncover additional launch sites which are presently undetected, but the extent of our coverage leads us to believe that such evidence would not drastically

- 2 -

T-O-P S-E-C-R-E-T PSALM

increase the total now deployed. On the other hand, new deployments could be started at any time.

5. The inventory of other major Soviet weapons now identified in Cuba includes:

a. 22 IL-28 jet light bombers, of which one is assembled and three others have been uncrated;

b. 39 MIG-21 jet fighters, of which 35 are assembled and four are still crates, and 62 other jet fighters of less advanced types;

c. 24 SA-2 sites, of which 16 are believed to be individually operational with some missiles on launcher;

d. 3 cruise missile sites for coastal defense, of which 2 are now operational;

e. 12 Komar cruise missile patrol boats, all probably operational or nearly so.

6. Cuban-based MRBMs and IRBMs with nuclear warheads would augment the present limited Soviet ICBM capability by virtue of their ability to strike at similar types of targets with warheads of generally similar yields. In the near future, therefore, Soviet gross capabilities for initial attack on US military and civilian targets can be increased considerably by Cuban-based missiles. However, the deployment of these missiles in Cuba will probably not, in the Soviet judgment, insure destruction of the US second strike capability to a degree which would

PSALM T-O-P S-E-C-R-E-T 

eliminate an unacceptably heavy retaliatory attack on the USSR. If the missile buildup in Cuba continues, the Soviet capability to blunt a retaliatory attack will be progressively enhanced.

PURPOSE OF SOVIET BUILDUP

7. A major Soviet objective in their military buildup in Cuba is to demonstrate that the world balance of forces has shifted so far in their favor that the US can no longer prevent the advance of Soviet offensive power even into its own hemisphere. In this connection they assume, of course, that these deployments sooner or later will become publicly known. At the same time, they expect their missile forces in Cuba to make an important contribution to their total strategic capability vis-a-vis the US.

8. Consequently, it is unlikely that the USSR is installing these missiles primarily in order to use them in bargaining for US concessions elsewhere. Moreover, the public withdrawal of Soviet missiles from Cuba would create serious problems in the USSR's relations with Castro; it would cast doubt on the firmness of the Soviet intention to protect the Castro regime and perhaps on their commitments elsewhere.

- 4 -

T-O-P S-E-C-R-E-T PSALM

US ACQUIESCENCE IN THE BUILDUP

9. If the US acquiesces to the presence of strategic missiles in Cuba, we believe that the Soviets will continue the buildup. We have no basis for estimating the force level which they would wish to reach, but it seems entirely clear now that they are going well beyond a token capability.

10. This course of US action would provide strong encouragement to Communists, pro-Communists, and the more anti-American sectors of opinion in Latin America. We believe that, especially over the long run, there would be loss of confidence in US power and determination and a serious decline of US influence, particularly in Latin America. Should any additional Latin American government fall to the Communists the Soviets would feel free to establish bases in the country in question if they chose. A major immediate consequence would be that the Soviets would probably estimate lower risks in pressing the US hard in other confrontations, such as Berlin.

EFFECT OF WARNING

11. If the US confronts Khrushchev with its knowledge of the MRBM deployment and presses for a withdrawal, we do not believe the Soviets would halt the deployment. Instead, they would propose negotiations on the general question of foreign bases, claiming equal right to establish Soviet bases and assuring the US of tight control over the missiles.

PSALM 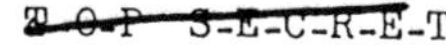 

They would probably link Cuba with the Berlin situation and emphasize their patience and preference for negotiations, implying that Berlin was held hostage to US actions in Cuba.

12. There is some slight chance that a warning to Castro might make a difference, since the Soviets could regard this as a chance to stand aside, but it also would give time for offers to negotiate, continued buildup, and counterpressures, and we think the result in the end would be the same.

13. Any warning would of course degrade the element of surprise in a subsequent US attack.

A US BLOCKADE

14. Two basic modes of blockade could be considered: total and selective. We believe that even under a total blockade individual aircraft and submarines might get through to deliver vital military items, e.g., nuclear warheads. Even the most severe blockade would not deprive the Soviets of the use of missiles already in Cuba for a nuclear strike on the US.

15. Under any form of blockade, the Soviets would concentrate on political exploitation, especially in the UN. They might risk violent encounters in attempts to penetrate the blockade, but they would not resort to major force in the area of Cuba or forceful retaliation elsewhere,

- 6 -

  PSALM

at least initially. If US enforcement of the blockade involved use of force by the US, the Soviets might respond on an equivalent level, but would seek to avoid escalation.

16. Thus any blockade situation would place the Soviets under no immediate pressure to choose a response with force. They could rely on political means to compel the US to desist, and reserve a resort to force until the US had actually used force. They would estimate that the inherent difficulties of enforcing the blockade and the generally adverse reactions, including those of US allies to it, would result in enormous pressures on the US to desist. They could heighten these pressures by threatening retaliation in Berlin or actually undertaking major harassments on the access routes, which could become tantamount to a blockade, and would probably do so at some stage.

17. We do not believe that even a severe blockade, of itself, would bring down the Cuban regime. Castro would tighten internal security and, unless action against the regime subsequently developed on Cuban soil, the Cuban population would be increasingly reluctant to oppose the regime. Direct action would still be required to bring down the Castro regime.

SOVIET REACTION TO USE OF MILITARY FORCE

18. In the case of US use of force against Cuban territory, the likelihood of a Soviet response by force, either locally or for retaliation elsewhere, would be greater than in the case of blockade. The

Soviets would be placed automatically under great pressure to respond in ways which, if they could not save Cuba, would inflict an offsetting injury to US interests. This would be true whether the action was limited to an effort to neutralize the stra .c missiles, or these missiles plus airfields, surface-to-air missile sites, or cruise missile sites, or in fact an outright invasion designed to destroy the Castro regime.

19. In reaction to any of the various forms of US action, the Soviets would be surprised and probably alarmed, since they appear to have estimated that the US would probably not take military action in the face of Soviet warnings of the danger of nuclear war. They would recognize that US military action posed a major challenge to the prestige of the USSR. We must of course recognize the possibility that the Soviets, under pressure to respond, would again miscalculate and respond in a way which, through a series of actions and reactions, could escalate to general war.

20. On the other hand, the Soviets have no public treaty with Cuba and have not acknowledged that Soviet bases are on the island. This situation provides them with a pretext for treating US military action against Cuba as an affair which does not directly involve them, and thereby avoiding the risks of a strong response. We do not believe that the USSR would attack the US, either from Soviet bases or with its missiles in Cuba, even if the latter were operational and not put out of action before they could be readied for firing.

67. *(Continued)*

PSALM ~~T-O-P S-E-C-R-E-T~~

21. Since the USSR would almost certainly not resort to general war and could not hope to prevail locally, we believe that the Soviets would consider retaliatory actions outside Cub The timing and selection of such moves would depend heavily up immediate context of events and the USSR's appreciation of US attitu The most likely location for broad retaliation outside Cuba appears to be Berlin. They would probably react here with major harassments, interruptions of access to the city or even a blockade, with or without the signing of a separate peace treaty. Retaliation against some US installation overseas is possible but in our view unlikely.

22. We believe that there would probably be a difference between Soviet reaction to all-out invasion and Soviet reaction to more limited US use of force against selected objectives in Cuba. We believe that the Soviets would be somewhat less likely to retaliate with military force in areas outside Cuba in response to speedy, effective invasion than in response to more limited forms of military action against Cuba. We recognize that such an estimate cannot be made with very great assurance and do not rule out the possibility of Soviet retaliation outside Cuba in case of invasion. But we believe that a rapid occupation of Cuba would be more likely to make the Soviets pause in opening new theaters of conflict than limited action or action which drags out.

23. Finally, we believe that, whatever course of retaliation the USSR elected, the Soviet leaders would not deliberately initiate general

- 9 -

~~T-O-P S-E-C-R-~~E T  PSALM

67. *(Continued)*

war or take military measures, which in their calculation, would run grave risks of general war.

68. *[Cline], DD/I Briefing, White House, 20 October 1962*

DDI Briefing
20 October
White House
OVAL Room
1430—1500

Mr. President:

We want to bring you up to ~~date on the~~ very briefly deployment of Soviet military weapons systems to Cuba. You have been briefed many times on the major buildup of equipment in Cuba prior to mid-October. ~~just about one week ago.~~

In the past week, ~~in intensive photo reconnaissance coverage beginning 14 October,~~ we have discovered unmistakable evidence of the deployment to Cuba of medium range ballistic missiles (i.e. 1020 NM range ~~SS-4~~) and intermediate range ballistic missiles (i.e. 2200 NM range ~~SS-5~~). These ranges imply coverage of targets ~~in the SE United States inside an arc running roughly from~~ from Dallas through Cincinnati and Washington, D. C. (~~on the part of~~ by MRBMs) and practically all of the continental United States (~~on the part of~~ by IRBMs).

There are at least four, and possibly five MRBM sites deployed in field-mobile installations, two (or possibly three) in Western Cuba, i.e. nearest the United States, and two somewhat more permanent looking, improved sites well to the East of Havana. There are, in accordance with standard Soviet military practice and what we see developing in Cuba, 4 launchers at each site. Two of these sites probably are in a state of at least limited operational readiness at this time, since the photography shows field-type launchers in place and missiles (eight at each site for a total of 16) on the ground -- not on launcher -- at the sites as of 14 and 17 October. All of the sites are in a state of continuous crash construction and improvement and we would expect the remaining two (or three) MRBM sites to become operational in about one week.

3

In addition ~~to these MRBM sites,~~ two fixed IRBM sites (with four launch pads and permanent storage facilities at each site) are being constructed near Havana. One of these sites appears to be in a stage of construction that ~~would~~ leads to an estimate of operational readiness ~~within~~ of six weeks from now, i.e. about 1 December and the other in a stage indicating operational readiness between 15 December and the end of the year.

We have not seen nuclear warheads for any of these missiles, but we do not rely on ever seeing them in our photography 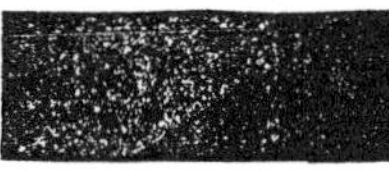

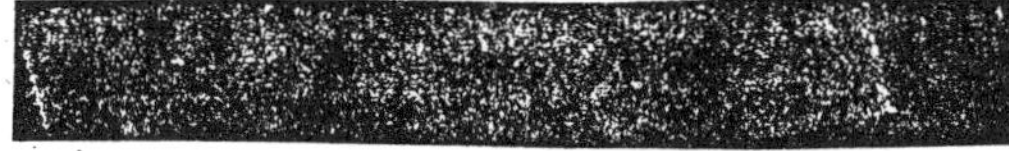 We have found what appears to be a nuclear warhead storage facility at one of the IRBM sites at Guanajay, near Havana. It will probably be completed about 1 December along with the ;missile site itself. ~~We also note a port nearby with very special security protection facilities that would be suitable for offloading nuclear weapons.~~

-4-

I should like to repeat that we do not have evidence of nuclear warheads in Cuba, but our estimate is that since the missile systems in question are relatively ineffective without them, we believe warheads either are or will be available. They could be in temporary storage prior to completion of the storage facility we have seen. The Poltava, a Soviet ship ; which we think is the most likely carrier of security-sensitive military cargoes into the tightly guarded port of Mariel has made two trips to Cuba and is due back in about ten days.

In summary, we believe the evidence indicates the probability that eight MRBM missiles can be fired from Cuba today. Naturally operational readiness is likely to be degraded by many factors, but if all eight missiles could be launched with nuclear warheads, they could deliver a total load of 16-24 Megatons (2 to 3 MT per warhead). If able to refire, they could theoretically deliver the same load approximately five hours later.

68. *(Continued)*

-5-

When the full installation of missile sites we now see under construction is completed at the end of the year, the initial salvo capability (if all missiles on launchers were to reach target) would be 56 - 88 MT.

68. *(Continued)*

— 6 —

These views are the considered judgment, concurred in unanimously by the ~~B~~ United States Intelligence Board. They are supported by the analyses of the National Photographic Intel Center, by the US Guided Missile and Astronautic Intel Committee, and the US Joint Atomic Energy Intel Committee. I have the chiefs of these three evaluation groups here to answer questions you may have.

First, however, we would like to run through the photographic evidence in ~~[illegible]~~ chronological sequence to show you the ~~[illegible]~~ rapid development of the crash deployment program I have just summarized.

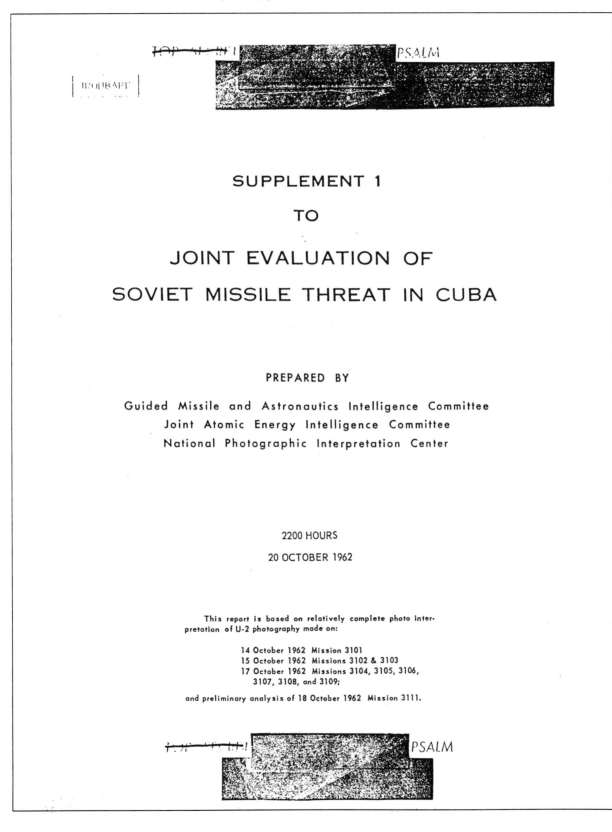

69. *Supplement 1 to Joint Evaluation of Soviet Missile Threat in Cuba, 20 October 1962 (Excerpt)*

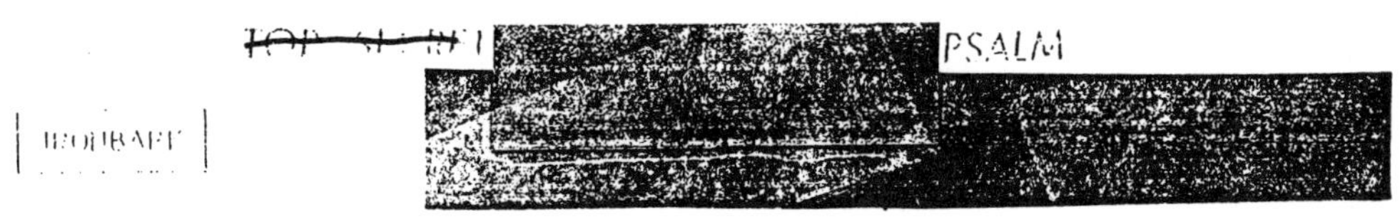

SUPPLEMENT 1

TO

JOINT EVALUATION OF

SOVIET MISSILE THREAT IN CUBA

PREPARED BY

Guided Missile and Astronautics Intelligence Committee
Joint Atomic Energy Intelligence Committee
National Photographic Interpretation Center

2200 HOURS

20 OCTOBER 1962

This report is based on relatively complete photo interpretation of U-2 photography made on:

14 October 1962 Mission 3101
15 October 1962 Missions 3102 & 3103
17 October 1962 Missions 3104, 3105, 3106, 3107, 3108, and 3109;

and preliminary analysis of 18 October 1962 Mission 3111.

TOP SECRET PSALM

IRONBARK

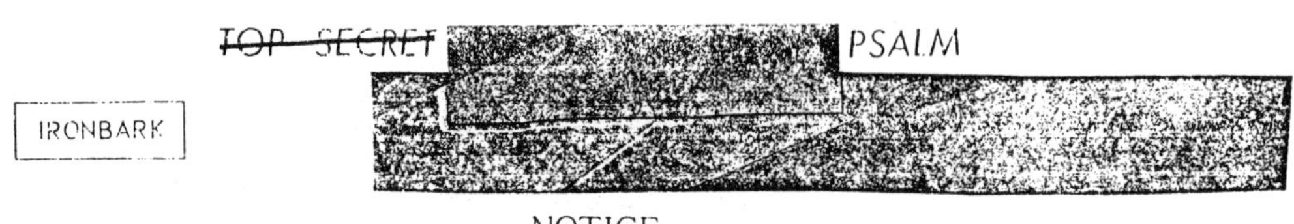

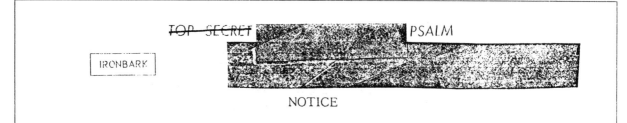

NOTICE

This supplement up-dates and amplifies [redacted] dated 2000 hours, 19 October 1962. Emphasis is on the READINESS status of the offensive missiles in Cuba.

Offensive Missile Readiness

General

1. Analysis of the comparative photographic coverage of the offensive-missile sites in Cuba now leads us to conclude that the Soviets did not have as their main objective an immediate operational capability at any of the identified sites. An emergency operational capability to launch some of the missiles on hand within about 8 hours could now exist at the four MRBM sites. They appear to be pursuing an urgent but systematic plan to achieve an operational capability which will maximize the effectiveness of the missile regiments. Within the sites the steps necessary to achieve an immediate operational capability have not occurred. For example, at San Cristobal Site 2 the three launchers and five missiles present continue to be bunched together in a field. Were an immediate launch capability intended one would expect deployment of the launcher to the vicinity of the intended launch positions.

San Cristobal Area

2. Activity in Site 1 and Site 2 continues to indicate an urgent effort to achieve full operational readiness. The launch crews, missiles and associated equipment are in the immediate area. From the status of the sites as of our last coverage (Mission 3111 on 18 October), we estimate that Site 1 could now have full operational readiness and that Site 2 could achieve

- 1 -

TOP SECRET PSALM

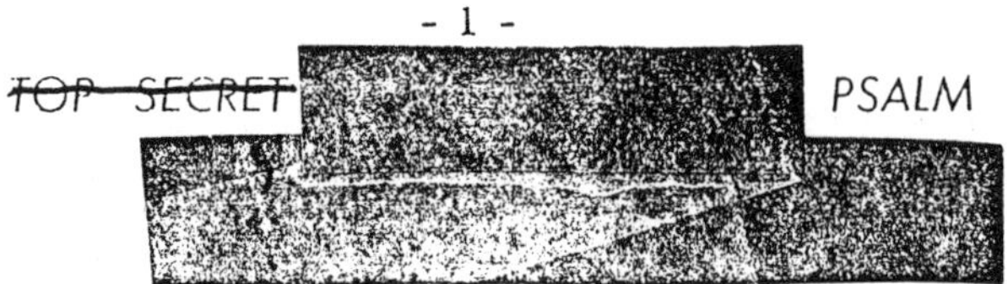

69. *(Continued)*

this status by 25 October. By full operational readiness we mean the ability to launch in salvo four missiles per site with a refire capability of four missiles per site within 4 to 6 hours.

Sagua La Grande Area

3. The MRBM sites at Sagua La Grande were first identified on 17 October and were covered by photography twice that day. (The last previous coverage was on 7 July and showed no evidence of missile activity.) The status of preparation at the two sites on 17 October was approximately the same. It is believed that the missile regiment was moving into the area on 17 October, inasmuch as 35 vehicles arrived in a support area at Site 1 within the 1 3/4 hour period between two photographic coverages.

4. Construction activity and random location of missile support equipment indicate that development of the area was not complete. The presence of missiles and launchers indicates that the sites have an emergency operational capability. However, the regiment could reach full operational readiness at these sites by 1 November.

Guanajay Area

5. A detailed reexamination of the evidence available at this time indicates that the operational date for these launch sites may be somewhat earlier than our previous estimate. Construction activity appears to be progressing at a more rapid pace than that observed in the USSR at similar facilities. Several features of the sites such as the control bunkers, excavations for fuel tanks, and blast walls for component protection are several days more advanced than previously determined. Mission 3111 on 18 October indicates that concrete is being installed at all four pads at Site 1.

- 2 -

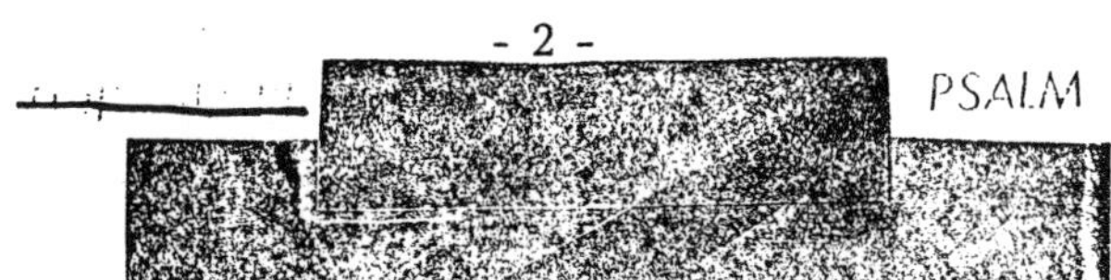

69. *(Continued)*

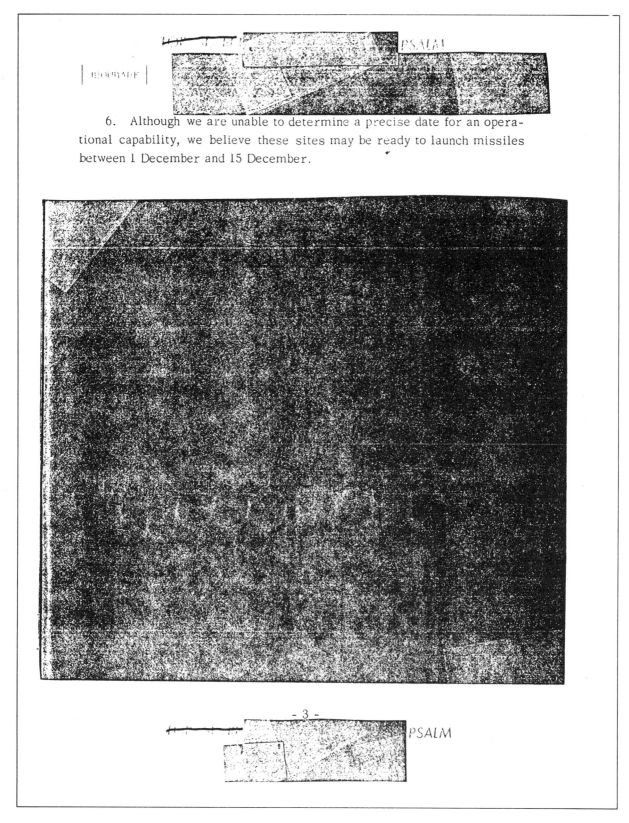

6. Although we are unable to determine a precise date for an operational capability, we believe these sites may be ready to launch missiles between 1 December and 15 December.

- 3 -

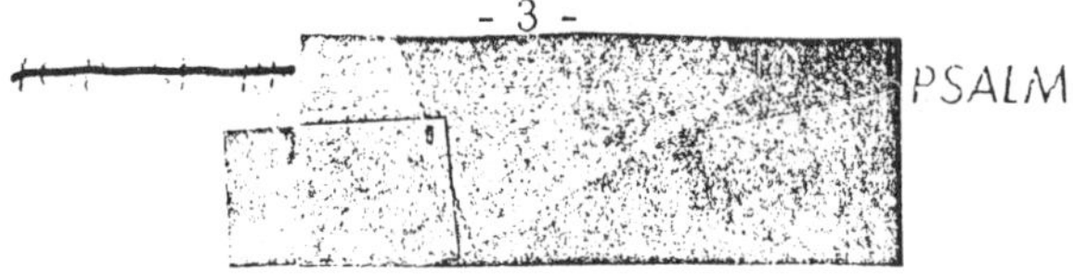

69. *(Continued)*

Nuclear Warheads for Offensive Missiles

9. At the probable nuclear storage site under construction adjacent to the Guanajay IRBM fixed missile launch Site 1, earth-moving activity at the 114 by 60 foot drive-through building continues at an apparent high rate.

10. A curved-roof building similar to that at Guanajay Site 1, but only about 35 by 67 feet has been observed at the newly identified possible missile site near Remedios.

11. Foundations of structures (approximately 60 by 35 feet) which might be intended to be future nuclear warhead storage facilities have been observed at the San Cristobal Sites 1 and 3 and at Sagua La Grande Site 1. The appearance of concrete arches nearby indicates that these buildings will be earth-covered.

12. The tank trailers observed in the quay area of the Punta Gerardo port facility are similar to those seen in 22 May 1962 photography taken before security fences were erected. This strongly suggests that these trucks have no nuclear association.

13. Search of the major airfields in Cuba has not as yet revealed any structures that can be identified as intended for nuclear storage.

Offensive Force Levels

See Table 2.

Support and Supply

No change.

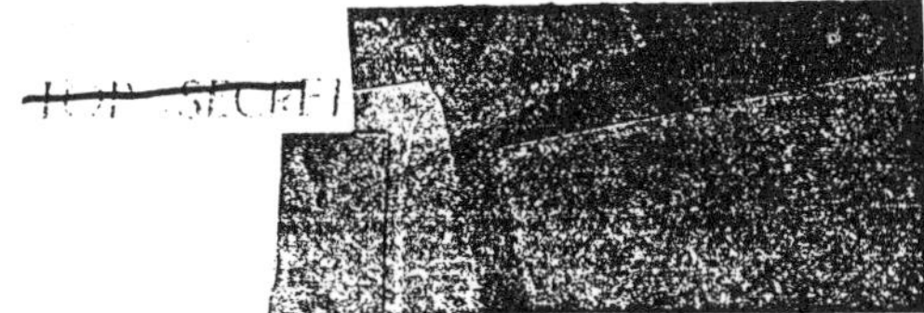

Coastal Defense Missiles

No change.

Air Defense Missiles

14. There are now 24 primary surface-to-air missile (SA-2) sites located in Cuba (see Figure 2). Two of these sites, Santa Lucia and Deleite, each have an alternate site located 3 to 5 nm from the primary site. These alternate sites are pre-surveyed, have no equipment and could possibly be used for mobility training exercises. Of the 24 primary sites, 20 are individually operational at the present time. The remaining primary SA-2 sites could be operational sites in approximately one week.

15. There are 6 surface-to-air missile assembly and support areas. Photography shows large quantities of surface-to-air missile cannisters and missile transporters. See Table 3 for a list of surface-to-air missile sites, missile assembly areas and associated equipment.

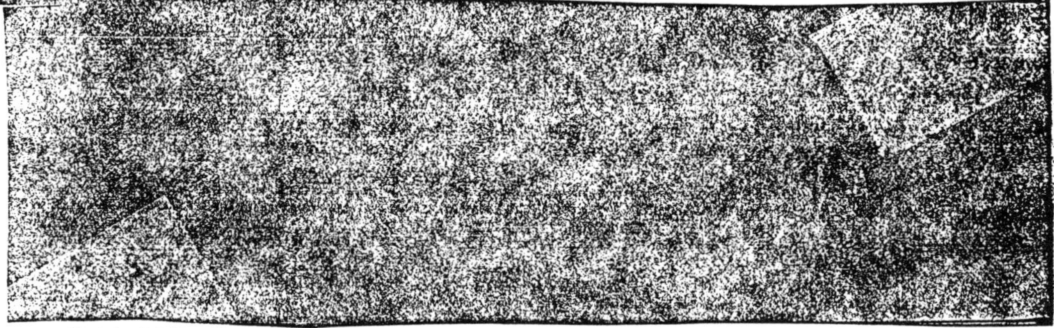

Guided Missile Patrol Craft

17. There are now a total of 12 KOMAR class patrol craft in Cuba. Each KOMAR craft carries two homing missiles which have an effective range of 10 to 15 nm and carry 2000 pound HE warheads. The KOMARs

- 5 -

69. *(Continued)*

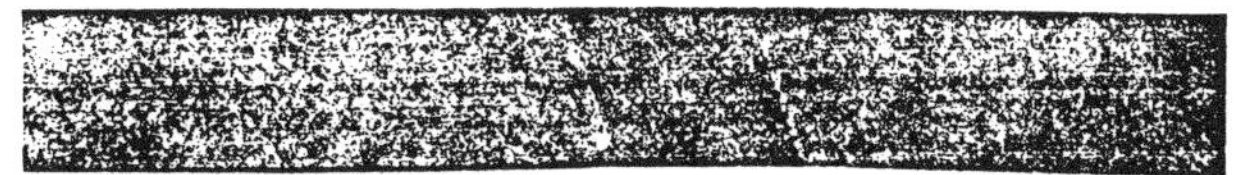

must return to base or to a tender for reloading. Tenders for these craft have not yet been identified in Cuba. All KOMARs in Cuba are considered to be operational. At least six are based at Havana and four at Banes. The remaining two have been observed operating in the Mariel area, but it is not known whether they are based there or were operating from the Havana base.

18. The KOMARs have all been transported to Cuba as deck cargo on Soviet ships, two and four per shipload. The first shipment arrived in Havana on 14 August 1962. Whereas it probably took several weeks to establish base and logistic support for the first KOMARs to become integrated fully operational units, additional units can probably become operational within one week after offloading.

Tactical Missiles

No change.

Significance

19. The apparent Soviet objective to rapidly achieve full operational status for their MRBM and IRBM regiments rather than to achieve an immediate operational capability at each site as the missiles and equipment arrive, may be very significant to the planners judging various Soviet courses of action.

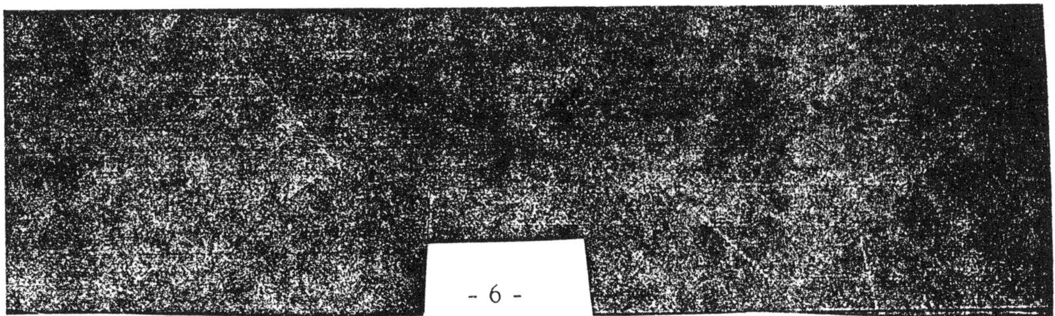

- 6 -

69. *(Continued)*

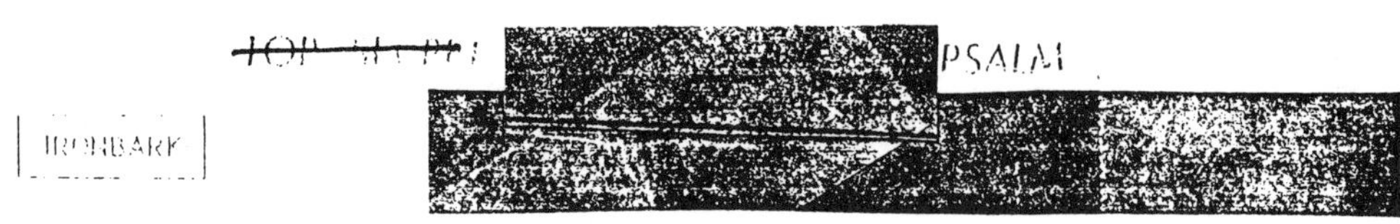

Addendum

Preliminary analysis of photography of 18 October reveals an unidentified secured installation in an early stage of construction 5 nm southwest of the town of REMEDIOS. It consists of 4 large excavations in a symmetrical pattern; however, their function cannot be determined at this time. This installation is, however, considered to be a suspected surface-to-surface missile site.

- 7 -

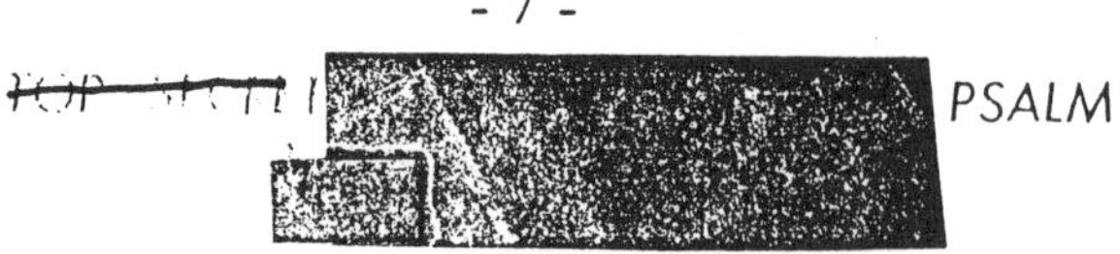

70. *Intelligence Memorandum, "Evaluation of Offensive Threat in Cuba," with cover memorandum, Carter to Members of United States Intelligence Board, 21 October 1962*

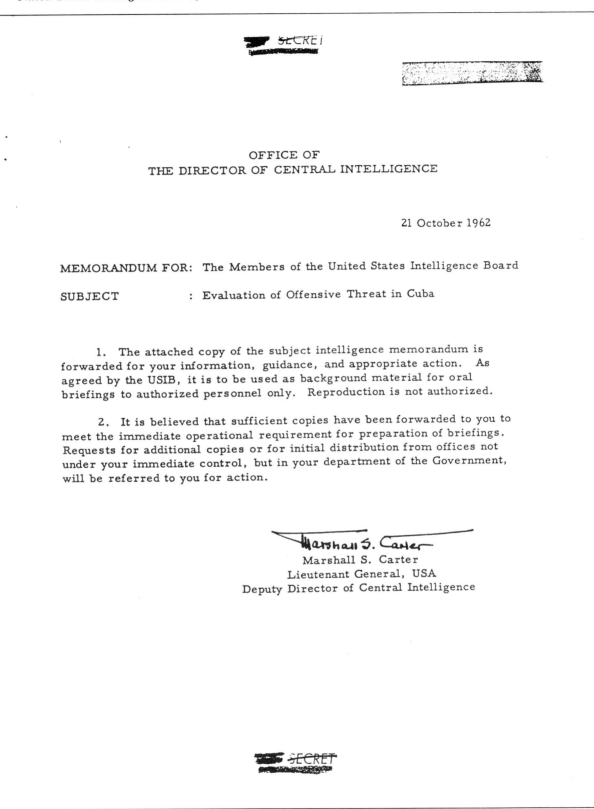

OFFICE OF
THE DIRECTOR OF CENTRAL INTELLIGENCE

21 October 1962

MEMORANDUM FOR: The Members of the United States Intelligence Board

SUBJECT : Evaluation of Offensive Threat in Cuba

1. The attached copy of the subject intelligence memorandum is forwarded for your information, guidance, and appropriate action. As agreed by the USIB, it is to be used as background material for oral briefings to authorized personnel only. Reproduction is not authorized.

2. It is believed that sufficient copies have been forwarded to you to meet the immediate operational requirement for preparation of briefings. Requests for additional copies or for initial distribution from offices not under your immediate control, but in your department of the Government, will be referred to you for action.

Marshall S. Carter

Marshall S. Carter
Lieutenant General, USA
Deputy Director of Central Intelligence

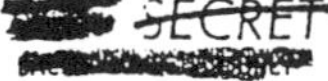

EVALUATION OF OFFENSIVE THREAT IN CUBA

Significance

1. A significant deployment of guided missiles to Cuba is already well advanced, and has proceeded by first deploying a large force of defensive weapons, followed quickly by long-range offensive guided missiles and aircraft. (See Figure 1.) A mixed force of 1000- and 2200-nm ballistic missiles in Cuba provides for the first time a significant strategic strike capability against almost all targets in the U. S., and against a large portion of Canada and Latin America. (See Figure 2.) The planning for this operation must have started at least one year ago and the actual deployment itself began last spring.

Offensive Deployment

2. The equipment for 1000-nm ballistic missiles is now being deployed in Western Cuba at four launch sites near San Cristobal. (See Figures 3-5.) Two of these are now operational and the other two are proceeding to this status on an accelerated basis. The missiles are probably those reported moving into this area during September. Each of the four sites contains eight missiles and four unrevetted, field type launchers which rely on mobile erection, checkout, and support equipment. This implies a refire capability from each unit.

3. Other 1000-nm ballistic missiles are also deployed at two sites nine miles apart, east of Havana in the Sagua La Grande area. (See Figures 8-9.) These sites closely resemble the sites at San Cristobal but appear to be more permanent in nature. Terrain features have dictated considerable clearing and grading for deployment of the system. Also, there are permanent structures at the launch positions at each site and we estimate an operational capability for each site within one week. The sizes of the missiles, associated equipment, and buildings found at the San Cristobal and Sagua La Grande sites are almost identical and are compatible with the 1000-nm missile system.

- 1 -

4. Two fixed sites for 2200-nm, ballistic missiles are under construction in the Guanajay area near Havana. (See Figures 6-7.) Four launchers, two blockhouses, and underground propellant storage are being built at each site. Site 1 is considered to be in a mid-to-late stage of construction and should be operational within six weeks. Site 2 is in an earlier stage of construction and could be operational between 15 and 30 December 1962. There are no missiles or support equipment detectable within the Guanajay Area at the present time.

5. An additional fixed site has been observed at Remedios in Eastern Cuba which is similar to those at Guanajay. This is probably a valid indicator of deployment of a second grouping of 2200-nm ballistic missiles.

6. In addition to missiles, IL-28 light bomber aircraft with a combat radius of about 750 miles are also arriving in Cuba. Approximately 22 of these bombers, most still in crates, are now present. These are in addition to the force of about 40 MIG-21 fighters there.

Nuclear Warheads

7. We believe that a nuclear warhead storage site is under construction adjacent to the more complete of the fixed missile launch sites near Guanajay. (See Figure 6.) Construction is proceeding at a high rate. This site could become operational at about the same time as the associated Launch Site 1.

8. A curved-roof building similar to that at Guanajay Site 1, but only about 35 by 67 feet has been observed at the newly identified possible missile site near Remedios.

9. Foundations of structures (approximately 60 by 35 feet) which may be intended to be future nuclear warhead storage facilities have been observed at the San Cristobal Sites 1 and 3 and at Sagua La Grande Site 1. The appearance of concrete arches nearby indicates that these buildings will be earth-covered.

- 2 -

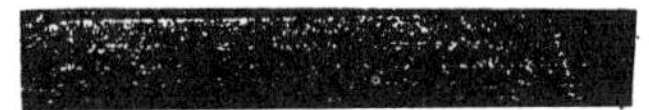

10. Search of the major airfields in Cuba has not as yet revealed any structures that can be identified as intended for nuclear storage.

11. There is still no evidence of currently operational nuclear storage facilities in Cuba. Nevertheless, one must assume that nuclear weapons could now be in Cuba to support the operational missile capability as it becomes available. The missiles would probably be equipped with thermonuclear warheads.

Support and Supply

12. Offensive missile systems are being introduced into Cuba through the Port of Mariel and perhaps other ports. A new Soviet ship, the Poltava, possibly designed as a ballistic missile transport, has been noted making frequent trips between the USSR and Cuba. (See Figure 11.) This ship has made two trips to Cuba since 17 July, and is next estimated to arrive in Cuba on or about 2 November 1962.

13. Possible central missile checkout, storage, and repair bases have been located at Soroa, between the two eastern deployment areas, and at Managua, south of Havana.

14. It is significant that all of the ballistic and air defense missiles now being deployed in Cuba probably use a common oxidizer, permitting exploitation of a common system for propellant supply and storage.

Coastal Defense Missiles

15. Three coastal defense missile sites have now been identified in Cuba, two of which must now be considered operational (Banes and Santa Cruz del Norte). (See Figure 10.) These cruise missiles have a range of 35 to 40 miles.

Air Defense Missiles

16. There are now 24 primary surface-to-air missile sites located in Cuba. (See Figure 10.) Two of these sites, Santa Lucia and Deleite,

- 3 -

each have an alternate site located 3 to 5 nm from the primary site. These alternate sites are pre-surveyed, have no equipment and could possibly be used for mobility training exercises. Of the 24 primary sites, 20 are individually operational at the present time. The remaining primary surface-to-air missile sites could be operational in approximately one week.

17. There are 6 surface-to-air missile assembly and support areas. Photography shows large quantities of surface-to-air missile cannisters and missile transporters.

Guided Missile Patrol Craft

18. There are now a total of 12 missile-launching patrol craft in Cuba. Each craft carries two homing missiles which have an effective range of 10 to 15 nm and carry 2000-pound, high-explosive warheads. They must return to base or to a tender for reloading, although tenders for these craft have not yet been identified in Cuba. All of these missile launching patrol craft in Cuba are considered to be operational. All have been recently observed operating in the Mariel area, but it is not known whether they are based there or were operating from other bases.

19. These craft have all been transported to Cuba as deck cargo on Soviet ships, two and four per shipload. The first shipment arrived in Havana on 14 August 1962. Whereas it probably took several weeks to establish base and logistic support for the first craft to become integrated fully operational units, additional units can probably become operational within one week after offloading.

———— • ————

- 4 -

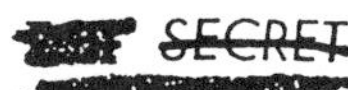

71. *McCone, "Memorandum of Meeting with the President, Attorney General, Secretary McNamara, General Taylor, and Mr. McCone, 10:00 a.m.—10/21/62"*

#43

October 21, 1962

MEMORANDUM OF MEETING WITH THE PRESIDENT, ATTORNEY GENERAL, SECRETARY McNAMARA, GENERAL TAYLOR, AND MR. McCONE. 10:00 A.M. — 10/21/62

1. General Sweeney reviewed in considerable detail the plans for an air strike against the missile bases, the air fields, a few SAM sites in critical locations and finally the plans for invasion.

2. It was decided that at a minimum an air strike must include both the missile sites and the air fields and such SAM sites as are necessary, and General Taylor was instructed to plan accordingly.

3. There was complete agreement that military action must include an invasion and occupation of Cuba.

4. Secretary McNamara and General Taylor told the President that an air strike could not provide absolute assurance that all missiles were destroyed; they indicated a 90 per cent probability. They also stated that any warning would very possibly cause the movement of missiles to obscure unknown locations from which they could become operational. General Taylor therefore recommended, on the basis of military grounds, that the air strike be conducted immediately, suggesting tomorrow morning, and that it be without warning. Secretary McNamara confirmed the military appraisal expressed above but made no recommendation as to policy.

5. In response to direct questioning from the President, the Attorney General and McCone advised against surprise attack for the reasons discussed at previous meetings. The Attorney General failed to make an absolute recommendation with respect to future military actions, indicating this question could be decided as the situation developed from day to day, and that only preparatory

~~TOP SECRET~~

TOP SECRET

steps should be taken now. McCone urged on the other hand that the President in a public statement indicate an intention to remove the missiles and other potential weapons by means and at a time of his own choosing if surveillance did not prove conclusively that the Soviets and the Cubans were removing them.

6. The meeting adjourned to be reconvened at 2:30, with additional principals in attendance.

John A. McCone
Director

JAM:at

- 2 -

TOP SECRET

72. *McCone, "Memorandum of Discussion with the President Alone, October 21, 1962"*

#4

TOP SECRET

October 21, 1962

MEMORANDUM OF DISCUSSION WITH THE PRESIDENT ALONE, OCTOBER 21, 1962. (Approx. 4:30 p.m.)

On my report of my discussion with General Eisenhower at my residence this morning, the following information was given later to the Attorney General. It is not to be given to anyone else.

After briefing by Lundahl, General Eisenhower and I engaged in a long discussion concerning the proper procedure to be followed. Eisenhower's conclusions are as follows:

1. Any military action would be inconclusive and therefore inadvisable unless it employed invasion and occupation of Cuba. Eisenhower gave this opinion on a basis of his experience in war in countless examples of air strikes which though most effective, were never completely conclusive.

2. From a military point of view a surprise attack would be most effective and most desirable if followed in a minimum time by invasion.

3. However, from a broader point of view, he opposed surprise attack because of the indictment, the resulting tensions, and the fact that such action by the United States would license other countries to resort to violent military action without notice.

4. Therefore Eisenhower would accept the handicaps from a military point of view, of warning or notice, and therefore would follow the suggested plan of initiating a blockade, conducting intense surveillance, and announcing the intention of taking military action if the Soviets and the Cubans either maintained the status quo of their missile installations or continued the construction of theil missile bases. The military action he envisaged would be air strikes and invasion.

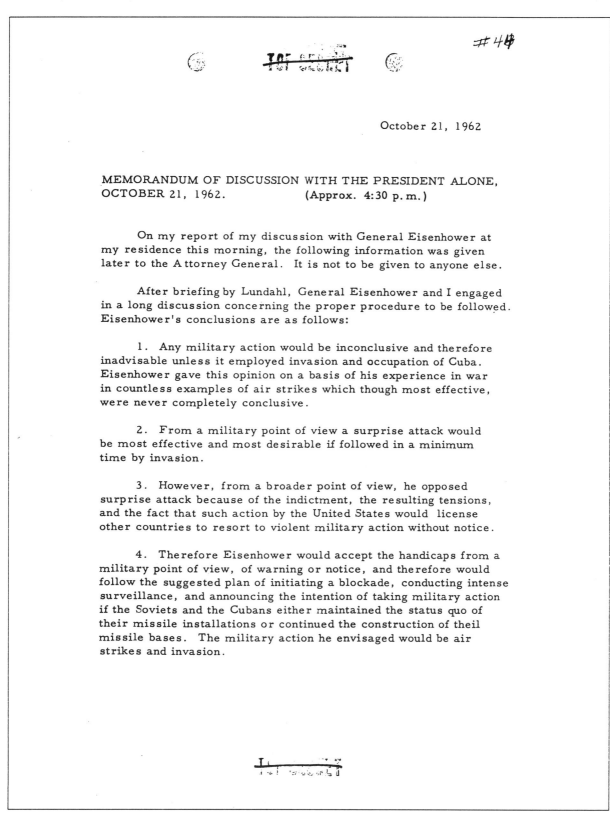

~~TOP SECRET~~

5. General Eisenhower emphasized he was giving his opinion based solely on intelligence and without the benefit of a study of the war plans or the most recent diplomatic exchanges with Castro, Khrushchev, our allies, etc. It seemed fair to conclude that his views as expressed above represent a flash judgment rather than a considered judgment arrived at with all facets of the problem laid before him.

John A. McCone
Director

- 2 -

~~TOP SECRET~~

73. *McCone, Memorandum for the File, "Meeting with the Vice President on 21 October 1962," 22 October 1962*

m/R #102

~~SECRET~~ EYES ~~ONLY~~

22 October 1962

MEMORANDUM FOR THE FILE

SUBJECT: Meeting with the Vice President on 21 October 1962

On Sunday night, October 21 at 8:30 I briefed Vice President Lyndon Johnson at the request of the President, conveyed through McGeorge Bundy.

The briefing involved a review of photography by Lundahl paralleling briefings given to General Eisenhower and others.

We then discussed policy and details of the proposed speech by the President in considerable detail.

The thrust of the Vice President's thinking was that he favored an unannounced strike rather than the agreed plan which involved blockade and strike and invasion later if conditions warranted. He expressed displeasure at "telegraphing our punch" and also commented the blockade would be ineffective because we in effect are "locking the barn after the horse was gone".

I followed the position and the arguments used in my briefing paper of 20 October. The Vice President finally agreed reluctantly but only after learning among other things the support indicated by General Eisenhower.

JOHN A. McCONE

TMLee/mfb

~~SECRET~~ EYES ~~ONLY~~

74. *"Soviet Military Buildup in Cuba," 21 October 1962*
[briefing notes for Heads of Government]

~~TOP SECRET~~

Sanitized version of Briefing notes for Heads of Government

~~TOP SECRET~~

~~TOP SECRET~~ C[illegible]0, 21 Oct 62

SOVIET MILITARY BUILD-UP
IN CUBA

I. Now clear to US that Khrushchev last spring made foreign policy decision on Cuba which involved unprecedented risks and which made it undeniable that Soviets are playing for very high stakes indeed.

A. Soviets believed decisive action necessary because:

1. Cuban economy was deteriorating;

2. There seemed to be mounting pressure in the US for intervention.

B. Soviets also saw opportunity to:

1. Demonstrate that the US can no longer prevent advance of Soviet offensive power even in its own hemisphere;

2. Significantly expand Soviet capabilities for initial attack on US targets;

3. Thus weaken Western resolve and unity in countering Soviet moves in the East-West global contest, particularly over Berlin and Germany.

II. The Soviet decision has since been implemented in two phases:

A. First, the build-up during the summer of defensive capabilities;

~~TOP SECRET~~

TOP SECRET 400, 21 Oct 62

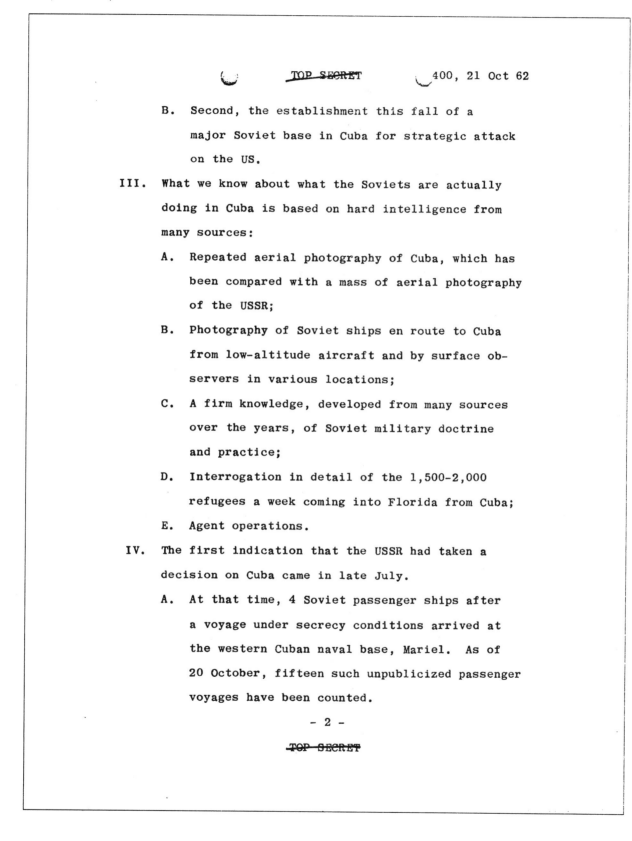

B. Second, the establishment this fall of a major Soviet base in Cuba for strategic attack on the US.

III. What we know about what the Soviets are actually doing in Cuba is based on hard intelligence from many sources:

A. Repeated aerial photography of Cuba, which has been compared with a mass of aerial photography of the USSR;

B. Photography of Soviet ships en route to Cuba from low-altitude aircraft and by surface observers in various locations;

C. A firm knowledge, developed from many sources over the years, of Soviet military doctrine and practice;

D. Interrogation in detail of the 1,500-2,000 refugees a week coming into Florida from Cuba;

E. Agent operations.

IV. The first indication that the USSR had taken a decision on Cuba came in late July.

A. At that time, 4 Soviet passenger ships after a voyage under secrecy conditions arrived at the western Cuban naval base, Mariel. As of 20 October, fifteen such unpublicized passenger voyages have been counted.

- 2 -

TOP SECRET

~~TOP SECRET~~ 0400, 21 Oct 62

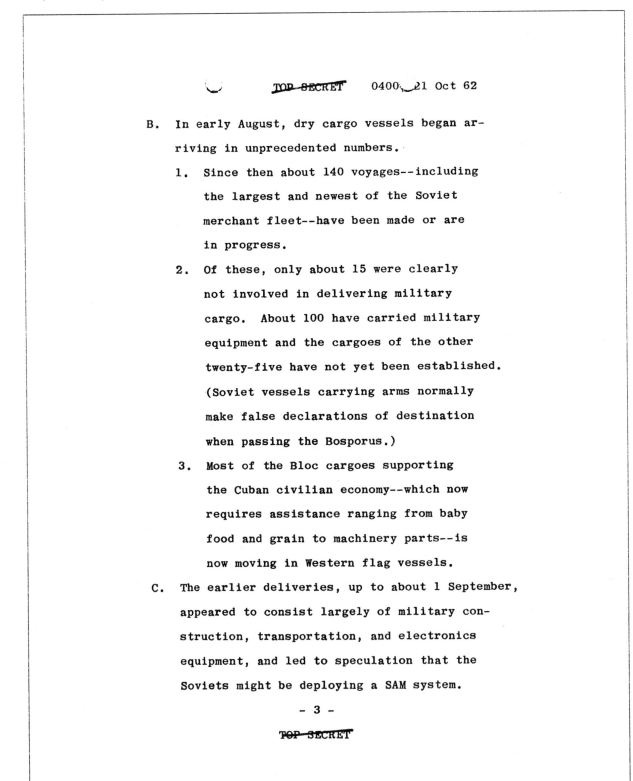

B. In early August, dry cargo vessels began arriving in unprecedented numbers.

1. Since then about 140 voyages--including the largest and newest of the Soviet merchant fleet--have been made or are in progress.

2. Of these, only about 15 were clearly not involved in delivering military cargo. About 100 have carried military equipment and the cargoes of the other twenty-five have not yet been established. (Soviet vessels carrying arms normally make false declarations of destination when passing the Bosporus.)

3. Most of the Bloc cargoes supporting the Cuban civilian economy--which now requires assistance ranging from baby food and grain to machinery parts--is now moving in Western flag vessels.

C. The earlier deliveries, up to about 1 September, appeared to consist largely of military construction, transportation, and electronics equipment, and led to speculation that the Soviets might be deploying a SAM system.

- 3 -

~~TOP SECRET~~

TOP SECRET 1430, 21 Oct 62

1. Photography of 29 August and 5 September confirmed that a SAM system was being deployed. Twelve sites were identified. One MIG-21 was seen, as were eight Komar-class missile boats and one land-based anti-shipping cruise missile site. During September the known number of each of these systems increased.

D. In early September, consequently, we had ample evidence of a significant buildup. All confirmed deliveries, however, fitted into a pattern of weapons which are essentially defensive in design and in normal operational employment. On basis of such evidence President issued his statements of 4 and 13 September that Soviet activity in Cuba was defensive in nature.

V. Our present knowledge of the state of these weapons in Cuba is as follows:

A. SAM sites (These are the standard Soviet six-launcher second-generation-type called in NATO terminology GUIDELINE).

1. At least 24 sites, with alternate positions for several. These sites cover most of the island. Three or four more will cover the entire island.

- 4 -

TOP SECRET

TOP SECRET  0400, 21 Oct 62

2. Support sites--six presently identified, still field-type, but signs of permanent-type installation appearing.

3. Readiness--as of 17 October, 17 sites appeared--in photography--to have both missiles on launchers and the essential radar in position. Only one, however, has emplaced around it the radar-controlled guns which normally are installed to provide some defense against low-flying aircraft. Known radar emissions have thus far been very few. However, at least one site has the C-band radar--the latest Soviet model now being widely deployed in the USSR and East Germany. The sites were installed with haste. Revetments were built at most sites only after setting up.

B. There are now about 100 MIG fighters in Cuba. About 60 15's, 17's and 19's arrived prior to 1 January '62, and there are now at least 39 MIG-21s.

1. Standard Soviet GCI units (one identified this far through photography) will control these fighters.

2. While there is no direct evidence of air-to-air missiles in Cuba, such equipment is

- 5 -

TOP SECRET

~~TOP SECRET~~ 430, 21 Oct 62

being supplied to Indonesia, Egypt, and probably to Iraq. We think it likely that Cuba will get at least equal treatment.

3. The MIG-21's have only recently become available. On 5 September we know that only one had been assembled. By 17 October, 35 had been assembled.

C. Coastal Defense.

1. We have identified 12 Komar-class patrol craft. Each carries two homing missiles, with a range of 10-15 n.m. and carrying 2,000-pound HE warheads. The first arrived in mid-August. All are now operational.

2. There are three coastal defense missile sites--two now operational. These anti-shipping missiles have a range of 35-40 miles and carry HE warheads.

VI. Soviet diplomacy and pronouncements have been carefully geared to military build-up; amounts to well-thought-out deception plan.

A. Soviets wanted to keep international tensions down until build-up completed;

- 6 -

~~TOP SECRET~~

B. Have tried to keep attention focussed on Berlin - but with emphasis on lull till after US elections;

C. Emphasized defensive nature of Soviet support for Cuba as justified by provocative US threat;

D. Made connection between Berlin and Cuba as part of effort to demonstrate seriousness of Soviet commitment to Castro, but discreetly enough to avoid Western counteraction.

VII. In early October we obtained our first hard information on the delivery of Soviet offensive weapons to Cuba.

A. We photographed 10 crates on a ship bound for Cuba of a kind especially designed to contain the fuselage of an IL-28 jet light bomber.

B. 21 of these crates were later photographed at San Julian airfield in the extreme west of Cuba.

C. As of 17 October, four aircraft had been uncrated, of which one is partially assembled.

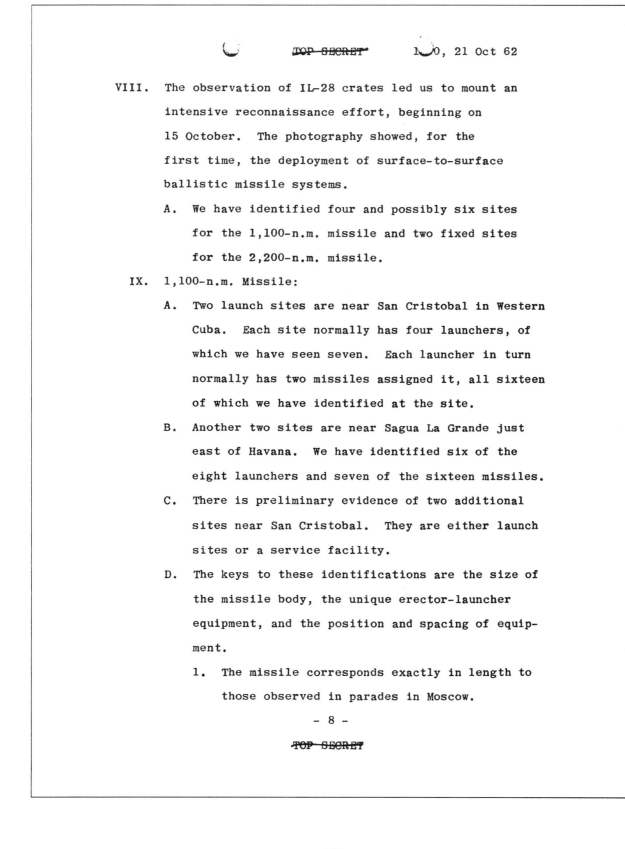

VIII. The observation of IL-28 crates led us to mount an intensive reconnaissance effort, beginning on 15 October. The photography showed, for the first time, the deployment of surface-to-surface ballistic missile systems.

A. We have identified four and possibly six sites for the 1,100-n.m. missile and two fixed sites for the 2,200-n.m. missile.

IX. 1,100-n.m. Missile:

A. Two launch sites are near San Cristobal in Western Cuba. Each site normally has four launchers, of which we have seen seven. Each launcher in turn normally has two missiles assigned it, all sixteen of which we have identified at the site.

B. Another two sites are near Sagua La Grande just east of Havana. We have identified six of the eight launchers and seven of the sixteen missiles.

C. There is preliminary evidence of two additional sites near San Cristobal. They are either launch sites or a service facility.

D. The keys to these identifications are the size of the missile body, the unique erector-launcher equipment, and the position and spacing of equipment.

1. The missile corresponds exactly in length to those observed in parades in Moscow.

~~TOP SECRET~~ 1430, 21 Oct 62

2. The handling equipment is similar to that photographed in the USSR.
3. The spacing of launchers corresponds to that discussed in secret Soviet military documents and to that observed in known missile sites in the USSR.

E. The 1,020-mile-range missile is a single-stage ballistic missile using storable liquid fuels.

1. It has an autonomous (i.e., all-inertial) guidance system giving a CEP of 1, to 1 1/2 nautical miles. It carries a warhead of 2,500-3,500 pounds, yielding 2-3 megatons.

F. Photography alone cannot permit us to be very precise about the operational readiness of these missiles.

1. The sites at San Cristobal are the nearest to completion. We are inclined to believe that one of them could now have full operational readiness -- i.e.: an ability to launch four missiles with a refire capability within 4 to 6 hours --and that the other could achieve this status in about two days.
2. The sites at Sagua La Grande will probably not achieve the same stage of construction until 1 November or later.

- 9 -

~~TOP SECRET~~

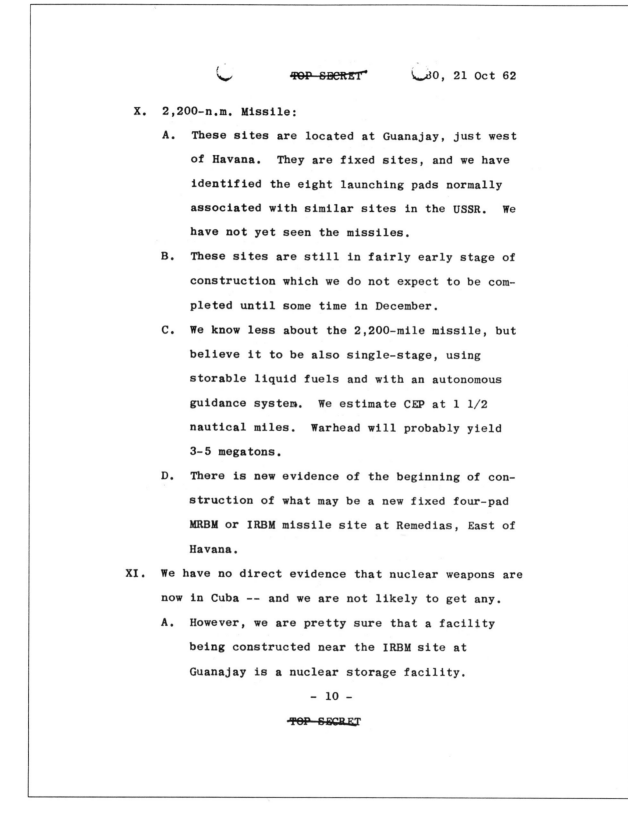

X. 2,200-n.m. Missile:

A. These sites are located at Guanajay, just west of Havana. They are fixed sites, and we have identified the eight launching pads normally associated with similar sites in the USSR. We have not yet seen the missiles.

B. These sites are still in fairly early stage of construction which we do not expect to be completed until some time in December.

C. We know less about the 2,200-mile missile, but believe it to be also single-stage, using storable liquid fuels and with an autonomous guidance system. We estimate CEP at 1 1/2 nautical miles. Warhead will probably yield 3-5 megatons.

D. There is new evidence of the beginning of construction of what may be a new fixed four-pad MRBM or IRBM missile site at Remedias, East of Havana.

XI. We have no direct evidence that nuclear weapons are now in Cuba -- and we are not likely to get any.

A. However, we are pretty sure that a facility being constructed near the IRBM site at Guanajay is a nuclear storage facility.

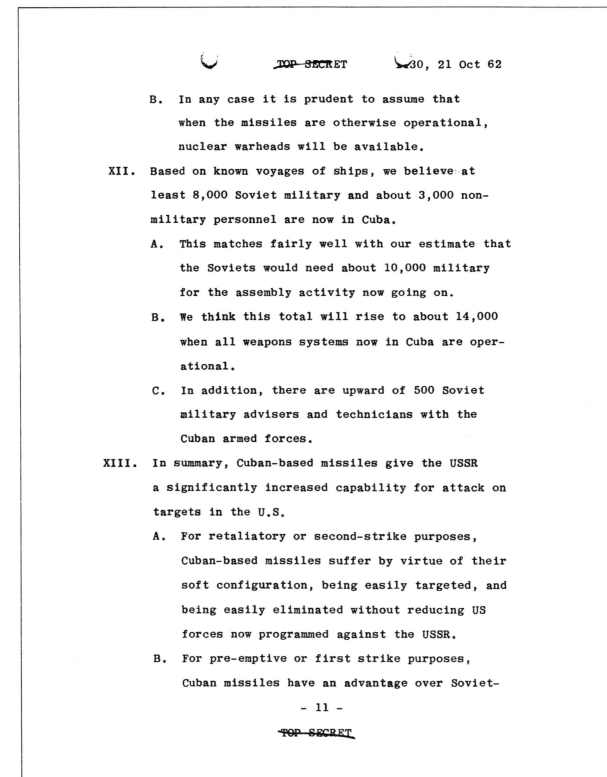

~~TOP SECR~~ET 30, 21 Oct 62

B. In any case it is prudent to assume that when the missiles are otherwise operational, nuclear warheads will be available.

XII. Based on known voyages of ships, we believe at least 8,000 Soviet military and about 3,000 non-military personnel are now in Cuba.

A. This matches fairly well with our estimate that the Soviets would need about 10,000 military for the assembly activity now going on.

B. We think this total will rise to about 14,000 when all weapons systems now in Cuba are operational.

C. In addition, there are upward of 500 Soviet military advisers and technicians with the Cuban armed forces.

XIII. In summary, Cuban-based missiles give the USSR a significantly increased capability for attack on targets in the U.S.

A. For retaliatory or second-strike purposes, Cuban-based missiles suffer by virtue of their soft configuration, being easily targeted, and being easily eliminated without reducing US forces now programmed against the USSR.

B. For pre-emptive or first strike purposes, Cuban missiles have an advantage over Soviet-

- 11 -

~~TOP SECRET~~

based ICBM's -- shorter flight times and no BMEWS detection.

C. Sites now identified will, when completed, give Soviets total of 36 launchers and 72 missiles. This compares with 60-65 ICBM launchers we now estimate to be operational in the USSR.

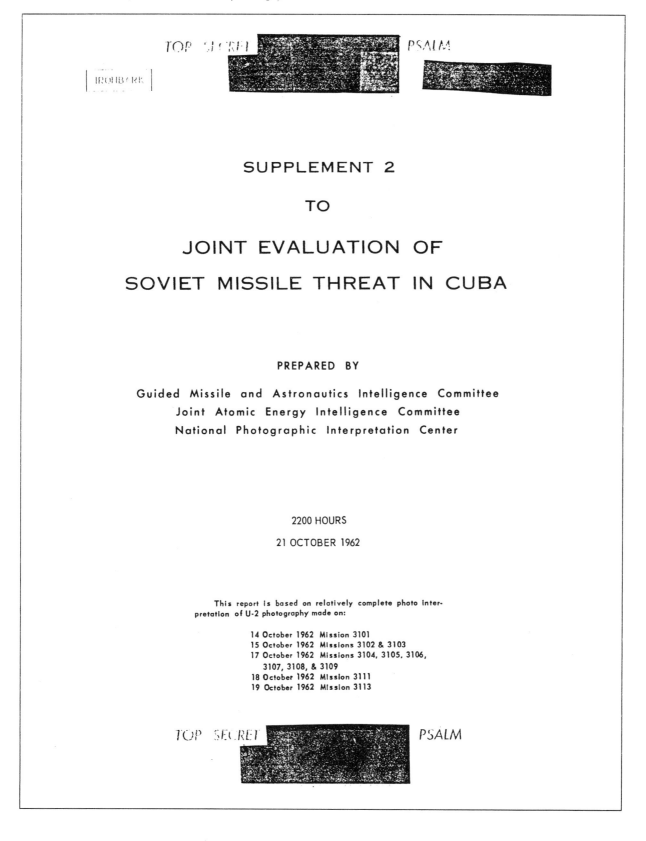

75. *Supplement 2 to Joint Evaluation of Soviet Missile Threat in Cuba, 21 October 1962 (Excerpt)*

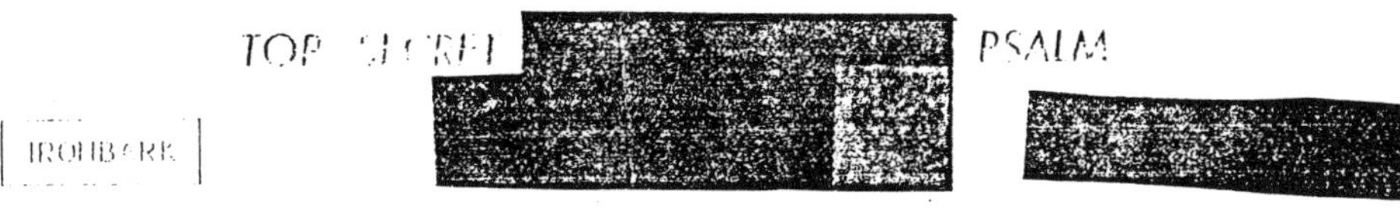

SUPPLEMENT 2

TO

JOINT EVALUATION OF

SOVIET MISSILE THREAT IN CUBA

PREPARED BY

Guided Missile and Astronautics Intelligence Committee
Joint Atomic Energy Intelligence Committee
National Photographic Interpretation Center

2200 HOURS

21 OCTOBER 1962

This report is based on relatively complete photo interpretation of U-2 photography made on:

14 October 1962 Mission 3101
15 October 1962 Missions 3102 & 3103
17 October 1962 Missions 3104, 3105, 3106, 3107, 3108, & 3109
18 October 1962 Mission 3111
19 October 1962 Mission 3113

TOP SECRET PSALM

75. *(Continued)*

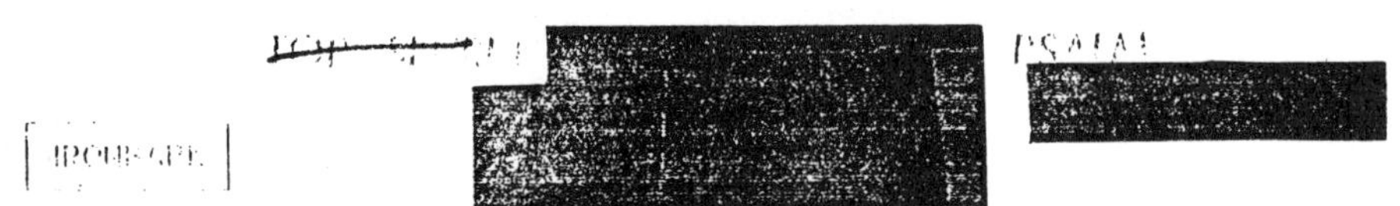

NOTICE

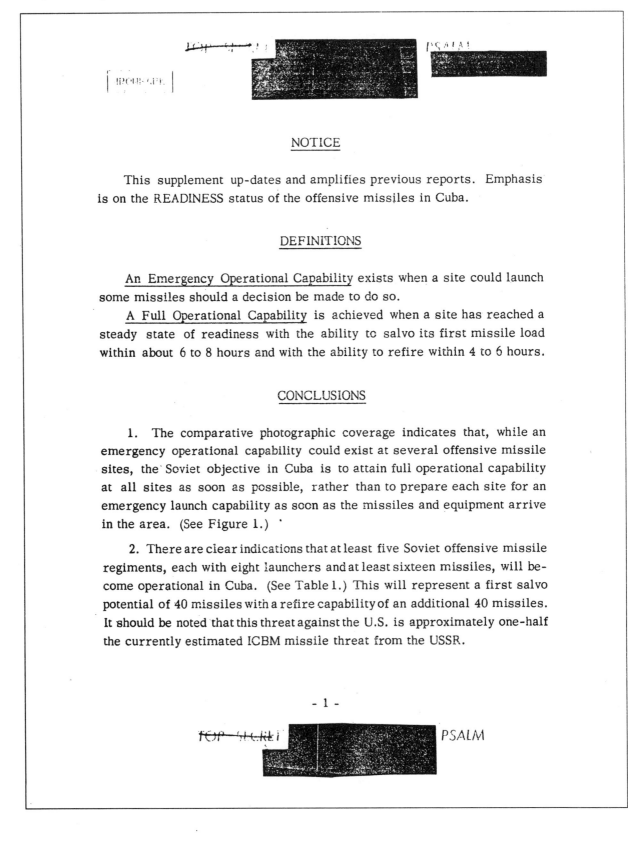

This supplement up-dates and amplifies previous reports. Emphasis is on the READINESS status of the offensive missiles in Cuba.

DEFINITIONS

An Emergency Operational Capability exists when a site could launch some missiles should a decision be made to do so.

A Full Operational Capability is achieved when a site has reached a steady state of readiness with the ability to salvo its first missile load within about 6 to 8 hours and with the ability to refire within 4 to 6 hours.

CONCLUSIONS

1. The comparative photographic coverage indicates that, while an emergency operational capability could exist at several offensive missile sites, the Soviet objective in Cuba is to attain full operational capability at all sites as soon as possible, rather than to prepare each site for an emergency launch capability as soon as the missiles and equipment arrive in the area. (See Figure 1.)

2. There are clear indications that at least five Soviet offensive missile regiments, each with eight launchers and at least sixteen missiles, will become operational in Cuba. (See Table 1.) This will represent a first salvo potential of 40 missiles with a refire capability of an additional 40 missiles. It should be noted that this threat against the U.S. is approximately one-half the currently estimated ICBM missile threat from the USSR.

- 1 -

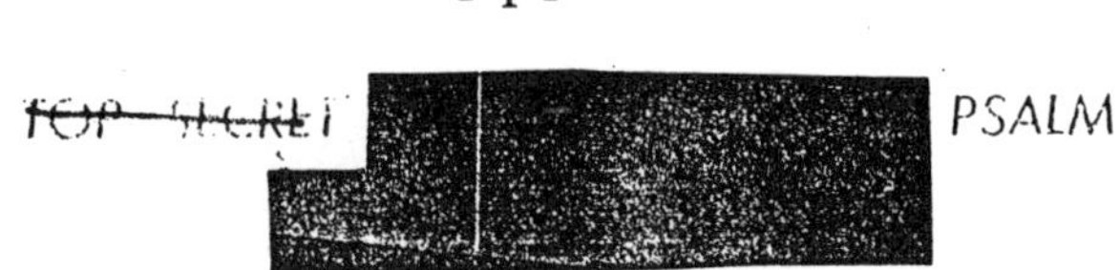

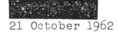

76. *Lundahl, Memorandum for Director of Central Intelligence and Director, Defense Intelligence Agency, "Additional Information—Missions 3111 and 3113," 21 October 1962*

21 October 1962

Copy ___

MEMORANDUM FOR: Director of Central Intelligence
Director, Defense Intelligence Agency

SUBJECT: Additional Information - Missions 3111 and 3113

1. A newly identified possible ▇▇▇ launch site, five previously reported MRBM launch sites and two IRBM launch sites were observed on Mission 3111. A newly identified confirmed MRBM launch site was located on Mission 3113.

2. The newly identified unimproved field type MRBM launch site is located 2.7 nm NNW of Candelaria at 22°47'45"N 82°58'40"W in the San Cristobal area. The site contains two tent areas totalling 26 tents and at least 60 vehicles. Seven missile trailers and two missile erectors were identified at the site.

3. The possible launch site under construction is located 5 nm SW of Remedios at 22°25'N 79°35'E. It consists of paired trench-like excavations 450 feet apart, clearing for a possible control bunker, an arched building, a tent camp and motor pool and a concrete batch plant. At three of the four excavations there are 10 to 12 precast hollow concrete objects.

4. A description of the three MR site areas in the San Cristobal area follows: MR Site 1 - The seven canvas covered missiles are now draped with netting and three of the four erectors are canvas covered. MR Site 2 - The six missiles and three erectors are parked in a common area. MR Site 3 - Cloud cover prevents a complete analysis; however, one erector and possibly two others are observed.

5. The Sauga La Grande area MR Site 4 consists of four launch positions, two containing erectors and six canvas covered missiles on trailers and MR Site 5 consists of four erectors on pads and four canvas covered missiles on trailers.

76. *(Continued)*

TOP SECRET  PSALM

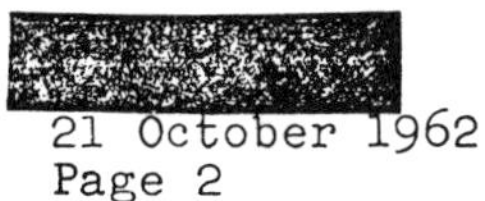

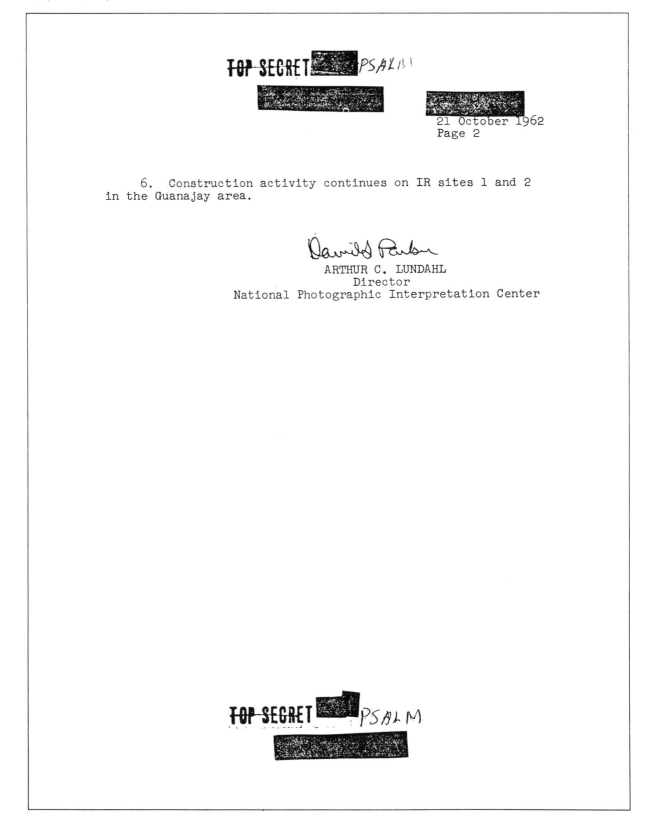

21 October 1962
Page 2

6. Construction activity continues on IR sites 1 and 2 in the Guanajay area.

David S. Parker
ARTHUR C. LUNDAHL
Director
National Photographic Interpretation Center

TOP SECRET PSALM

77. *THK [Thomas H. Karamessines] to [Walter] Elder, 22 October 1962, with copies of two cables sent to all Chiefs of Station*

EK

22 October 1962

~~EYES ONLY~~

Executive Registry

EC 62-7738

Mr. Elder:

Attached are copies of the cables Mr. Karamessines discussed with you yesterday. They have been sent to all Chiefs of Stations with some minor variations to cover local conditions.

THK (JMA)
for THK

~~EYES ONLY~~

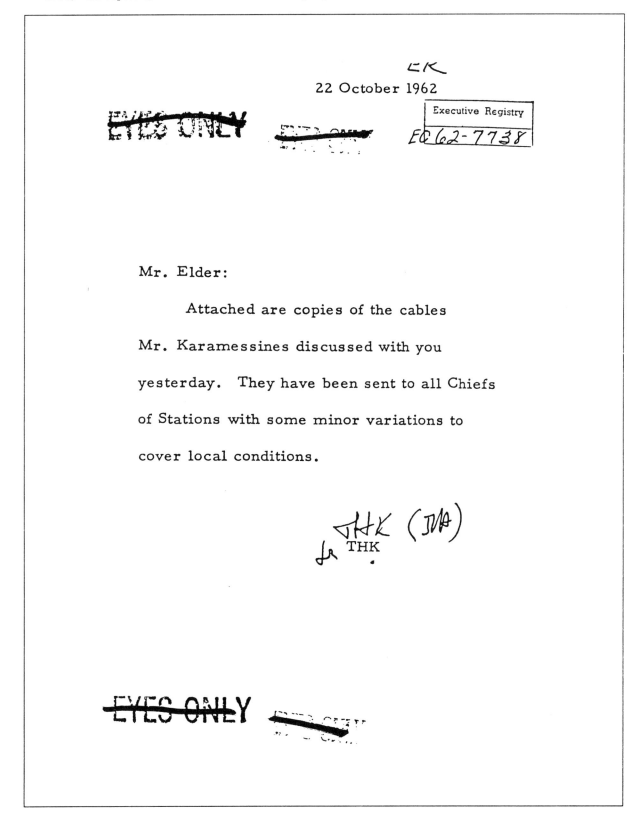

77. *(Continued)*

SECRET

IN CONNECTION WITH CERTAIN INSTRUCTIONS WHICH STATE'S [redacted] CHIEF OF MISSION YOUR AREA MAY RECEIVE SUNDAY 21 OCTOBER OR SHORTLY THEREAFTER, YOU ARE REQUESTED TO BE STANDING BY AS OF THAT TIME. CANCEL ANY OTHER PLANS FOR BEING ABSENT FROM STATION.

NATURE AND DETAILS OF STATE'S [redacted] INSTRUCTION NOT YET AVAILABLE BUT OBVIOUSLY WOULD DEAL WITH MATTER OF URGENCY. THEREFORE DO NOT DISCUSS THIS REQUEST WITH ANYONE OTHER THAN YOUR CHIEF OF MISSION.

77. *(Continued)*

SECRET

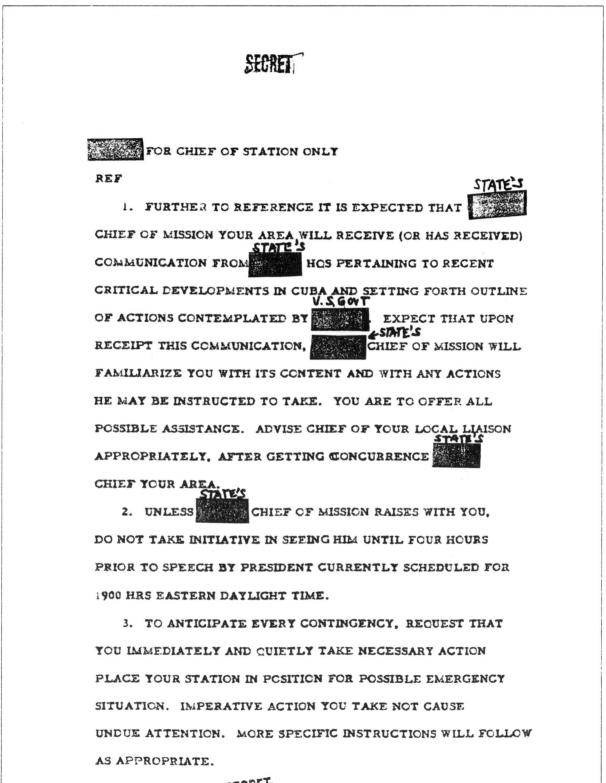

[redacted] FOR CHIEF OF STATION ONLY

REF

1. FURTHER TO REFERENCE IT IS EXPECTED THAT [STATE'S] CHIEF OF MISSION YOUR AREA WILL RECEIVE (OR HAS RECEIVED) COMMUNICATION FROM [STATE'S] HQS PERTAINING TO RECENT CRITICAL DEVELOPMENTS IN CUBA AND SETTING FORTH OUTLINE OF ACTIONS CONTEMPLATED BY [U.S. GOVT]. EXPECT THAT UPON RECEIPT THIS COMMUNICATION, [STATE'S] CHIEF OF MISSION WILL FAMILIARIZE YOU WITH ITS CONTENT AND WITH ANY ACTIONS HE MAY BE INSTRUCTED TO TAKE. YOU ARE TO OFFER ALL POSSIBLE ASSISTANCE. ADVISE CHIEF OF YOUR LOCAL LIAISON APPROPRIATELY, AFTER GETTING CONCURRENCE [STATE'S] CHIEF YOUR AREA.

2. UNLESS [STATE'S] CHIEF OF MISSION RAISES WITH YOU, DO NOT TAKE INITIATIVE IN SEEING HIM UNTIL FOUR HOURS PRIOR TO SPEECH BY PRESIDENT CURRENTLY SCHEDULED FOR 1900 HRS EASTERN DAYLIGHT TIME.

3. TO ANTICIPATE EVERY CONTINGENCY, REQUEST THAT YOU IMMEDIATELY AND QUIETLY TAKE NECESSARY ACTION PLACE YOUR STATION IN POSITION FOR POSSIBLE EMERGENCY SITUATION. IMPERATIVE ACTION YOU TAKE NOT CAUSE UNDUE ATTENTION. MORE SPECIFIC INSTRUCTIONS WILL FOLLOW AS APPROPRIATE.

SECRET

78. *Central Intelligence Agency, Office of Current Intelligence, Current Intelligence Memorandum, "Timing of the Soviet Military Buildup in Cuba," 22 October 1962*

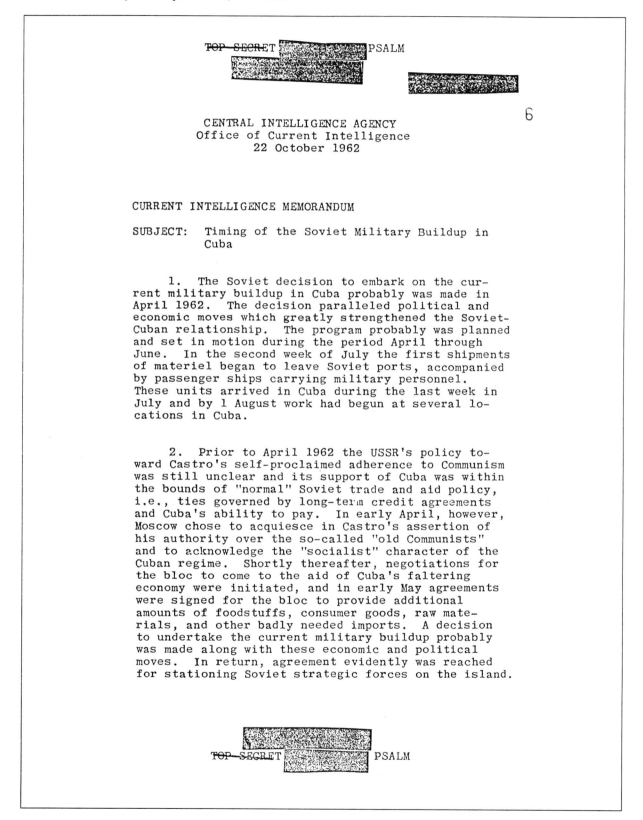

~~TOP SECRET~~ 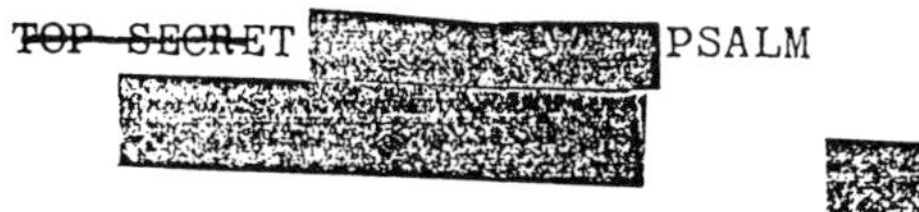 PSALM

6

CENTRAL INTELLIGENCE AGENCY
Office of Current Intelligence
22 October 1962

CURRENT INTELLIGENCE MEMORANDUM

SUBJECT: Timing of the Soviet Military Buildup in Cuba

1. The Soviet decision to embark on the current military buildup in Cuba probably was made in April 1962. The decision paralleled political and economic moves which greatly strengthened the Soviet-Cuban relationship. The program probably was planned and set in motion during the period April through June. In the second week of July the first shipments of materiel began to leave Soviet ports, accompanied by passenger ships carrying military personnel. These units arrived in Cuba during the last week in July and by 1 August work had begun at several locations in Cuba.

2. Prior to April 1962 the USSR's policy toward Castro's self-proclaimed adherence to Communism was still unclear and its support of Cuba was within the bounds of "normal" Soviet trade and aid policy, i.e., ties governed by long-term credit agreements and Cuba's ability to pay. In early April, however, Moscow chose to acquiesce in Castro's assertion of his authority over the so-called "old Communists" and to acknowledge the "socialist" character of the Cuban regime. Shortly thereafter, negotiations for the bloc to come to the aid of Cuba's faltering economy were initiated, and in early May agreements were signed for the bloc to provide additional amounts of foodstuffs, consumer goods, raw materials, and other badly needed imports. A decision to undertake the current military buildup probably was made along with these economic and political moves. In return, agreement evidently was reached for stationing Soviet strategic forces on the island.

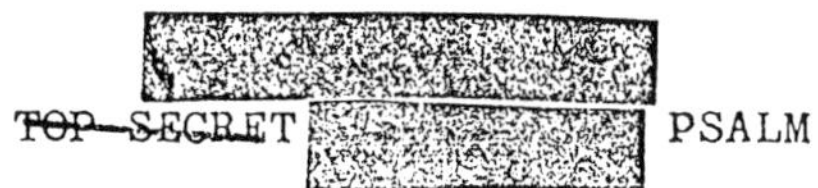

~~TOP SECRET~~ PSALM

3. The buildup in Cuba has been taking place in stages which can be distinguished reasonably well. The first deliveries of men and equipment arrived in late July, and through most of August they appear to have been primarily of equipment for SAM and coastal defense missile installations. Work started first in western Cuba and gradually spread throughout the island. Eight of the 12 Komar guided-missile boats were delivered in August, as well as some land armaments. We cannot determine precisely when the first equipment for MRBM/IRBM installations arrived, but available information suggests work on the first site began about 29 August and the first missiles of this kind probably arrived in the first half of September. Two top-level meetings between the Cubans and Khrushchev were held in this period; one when Raul Castro visited Moscow in July at the start of the shipments and one in late August - early September when Che Guevara traveled to tne USSR.

4. Since early September, military shipments probably have included equipment for all the missile installations as well as aircraft and land armaments. Most of the 39 or more MIG-21s arrived during the first week of September. Two shipments of IL-28 bombers--22 aircraft in all--appear to have arrived in late September, and a third shipment may be en route. There is no sign of a slowdown in the military shipments; about 20 Soviet vessels are en route with probable military cargoes, and one or two are leaving Soviet ports almost daily.

-2-

TOP SECRET [redacted] PSALM

79. *[Cline], "DDI notes for DCI for NSC Briefing at 3 PM in Cabinet Room," 22 October 1962*

~~TOP SECRET EYES ONLY~~

DDI notes for DCI for NSC Briefing at 3 PM in Cabinet Room

22 October 1962

Mr. President,

We have now read out the film from all missions flown over Cuba through Saturday 20 October (this means 17 missions between 14 and 20 October).

There is no evidence of new missile sites in Cuba since the report given to you at 2:30 p.m. yesterday.

Thus what we have seen to date completed or underway is still 24 launcher positions for Medium Range Ballistic Missiles (1,020 mile range) located at six base complexes, and 12 launch pads for Intermediate Range Ballistic Missiles (2,200 mile range), located at three bases -- a total of 36 launchers at nine separate bases.

~~TOP SECRET EYES ONLY~~

~~TOP SECRET EYES ONLY~~

As explained, we expect deployment of 2 missiles per launch position, but to date what we have actually seen are 30 and possibly 32 Medium Range Missiles. (We have not yet seen any Intermediate Range Missiles, although they may be in Cuba under cover or on the Soviet ship POLTAVA, which is due to arrive in Cuba in about five days, and is peculiarly arranged to carry long cylindrical items of cargo.)

The sites are in varying degrees of operational readiness. On the basis of latest evidence we now believe 4 MRBM sites (containing 16 launchers) are in full operational readiness as of today (22 October). We now estimate the remaining 2 MRBM sites (containing 8 additional launchers) will come into full operational readiness on 25 October/and 29 October respectively. These MRBM's are considered mobile; they are fired from a trailer bed type of launcher, and their location as now established

- 2 -

~~TOP SECRET EYES ONLY~~

might suddenly shift to a new location difficult to determine by surveillance.

The 3 IRBM sites (containing 12 launch pads) still seem likely to reach full operational readiness in December. However, emergency operational readiness of some of the IRBMs might be reached somewhat earlier.

Of the 24 primary surface-to-air missile sites in Cuba, we believe 22 are now operational.

The Soviet fleet support vessel, TEREK, is now in the Atlantic on a high-speed run from the Kola Inlet Northern Fleet Base near Murmansk in Russia. It could reach Cuba in four or five days. Its mission is unknown.

- 3 -

~~TOP SECRET EYES ONLY~~

80. *McCone, Memorandum for the File, "Leadership Meeting on October 22nd at 5:00 p.m.," 24 October 1962*

#46

24 October 1962

MEMORANDUM FOR THE FILE

SUBJECT: Leadership meeting on October 22nd at 5:00 p.m.

ATTENDED BY: The Leadership, except for Senator Hayden, The President, Rusk, McNamara, McCone and Ambassador Thompson

McCone read a summary of the situation, copy of which is attached. This statement had been discussed with the President, Attorney General and Bundy and had been modified to conform to their views.

There were a few questions of a substantive nature, Hickenlooper asking when missiles would be in operational status. McCone replied with the existing figures as reported in the morning report. Hickenlooper then asked if the Cuban situation is tied in to the China/India confrontation. McCone replied that we have no information one way or the other. Thompson ~~then/it was~~ indicated more probable that Cuba may force a showdown on Berlin.

Secretary Rusk then reviewed his current appraisal of the Soviet Union indicating there had been some radical moves within the USSR which were indicating a tougher line. It appeared the hard-liners are coming in to ascendency and the soft co-existent line seems to be disappearing. Peiping seems somewhat more satisfied with Moscow now. Rusk stated that he did not wish to underestimate the gravity of the situation; the Soviets were taking a very serious risk, but this in his opinion represents the philosophy of the "hard-liners". Russell questioned the Secretary as to whether things will get better in the future, whether we will have a more propitious time to act than now, the thrust of his questioning being, "Why wait". Rusk answered that he saw no opportunity for improvement.

The President then reviewed the chronology of the situation, starting on Tuesday, October 16th, when the first information was received from the photographic flight of October 14th. He stated

TOP SECRET ~~EYES ONLY~~

that he immediately ordered extensive overflights; that McCone briefed President Eisenhower; that we must recognise that these missiles might be operational and therefore military action on our part might cause the firing of many of them with serious consequences to the United States; furthermore the actions taken, and further actions which might be required, might cause the Soviets to react in various areas, most particularly Berlin, which they could easily grab and if they do, our European Allies would lay the blame in our lap. The President concluded whatever we do involves a risk; however we must make careful calculations and take a chance. To do nothing would be a great mistake. The blockade of Cuba on the importation of offensive weapons was to be undertaken, all ships would be stopped and those containing offensive weapons would not be permitted to proceed. We have no idea how the Bloc will react but the indications are, from unconfirmed sources, they will attempt to run the blockade. Initially the blockade would not extend to petroleum. This might be a further step. We are taking all military preparations for either an air strike or an invasion. It was the President's considered judgment that if we have to resort to active military actions, then this would involve an invasion. Rusk then stated that our proposed action gave the other side a chance to pause. They may pull back or they may rapidly intensify the entire situation existing between the Soviet Union and the United States.

Senator Russell then demanded stronger steps, stated he did not think we needed time to pause. The President had warned them in September and no further warning was necessary. We must not take a gamble and must not temporize; Khrushchev has once again rattled his missiles; he can become firmer and firmer, and we must react. If we delay, if we give notification, if we telegraph our punches, the result will be more a difficult military action and more American lives will be sacrifieed. The thrust of Senator Russell's remarks were to demand military action. He did not specifically say by surprise attack; however he did not advocate warning.

- 2 -

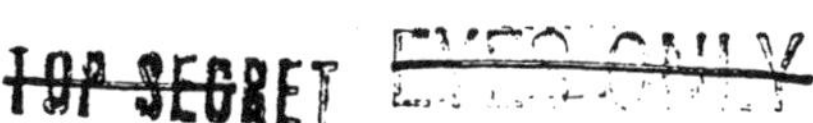

TOP SECRET EYES ONLY

McNamara then described the blockade, indicating that this might lead to some form of military action; that there would be many alternative courses open to us. The President then reviewed in some detail time required

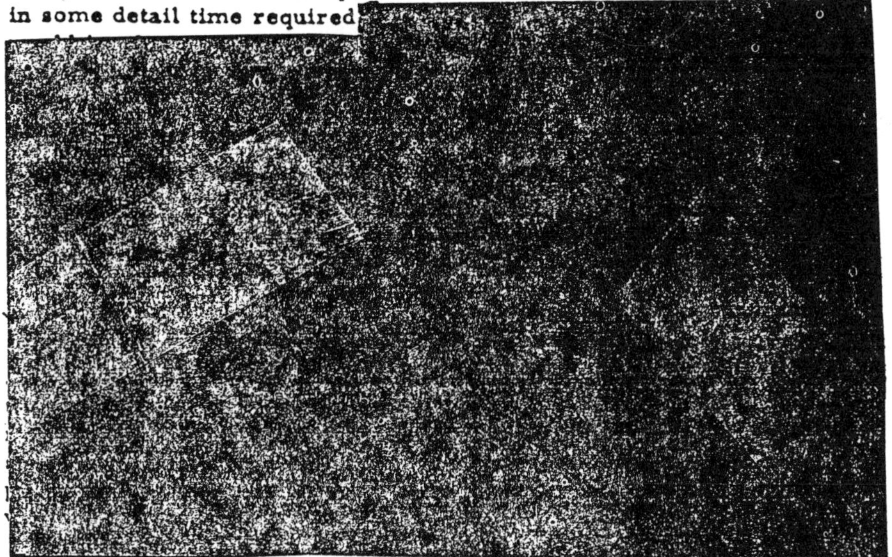

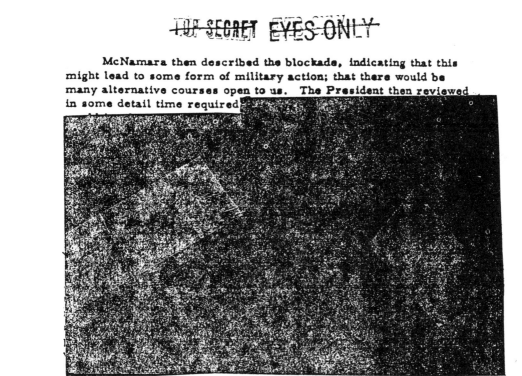

Vinson then asked if the Joint Chiefs of Staff actually approved the plans for the invasion. McNamara answered, "Yes." The plans had been developed over a 10-month period and had been submitted to the President by the JCS on a number of occasions.

NOTE: This question did not refer to whether the JCS did or did not approve the proposed actions of blockade against Cuba.

The President then reviewed matters again, read an intelligence note from a United Nations source which indicated Soviet intention to grab Berlin. Russell promptly replied that Berlin will always be a hostage. He then criticized the decision, stated we should go now and not wait.

Halleck questioned whether we were absolutely sure these weapons were offensive. The President answered affirmatively. McNamara then made a most unusual statement. He said, "One might question whether the missiles are or are not offensive. However there is no question about the IL 28s." NOTE: This was the first time anyone has raised doubt as to whether the MRBMs and the IRBMs are offensive missiles.

- 3 -

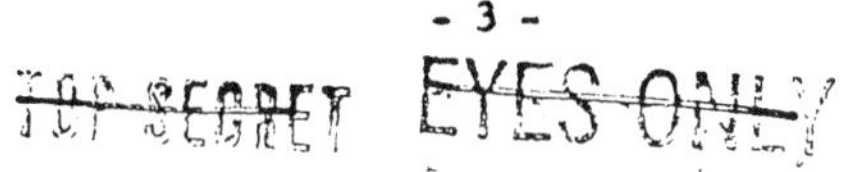

80. *(Continued)*

TOP SECRET EYES ONLY

Questions were then raised concerning the attitude of our Allies. The President advised steps taken to inform our major Allies. He then read the message received from the Prime Minister which in effect agreed to support us in the United Nations and then raised many warnings including the dangers to Berlin, Turkey, Pakistan, Iran, etc., etc.

Senator Saltonstall brought up the question of the legality of the blockade. A great many Senators expressed concern over the proposed action with the OAS, indicating that they felt the OAS would delay rather than act. Saltonstall then asked whether a blockade would be legal if the OAS did not support it. The President answered that it probably would not; however we would proceed anyway.

Fulbright then stated that in his opinion the blockade was the worst of the alternatives open to us and it was a definite affront to Russia and that the moment that we had to damage or sink a Soviet ship because of their failure to recognize or respect the blockade we would be at war with Russia and the war would be caused because of our own initiative. The President disagreed with this thinking. Fulbright then repeated his position and stated in his opinion it would be far better to launch an attack and to take out the bases from Cuba. McNamara stated that this would involve the spilling of Russian blood since there were so many thousand Russians manning these bases. Fulbright responded that this made no difference because they were there in Cuba to help on Cuban bases. These were not Soviet bases. There was no mutual defense pact between the USSR and Cuba. Cuba was not a member of the Warsaw Pact. Therefore he felt the Soviets would not react if some Russians got killed in Cuba. The Russians in the final analysis placed little value on human life. The time has come for an invasion under the President's statement of February 13th. Fulbright repeated that an act on Russian ships is an act of war against Russia and on the other hand, an attack or an invasion of Cuba was an act against Cuba, not Russia. Fulbright also expressed reservations concerning the possible OAS action.

The President took issue with Fulbright, stating that he felt that an attack on these bases, which we knew were manned by Soviet personnel, would involve large numbers of Soviet casualities and this would be more provocative than a confrontation with a Soviet ship.

- 4 -

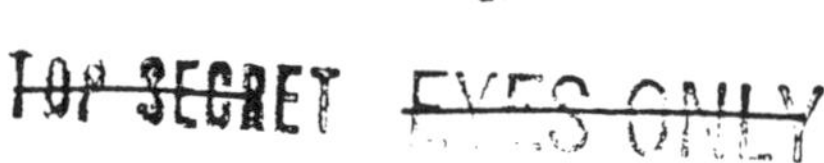

TOP SECRET ~~EYES ONLY~~

Vinson urged that if we strike, we strike with maximum force and wind the matter up quickly as this would involve the minimum of American losses and insure the maximum support by the Cuban people at large who, he reasoned, would very quickly go over to the side of the winner.

The meeting was concluded at 6:35 6o permit the President to prepare for his 7:00 o'clock talk to the nation.

It was decided to hold a meeting on Wednesday, October 24th. During this meeting Senator Hickenlooper expressed himself as opposed to the action and in favor of direct military action. He stated that in his opinion ships which were accosted on the high sea and turned back would be a more humiliating blow to the Soviets and a more serious involvement to their pride than the losing of as many as 5,000 Soviet military personnel illegally and secretly stationed in Cuba.

JOHN A. McCONE
Director

mfb

- 5 -

TOP SECRET ~~EYES ONLY~~

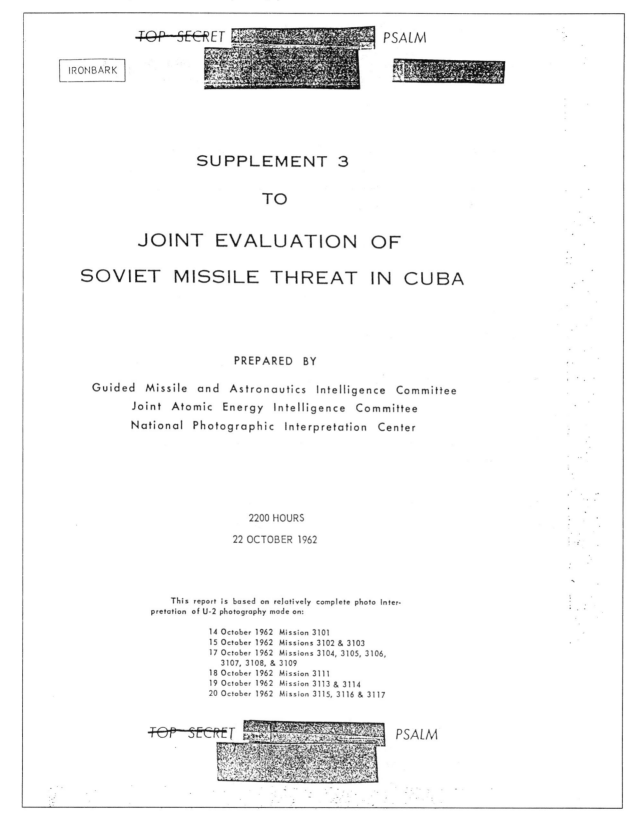

81. *Supplement 3 to Joint Evaluation of Soviet Missile Threat in Cuba, 22 October 1962 (Excerpt)*

~~TOP SECRET~~ PSALM

IRONBARK

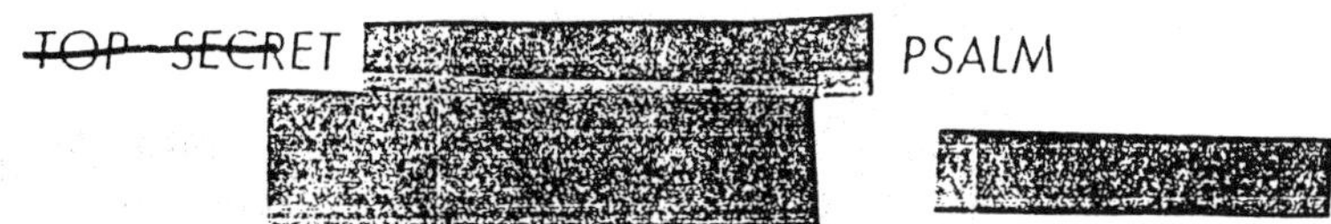

SUPPLEMENT 3

TO

JOINT EVALUATION OF

SOVIET MISSILE THREAT IN CUBA

PREPARED BY

Guided Missile and Astronautics Intelligence Committee
Joint Atomic Energy Intelligence Committee
National Photographic Interpretation Center

2200 HOURS

22 OCTOBER 1962

This report is based on relatively complete photo interpretation of U-2 photography made on:

14 October 1962 Mission 3101
15 October 1962 Missions 3102 & 3103
17 October 1962 Missions 3104, 3105, 3106, 3107, 3108, & 3109
18 October 1962 Mission 3111
19 October 1962 Mission 3113 & 3114
20 October 1962 Mission 3115, 3116 & 3117

~~TOP SECRET~~ PSALM

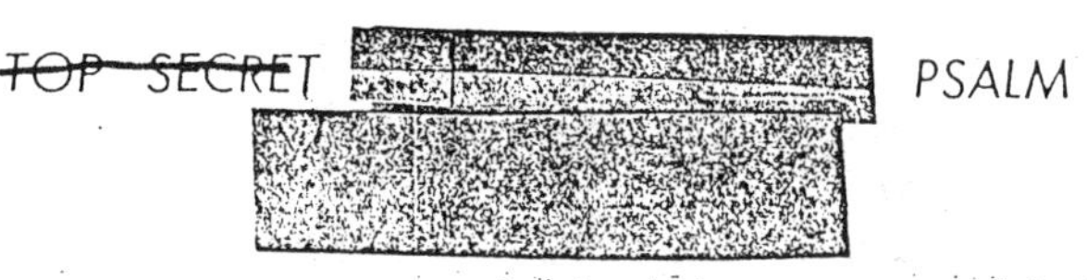

81. *(Continued)*

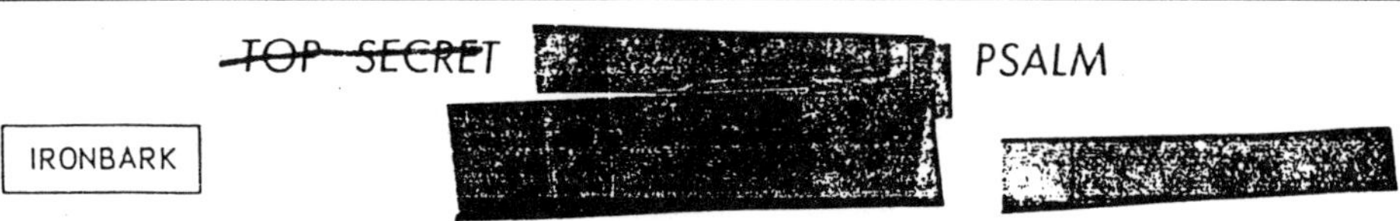

NOTICE

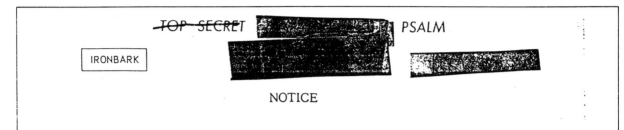

This supplement up-dates and amplifies previous reports. Emphasis continues to be placed on the READINESS status of the offensive missiles in Cuba. This report is based on photographic coverage through Mission 3117 of 20 October 1962. (See Figure 1)

SUMMARY

1. There are no changes in the estimates of operational readiness for the nine offensive missile sites. (See Figure 2)

2. No new missile sites have been identified.

3. The observed missile and launcher count is increasing as estimated. Three additional MRBMs and four additional MRBM launchers raise the totals to 33 missiles and 23 launchers. No IRBMs have been identified. (See Table 1)

4. One additional SAM site is now considered operational, bringing the total individually operational sites to 23 of the 24 active sites so far identified. (See Table 2)

5. No new intelligence information has been received which modifies the nuclear storage situation since the last joint supplement.

- 1 -

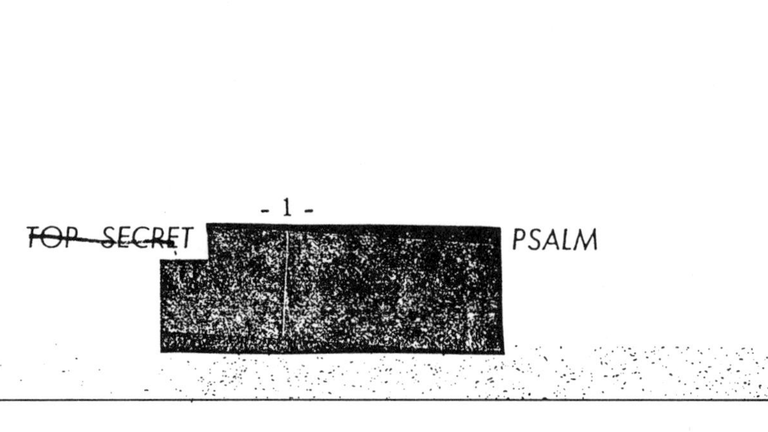

82. *McCone, "Memorandum of Meeting of Executive Committee of the NSC, 10:00 a.m., October 23, 1962"*

23 October 1962

MEMORANDUM OF MEETING OF EXECUTIVE COMMITTEE OF THE NSC. 10:00 a.m., October 23, 1962

PRESENT: The President, Vice President, Secty. McNamara, Secty. Gilpatric, Gen. Taylor, Mr. Bundy, Secty. Ball, Secty. Johnson, Amb. Thompson, Attorney General, DCI

1. McCone gave a brief intelligence report as covered by the attached documents. (Descriptive note attached). Lundahl displayed the most recent photographs and a map showing 97 per cent coverage of the island.

2. Robert Kennedy stated that the question had been raised as to why the situation was not reported earlier, what was wrong with our intelligence. It was agreed that the rapidity with which the MRBM site construction took place, and other events took place, accounted for the suddenness of the findings and that the leadership and selected press should be contacted privately.

Action: DCI was requested to contact Fulbright, Russell, Vinson, Halleck, Dirksen, and Hickenlooper, and for the press, Alsop, Krock and David Lawrence.

3. McNamara raised questions of when blockade proclamation will be issued, become effective, and discussed plans for the intercept of the first ship which would be the Kimovsk. It was decided that if OAS acted on Tuesday, the proclamation would be issued, effective Wednesday morning, October 24. Probably the first intercept would be made on that day.

4. The President discussed the program, defending the steps taken, stated earlier action would not have been supported and would not have shut off the possibility of missiles, emphasized that mobile missiles ca[n] come in at any time and be set up rapidly.

5. McNamara discussed several military actions, including extension of tours of duty of Navy and Marine Corps personnel, and these were approved.

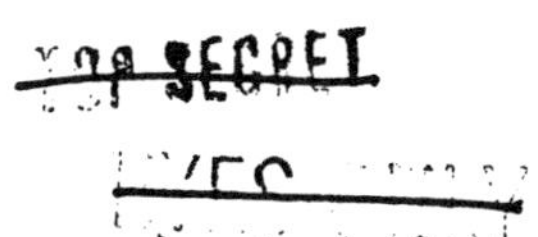

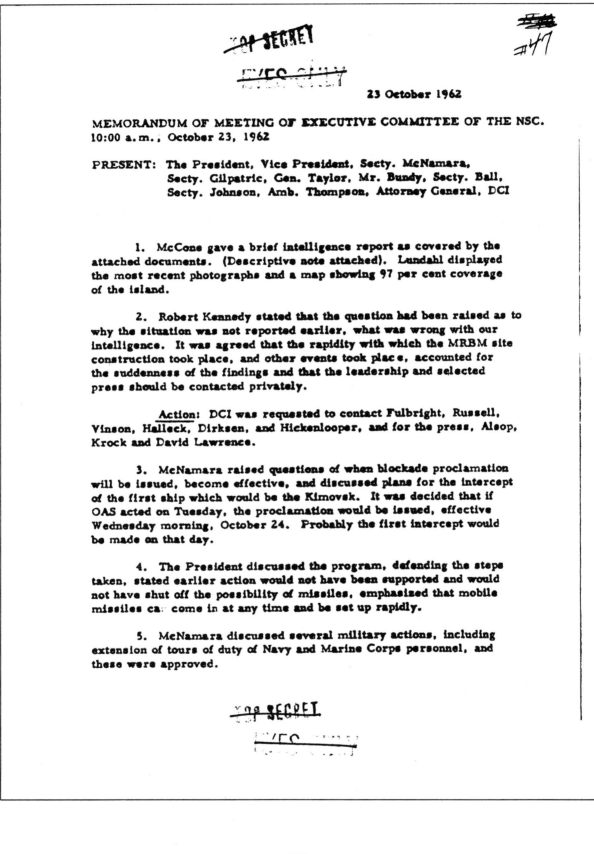

6. McNamara then raised question of reaction to firing on a U-2, indicated pilots instructed to take evasive action. It was decided that we would be immediately informed through JCS to the Secretary of Defense and a prompt decision for retaliation would then be made by the President. Taylor reported eight attack aircraft are maintained in hot alert and can destroy SAM sites within two hours or approximately the time that the U-2 would get back if the attack on it failed. McNamara confirmed that air-sea rescue was continuing. It was decided that if the President was not available, McNamara would have authority to act.

Action: General Taylor agreed that he would take up and confirm today CIA request that our representatives be stationed with JCS planning staff and in the Flag Plot and in the JCS War Room. If there is any delay on this please inform me so that I can again communicate with Taylor.

7. McNamara noted that they had no air intercept capability and would not attempt at this time to develop their plan of air intercept.

Action: It was requested that CIA and Defense carefully analyze air traffic and report currently so that if there is a marked build-up, the Committee will be advised and appropriate action can be taken.

8. McNamara then presented the need for shipping, indicating between 125 and 130 Merchant ships were needed to support an invasion and that a few had been chartered as of yesterday. He felt perhaps 20 more could be secured promptly, but this would leave about 100 short, and this would involve extensive requisitioning. McCone pointed out the serious consequences to American business, inter-coastal and coast-wise shipping, the Northwest lumber industry, et cetera, et cetera. McCone suggested consideration be given to taking foreign flag ships on a bare boat basis. Defense was asked to explore the possibility of temporary waiver of laws regulating operation of foreign flag ships, et cetera, et cetera.

9. McCone and McNamara raised the question of low level flights.

Action: Six flights were approved and General Taylor ordered them off immediately. It was presumed that they will return not later than 1:00 o'clock today.

EYES ONLY

- 2 -

TOP SECRET

<u>Action</u>: <u>It is very important that NPIC and DCI's office receive prints at earliest moment. DDCI to follow. Also important that if the photography is productive of new and more convincing information, prints should be sent to Governor Stevenson at once.</u>

10. The President raised question of security of our own air fields in Florida during surprise strafing, etc. McNamara and Gilpatric assumed responsibility.

11. After a brief discussion of communications Bundy stated that subject under study by Dr. Wiesner, and urged State, Defense and CIA communications specialists to contact Wiesner.

<u>Action</u>: Following meeting McCone, Wiesner, Smith and Edwards met and reviewed the CIA Latin American communication system. Subject left for further discussion today.

<u>Action</u>: This whole communication problem is to be followed up energetically by CIA with Wiesner and all appropriate actions taken.

12. Secretary Ball reported Governor Stevenson and Mr. McCloy felt they did not have enough information to make a convincing case before the UN Security Council. They requested (1) a large map marked in color, showing the actual locations of a few of the sites, possibly one MRBM site, one IRBM site and one or two air fields; (2) pictures of the sites showing progressive construction with dates indicated; (3) indication, but not necessarily the numbers, of all of the sites; (4) a pre-May 1, 1960 U-2 picture of the Soviet MRBM/IRBM site to show similarity.

<u>Action</u>: The Committee left matter of disclosure to McCone, despatch of Lundahl and Cline to New York for discussions, and assistance in developing Stevenson's scenario. McCone authorized items one, two and three above but refused item 4. Also agreed transmit low-level product to Stevenson if same useful.

13. Bundy explained idea of creating a staff to support the Committee indicating each member should have a working staff member, details to be worked out later.

<u>Action</u>: DDCI should consider appropriate assignment after conferring with State and Defense and determining their nominees. This will be more or less full time and this staff man can handle Agency representation and also support me.

JAM/at/mfb

John A. McCone
Director

- 3 -

~~TOP SECRET~~

83. *McCone, Memorandum for the File, "Meetings with Mr. Krock, Mr. David Lawrence, and Mr. Scott," 23 October 1962*

~~TOP SECRET~~ ~~EYES ONLY~~

MR 104

October 23, 1962

MEMORANDUM FOR THE FILE

SUBJECT: Meetings with Mr. Krock, Mr. David Lawrence, and Mr. Scott

At 12:40 Mr. Arthur Krock called at my office at my invitation. I reviewed the situation generally with him, answering questions concerning the background of the decisions, the arguments in favor of the course of action versus a blockade coupled with the political debate on the one hand and surprise military action on the other. Krock seemed in general agreement with the course of action.

At 5:00 o'clock at my invitation Mr. David Lawrence and Mr. Scott called at my office and I reviewed the situation with them. They questioned me concerning the evidence and I showed them several pictures which they accepted as convincing evidence. They questioned me in considerable detail as to why we did not know this sooner, how Keating got his information and the penetration of intelligence activities during the months of August and September. I explained the situation substantially as outlined to the leadership at their meeting. I felt that neither was convinced and that both attached some "other motive" to the timing. However, they did recognize that MRBM sites can be installed quickly and with very little advanced preparation which can be detected. Both gentlemen questioned me at considerable length as to why Administration spokesmen spoke so categorically that the build-up was purely defensive and that no offensive capability was being installed. They were concerned about repeated statements by the President, Chester Bowles, the Vice President and other Administration spokesmen, but most particularly the State Department briefing held on Thursday, October 18th, which was two or three days after the original data was in our hands, at which time the briefers again repeated the statement that the "build-up involved defensive and no offensive weapons." They said they thought this briefing was a deceptive mistake and wondered why the briefing was carried on.

~~TOP SECRET~~ ~~EYES ONLY~~

83. *(Continued)*

~~TOP SECRET~~ ~~EYES ONLY~~

I inadvertently met with Mr. Scott of the Scott/Allen combination who accosted me as I headed Senate Office Building. He said, "McCone, I guess we're going to have to blow you out of this (waters) for not reorganizing your estimating processes, most particularly your Board of National Estimates. In answer to my question as to why, he said, "On October the 4th, the Board put out a National Estimate which has served to guide our government in its policy and this Estimate stated that the Soviets would not install offensive missiles in Cuba as doing so would constitute a change in policy on their part and would confront them with problems all over the world which they, the Soviets did not wish to face at this time." Scott said that he felt that such an Estimate was reckless, it did not serve the Government in establishing policy, and it was a frightful disservice to the people of the United States. He said this was just another example of how the CIA estimating processes were not objective and served special interests. Hence, he said, they were going to prepare an article and expose the whole situation to the public. I merely stated I knew nothing about any such estimate.

ACTION: Scott apparently has read the latest Cuban estimate published about September 20th, which contains wording as quoted above. Source of his information is unknown. I feel Grogan should talk with him and perhaps I should talk with him also.

NOTE: In my discussions with all the above people, Congressional and Press, I have been forced to defend the Executive Branch of the Government and CIA against the questions (1) why did we not know about this sooner and (2) did we not estimate or forecast this eventuality.

JOHN A. MC CONE

84. *McCone, Memorandum for the File, "Meetings with Senator Russell, Senator Hickenlooper, and Chairman Vinson," 23 October 1962*

#108

~~TOP SECRET~~ ~~EYES ONLY~~

October 23rd, 1962

MEMORANDUM FOR THE FILE

SUBJECT: Meetings with Senator Russell, Senator Hickenlooper, and Chairman Vinson

1. At the President's request I contacted several members of the leadership of the Congress with the following results. In a meeting on ~~August~~ October 23rd, Senator Russell indicated a less critical attitude toward Administration policy than was evident at the leadership meeting the night before. He in general approved the plan of actions, indicating strong reservations concerning the effectiveness and the utility of the blockade, expressed serious concern over the Soviet/U.S. confrontation which would result from the blockade, and accepted the course of action only because it would lead to the next phase which would be that of taking the missiles and offensive weapons out of Cuba at a time and by means of our own determination. Russell favored more positive action against Cuba which would involve not only air strike but invasion. In the initial part of the discussion he felt the President's speech had not established a clear-cut right for military action; however, by careful reference to the speech (a copy of which I had with me) he agreed that the wording did give the President right of action without further notification. In general, Russell's attitude was considerably different than the leadership meeting and might be summed up as reserved approval.

During the conversation, I outlined my feelings that our purposes must be to remove the missiles and also to remove Castro as is outlined in a separate memorandum,

2. Senator Hickenlooper approved the speech, the action, and the anticipated further action without reservation. He expressed confidence in the President as did Senator Russell but serious reservations concerning some of the President's advisors who he felt would influence the President to follow a very weak and compromising line. However, it appeared to me that Hickenlooper was greatly relieved by the speech and more satisfied with our Cuban policy than was evident at the leadership meeting.

~~TOP SECRET~~ ~~EYES ONLY~~

TOP SECRET EYES ONLY

3. Chairman Vinson stated that he thought the speech was good. He approved it but he had concluded that military action would be necessary and this he heartily approved. Vinson feels that we must dispose of the Castro problem as well as the missiles. In this regard, I outlined my feelings as covered by separate memorandum. Vinson tended to review the activities of the Navy with Admiral Anderson and others, insisting that we must be sure that we are going to do enough, that our blockade is going to be effective, and that if we invade, we must invade with great force, an assured victory, quick victory, otherwise Cuban resistance will be rallied and our casualties will be great. He stated that 250,000 men would be not enough, that it would take 500,000 men; that we should land at at least 10 or more points in Cuba at one time, and if we did this, the entire Cuban population would come to our side.

Note: Both Vinson and Russell were very inquisitive as to the position of the Joint Chiefs. I explained this as expressed by Taylor, pointing out that their position of a sudden unannounced military strike was reasonable in view of their responsibilities, however, it must also be recognized that civilians with broader responsibilities, i.e. military and political as well, necessarily had to moderate the JCS view. I stated that I felt the JCS view would insure the most successful military operations with the least American losses but that I opposed it and felt that the military handicaps resulting from our course of action (in military operations) must be reverted to, can be overcome by increase in the weight of the military operation. None of the three felt that we should have undertaken a surprise attack; however, Russell in particular felt that a warning and a following military operation might have been preferable to the blockade. I pointed out that the warning now had been given and action could be taken now "at a time of our own choosing and by means of our own determination" and after again reviewing the wording of the speech, Russell agreed this was correct.

JOHN A. MC CONE

JAM/mfb

TOP SECRET EYES ONLY

85. *McCone, Memorandum for the File, "Executive Committee Meeting on 23 October 1962, 6:00 p.m."*

TOP SECRET ~~EYES ONLY~~ #48

23 October 1962

MEMORANDUM FOR THE FILE

SUBJECT: Executive Committee Meeting on 23 October 1962 6:00 p.m. All members present plus Counsel for Defense Department

1. Committee reviewed the blockade proclamation and approved it. It was signed by the President at 6:00 p.m.

2. The President instructed McNamara to review all details of instructions to the Fleet Commanders regarding procedures to be followed in the blockade. There was an extended discussion of actions to be taken under various assumed Soviet resistance activities such as (a) failing to stop, (b) refusing right to board, (c) ships turning around, heading in another direction, etc.

3. Discussion of the effect on U.S. industry by chartering and preempting the use of 20 or 30 American ships. Gilpatric reported that this would have little or no effect on the American economy. McCone questioned these findings; however Gilpatric said that this had been thoroughly studied and McCone's concerns as expressed at the morning meeting were unfounded. The Attorney General stated that it was within the law to use foreign bottoms, however decision was made to preempt U.S. bottoms and not worry about the consequences because they would not be serious.

4. The President urged that Norstad be retained at SHAPE during the period of crisis, perhaps until 1 February 63. He indicated Lemnitzer might be used as CINCEUR with Norstad remaining as SACEUR. Bundy stated that this is complicated as the two posts are so co-mingled that they really must be held by one man. Taylor raised question that if this was done it would hurt Lemnitzer's prestige. The President said that he felt that Norstad was so experienced and so capable and his judgment so sound, as evidenced by today's cable, copy of which I have not seen, that he would take the risk of NATO country criticisms, he did not think that Lemnitzer would be hurt, and he wished Norstad to remain. Defense to take under advisement and report within 24 hours.

4. In the prolonged discussion of report on Civil Defense problems, the President seemed particularly concerned over the situation if we should launch attacks which might result in four or five missiles being delivered on the United States. DOD spokesmen stated that the area covered by the 1100 mile missiles involved 92 million people. They felt that fall-out space was available though

TOP SECRET ~~EYES ONLY~~

~~TOP SECRET~~ ~~EYES ONLY~~

not equipped for about 40 million. The President asked what emergency steps could be taken. Replied that many arrangements could be made without too much publicity, such as repositioning food, actually obtaining space, putting up shelter signs, etc. I got the conclusion that not very much could or would be done; that whatever was done would involve a great deal of publicity and public alarm.

Prior to the departure of Secretary McNamara at approximately 7:00 o'clock, McCone (who had not been called upon for an intelligence appraisal) stated to the President that he felt certain intelligence should be reported to the meeting prior to the departure of Secretary McNamara as some items observed by the Intelligence Community might prove of great significance.

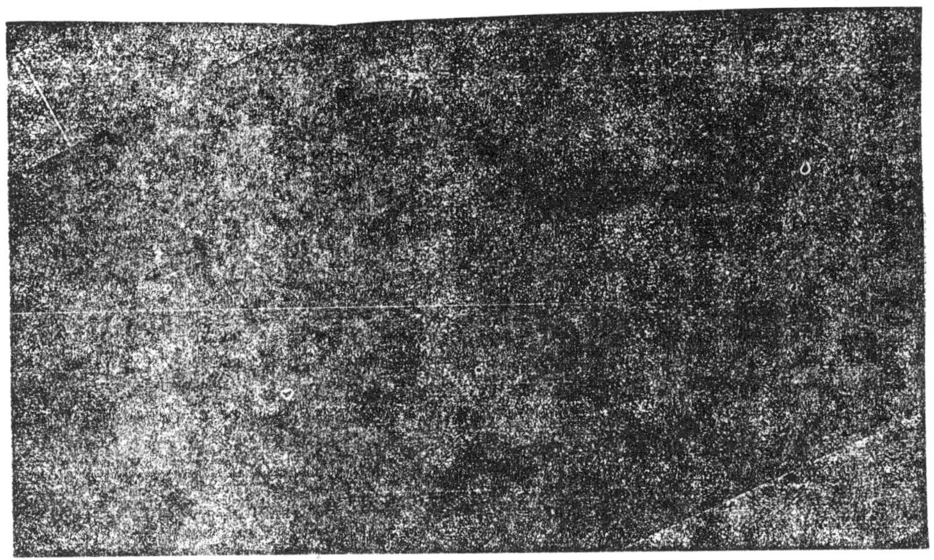

JOHN A. McCONE
Director

JAM/mfb

~~TOP SECRET~~ ~~EYES ONLY~~

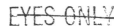

86. *Supplement 4 to Joint Evaluation of Soviet Missile Threat in Cuba, 24 October 1962 (Excerpt)*

TOP SECRET

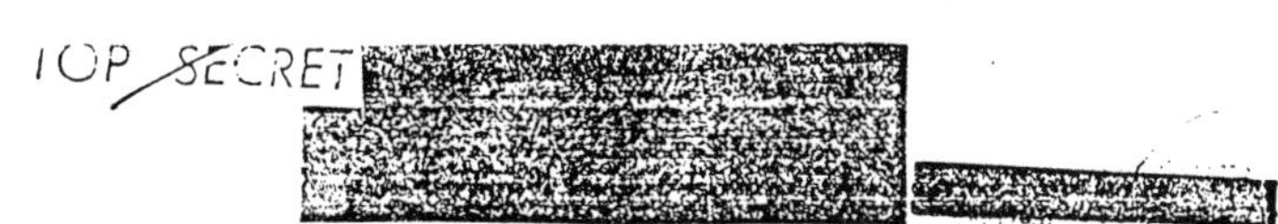

IRONBARK

SUPPLEMENT 4
TO
JOINT EVALUATION OF SOVIET MISSILE THREAT IN CUBA

PREPARED BY

Guided Missile and Astronautics Intelligence Committee
Joint Atomic Energy Intelligence Committee
National Photographic Interpretation Center

0100 HOURS

24 OCTOBER 1962

This report is based on relatively complete photo interpretation of U-2 photography made on:

14 October 1962 Mission 3101
15 October 1962 Missions 3102 & 3103
17 October 1962 Missions 3104, 3105, 3106, 3107, 3108, & 3109
18 October 1962 Mission 3111
19 October 1962 Mission 3113 & 3114
20 October 1962 Mission 3115, 3116 & 3117
22 October 1962 Mission 3118 & 3119

and a very preliminary analysis of Mission 5002 of 23 October 1962 has been included.

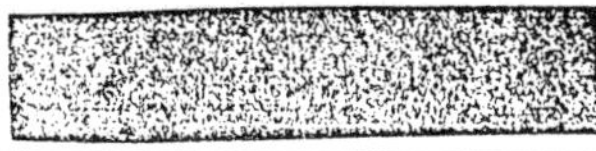

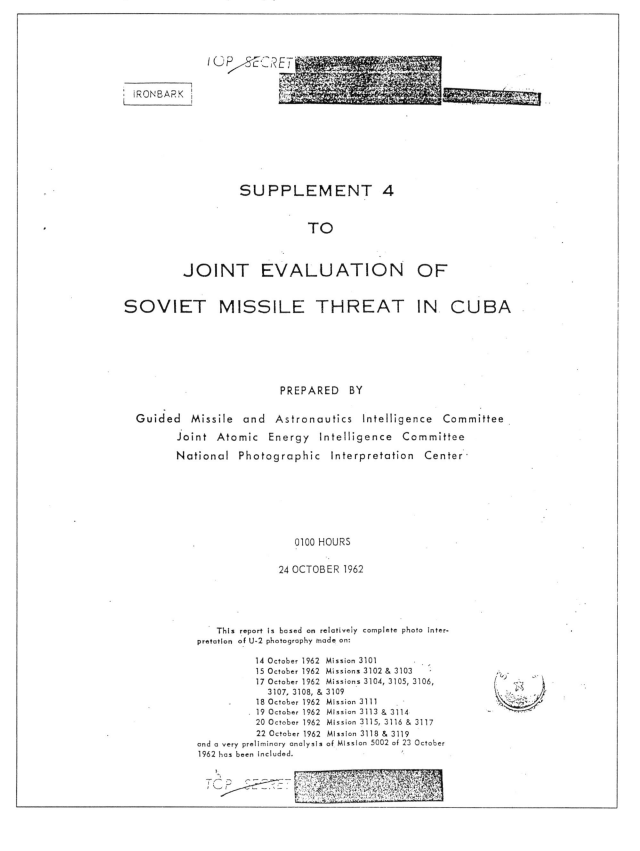

IRONBARK

NOTICE

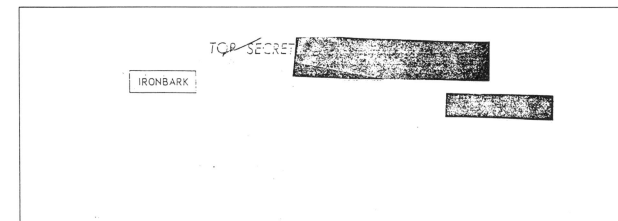

This supplement updates and amplifies previous reports. Emphasis continues to be placed on the READINESS status of the offensive missiles in Cuba. This report is based on U-2 photographic coverage through Mission 3119 of 22 October 1962 (see Figure 1). Some of Mission 5002, the low altitude photographic coverage of 23 October 1962, arrived during the preparation of this report and preliminary comments have been incorporated in the discussion of the Guanajay IRBM sites. Analysis has just started and will require many hours for completion.

SUMMARY

1. There are two changes in the estimated dates of full operational capability. San Cristobal MRBM Site 2 and Sagua La Grande MRBM Site 1 are now estimated to achieve this status on 25 October instead of 22 October as previously estimated.

2. No new missile sites have been identified (See Table 1).

3. No IRBMs per se have yet been identified.

4. Seven Soviet ships with cargo hatch openings of 75 feet or longer have now been identified as possible ballistic missile carriers. They have made 13 trips to Cuba to date, and three are currently enroute to Cuba.

5. No new intelligence information has been received which modifies the nuclear storage situation.

- 1 -

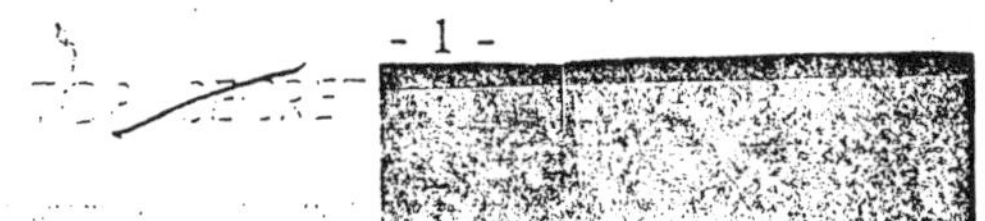

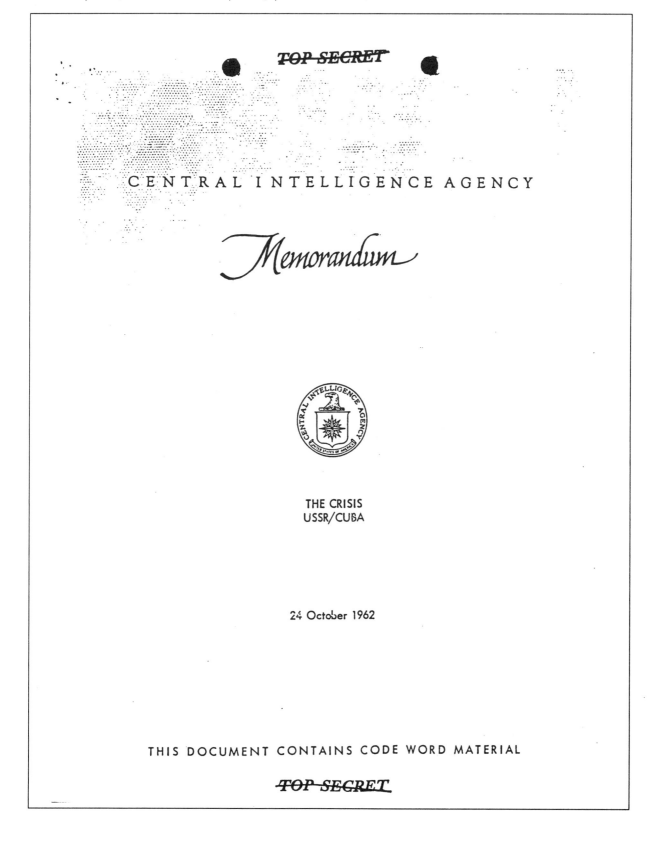

87. *Central Intelligence Agency Memorandum, "The Crisis, USSR/Cuba," 24 October 1962 (Excerpt)*

~~TOP SECRET~~

CENTRAL INTELLIGENCE AGENCY

THE CRISIS
USSR/CUBA

24 October 1962

THIS DOCUMENT CONTAINS CODE WORD MATERIAL

~~TOP SECRET~~

87. *(Continued)*

TOP SECRET 

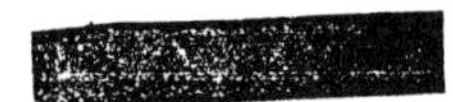

24 October 1962

SUMMARY CONTENTS

1. We do not believe the measures to achieve a higher degree of action readiness for Soviet and bloc forces are being taken on a crash basis. Communist reaction to the US quarantine action against Cuba has not gone beyond the highly critical but uncommitting statement issued yesterday by the Soviet government.

2. Surveillance of Cuba indicates continued rapid progress in completion of IRBM and MRBM missile sites. No new sites have been discovered. Buildings believed to afford nuclear storage are being assembled with great rapidity. Cuban naval units have been ordered to blocking positions at Banes and Santiago Bays.

3. Survey of Soviet shipping shows 16 dry cargo and 6 tanker ships en route to Cuba. Of these 22, nine are in positions which would permit arrival by the end of October. Three ships have hatches suitable for missile handling

4. Official world reaction shows a generally favorable response to the US action, particularly in Latin America. The OAS representatives approved a resolution endorsing the quarantine without opposition, one abstention was due to lack of instructions.

5. There are no indications of any Soviet aircraft movements to Cuba.

TOP SECRET 

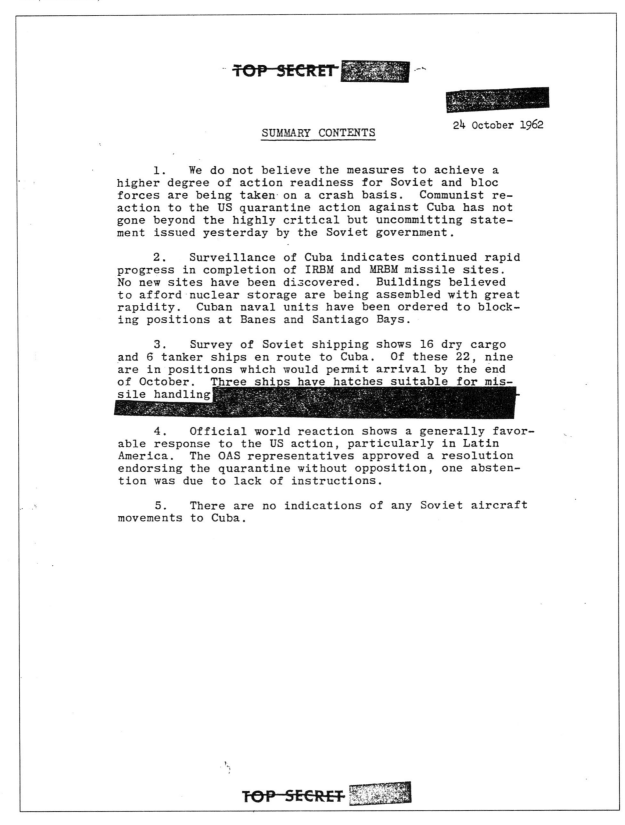

88. *McCone, Memorandum for the File, "Notes on Leadership Meeting on October 24th, 1962, at 5:00 p.m.," 25 October 1962*

October 25, 1962

MEMORANDUM FOR THE FILE

SUBJECT: Notes on Leadership Meeting on October 24th, 1962, at 5:00 p.m.

Attended by: Congressional Leadership (except Senator Hayden), the President, Rusk, McNamara, McCone and Robert Lovett.

McCone gave a brief intelligence summary, copy attached.

Secretary Rusk reported on the United Nations, stated there is no confirmed Soviet reaction or statement of intentions but discussed exchange with Bertrand Russell and dismissed this as unofficial. The President categorically stated on several occasions through the meeting there was no formal or informal direct approach for a Kennedy/Khrushchev meeting and no negotiations toward that end.

McNamara reported on military operations, stated that as of this hour there had been "no interceptions of Soviet ships; none were necessary." McNamara very carefully avoided any statements that ships had turned around. (Note: McNamara's statements were not consistent with reports that an intercept had been attempted at 10:35 a.m. with the KIMOVSK, and that the ship had turned around when confronted by a Navy vessel).

Mansfield spoke of the importance of confidential nature of the meeting, referring to Roland Evans' article in the Herald Tribune which summarized in accurate detail views of all who attended the prior meeting. It was the consensus that the discussions at leadership meetings must be kept most confidential.

Russell complimented Secretary Rusk on the unanimous OAS action and his unusually complimentary remarks were strongly supported by Dirksen, Hickenlooper and Mansfield.

Rusk then reported that Secretary General U Thant would issue a statement calling for a two-week moratorium. There was no conclusion as to the United States answer.

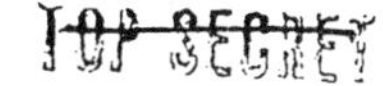

EYES ONLY

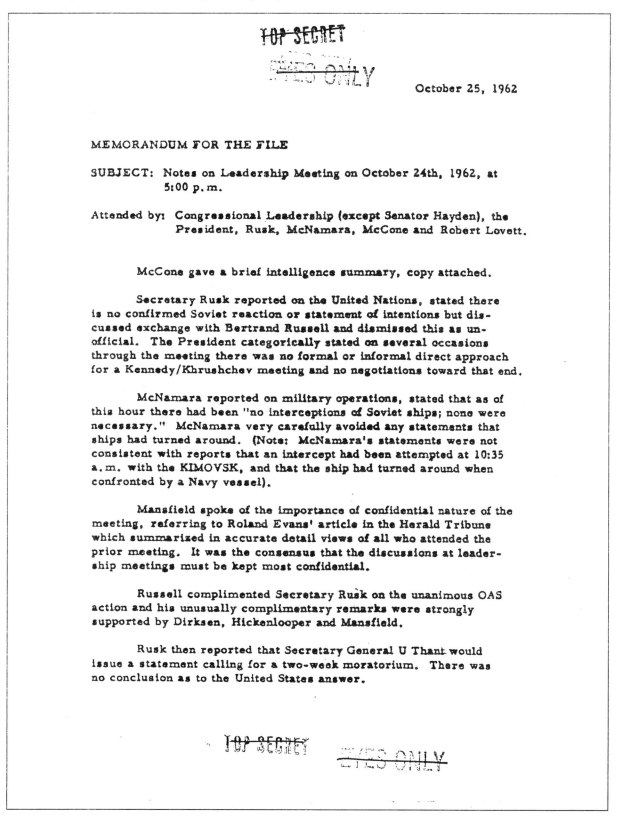

~~TOP SECRET~~ ~~EYES ONLY~~

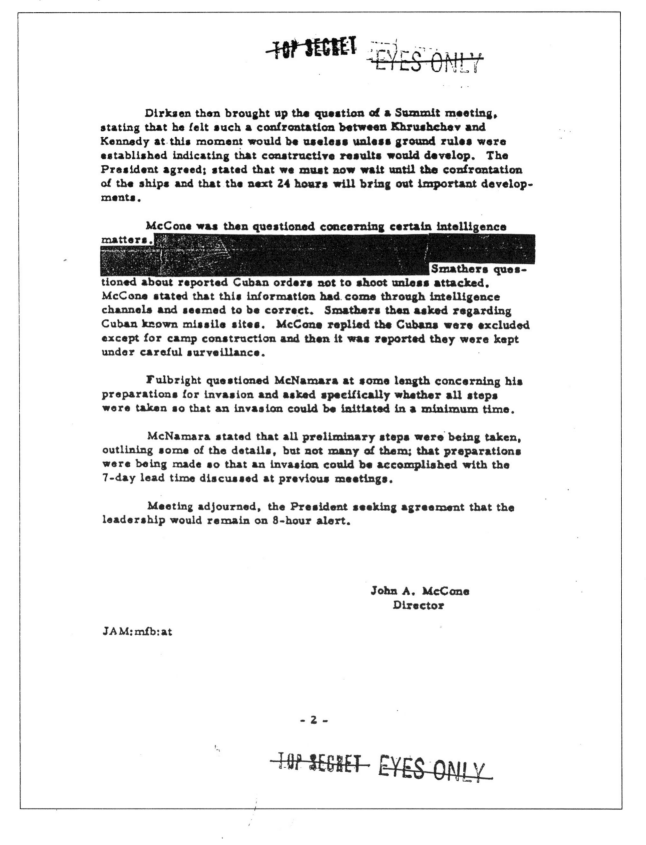

Dirksen then brought up the question of a Summit meeting, stating that he felt such a confrontation between Khrushchev and Kennedy at this moment would be useless unless ground rules were established indicating that constructive results would develop. The President agreed; stated that we must now wait until the confrontation of the ships and that the next 24 hours will bring out important developments.

McCone was then questioned concerning certain intelligence matters. [redacted] Smathers questioned about reported Cuban orders not to shoot unless attacked. McCone stated that this information had come through intelligence channels and seemed to be correct. Smathers then asked regarding Cuban known missile sites. McCone replied the Cubans were excluded except for camp construction and then it was reported they were kept under careful surveillance.

Fulbright questioned McNamara at some length concerning his preparations for invasion and asked specifically whether all steps were taken so that an invasion could be initiated in a minimum time.

McNamara stated that all preliminary steps were being taken, outlining some of the details, but not many of them; that preparations were being made so that an invasion could be accomplished with the 7-day lead time discussed at previous meetings.

Meeting adjourned, the President seeking agreement that the leadership would remain on 8-hour alert.

John A. McCone
Director

JAM:mfb:at

- 2 -

~~TOP SECRET~~ ~~EYES ONLY~~

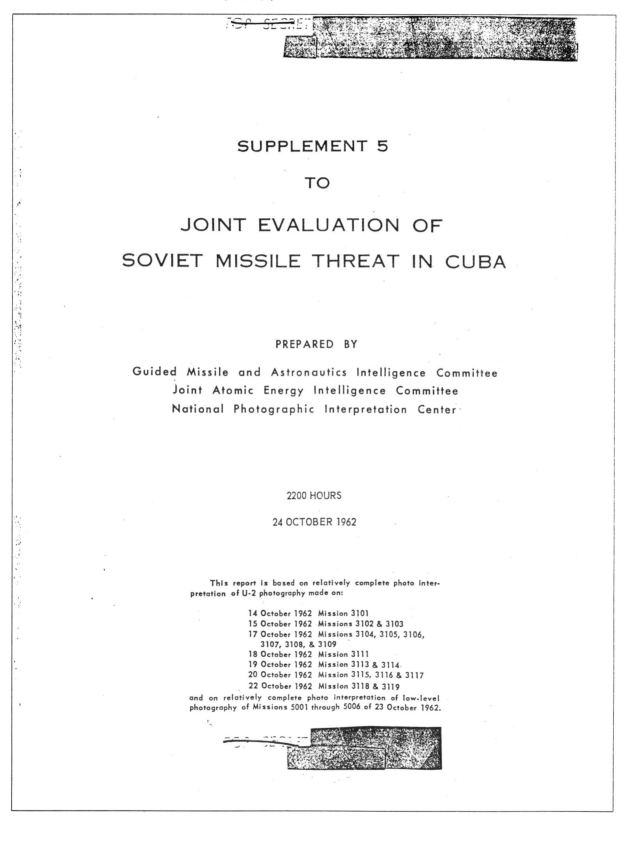

89. *Supplement 5 to Joint Evaluation of Soviet Missile Threat in Cuba, 24 October 1962 (Excerpt)*

TOP SECRET

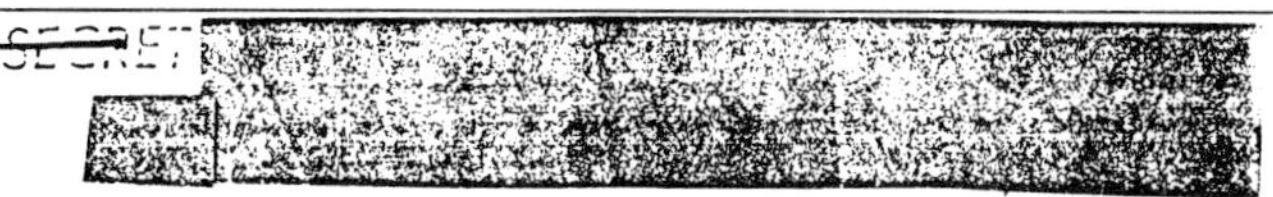

SUPPLEMENT 5

TO

JOINT EVALUATION OF SOVIET MISSILE THREAT IN CUBA

PREPARED BY

Guided Missile and Astronautics Intelligence Committee
Joint Atomic Energy Intelligence Committee
National Photographic Interpretation Center

2200 HOURS

24 OCTOBER 1962

This report is based on relatively complete photo interpretation of U-2 photography made on:

14 October 1962 Mission 3101
15 October 1962 Missions 3102 & 3103
17 October 1962 Missions 3104, 3105, 3106, 3107, 3108, & 3109
18 October 1962 Mission 3111
19 October 1962 Mission 3113 & 3114
20 October 1962 Mission 3115, 3116 & 3117
22 October 1962 Mission 3118 & 3119

and on relatively complete photo interpretation of low-level photography of Missions 5001 through 5006 of 23 October 1962.

TOP SECRET

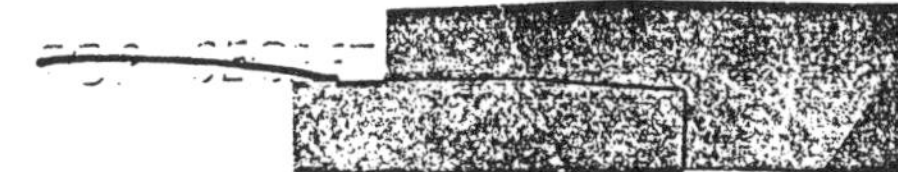

89. *(Continued)*

TOP SECRET 

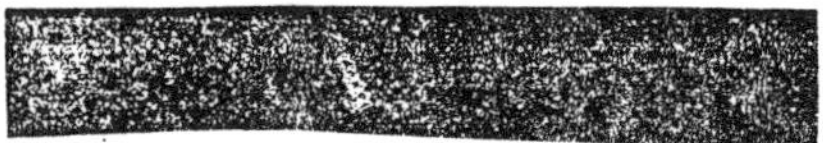

NOTICE

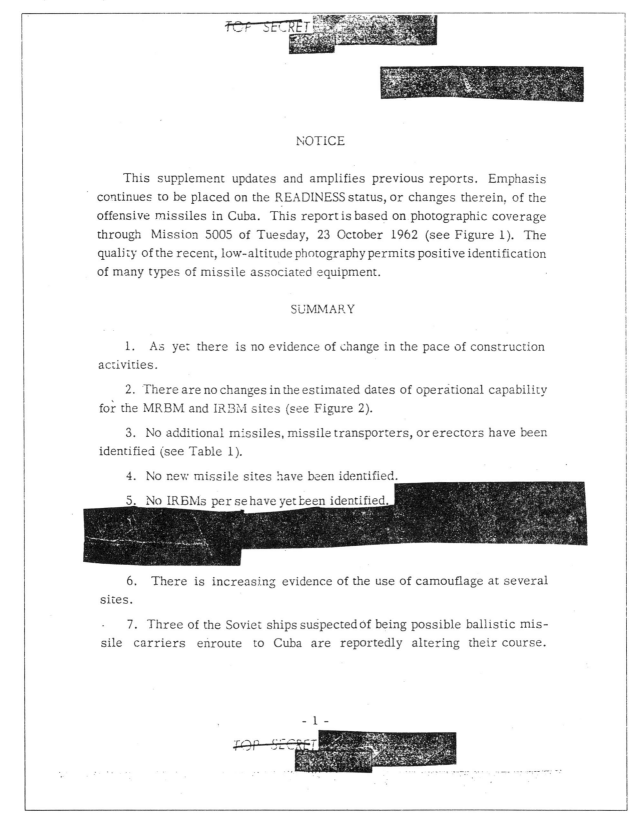

This supplement updates and amplifies previous reports. Emphasis continues to be placed on the READINESS status, or changes therein, of the offensive missiles in Cuba. This report is based on photographic coverage through Mission 5005 of Tuesday, 23 October 1962 (see Figure 1). The quality of the recent, low-altitude photography permits positive identification of many types of missile associated equipment.

SUMMARY

1. As yet there is no evidence of change in the pace of construction activities.

2. There are no changes in the estimated dates of operational capability for the MRBM and IRBM sites (see Figure 2).

3. No additional missiles, missile transporters, or erectors have been identified (see Table 1).

4. No new missile sites have been identified.

5. No IRBMs per se have yet been identified. 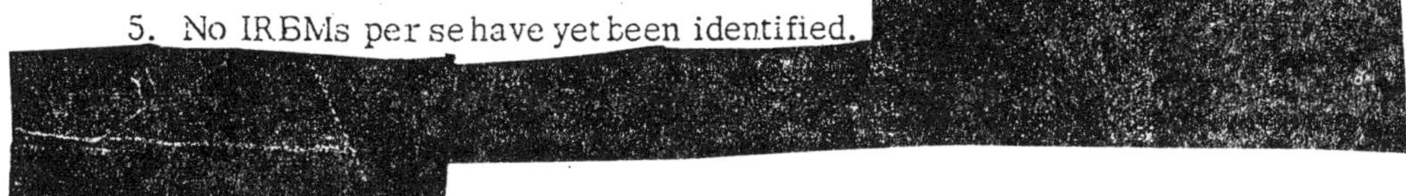

6. There is increasing evidence of the use of camouflage at several sites.

7. Three of the Soviet ships suspected of being possible ballistic missile carriers enroute to Cuba are reportedly altering their course.

- 1 -

TOP SECRET 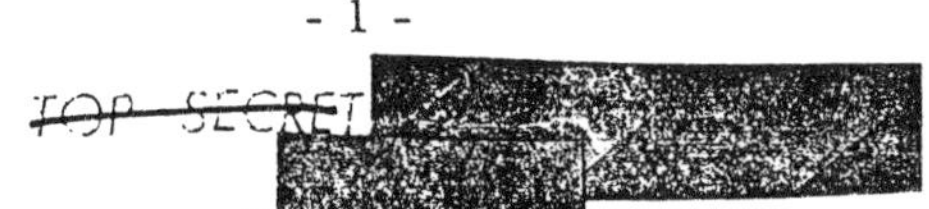

TOP SECRET 

8. We have analyzed the capability of the Soviets to transport nuclear warheads for these missiles from the USSR to Cuba using submarines and aircraft. While submarine transport is possible, air transport is more likely. A TU-114 can fly non-stop from Olenya in the Soviet Union to Cuba with up to 10 nuclear warheads on an approximate great circle route which would not pass over any other country.

9. New, low-altitude photography of 23 October confirms previous estimates of the general characteristics and rate of construction of the probable nuclear warhead bunkers at several sites. We are at this time unable to determine whether these bunkers are for storage or checkout of nuclear warheads, or for both of these functions.

- 2 -

TOP SECRET 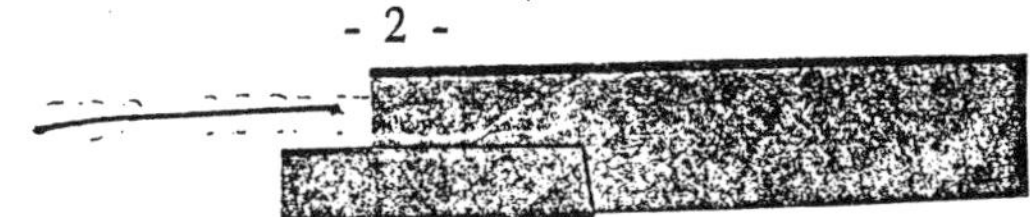

90. *Central Intelligence Agency Memorandum, "The Crisis, USSR/Cuba," 25 October 1962 (Excerpt)*

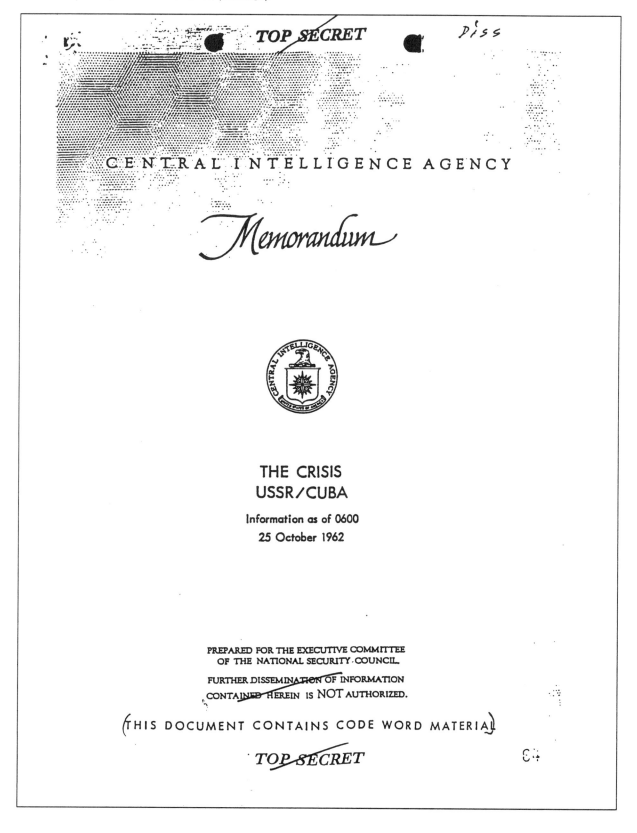

TOP SECRET

Diss

CENTRAL INTELLIGENCE AGENCY

Memorandum

THE CRISIS
USSR/CUBA

Information as of 0600
25 October 1962

PREPARED FOR THE EXECUTIVE COMMITTEE
OF THE NATIONAL SECURITY COUNCIL

FURTHER DISSEMINATION OF INFORMATION
CONTAINED HEREIN IS NOT AUTHORIZED.

(THIS DOCUMENT CONTAINS CODE WORD MATERIAL)

TOP SECRET

90. *(Continued)*

~~TOP SECRET~~ 

25 October 1962

SUMMARY CONTENTS

I. No change has been noted in the scope or pace of the construction at the IRBM and MRBM missile sites in Cuba. Cuban armed forces continue their alert, with military aircraft on standdown since the morning of 23 October. There are indications that known and suspected dissidents are being rounded up.

II. As of 0600 EDT at least 14 of the 22 Soviet ships which were known to be en route to Cuba had turned back. Five of the remaining eight are tankers. Two of the dry cargo ships not known to have reversed course may be carrying non-military cargo, but the BELOVODSK [redacted] has 12 HOUND helicopters. Changes in course appear to have been executed in midday on 23 October, before the President signed the proclamation establishing the quarantine.

III. We still see no signs of any crash procedure in measures to increase the readiness of Soviet armed forces. Bloc media are playing up Khrushchev's 24 October statement that he would consider a top-level meeting "useful."

IV. There is as yet no reaction to the turn-around of Soviet shipping, which had not become publicly apparent. Attention remains centered on neutralist efforts in the UN to find machinery for easing tension. Canada has searched a Cubana airliner flying from Prague to Havana. Latin American countries are beginning to offer military units for the quarantine, and there is generally little adverse reaction in the hemisphere.

~~TOP SECRET~~ 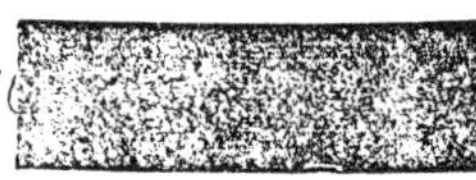

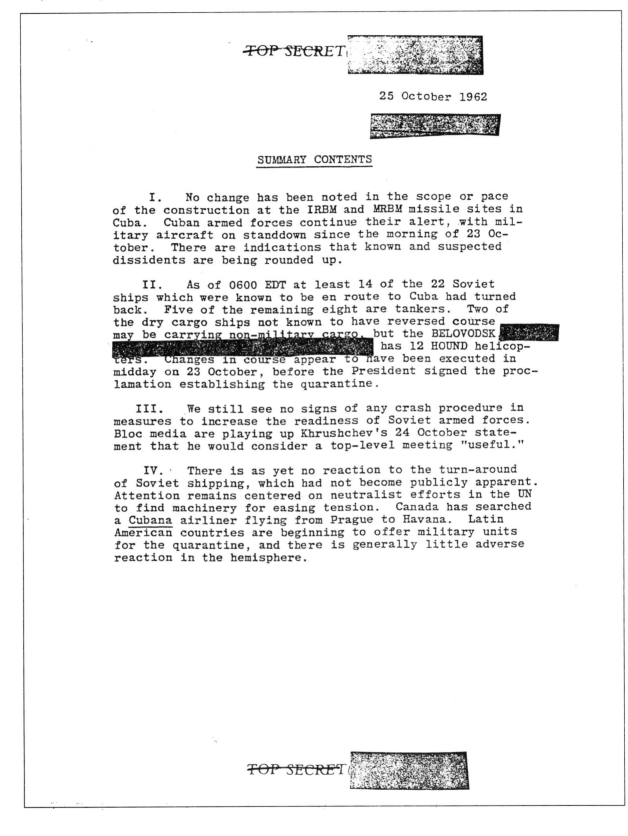

91. *McCone, Memorandum for the File, "Executive Committee Meeting 10/25/62—10:00 a.m."*

~~TOP SECRET~~

#50

October 25, 1962

MEMORANDUM FOR THE FILE

SUBJECT: Executive Committee Meeting 10/25/62 -- 10:00 a.m.
All Members present.

McCone reported on intelligence, reviewing summary of 25 October, including penciled memorandums as indicated, plus Cline memorandum of 25 October on talks with Sir Kenneth Strong, and the Watch Report of same date.

I called special attention to the BELOVODSK and reported on Page II-5 and the searching of the Cubana airplane by Canadians as reported on page IV-2. Also the shipping schedule.

McNamara reported that at 7:00 o'clock a destroyer intercepted the tanker BUCHAREST which responded destination was Havana, cargo was petroleum and the BUCHAREST was permitted to proceed under surveillance. He stated that no United States Navy ships had orders to board. He recommended orders be issued to immediately board Bloc ships and then the BUCHAREST be boarded. Decision was reached that Navy be instructed to board the next Soviet ship contacted which would be the GROZNY, a tanker but which was carrying a deck load which might be missile field tanks. Later in the meeting decision was reached not to board the BUCHAREST. Contact was to be made with the GROZNY as early as possible and that was estimated to be about 8:00 o'clock in the evening, Friday, October 26th.

~~TOP SECRET~~

McCone then noted the number of ships in the Eastern Atlantic and in the Baltic and Mediterranean which had turned back. Dillon asked about ships in the Pacific. The President asked whether Soviet ships bound elsewhere than Cuba had changed course. McCone said he would report on this in the afternoon.

There was a further discussion of the policy of stopping or hailing non-Bloc ships. It was decided that all ships must be hailed.

Rusk raised the question of discussions with the United Nations. Draft of U.S. reply to the U Thant letter was approved with modifications. It was agreed at the meeting that we must insist upon the removal of missiles from Cuba in addition to demands that construction be stopped and that UN inspectors be permitted at once.

Bundy reviewed Khrushchev letter to the President of the 24th of October and the Kennedy reply. McNamara raised the question of accelerating or raising the escalation of the actions we have so far taken, expressing concern over the plateau, indicating determination to meet our ultimate objective of taking out the missile sites.

- 2 -

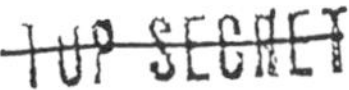

~~TOP SECRET~~

Rusk then asked certain actions on the part of CIA as follows: (1) An answer to questions of the effect on Cuba because ships were turned about as indicated in recent reports; (2) What had happened to Soviet ships which were bound elsewhere than Cuba; (3) The general Cuban reaction to our actions to date:

(a) Do they know about Soviet missiles?

(b) Have they heard the President's speech?

(c) What is the morale in Cuba?

McCone promised answers.

John A. McCone
Director

JAM:mfb:at

- 3 -

~~TOP SECRET~~

92. *McCone, Memorandum for the File, "Meeting of the NSC Executive Committee, 25 October, 5:00 p.m.," 26 October 1962*

~~TOP SECRET~~

Chons

26 October 1962

MEMORANDUM FOR THE FILE

SUBJECT: Meeting of the NSC Executive Committee, 25 October, 5:00 P.M.

ALL MEMBERS PRESENT

McCone gave intelligence briefing covered by Situation Report of 10/25 and followed with resume of Bloc shipping (SC 11064/62) dated 10/25 and summarized answers to specific questions as indicated on the third page; also referred briefly to [redacted] reaction to the Soviet government statement.

There followed a long discussion of policy matters, notes of which are covered in the attached.

The meeting considered three drafts of scenarios of three possible courses of action, that is, air strike, the political path and progressive economic blockade, all of which are attached.

JOHN A. McCONE
Director

Attached:
Two pages of notes on small White House note paper
Situation Report 10/25 - 3 pages
SC 11064/62
Canadian Reaction (OCI 3569/62
Draft: Scenario for Airstrike; Political Path; Progressive Economic Blockade

JAM/mfb

~~TOP SECRET~~

93. *MSC [Carter], Memorandum for the Director, "MONGOOSE Operations and General Lansdale's Problems," 25 October 1962*

~~SECRET~~

25 October 1962

MEMORANDUM FOR THE DIRECTOR

SUBJECT: MONGOOSE Operations and General Lansdale's Problems

1. You asked me to give you a paper by 5:00 p.m. today on the San Roman/Attorney General/Harvey/Lansdale/MONGOOSE problem in connection with submarines and the 50-Cuban project. I have talked only to Bill Harvey but in the light of my prior knowledge of Special Group/MONGOOSE/Lansdale/voice level, etc., it is my clear opinion that this whole problem is centered around jurisdictional bureaucracy not unlike the tangle I had with Gilpatric and the Air Forces.

2. Lansdale feels badly cut out of the picture and appears to be seeking to reconstitute the MONGOOSE Special Group operations during this period of impending crisis. I need not tell you that Lansdale's organization and the MONGOOSE concept of clearing actions through Special Group is an impossible procedure under current circumstances.

3. The deliberative MONGOOSE system was not utilized for this particular project. Harvey rightly realized that intelligence collection was essential and that it should be geared to a turnover of the assets to the military in place in the event military operations took place. It was this requirement that generated the need for submarines and the need for the 50-odd Cubans. General Johnson of the JCS Staff was knowledgeable and General Lansdale was subsequently informed and assisted in obtaining the submarines. The detailed planning is still going on but cannot be firm until the submarine commanders are available. The Cubans are not owned by San Roman but have been recruited and checked out by CIA and in a number of cases have been CIA agents for a long time. Unfortunately San Roman, like other exile group leaders, is looking out for the future of San Roman.

~~SECRET~~

SECRET

- 2 -

4. The targets planned for this operation as have been previously indicated to you, are to include the MRBM and IRBM sites. This is pure intelligence collection and the establishment of intelligence assets in place. It is being closely coordinated with the JCS Planning Staff and Lansdale knows about it. It obviously cannot be planned, controlled, and operated through the cumbersome procedures of MONGOOSE and therefore it is not in MONGOOSE channels.

5. I am convinced that if we are to have military operations in Cuba, and even now during this doubtful period of heavy military involvement in planning for such operations, the direct CIA-JCS coordinated liaison and control must be effected -- the time has long since passed for MONGOOSE-type, Special Group-type consideration.

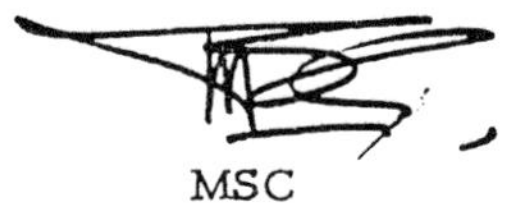

MSC

SECRET

94. *Supplement 6 to Joint Evaluation of Soviet Missile Threat in Cuba, 26 October 1962 (Excerpt)*

~~TOP SECRET~~

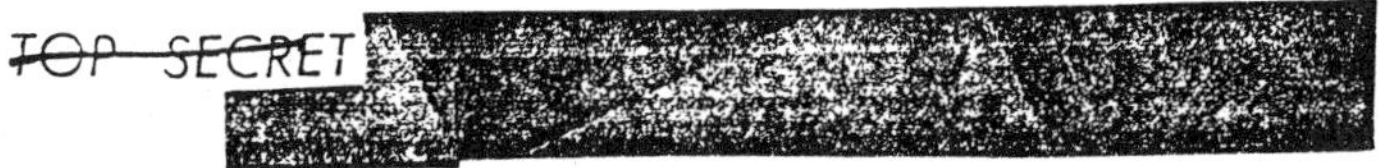

SUPPLEMENT 6

TO

JOINT EVALUATION OF

SOVIET MISSILE THREAT IN CUBA

PREPARED BY

Guided Missile and Astronautics Intelligence Committee
Joint Atomic Energy Intelligence Committee
National Photographic Interpretation Center

0200 HOURS

26 OCTOBER 1962

This report is based on relatively complete photo interpretation of U-2 photography made on:

14 October 1962 Mission 3101
15 October 1962 Missions 3102 & 3103
17 October 1962 Missions 3104, 3105, 3106, 3107, 3108 & 3109
18 October 1962 Mission 3111
19 October 1962 Missions 3113 & 3114
20 October 1962 Missions 3115, 3116 & 3117
22 October 1962 Missions 3118, 3119 & 3120
23 October 1962 Missions 3121, 3122, 3123, & 5002, 5003, 5004, 5005 & 5006
25 October 1962 Mission 3125

and preliminary analysis of low-altitude photography of Missions 5007, 5008, 5009, 5011, 5012, 5013, 5014, 5015 & 5016.

~~TOP SECRET~~

~~TOP SECRET~~

NOTICE

This supplement updates and amplifies previous reports. Emphasis is placed on the READINESS status, construction pace and any significant changes at the offensive missile sites in Cuba. This report is based primarily on preliminary analysis of the 25 October low-altitude photography, portions of which arrived during the preparation of this report (see Figure 1).

SUMMARY

1. The 25 October photography of four MRBM sites shows continued rapid construction activity at each site. This activity apparently continues to be directed toward achieving a full operational capability as soon as possible. Camouflage and canvas covering of critical equipment is also continuing. As yet there is <u>no</u> evidence indicating any intention to move or dismantle these sites.

2. There is one change in the estimated dates of operational capability. San Cristobal MRBM Site 2 is estimated to achieve a full operational capability on 26 October instead of 25 October, probably as a result of the heavy rain that has recently hit this site (see Figure 2).

3. No additional missiles, missile transporters, or erectors have been identified (see Table 1).

4. No new missile sites have been identified, although continued analysis of previous photography has revealed some road improvement activity in the Remedios area which is considered indicative of plans for the second IRBM site estimated for this area.

5. The three Soviet ships suspected of being possible ballistic missile carriers continue their eastward course towards the USSR.

- 1 -

~~TOP SECRET~~

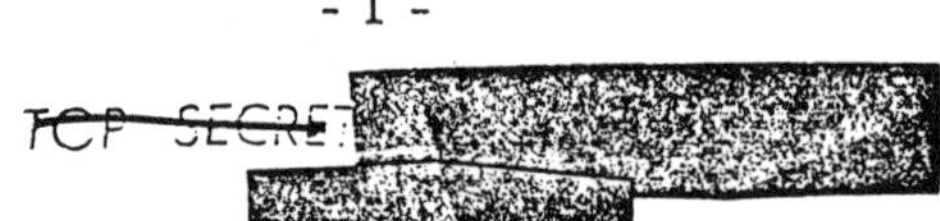

95. *Central Intelligence Agency Memorandum, "The Crisis, USSR/Cuba," 26 October 1962 (Excerpt)*

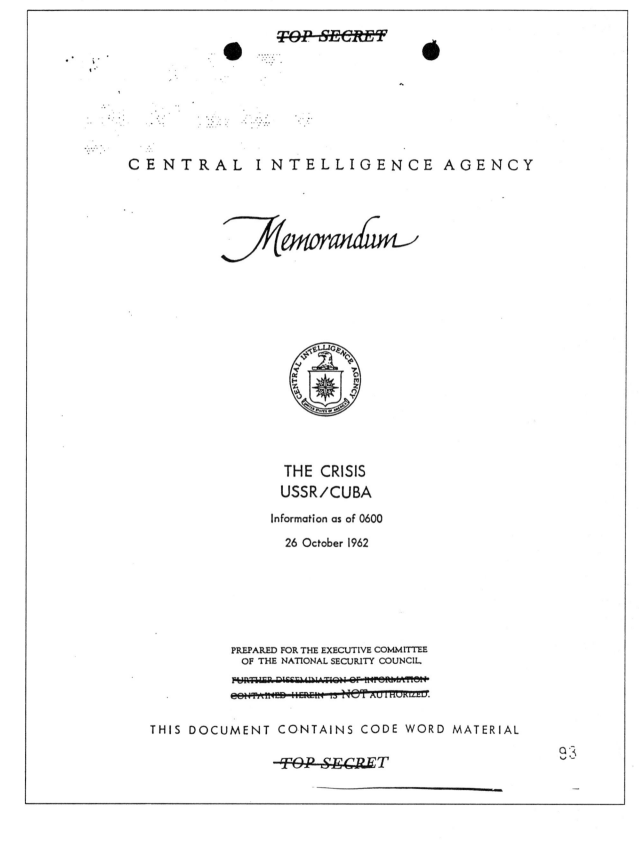

~~TOP SECRET~~

CENTRAL INTELLIGENCE AGENCY

THE CRISIS
USSR/CUBA

Information as of 0600

26 October 1962

PREPARED FOR THE EXECUTIVE COMMITTEE
OF THE NATIONAL SECURITY COUNCIL

~~FURTHER DISSEMINATION OF INFORMATION~~
~~CONTAINED HEREIN IS NOT AUTHORIZED.~~

THIS DOCUMENT CONTAINS CODE WORD MATERIAL

~~TOP SECRET~~

93

~~TOP SECRET~~ 

26 October 1962

SUMMARY CONTENTS

I. Surveillance of 25 October shows that the construction of IRBM and MRBM bases in Cuba is proceeding largely on schedule; now level photography confirms that the MRBM bases will use the 1,020-nautical-mile SS-4 missile. No additional sites, launchers or missiles have been located, but there is road construction around Remedios which suggests the fourth IRBM site we have been expecting there. We estimate that it would cost the USSR more than twice as much and take considerably longer to add to its ICBM strike capability from the USSR as great an increment as the potential salvo from Cuban launching sites.

II. Only two Soviet freighters--and five tankers, one of them already past the quarantine line--still are headed for Cuba. The BELOVODSK, with twelve MI-4 helicopters, is inthe North Atlantic; the PUGACHEV appears to have slowed or stopped several days west of the Panama Canal. A total of 16 dry cargo ships now are carried as having turned back toward the USSR on 23 October.

Two Soviet civil air flights are scheduled for Havana with passengers; cargo, if any, is not known. One may be turned back by Guinea today. A TU-114 is scheduled via Senegal to reach Havana 1 November.

III. There are further indications that some Soviet and satellite elements, particularly air and ground elements in Eastern Europe and European Russia, are on an alert or readiness status. No major deployments have been detected, however [redacted] There is some evidence that additional tactical aircraft have been placed on five-minute alert in East Germany, where two areas along the West German border have been closed off for exercises.

Moscow highlights Khrushchev's acceptance of U Thant's appeal in a bid to start US-Soviet negotiations. Peiping, however, is irritated that the Soviet response to US action is not stronger. The Communists still deny there are any offensive weapons in Cuba.

IV. There is no major change or significant new development in non-bloc reaction to the crisis. Most of the OAS nations have offered to participate in some form in the quarantine, and NATO members have agreed with minor reservations to deny landing and overflight rights to Soviet planes bound for Cuba.

~~TOP SECRET~~ [redacted]

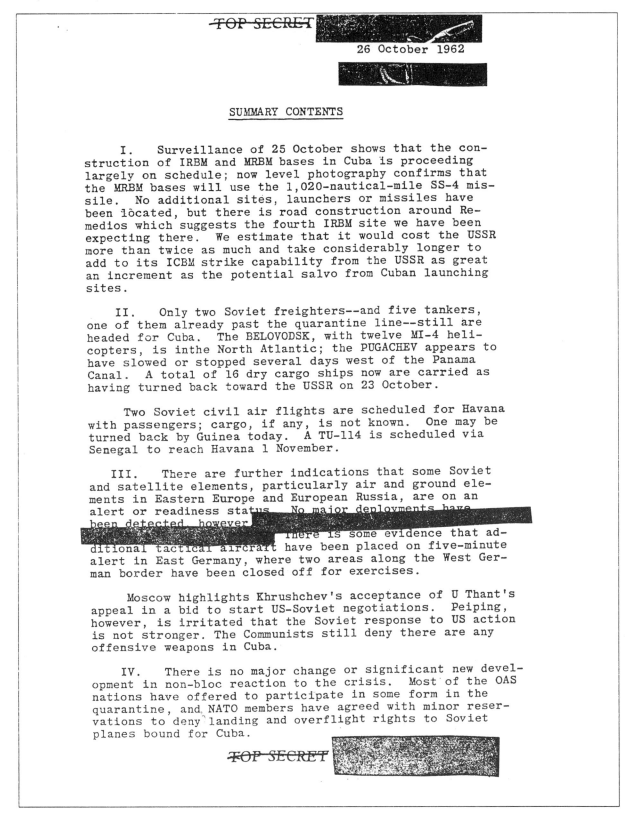

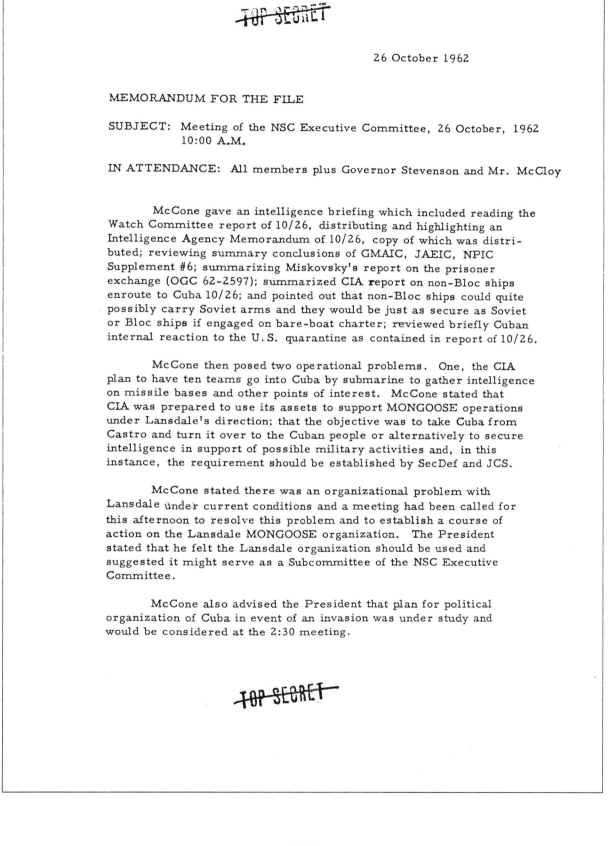

96. *McCone, Memorandum for the File, "Meeting of the NSC Executive Committee, 26 October, 1962, 10:00 a.m."*

~~TOP SECRET~~

26 October 1962

MEMORANDUM FOR THE FILE

SUBJECT: Meeting of the NSC Executive Committee, 26 October, 1962 10:00 A.M.

IN ATTENDANCE: All members plus Governor Stevenson and Mr. McCloy

McCone gave an intelligence briefing which included reading the Watch Committee report of 10/26, distributing and highlighting an Intelligence Agency Memorandum of 10/26, copy of which was distributed; reviewing summary conclusions of GMAIC, JAEIC, NPIC Supplement #6; summarizing Miskovsky's report on the prisoner exchange (OGC 62-2597); summarized CIA report on non-Bloc ships enroute to Cuba 10/26; and pointed out that non-Bloc ships could quite possibly carry Soviet arms and they would be just as secure as Soviet or Bloc ships if engaged on bare-boat charter; reviewed briefly Cuban internal reaction to the U.S. quarantine as contained in report of 10/26.

McCone then posed two operational problems. One, the CIA plan to have ten teams go into Cuba by submarine to gather intelligence on missile bases and other points of interest. McCone stated that CIA was prepared to use its assets to support MONGOOSE operations under Lansdale's direction; that the objective was to take Cuba from Castro and turn it over to the Cuban people or alternatively to secure intelligence in support of possible military activities and, in this instance, the requirement should be established by SecDef and JCS.

McCone stated there was an organizational problem with Lansdale under current conditions and a meeting had been called for this afternoon to resolve this problem and to establish a course of action on the Lansdale MONGOOSE organization. The President stated that he felt the Lansdale organization should be used and suggested it might serve as a Subcommittee of the NSC Executive Committee.

McCone also advised the President that plan for political organization of Cuba in event of an invasion was under study and would be considered at the 2:30 meeting.

~~TOP SECRET~~

96. *(Continued)*

~~TOP SECRET~~

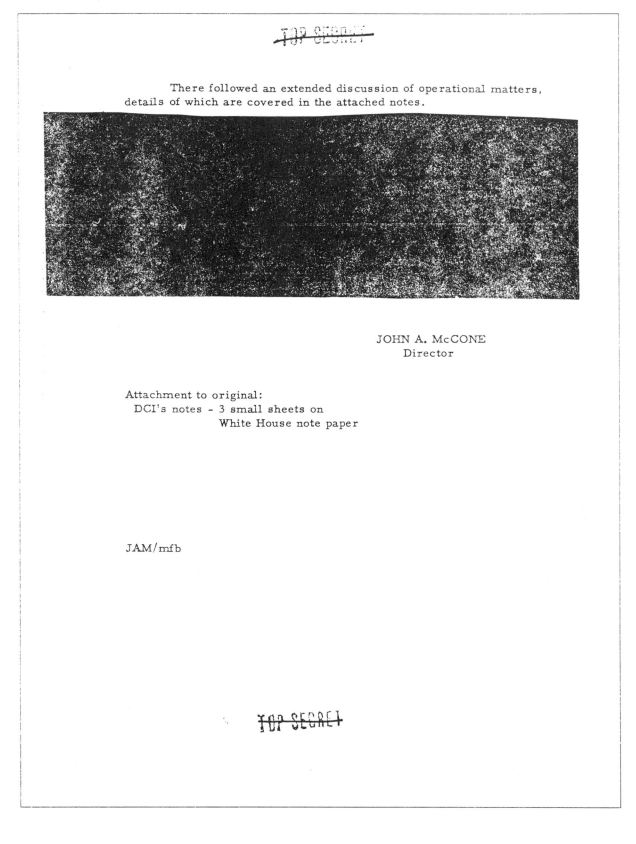

There followed an extended discussion of operational matters, details of which are covered in the attached notes.

JOHN A. McCONE
Director

Attachment to original:
DCI's notes - 3 small sheets on
White House note paper

JAM/mfb

~~TOP SECRET~~

97. *McCone, "Memorandum of MONGOOSE Meeting in the JCS Operations Room, October 26, 1962, at 2:30 p.m.," 29 October 1962*

~~SECRET,~~ EYES ONLY

B-28

October 29, 1962

MEMORANDUM OF MONGOOSE MEETING IN THE JCS OPERATIONS ROOM, OCTOBER 26, 1962, AT 2:30 p.m.

Attended by: McNamara, Gilpatric, General Taylor, Johnson, Ed Martin, Don Wilson, the Attorney General, McCone, Lansdale, Harvey, and Parrott.

The purpose of the meeting was to give guidance to operation MONGOOSE. It became immediately apparent that Lansdale felt himself lacking in authority and not in channel of either operations or information with JCS or SecDef's office. There was considerable criticism by innuendo of the CIA/Lansdale relationship.

McCone stated that he understood the MONGOOSE goal was to encourage the Cuban people to take Cuba away from Castro and to set up a proper form of government. He said CIA had, and would continue to support Lansdale whom we recognized as the director of this operation. He felt that any indication that CIA was not affording such support to Lansdale was completely erroneous.

On the other hand, CIA by long-standing arrangements, details of which were most recently confirmed, are obligated to support the military to the extent desired by the JCS in any combat theatre, and therefore probably some CIA moves made for the purpose of meeting this objective had been misunderstood by Lansdale. Lansdale had distributed the attached paper headed "Main Points to be Considered, 10/26."

~~SECRET,~~ EYES ONLY

97. *(Continued)*

~~SECRET EYES ONLY~~

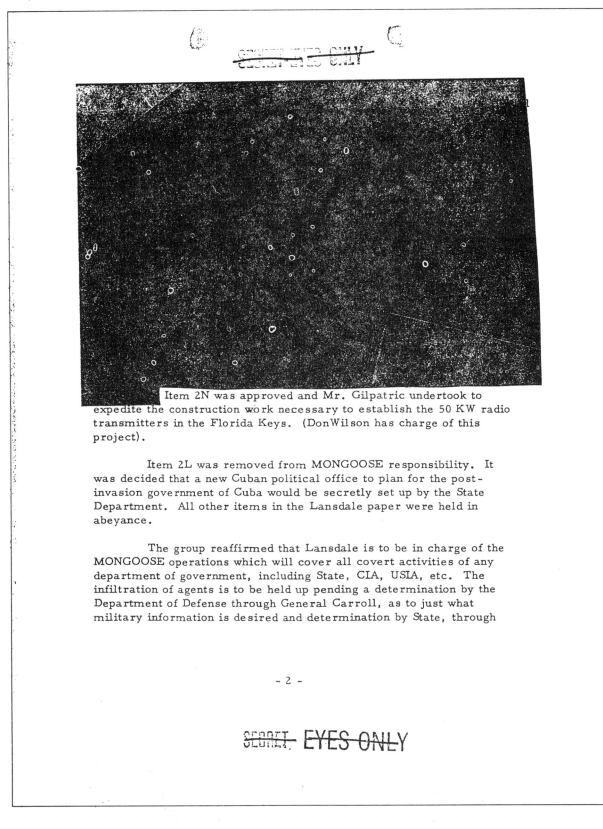

Item 2N was approved and Mr. Gilpatric undertook to expedite the construction work necessary to establish the 50 KW radio transmitters in the Florida Keys. (DonWilson has charge of this project).

Item 2L was removed from MONGOOSE responsibility. It was decided that a new Cuban political office to plan for the post-invasion government of Cuba would be secretly set up by the State Department. All other items in the Lansdale paper were held in abeyance.

The group reaffirmed that Lansdale is to be in charge of the MONGOOSE operations which will cover all covert activities of any department of government, including State, CIA, USIA, etc. The infiltration of agents is to be held up pending a determination by the Department of Defense through General Carroll, as to just what military information is desired and determination by State, through

- 2 -

~~SECRET~~ ~~EYES ONLY~~

97. *(Continued)*

Alexis Johnson, as to just what political information is desired. General Lansdale is then to determine if assets available in the government (all of which rest in CIA) can produce the information desired by Defense and State, and then program a procedure to be followed.

It is expected that Lansdale will make these determinations at the earliest moment and confer further with the committee or individual representatives thereof.

John A. McCone
Director

JAM:at

- 3 -

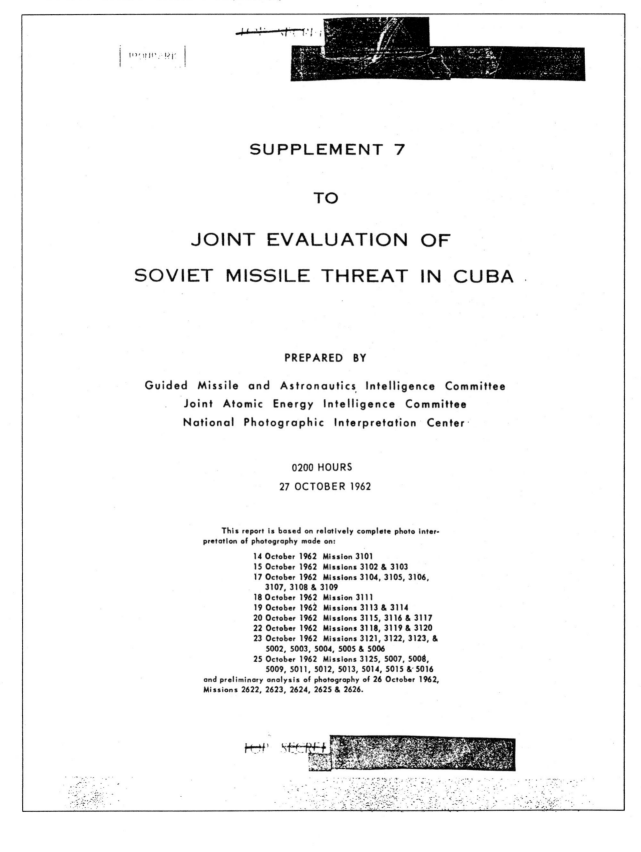

98. *Supplement 7 to Joint Evaluation of Soviet Missile Threat in Cuba, 27 October 1962 (Excerpt)*

SUPPLEMENT 7

TO

JOINT EVALUATION OF SOVIET MISSILE THREAT IN CUBA

PREPARED BY

Guided Missile and Astronautics Intelligence Committee
Joint Atomic Energy Intelligence Committee
National Photographic Interpretation Center

0200 HOURS
27 OCTOBER 1962

This report is based on relatively complete photo interpretation of photography made on:

14 October 1962 Mission 3101
15 October 1962 Missions 3102 & 3103
17 October 1962 Missions 3104, 3105, 3106, 3107, 3108 & 3109
18 October 1962 Mission 3111
19 October 1962 Missions 3113 & 3114
20 October 1962 Missions 3115, 3116 & 3117
22 October 1962 Missions 3118, 3119 & 3120
23 October 1962 Missions 3121, 3122, 3123, & 5002, 5003, 5004, 5005 & 5006
25 October 1962 Missions 3125, 5007, 5008, 5009, 5011, 5012, 5013, 5014, 5015 & 5016

and preliminary analysis of photography of 26 October 1962, Missions 2622, 2623, 2624, 2625 & 2626.

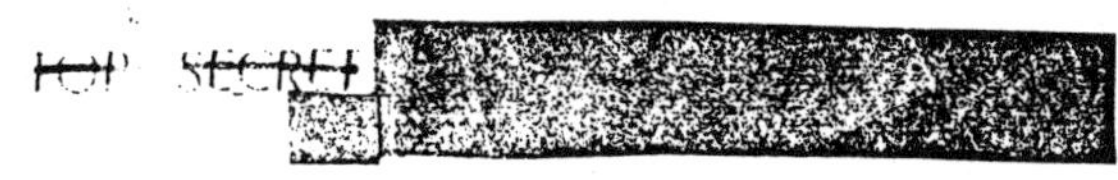

98. *(Continued)*

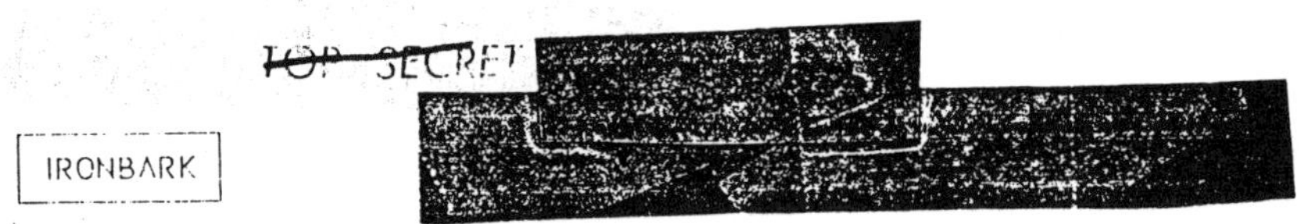

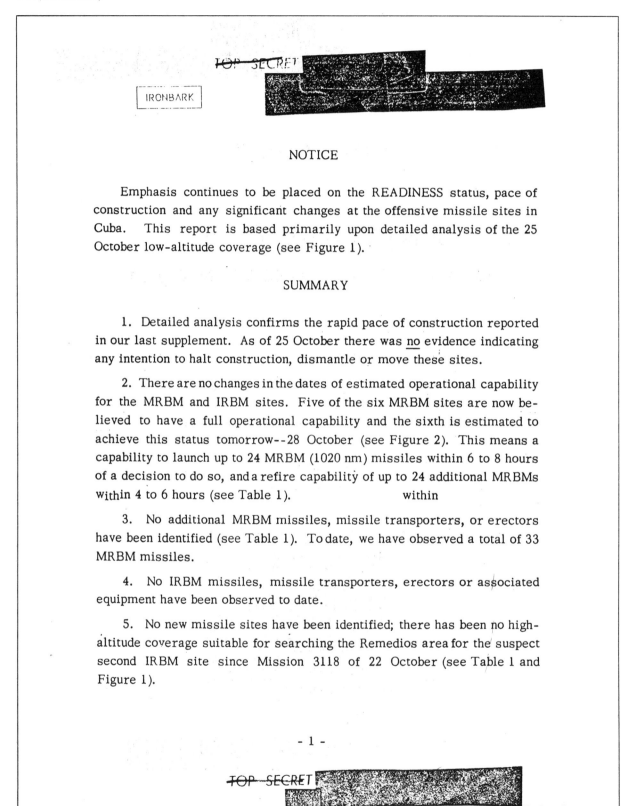

NOTICE

Emphasis continues to be placed on the READINESS status, pace of construction and any significant changes at the offensive missile sites in Cuba. This report is based primarily upon detailed analysis of the 25 October low-altitude coverage (see Figure 1).

SUMMARY

1. Detailed analysis confirms the rapid pace of construction reported in our last supplement. As of 25 October there was no evidence indicating any intention to halt construction, dismantle or move these sites.

2. There are no changes in the dates of estimated operational capability for the MRBM and IRBM sites. Five of the six MRBM sites are now believed to have a full operational capability and the sixth is estimated to achieve this status tomorrow--28 October (see Figure 2). This means a capability to launch up to 24 MRBM (1020 nm) missiles within 6 to 8 hours of a decision to do so, and a refire capability of up to 24 additional MRBMs within 4 to 6 hours (see Table 1). within

3. No additional MRBM missiles, missile transporters, or erectors have been identified (see Table 1). To date, we have observed a total of 33 MRBM missiles.

4. No IRBM missiles, missile transporters, erectors or associated equipment have been observed to date.

5. No new missile sites have been identified; there has been no high-altitude coverage suitable for searching the Remedios area for the suspect second IRBM site since Mission 3118 of 22 October (see Table 1 and Figure 1).

- 1 -

98. *(Continued)*

TOP SECRET

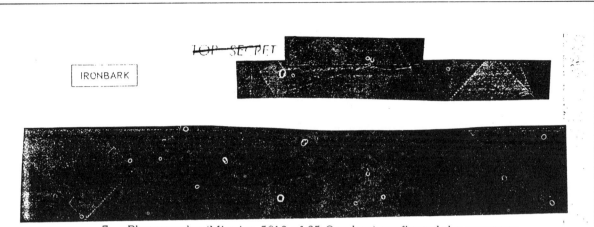

IRONBARK

7. Photography (Mission 5012 of 25 October) confirmed the presence of a FROG missile launcher in a vehicle park near Remedios. (The FROG is a tactical unguided rocket of 40,000 to 50,000 yard range, and is similar to the U.S. Honest John).

8. There has been no [redacted] evidence of attempts at interdiction of U.S. reconnaissance aircraft.

9. Despite Krushchev's statement to Mr. Knox of 24 October, we still lack positive evidence that nuclear weapons are deployed in Cuba.

10. The probable nuclear bunkers adjacent to the MRBM sites are not yet ready for storage, assembly or checkout.

- 2 -

TOP SECRET

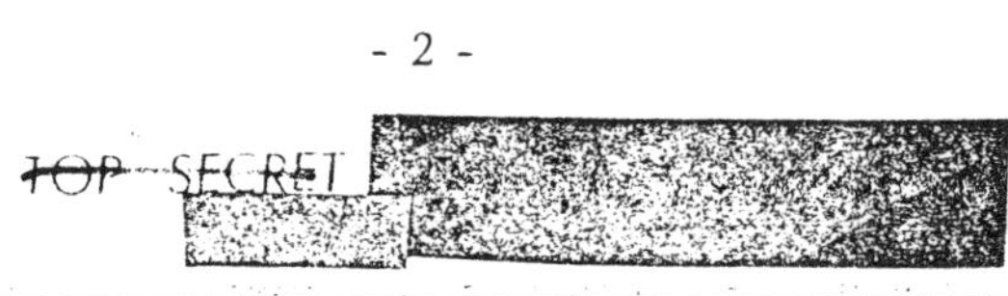

99. *Central Intelligence Agency Memorandum, "The Crisis, USSR/Cuba," 27 October 1962 (Excerpt)*

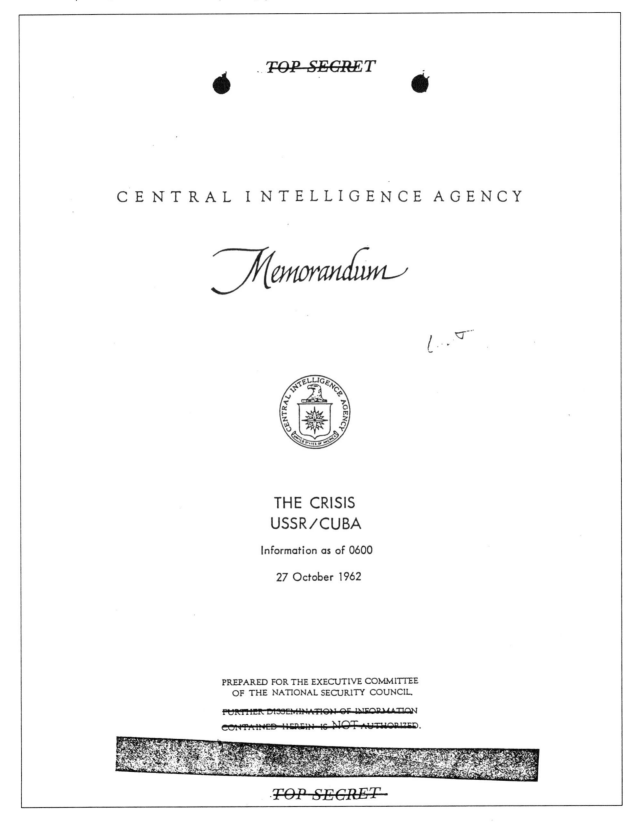

~~TOP SECRE~~T

CENTRAL INTELLIGENCE AGENCY

Memorandum

THE CRISIS
USSR/CUBA

Information as of 0600

27 October 1962

PREPARED FOR THE EXECUTIVE COMMITTEE
OF THE NATIONAL SECURITY COUNCIL.

~~FURTHER DISSEMINATION OF INFORMATION CONTAINED HEREIN IS~~ NOT ~~AUTHORIZED~~.

~~TOP SECRET~~

99. *(Continued)*

~~TOP SECRET~~ 

27 October 1962

SUMMARY CONTENTS

I. Based on the latest low-level reconnissance mission, three of the four MRBM sites at San Cristobal and the two sites at Sagua La Grande appear to be fully operational. No further sites or missiles have been identified.

The mobilization of Cuban military forces continues at a high rate. However, they remain under orders not to take any hostile action unless attacked.

Steps toward establishing an integrated air defense system are under way. On the diplomatic front, Cuban representatives are trying to plant the idea that Havana would be receptive to UN mediation. They indicate, however, that a prerequisite must be "proof" that the US does not intend to attack Cuba.

II. Despite Khrushchev's declaration to U Thant that Soviet ships would temporarily avoid the quarantine area, we have no information as yet that the six Soviet and three satellite ships en route have changed course. A Swedish vessel, believed to be under charter to the USSR, refused to stop yesterday when intercepted by a US destroyer and was allowed to continue to Havana.

III. No significant redeployment of Soviet ground, air or naval forces have been noted. However, there are continuing indications of increased readiness among some units. Three F-class submarines have been identified on the surface inside or near the quarantine line.

IV. There has been no distinct shift in the pattern of reaction. In Western Europe, further support for the US has come from several quarters and unfavorable reactions are decidedly in the minority.

Official London seems intent on checking premature optimism which is showing up in widely scattered parts of the world, particularly among the neutrals. French support for the US is hardening.

There are reports that anti-US demonstrations have broken out in several Latin American capitals, including Buenos Aires, Caracas, and La Paz.

~~TOP SECRET~~

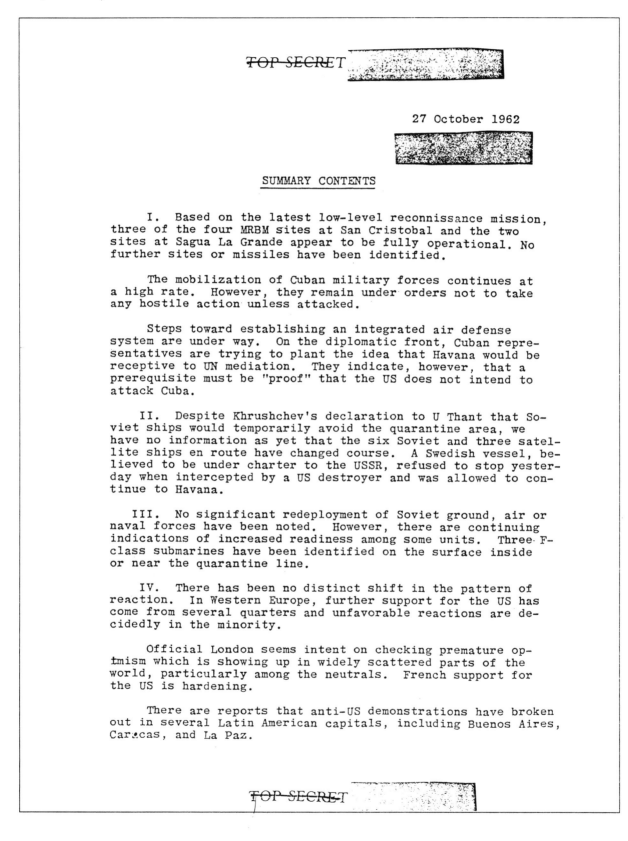

99. *(Continued)*

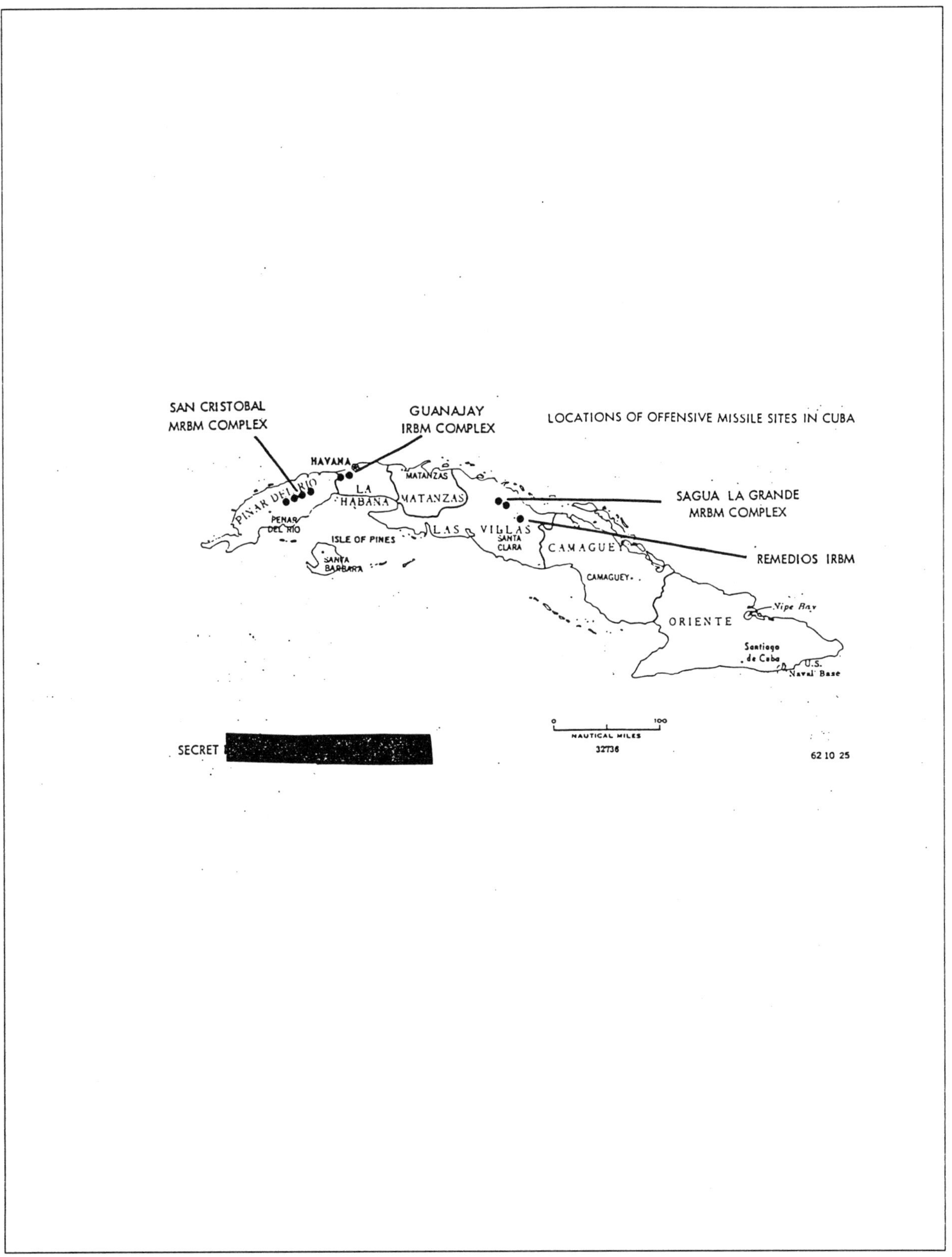

100. *[McCone], notes from 10:00 a.m. NSC Executive Committee meeting, 27 October 1962*

THE WHITE HOUSE

10/27 10 AM all

McCone – Brief intelligence briefing

McN – Report on ground equipment authorized – 2 daily flights of 8 planes each – 1 night flight planned – to be released at 4 PM if to be run –

Ball and Nitze – discussed the removal of Jupiters to Turkey because of press report that we have offered to exchange Turk missiles for Cuban missiles. This report is different from the private letter K to Kennedy of 10/26.

R Kennedy – Cuban bases must be removed promptly and negotiations cannot delay this – Turkey relates to security of Europe and USSR and this we can suggest

100. *(Continued)*

2) 10/27 —

THE WHITE HOUSE

This followed a long discussion of these communications from Kru —
1) to U Thant 2) to Kennedy 10/26
2) Kennedy 10/28 - all contradictory
The latter formally proposes the Turkish - Cuban quid pro quo.
Kennedy position we must insist work be stopped and this is pre requisite to any talks.

101. *[McCone], notes from 4:00 p.m. NSC Executive Committee meeting, 27 October 1962*

THE WHITE HOUSE

10/27 – 4:00 PM – Ex Comm. All present

No intelligence developments to report

Reviewed state draft letter ~~to do~~ Kennedy to K.—

Taylor reported that 8 planes low-level took off at 3 PM – 1 pair aborted because of mechanical trouble, 1 pair aborted because of AA fire – 2 pairs completed and are due back about 5 PM.

Rusk reported results of U2 flight of Russia – 100 miles off K-sail – Instrument failure caused plane to go over Sov. territory. Decided not to announce incident.

Meeting reviewed and approved draft reply to K's letter to Pres. 10/26 and instructions to U Thant at the U.N.

McN raised question of recon on Sunday agreed to send in flights until no chance – If ~~decided~~ fired upon we will then decide on action to be taken.

101. *(Continued)*

2) 10/27 THE WHITE HOUSE

Taylor reported that a U-2 was shot down over Banes –

Turkey and ~~[illegible]~~ Italy missiles to be made inoperational prior to further action in Cuba

102. *[McCone], notes from 9:00 p.m. NSC Executive Committee meeting, 27 October 1962*

10/27 9 00 PM THE WHITE HOUSE All present

Rusk – Castro broadcast at 21 00 this evening did not bring up Turk bases. Try to get K back on last night track.

Taylor – Planes today encountered ack-ack on low level operations against missile sites.

Pres. read message of even date from Norstad advising procedure to be followed in N.A.C. meeting on Sun AM.

Consideration of draft of TWX to K — Decided not to send the message in view of several messages and statements and U Thant proposed trip to Havana — Therefore McCone message (attached) not sent.

ExCom 10/27/62 9:00 p.m. - No other info/No M/R

103. *Supplement 8 to Joint Evaluation of Soviet Missile Threat in Cuba, 28 October 1962 (Excerpt)*

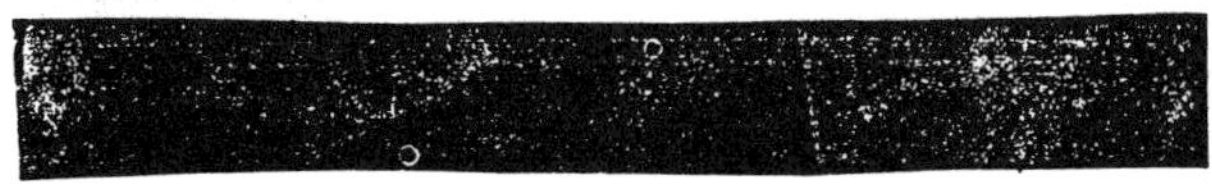

SUPPLEMENT 8

TO

JOINT EVALUATION OF

SOVIET MISSILE THREAT IN CUBA

PREPARED BY

Guided Missile and Astronautics Intelligence Committee
Joint Atomic Energy Intelligence Committee
National Photographic Interpretation Center

0200 HOURS

28 OCTOBER 1962

NOTICE

This report is based primarily on detailed analysis of low-altitude photography taken on Friday, 26 October, as well as preliminary evaluation of the results of similar missions from Saturday, 27 October 1962 (Figure 1). The primary emphasis is placed here on a technical evaluation of force readiness, pace of construction, and changes in the deployment program (Table 1). This report does not attempt to estimate Soviet intent to attack the United States.

SUMMARY

1. We still have no direct knowledge of thermonuclear warheads in Cuba, but believe it prudent to assume that the Soviet missile force there is so armed.

2. We estimate that all 24 MRBM launchers are now fully operational, representing a capability to salvo 24 1000-mile missiles within 6 to 8 hours of a decision to launch.

3. The present and estimated operational capability of all Soviet defensive missiles in Cuba is summarized in Figure 2.

4. No new MRBM or IRBM sites have been detected in the past day, although we have not had high-altitude coverage appropriate for search since 23 October 1962.

5. Construction at the Soviet IRBM sites in Cuba continues at a rapid pace and missile support equipment is now being moved to the vicinity of Guanajay Site 1. No IRBM's per se have yet been observed.

6. The entire missile-launching force at the Soviet MRBM sites in Cuba is being checked out on a rapid basis. This provides an increasing, integrated, operational readiness posture.

- 1 -

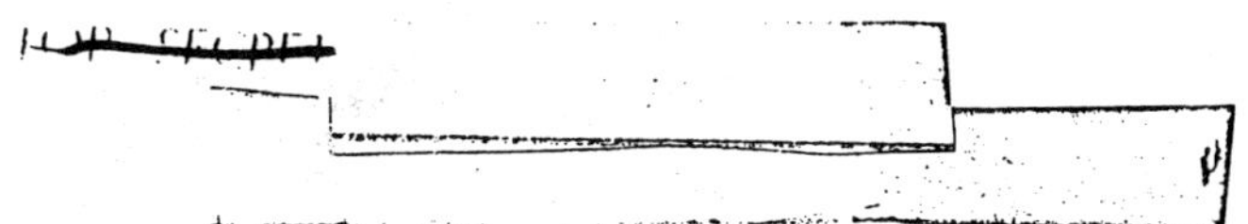

7. Automatic anti-aircraft weapons and personnel trenches for protection against air attack are now evident at many of the MRBM sites. These weapons have been introduced in the last few days and probably account for the ground fire now being noted on the low-level photographic missions.

8. Camouflage against aerial photography is being extended at the missile sites and is becoming more effective. Force dispersion is also evident.

9. A missile propellant offloading and transhipping facility has now been identified at the double-fenced area at Punta Gerada in Bahia Honda. This was suspected formerly of being a port of entry for nuclear weapons.

10. We now estimate an integrated operational capability for the SA-2 air defense network in Cuba

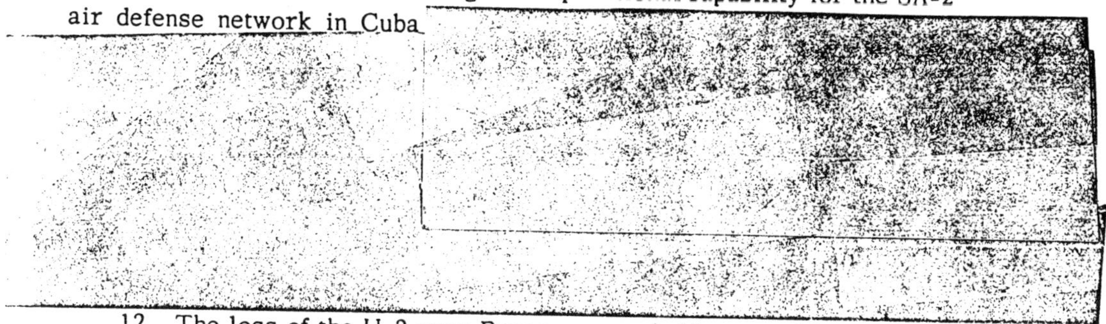

12. The loss of the U-2 over Banes was probably caused by intercept by an SA-2 from the Banes site, or pilot hypoxia, with the former appearing more likely on the basis of present information.

13. Microwave relay towers have been noted at some of the MRBM and IRBM site areas covered on 27 October, indicating that an integrated microwave command and control communication system will be utilized in Cuba. However, the use of high frequency radio is also indicated by the presence of high frequency antennae at Sagua La Grande sites 1 and 2.

- 2 -

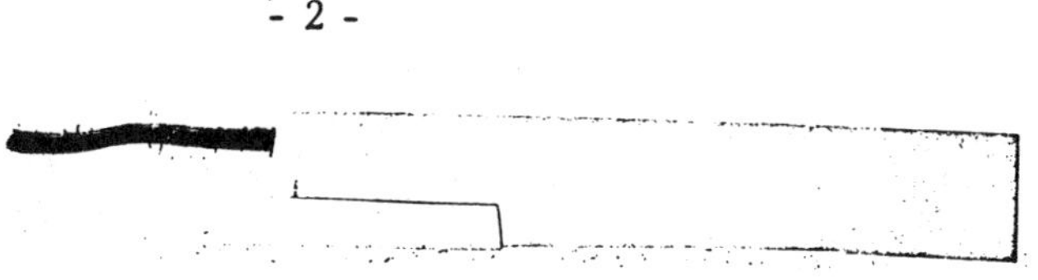

[illegible]

14. Construction of probable nuclear storage facilities was continuing on 26 and 27 October. None of the bunkers observed at probable nuclear storage sites are yet believed to be in operation although that at Guanajay IRBM Site No. 1 is essentially complete.

15. A new, probable nuclear storage facility has been identified at Sagua La Grande MRBM Site No. 2. Construction materials were being moved into this area on 27 October. The existence of a second, probable nuclear storage area at the Sagua La Grande launch complex indicates that each launch site is probably intended to have individual, permanent nuclear storage.

- 3 -

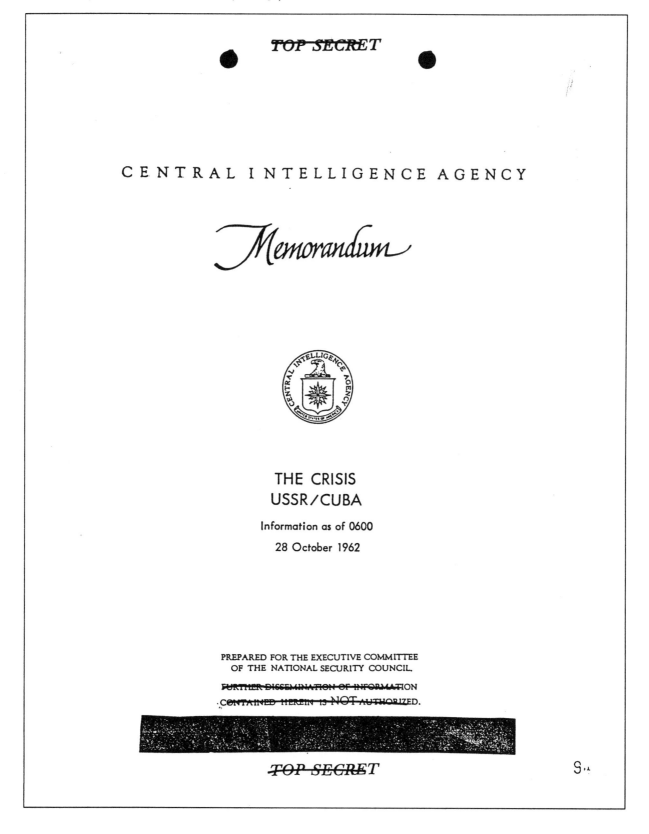

104. *Central Intelligence Agency Memorandum, "The Crisis, USSR/Cuba," 28 October 1962 (Excerpt)*

~~TOP SECRE~~T

CENTRAL INTELLIGENCE AGENCY

Memorandum

THE CRISIS
USSR/CUBA

Information as of 0600

28 October 1962

PREPARED FOR THE EXECUTIVE COMMITTEE OF THE NATIONAL SECURITY COUNCIL.

~~FURTHER DISSEMINATION OF INFORMA~~TION ~~CONTAINED HEREIN IS~~ NOT ~~AUTHORIZE~~D.

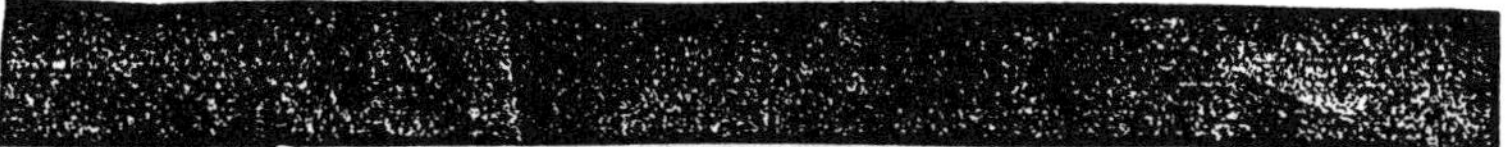

~~TOP SECRE~~T

104. *(Continued)*

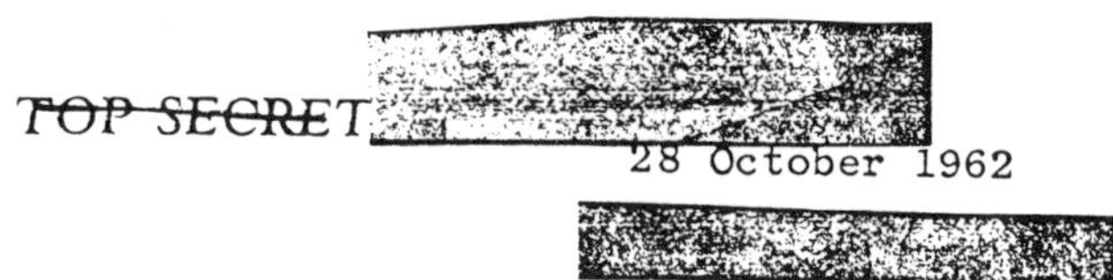

~~TOP SECRET~~

28 October 1962

SUMMARY CONTENTS

I. Surveillance of 26 October and preliminary analysis of yesterday's coverage shows that the development of both IRBM and MRBM sites in Cuba is continuing its rapid pace. All 24 MRBM launchers now appear to have reached full operational readiness. One nuclear storage facility is essentially complete, but none of the bunkers observed is yet believedto be in operation.

There are some indications that the U-2 lost yesterday over Banes was brought down by the SA-2 system.

Cuban military units remain at a high state of alert and the Castro regime is making a maximum effort to whip up troop and public morale.

II. As of 0700 EST, two or possibly three more Soviet ships are heading for Cuba in addition to the two dry cargo ships and four tankers we have been watching. The tanker GROZNY should have reached the quarantine line early this morning. One Soviet transport aircraft which reached Brazil is there to pick up the body of the Soviet ambassador. Another scheduled for Cuba via North Africa and Brazil turned back at Morocco.

III. No significant redeployment of major Soviet ground, air or naval forces has been noted. The general posture of Soviet ground forces in forward areas is one of precautionary defensive readiness. The overall total of Soviet submarines on extended operations is somewhat greater than normal, and a fourth F-class submarine may be in the area of the Cuban quarantine line.

In non-military developments, Khrushchev's bid for reciprocal withdrawal of offensive weapons from Cuba and Turkey looks like the first step in a series of moves to demonstrate the USSR's readiness for a negotiated solution. Soviet spokesmen continue to play down the possibility that the Cuban crisis could lead to general war.

~~TOP SECRET~~

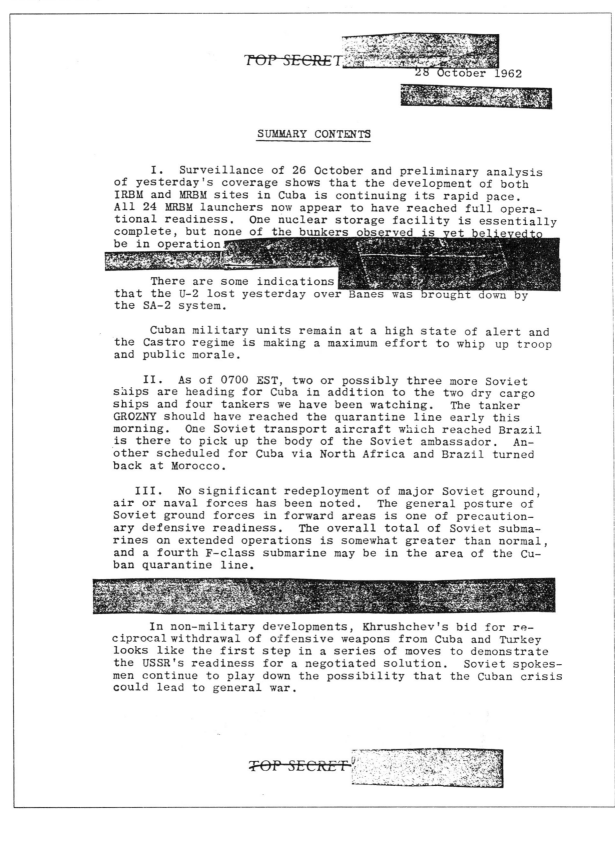

~~TOP SECRET~~ 

IV. U Thant is thinking seriously of accepting Castro's invitation to visit Cuba, and might go as early as Tuesday. There is thus far only fragmentary mixed reaction to the President's rejection of Khrushchev's Cuba-Turkey proposal.

~~TOP SECRET~~ 

104. *(Continued)*

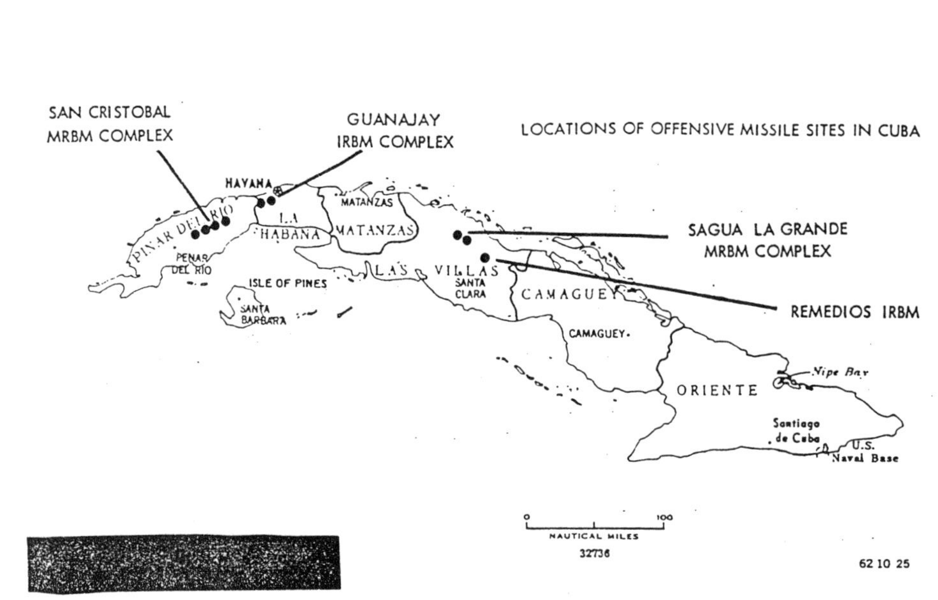

LOCATION OF MRBM AND IRBM SITES IN CUBA

A. MRBM SITES

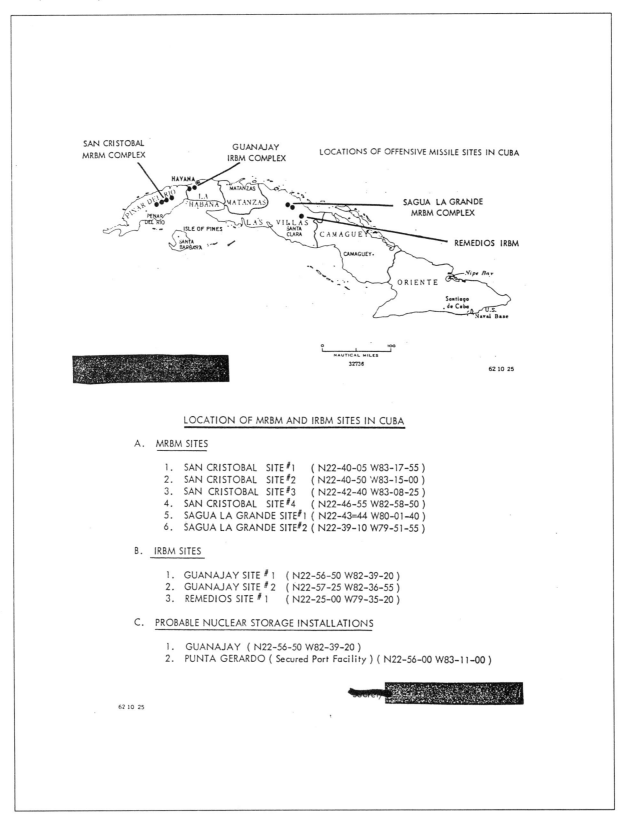

1. SAN CRISTOBAL SITE #1 (N22-40-05 W83-17-55)
2. SAN CRISTOBAL SITE #2 (N22-40-50 W83-15-00)
3. SAN CRISTOBAL SITE #3 (N22-42-40 W83-08-25)
4. SAN CRISTOBAL SITE #4 (N22-46-55 W82-58-50)
5. SAGUA LA GRANDE SITE #1 (N22-43=44 W80-01-40)
6. SAGUA LA GRANDE SITE #2 (N22-39-10 W79-51-55)

B. IRBM SITES

1. GUANAJAY SITE # 1 (N22-56-50 W82-39-20)
2. GUANAJAY SITE # 2 (N22-57-25 W82-36-55)
3. REMEDIOS SITE # 1 (N22-25-00 W79-35-20)

C. PROBABLE NUCLEAR STORAGE INSTALLATIONS

1. GUANAJAY (N22-56-50 W82-39-20)
2. PUNTA GERARDO (Secured Port Facility) (N22-56-00 W83-11-00)

62 10 25

105. *[McCone], notes, "National Security Council Meeting–Executive Committee, October 28–11:00 a.m."*

TOP SECRET

#5Ø

National Security Council Meeting - Executive Committee

October 28 - 11:00 a.m. - All present

Rusk	Rec no plane surveillance
McNamara	Noted difference in Chiefs - Personally agree with Rusk recommendations
Nitze	UN ask what we want to prove inoperable of weapons
McNamara	Have as our objectives a UN recon. plane on Monday
President	Secy. not go today - but let's go on assumption either we or UN will go on Monday

Decision made to release a brief statement welcoming the K message

McCone [redacted]

TOP SECRET

106. *Walter Elder, "Memorandum of Executive Committee of NSC Meeting on Sunday, 28 October 1962 Dictated by the Undersigned based on Debriefing of DCI"*

~~SECRET~~, ~~EYES ONLY~~

MEMORANDUM OF EXECUTIVE COMMITTEE OF NSC MEETING ON SUNDAY, 28 OCTOBER 1962 DICTATED BY THE UNDERSIGNED BASED ON DEBRIEFING OF DCI

1. No reconnaissance flights today despite a recommendation of the Secretary of State supported by the Secretary of Defense. It was decided to use RB-66's, which are now in Florida with UN observers aboard if arrangements can be made by the UN in time.

2. If not, the US will fly our own reconnaissance.

3. The DCI has been authorized to release to General Rickhye all pertinent information on the buildup in Cuba, protecting only intelligence sources [redacted] Therefore, the portfolios can be released. Competent people are to go with Charyk and Forrestal to New York to support General Rickhye on this operation.

4. Action: Bill Tidwell and Colonel Parker were dispatched to New York by Ray Cline. This action is underway.

5. A draft reply to Khrushchev is to be written by Ambassador Llewellyn Thompson in Alexis Johnson's office.

6. Action. DD/I is to insure that the CIA input is taken account of. Cline was instructed to support the DCI's position that the removal of the missiles should not end by giving Castro's a sanctuary and thus sustain his subversive threat to other Latin American nations.

7. Action: Action was taken by Ray Cline.

Walter Elder

~~SECRET~~, ~~EYES ONLY~~

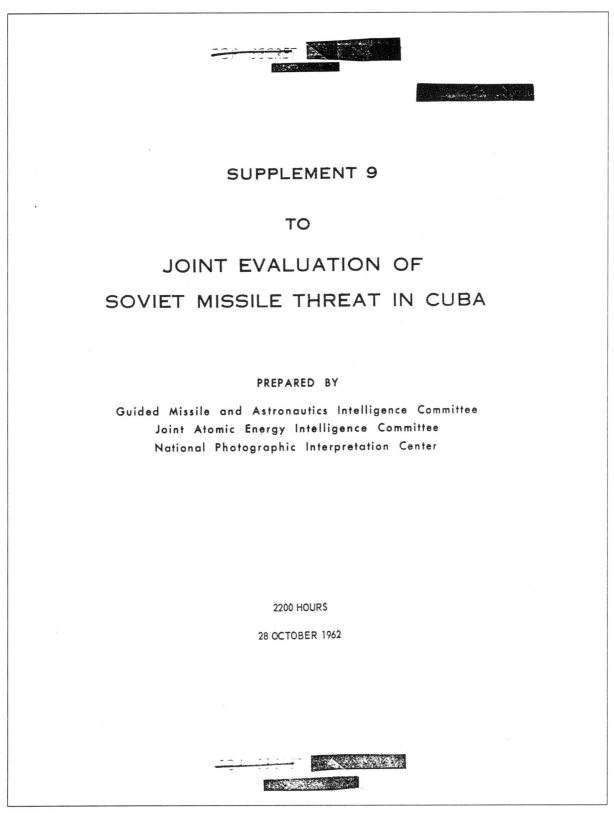

107. *Supplement 9 to Joint Evaluation of Soviet Missile Threat in Cuba, 28 October 1962 (Excerpt)*

SUPPLEMENT 9

TO

JOINT EVALUATION OF

SOVIET MISSILE THREAT IN CUBA

PREPARED BY

Guided Missile and Astronautics Intelligence Committee
Joint Atomic Energy Intelligence Committee
National Photographic Interpretation Center

2200 HOURS

28 OCTOBER 1962

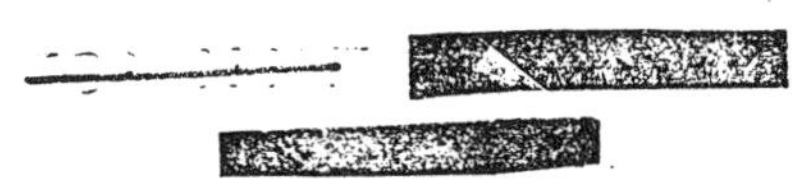

TOP SECRET 

NOTICE

This report is based primarily on detailed analysis of low-altitude photography taken on Saturday, 27 October 1962. (See Figure 4 for tracks.) The primary emphasis is placed here on a technical evaluation of force readiness, pace of construction, and changes in the deployment program (Table 1). This report does not attempt to estimate Soviet intent to attack the United States.

SUMMARY

1. All 24 MRBM launchers are believed to be fully operational. (See Figure 2.)

2. Activity was continuing at all the MRBM and IRBM missile sites covered on Saturday, 27 October. (See Figures 1 and 2.) Camouflage and covering with canvas and natural concealment was continuing at the MRBM sites and is becoming more effective.

3. No IRBM missiles, missile transports or erectors have been identified. However, we have identified oxidizer trailers and possible fuel transporters among the support equipment near Guanajay IRBM Site 1. These fuel transporters are larger in size than similar fuel transporters at MRBM sites.

4. No new MRBM or IRBM sites have been detected; however, we have had no high altitude coverage appropriate for search since 23 October 1962.

5. 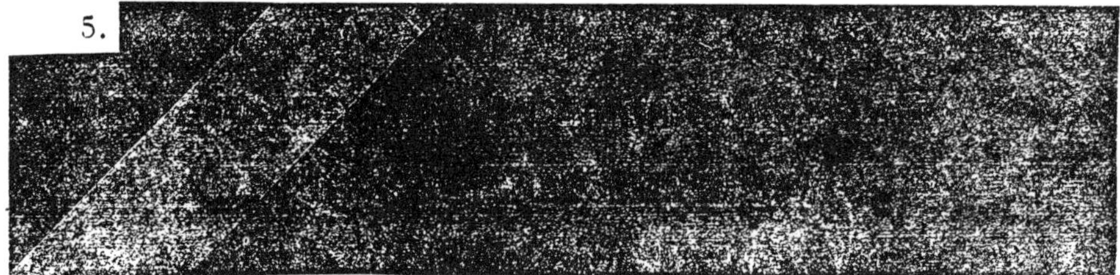

6. There is more evidence of the intent to have nuclear warhead bunkers at each launch site.

- 1 -

TOP SECRET 

PART III

THE AFTERMATH

Withdrawal of Soviet offensive weapons from Cuba

. . . Postcrisis reviews and assessments . . .

108. *Memorandum, "Soviet Offensive Weapons in Cuba," 29 October 1962, with attachment, "Table of Special Purpose Missile System Equipment"*

29 October 1962

MEMORANDUM

SUBJECT: Soviet Offensive Weapons in Cuba

1. The enclosed table includes a list of Soviet offensive missile weapons and associated equipment in Cuba.

2. Very little equipment has been observed at the three IRBM sites in Cuba. The only equipment identified, in addition to structures under construction, has been two possible fuel trucks and two possible oxidant trucks. If the IRBMs and other associated equipment are in Cuba they are probably in an unlocated facility between the port of Mariel and the sites. A study of Soviet sea shipments to Cuba, however, indicates that it is unlikely that many IRBMs had reached Cuba prior to the institution of the Quarantine.

3. No nuclear weapons or missile nosecones have been identified in Cuba. There are, however, nuclear weapon storage bunkers under construction at each of the MRBM and IRBM sites. These buildings are about 35 feet in width and are about 80 feet in length at the MRBM sites and 112 feet in length at the IRBM sites. If nuclear weapons are in Cuba they are probably in an unlocated facility between the entry port of Mariel and the sites.

4. All IL-28 aircraft are at San Julian in western Cuba; three or four appear to be assembled. An additional 23 or 24 aircraft in crates have also been observed at this airfield. Each disassembled aircraft consists of 1 fuselage crate 60X8X10 feet; 2 wing crates 9X40X8 feet; and 2 engine crates 9X30X8 feet.

Enclosure: Table of Special Purpose
Missile System Equipment

TABLE OF SPECIAL PURPOSE MISSILE SYSTEM EQUIPMENT

SECRET

Site Name and Number	Missiles and Missile Transports		Tracked Prime Movers for Transports		Erector Vehicles		Fuel Tank Trailers		Wheeled Prime Movers For Fuel Trailers		Oxidizer Tank Trailers		Tracked Prime Movers For Oxidizer Trailers		Launch Stands		Power Generators		Electronics Vans		Theodolites on Pedestal	
Medium-Range Ballistic Missile Sites	Seen	Im.	Seen	Im.	Seen	Im.	Seen	Im.	Seen	Im.	Seen	Im.	Seen	Im.	Seen	Im.	Seen	Im.	Seen	Im.	Seen	Im
Site Name and Number																						
San Cristobal #1 (20°40'05"N-83°17'50"W)	8	8	?	4	4	4	8	8	?	8	16	16	?	16	4	4	6	? 6	10	? 10	4	4
San Cristobal #2 (22°41'00"n-83°15'00"W)	6	8	?	4	4	4	7	8	?	8	16	16	?	16	4	4	1	? 6	0	? 10	4	4
San Cristobal #3 (22°42'40"N-83°08'25"W)	2	8	?	4	4	4	0	8	?	8	0	16	?	16	4	4	2	? 6	7	? 10	4	4
San Cristobal #4 (22°42'40"N-83°08'25"W)	7	8	?	4	4	4	0	8	?	8	7	16	?	16	4	4	0	? 6	0	? 10	0	4
Saqua La Grande #1 (22°43'44"N-80°01'40"W)	6	8	?	4	4	4	8	8	?	8	16	16	?	16	4	4	0	? 6	3	? 10	4	4
Saqua La Grande #2 (22°39'10"N-79°51'55"W)	4	8	?	4	4	4	8	8	?	8	16	16	?	16	3	4	5	? 6	3	? 10	3	4
TOTALS	33	48	?	24	24	24	31	48	?	48	71	96	?	96	23	24	14	? 36	14	? 60	19	21
Intermediate-Range Ballistic Missile Sites																						
Site Name and Number Co-ordinates																						
Guanajay 1	0	8	0	4	0	4	4	?	0	?	2	?	0	?	4	4	0	?	0	?	0	?
Guanajay 2	0	8	0	4	0	4	0	?	0	?	0	?	0	?	4	4	0	?	0	?	0	?
Remedios 1	0	8	0	4	0	4	0	?	0	?	0	?	0	?	4	4	0	?	0	?	0	?
Remedios 2 (unlocated)	0	8	0	4	0	4	0	?	0	?	0	?	0	?	0	4	0	?	0	?	0	?
TOTALS	0	32	0	16	0	16	4	?	0	?	2	?	0	?	12	16	0	?	0	?	0	?
Equipment at Logistical Support Points																						
Punta Gerardo Propellant Loading Point	NA	NA	NA	NA	NA	NA	UNK NO.	NA	NA	NA	2	NA	NA	NA	NA	NA	NA	NA	NA	NA	NA	NA
GRAND TOTALS	33	80	?	40	24	40	35	?	?	?	73	?	?	?	35	40	?	?	?	?	?	?

Footnote: 1. There are also numerous general purpose support equipment associated with MRBM/IRBM units, such as trucks, vehicles etc.
2. Implied numbers are those we estimate to be organic with Soviet MRBM/IRBM units or represent the highest number observed.

SECRET

109. *Memorandum for the Director, "Your Briefings of the NSC Executive Committee," 3 November 1962*

TOP SECRET

EYES ONLY

3 November 1962

MEMORANDUM FOR THE DIRECTOR

SUBJECT: Your Briefings of the NSC Executive Committee

1. On 23 October you gave a brief intelligence report saying that construction at the sites was continuing. Lundahl briefed on the most recent photographs. It was at this meeting that it was left to your discretion to consider the matter of disclosures of photos and you sent Lundahl and Cline to New York to assist Stevenson.

At an evening meeting that day you briefed on military developments within the WARSAW pact countries, describing an increased level of Soviet military communications.

2. On 24 October you briefed on the continued rapid progress in the completion of the missile sites and of the fact that 22 Soviet missile ships were en route to Cuba.

3. On 25 October you told the Group there had been no change in the construction pace; you covered the Watch Committee report, 'stating' that Soviet armed forces were increasing their state of readiness; you described the Soviet ships en route to Cuba carrying helicopters; you covered the departure of a Cubana plane from Canada to Havana; and also briefed on the turn-around of 15 of the 22 Soviet ships.

At an evening meeting you briefed in detail on the status of Soviet shipping [redacted]

4. On 26 October, which was attended by Stevenson, you covered the Watch Committee report which concluded that Soviet armed forces had completed measures for an alert but that there were no significant deployments. You noted continued construction at the missile bases, estimating that it had cost the Soviet less than one-half as much to put these in Cuba rather than build ICBM's in the USSR. You summarized the status of shipping and made the point that non-Bl ships could carry Soviet arms. You reviewed briefly Castro's apprehensive reaction to the US quarantine. He seems to fear an uprising.

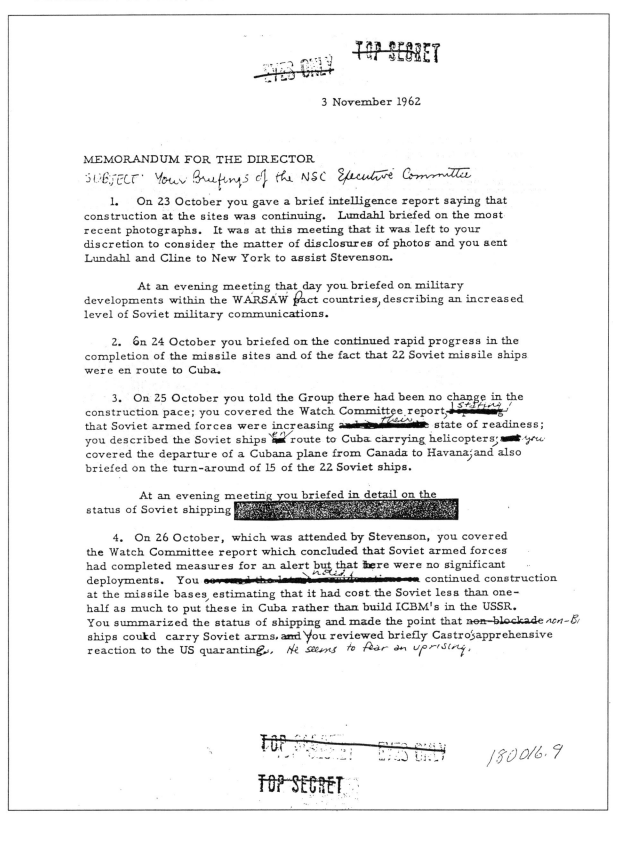

TOP SECRET EYES ONLY

180016.9

TOP SECRET

~~TOP SECRET~~

~~EYES ONLY~~

-2-

5. On 27 October you told the Group that three of the four MRBM sites at Sam Cristobal and two sites at Sagua la grande appeared fully operational and covered the latest Watch Committee report on Soviet military developments. [redacted]

6. On 28 October you agreed to lend all appropriate support to the effort to brief General Rikhye at the UN. You directed that Ray Cline participate in the draft reply to Khrushchev's letter. You asked that Cline insure supporting your position ~~but~~ that the removal of the missiles should not end by giving Castro a sanctuary.

7. On 29 October you covered the following:

a. Construction continues;

b.

c.

d.

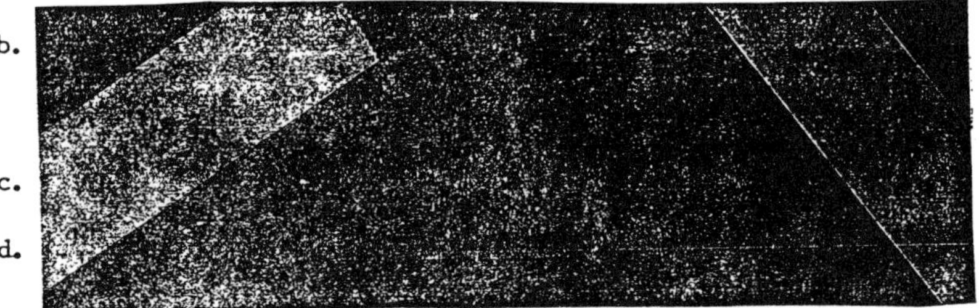

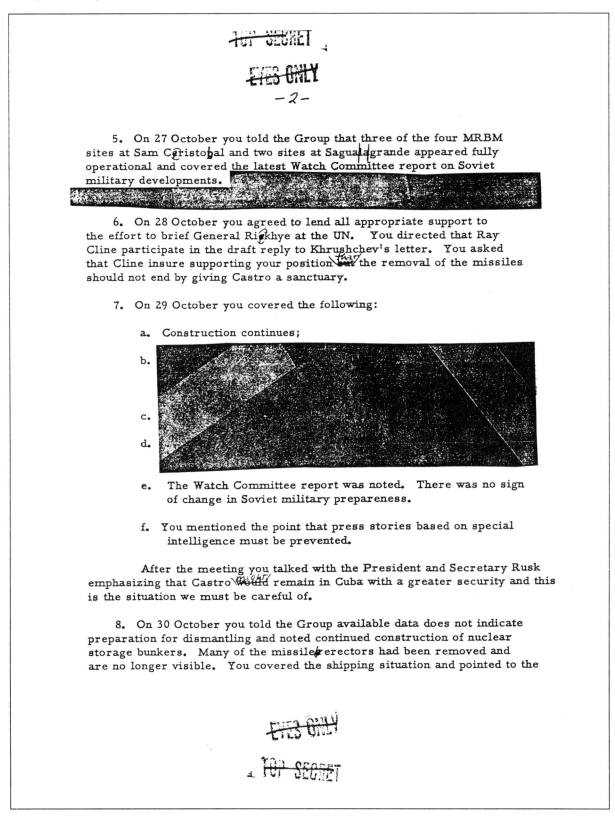

e. The Watch Committee report was noted. There was no sign of change in Soviet military prepareness.

f. You mentioned the point that press stories based on special intelligence must be prevented.

After the meeting you talked with the President and Secretary Rusk emphasizing that Castro ~~would~~ might remain in Cuba with a greater security and this is the situation we must be careful of.

8. On 30 October you told the Group available data does not indicate preparation for dismantling and noted continued construction of nuclear storage bunkers. Many of the missile erectors had been removed and are no longer visible. You covered the shipping situation and pointed to the

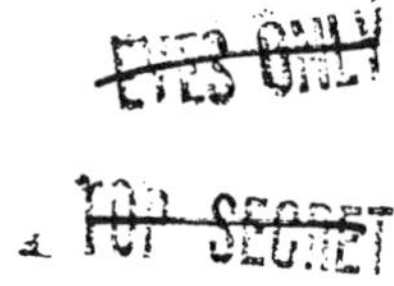

~~EYES ONLY~~

~~TOP SECRET~~

TOP SECRET -3- EYES ONLY

danger of sabotage in Latin American countries urging that all Embassies and consulates be alerted. You also covered the Watch Committee Report which concluded that Soviet armed forces remain on alert and you reviewed briefly current developments in Laos, South Vietnam, and India, Soviet nuclear subs, and Soviet nuclear tests and you pointed out that our ability to analyze these tests had been impared by DOD withdrawal of collection vehicles.

9. On 31 October you told the Group that there was continued evidence of construction and concealment but noted that evidence that some of the launchers had been moved from the MRBM sites might be construed as the first step at dismantling. You further pointed out that photos were compared with those taken on Saturday and orders to cease were probably not issued until Sunday night or Monday morning. There was discussion of the "intelligence gap" and you reviewed the Cuban SNIE of 19 September, noting that it failed to fully appraise all reports available.

10. On 1 November you briefed on details concerning U Thant's mission to Havana. You pointed out that Cuba probably would engage in reconnaissance with anti aircraft fire since they had claimed that they had developed a pattern of reconnaissance. Evidence indicates Soviets in command and control of SAM system. You noted there had been no reconnaissance in Eastern Cuba since 23 October. Decision was made at this meeting to cover ~~Isle 28~~, IL-28 base at San Julian and MRBM sites.

11. On 2 November you told the Group there was evidence that the Soviets were dismantling missiles, but the assembly of IL-28 bombers was continuing.

TOP SECRET EYES ONLY

110. *Central Intelligence Agency Memorandum, "Deployment and Withdrawal of Soviet Missiles and Other Significant Weapons in Cuba," 29 November 1962*

~~TOP SECRET~~

SC No. 11173/62

29 November 1962

CENTRAL INTELLIGENCE AGENCY

MEMORANDUM: Deployment and Withdrawal of Soviet Missiles and Other Significant Weapons in Cuba

NOTE

This memorandum assesses our evidence concerning the number of Soviet missiles deployed to and subsequently withdrawn from Cuba, the chances that Soviet missiles remain in Cuba, and the situation and outlook with respect to rates of withdrawal of IL-28s and other significant Soviet weapons in Cuba.

CONCLUSION

The Soviet claim to have delivered only 42 missiles to Cuba, and to have now withdrawn these, is consistent with our evidence. We cannot exclude the possibility that more actually arrived, and that some therefore remain, but we think that any such number would be small. Available evidence also warrants the conclusion that the Soviets are preparing to withdraw the IL-28s.

1. The Soviets almost certainly intended to deploy substantially more than the 42 missiles which they acknowledged and have withdrawn. We reach this conclusion from the following factors:

a. Nine sites with four launchers each have been identified in Cuba. The Soviets normally provide two missiles for every MRBM and IRBM launcher and, since several of the launchers already had two, we believe that they intended to provide two each for the others, or a total of 72 for the 36 launchers identified. Of these, 48 would be MRBMs, of which we identified 33, and the remainder would be IRBMs, of which we have no evidence that any had reached Cuba by 22 October.

b. The pattern of the nine identified sites strongly suggests that at least one more was planned to form a pair with the ninth. In addition, there is some evidence suggesting that the Soviets planned a third deployment area, in eastern Cuba, to follow upon those in the western and central parts of the country.

~~TOP SECRET~~ 

TOP SECRET 

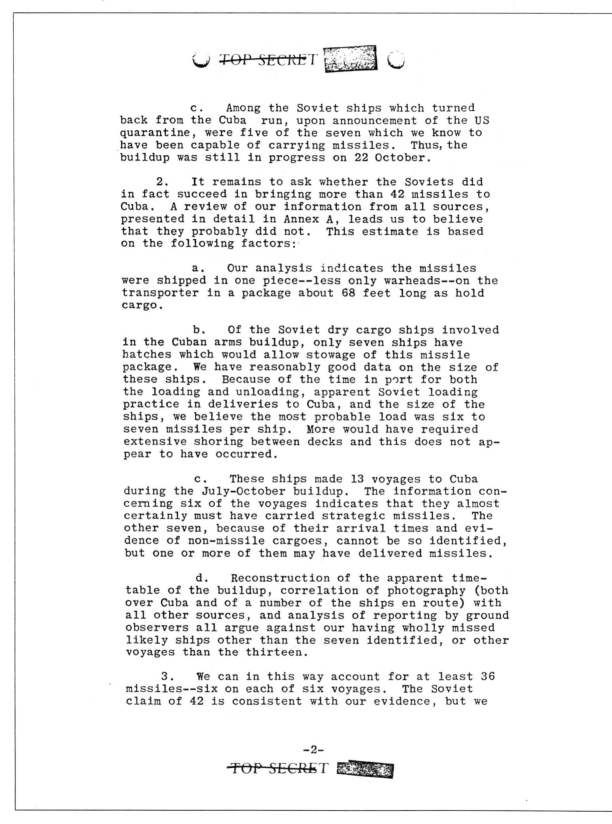

c. Among the Soviet ships which turned back from the Cuba run, upon announcement of the US quarantine, were five of the seven which we know to have been capable of carrying missiles. Thus, the buildup was still in progress on 22 October.

2. It remains to ask whether the Soviets did in fact succeed in bringing more than 42 missiles to Cuba. A review of our information from all sources, presented in detail in Annex A, leads us to believe that they probably did not. This estimate is based on the following factors:

a. Our analysis indicates the missiles were shipped in one piece--less only warheads--on the transporter in a package about 68 feet long as hold cargo.

b. Of the Soviet dry cargo ships involved in the Cuban arms buildup, only seven ships have hatches which would allow stowage of this missile package. We have reasonably good data on the size of these ships. Because of the time in port for both the loading and unloading, apparent Soviet loading practice in deliveries to Cuba, and the size of the ships, we believe the most probable load was six to seven missiles per ship. More would have required extensive shoring between decks and this does not appear to have occurred.

c. These ships made 13 voyages to Cuba during the July-October buildup. The information concerning six of the voyages indicates that they almost certainly must have carried strategic missiles. The other seven, because of their arrival times and evidence of non-missile cargoes, cannot be so identified, but one or more of them may have delivered missiles.

d. Reconstruction of the apparent timetable of the buildup, correlation of photography (both over Cuba and of a number of the ships en route) with all other sources, and analysis of reporting by ground observers all argue against our having wholly missed likely ships other than the seven identified, or other voyages than the thirteen.

3. We can in this way account for at least 36 missiles--six on each of six voyages. The Soviet claim of 42 is consistent with our evidence, but we

-2-

TOP SECRET 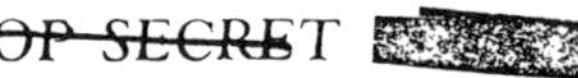

~~TOP SECRET~~

cannot rule out a somewhat higher number, primarily because of the possibility that two or more of the seven other voyages delivered missiles. The analysis of these thirteen voyages in Annex B inclines us to accept a figure not much higher than the 36 we can account for.

4. Sources inside Cuba have provided numerous reports in recent weeks claiming that strategic missiles have been retained in Cuba and concealed from aerial reconnaissance. Most of these sources are untested, and some of their reports are manifestly erroneous. Checks by other methods, including photographic intelligence, have failed to produce clear confirmation of any of these reports, but we are not able to disprove some of them.* Specifically, at Mayari Arriba--about 40 miles northwest of Guantanamo--we have identified both from photography and ground sources a Soviet installation which may be missile-associated. We have not, however, identified any equipment which can be associated with strategic missiles.

5. Since the foregoing evidence is not fully conclusive, we must also consider whether the Soviets would wish to secrete strategic missiles in Cuba. It is doubtful, in our view, that they would do so for strictly military reasons. In the first place, our shipping analysis leaves little room for a number of remaining missiles large enough to be strategically significant at some later date. Such missiles could not participate in an all-out Soviet surprise attack without great risk that preparations would be detected by the US and the entire strategic plan compromised. Neither could the Soviets count on being able to use them in a retaliatory second strike.

6. In contemplating concealment, the Soviets would be aware of great risk. They would foresee that, if the US found out, a second Cuban crisis would ensue which would be unlikely to leave the Castro regime intact. Such a renewed crisis would find the Soviets in an even more disadvantageous position than before to protect their interests or avoid humiliation.

*A summary review of these reports, including the identification of certain areas which remain suspicious, is presented in Annex C.

-3-

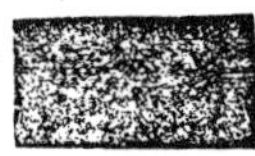

~~TOP SECRET~~ [redacted]

Jet Bombers

7. We have confidence in our estimate, based on repeated high- and low-altitude photography over Cuba and photography of deck cargo en route to Cuba, that no more than 42 IL-28s were delivered before the quarantine began. Photography of 25 November indicates that 20 IL-28 fuselage crates remained unopened at San Julian air base and some of the remaining 13 which had previously been partially or fully assembled were being dismantled. Photography indicates that the other nine crates, located at Holguin airfield, were still unopened on 25 November and had been removed to an undetermined location on 27 November.

8. The Soviets could easily ship out all these aircraft by mid-December. Shipping suitable for this purpose is continually available, and almost any four of the Soviet dry-cargo vessels in the Cuban trade could carry the entire number. Those still in crates could be moved to ports in a day or two, and the remainder could be disassembled and moved to ports by the agreed date.

Other Soviet Forces

9. Other Soviet weapon systems in Cuba include surface-to-air missiles, coastal defense missiles, Komar missile boats, and fighter aircraft. In addition, the equipment for four armored combat groups (including possibly 6-10,000 men) remains on the island. We have no evidence of any preparations in Cuba to withdraw these elements. At least four months and on the order of 100 voyages by Soviet ships were required to move these forces to Cuba, and their removal would require an equally large effort. The SA-2 system and the armored combat groups are the bulkiest of these elements, and might require several months for return to the USSR.

-4-

~~TOP SECRET~~ 

111. *President's Foreign Intelligence Advisory Board, James R. Killian, Jr., Chairman, Memorandum for the President and report, 4 February 1963*

THE WHITE HOUSE

WASHINGTON

~~TOP SECRET~~

February 4, 1963

PRESIDENT'S FOREIGN INTELLIGENCE ADVISORY BOARD

MEMORANDUM FOR THE PRESIDENT

Attached is the report of your Foreign Intelligence Advisory Board based on our review of the intelligence coverage, assessment and reporting by U. S. intelligence agencies concerning the Soviet military build-up in Cuba during the months preceding October 22, 1962.

Inasmuch as the most urgent recommendations growing out of our review of the Cuba situation have already been submitted to you in the Board's interim report dated December 28, 1962, we are not submitting further recommendations at this time. When the Board next meets we will complete consideration of the comments which have now been received from the Director of Central Intelligence and the U. S. intelligence agencies with respect to the recommendations of our interim report. At that time I anticipate that the Board may wish to present to you additional recommendations on important aspects of our intelligence program.

In undertaking its review the Board requested and received a comprehensive report by the intelligence community. This report, addressed to the Board, is available in the Board's office.

In Annex B to our report we list the principal sources of information considered in our review. We express our deep appreciation of the cooperation and assistance which was freely and promptly given.

While the Board had the benefit of helpful background information, the Board's observations and conclusions are wholly its own.

Respectfully,

FOR THE BOARD

James R. Killian, Jr.

James R. Killian, Jr.
Chairman

Enclosure

~~TOP SECRET~~

~~TOP SECRET~~

THE WHITE HOUSE

WASHINGTON

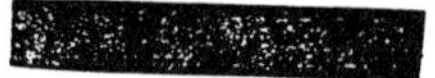

PRESIDENT'S FOREIGN INTELLIGENCE ADVISORY BOARD

February 4, 1963

MEMORANDUM FOR THE PRESIDENT

Your Foreign Intelligence Advisory Board has completed a review of actions which were taken by the foreign intelligence agencies of our Government to discharge their responsibility for intelligence coverage, assessment and reporting on the Soviet military build-up in Cuba during the months preceding your report to the Nation on October 22, 1962, concerning the USSR's establishment of offensive missile sites in Cuba.

In the course of our review we sought to determine whether there were lessons to be learned from an objective appraisal of the strengths and weaknesses of the U. S. foreign intelligence effort as disclosed by the Cuba experience. We directed particular attention to those areas of the intelligence process which are concerned with such matters as (1) the acquisition of intelligence, (2) the analysis of intelligence, and (3) the production and dissemination of intelligence reports and estimates in support of national policy formulation and operational requirements.

In our reconstruction of intelligence coverage of Soviet activities on the island of Cuba, it is noted that two principal, consecutive phases were involved. The first phase covered the period prior to October 14, 1962. The second phase consisted of a much briefer period beginning on October 14 and culminating with the Presidential announcement on October 22 concerning measures for meeting the Soviet offensive threat in Cuba. The event, of course, which provided a demarcation of these two phases was the acquisition on October 14 of U-2 photographic evidence that the Soviet Union had taken steps to establish a strategic nuclear missile complex in Cuba.

THE POST-OCTOBER 14 PHASE

We note that the definitive photographic evidence obtained as a result of the October 14 and subsequent overflights of Cuba was promptly processed and submitted to the President in time for

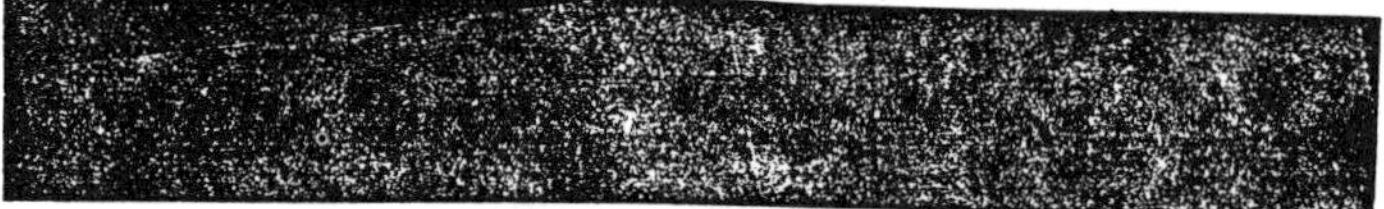

~~TOP SECRET~~

decisive action before the Soviet MRBM and IRBM systems became fully operational. Beginning with the President's initial receipt of this crucial intelligence there was an effective performance on the part of the U. S. intelligence community in providing the President and his top policy advisers promptly with the coordinated intelligence necessary to enable our Government to respond effectively to the offensive missile threat in Cuba.

We also note that in addition to photographic surveillance other factors contributed substantially to the intelligence success achieved during this period. They were (1) the skillful analysis of the data produced by photographic interpreters, [redacted] and (3) the use of intelligence previously obtained concerning strategic missile and air defense installations within the Soviet Union in determining the nature and extent of similar capabilities in Cuba.

In pointing to the high performance which was achieved by our foreign intelligence agencies during the post-October 14 period, we recognize that it would be difficult for the intelligence community to operate with the same intensity and efficiency under less critical conditions. Thus one of our major problems remains the achievement of very high performance between crises.

THE PRE-OCTOBER 14 PHASE

As to the pre-October 14 period, we conclude that our foreign intelligence effort should have been more effective in (1) obtaining adequate and timely intelligence as to the nature and scope of the Soviet military build-up as it developed over a period of months, and (2) exploiting the available intelligence as a basis for estimating Soviet and Cuban plans and intentions.

In view of the fact that the Soviet move came dangerously close to success in an area less than ninety miles from our shores, the absence of useful early warning of the enemy's intention must be stressed. We did not find that during this period there was within the intelligence community the focused sense of urgency or alarm which might well have stimulated a greater effort.

Intelligence Acquisition

In the intelligence collection area the most significant deficiencies involved (1) clandestine agent coverage, and (2) aerial photographic surveillance.

~~TOP SECRE~~T

Clandestine agent coverage within Cuba was inadequate. Although the limited agent assets of the Central Intelligence Agency and of Army Intelligence did produce some valuable reports on developments in Cuba, we believe that the absence of more effective clandestine agent coverage, as an essential adjunct to other intelligence collection operations, contributed substantially to the inability of our Government to recognize at an earlier date the danger of the Soviet move in Cuba. It would appear that over the years there has been a lack of foresight in the long-term planning for the installation of these agents.

We find also that full use was not made of aerial photographic surveillance, particularly during September and October when the influx of Soviet military personnel and armaments had reached major proportions. We recognize that in September inclement weather delayed some of the scheduled U-2 missions. However, we note that from September 8 to September 15 U-2 missions over Cuba were suspended apparently because of the loss of a Chinese Nationalist U-2 over the China mainland on September 8. We also note with concern that during the period of increasing emergency, as pointed up by intelligence indicators, there was not a corresponding intensification of the scheduling of U-2 missions over the island.

With regard to proposals for aerial photographic surveillance of Cuba, we make the following additional observations:

(1) The President granted authorization for all U-2 flights which were recommended to him by his policy advisers on the Special Group having responsibility for such matters.

(2) The Special Group approved, in one instance with modifications, all U-2 overflights recommended to it. (We surmise that on its own the Special Group could have initiated overflight recommendations.)

(3) Until October 3, when the Defense Intelligence Agency urged that suspicious areas of Cuba be covered by U-2 photographic missions, it appears that there was a failure on the part of the intelligence community as a whole to propose to the Special Group U-2 reconnaissance missions on a scale commensurate with the nature and intensity of the Soviet activity in Cuba. The need for more frequent and extensive aerial photographic surveillance during the summer and fall was even more pressing in view of the inadequacy of clandestine agent resources and the limited effectiveness of

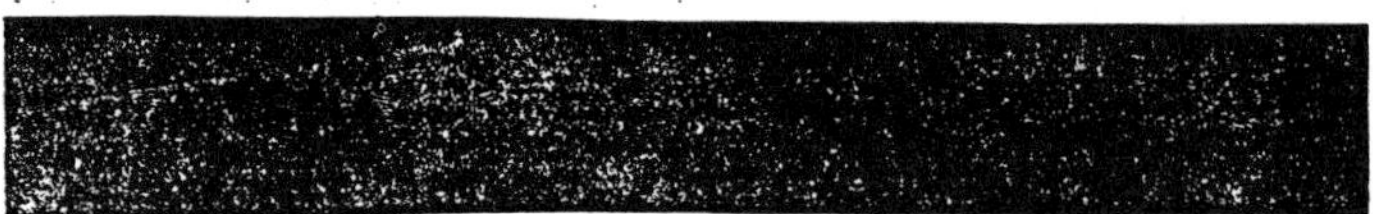

~~TOP SECRE~~T

- 3 -

TOP SECRET

other collection methods such as legal traveler, third country diplomat, refugee interrogation, and signals intelligence coverage.

(4) Although we were unable to establish the existence of a policy which prevented overflying areas of Cuba where surface-to-air missile installations were present, the Central Intelligence Agency and others believed that such a restriction did in fact prevail. We note in this regard that in the December 26 report of the Director of Central Intelligence it is stated that although the paucity of records makes it impossible to determine whether or not there was such a restriction, it is nevertheless clear that operational elements were under the impression that such an injunction was in effect.

(5) Apparently the Special Group was not made fully aware of the delaying effects on the acquisition of aerial intelligence which could and did result from changes in a CIA proposal for the conduct of a U-2 mission. On September 10 the CIA proposed that the Special Group approve and recommend the scheduling of a U-2 flight to provide extensive peripheral coverage of Cuba as well as two legs directly over Cuban air space. The Secretary of State objected to this combining of an actual overflight with the overflying of international waters. He felt that the long peripheral flight would draw attention, and if the aircraft were to fall into enemy hands after an overflight of Cuba, this would put the United States in a poor position to stand on its rights to overfly international waters. Accordingly, the Secretary of State proposed that the September flights be broken into four separate missions, two of them peripheral and two directly over Cuba, and the CIA made plans to do so. However, CIA made it an operational practice not to overfly if there was more than 25 per cent overcast, and the Director of Central Intelligence points out in his December 26 report that the poor weather in September plus the necessity for flying four separate missions instead of one resulted in prolonging the time required to get the desired coverage of Cuba. In fact, the next successful U-2 mission was not flown until September 26. We feel that under these circumstances the Special Group should have been informed of the factors operating to delay the four-flight coverage, and given an opportunity to reconsider the advisability of a mission over the critical target areas urgently requiring surveillance. We also feel that the Special Group should be possessed of a mechanism which would automatically pick up such omissions of reporting.

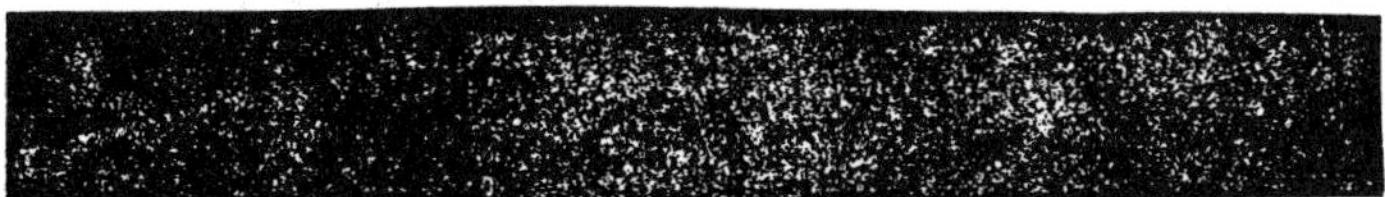

TOP SECRET

- 4 -

~~TOP SECRET~~

(6) It appears that within the Special Group further consideration should have been given to proposals by the Acting Director of Central Intelligence in August and September for low-level photographic reconnaissance of certain targets in Cuba. When the Special Group took up the matter on September 14, note was taken that the Secretary of Defense did not wish the low-level operations to be considered until results of U-2 coverage of the same area became available. Granting the obvious appropriateness of the recommendation of the Secretary of Defense, we must point out that when the U-2 flights were delayed there should have been immediate re-examination of the proposal for low-level flights. (No low-level reconnaissance missions were flown over Cuba until October 23.)

Intelligence Analysis

We find the need for improvement of the processes used in making national intelligence estimates and the processes used in making current intelligence analyses, and also in the techniques for relating these two functions.

The President and policy-advisory officials were ill served by the Special National Intelligence Estimate issued by the intelligence community on September 19, on "The Military Buildup in Cuba." This estimate concluded that the establishment of Soviet medium and intermediate range ballistic missiles in Cuba would be inconsistent with Soviet practice to date and with Soviet policy as the community then assessed it. This mistaken judgment, made at the very time when the Soviets were installing MRBMs and IRBMs in Cuba, we attribute to (1) the lack of adequate intelligence coverage of Cuba, (2) the rigor with which the view was held that the Soviet Union would not assume the risks entailed in establishing nuclear striking forces on Cuban soil, and (3) the absence of an imaginative appraisal of the intelligence indicators which, although limited in number, were contained in reports disseminated by our intelligence agencies. (We reach this conclusion even though we recognize the absence at the time of any conclusive photographic intelligence.)

The Estimate of September 19 pointed away from the likelihood of the establishment of Soviet nuclear missile systems in Cuba. An important cautionary statement appeared in a discussion paragraph, namely, that the contingency of such a development should be examined carefully, even though it would run counter to current Soviet policy. This cautionary statement, however, was not carried forward into the conclusions of the Estimate.

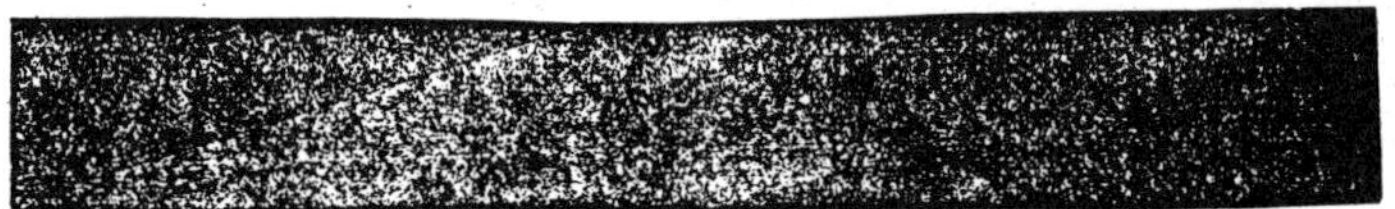

~~TOP SECRET~~

- 5 -

TOP SECRET

We believe that since this statement was of momentous significance and was in direct contradiction to the Estimate's principal finding, it should have been highlighted so as to alert policy makers and intensify the intelligence collection efforts of the agencies involved.

Turning to another important aspect of the intelligence assessment function, we find that in the analysis of intelligence indicators and in the production of current intelligence reports, the intelligence community failed to get across to key Government officials the most accurate possible picture of what the Soviets might be up to in Cuba, during the months preceding October 14. The importance of this conclusion is not diminished by the fact that hindsight is easier to apply than foresight in determining the significance of particular indicators included in the mass of reports available for intelligence analysis.

We believe that the near-total intelligence surprise experienced by the United States with respect to the introduction and deployment of Soviet strategic missiles in Cuba resulted in large part from a malfunction of the analytic process by which intelligence indicators are assessed and reported. This malfunction diminished the effectiveness of policy advisers, national intelligence estimators, and civilian and military officers having command responsibilities.

We believe that the manner in which intelligence indicators were handled in the Cuba situation may well be the most serious flaw in our intelligence system, and one which, if uncorrected, could lead to the gravest consequences. In this instance, the major consequences were the following:

(1) Our Government was not provided with the degree of early warning of hostile intentions and capabilities which should have been derived from the indicators contained in the incoming intelligence.

(2) Neither you nor your principal policy advisers were provided at appropriate intervals with meaningful, cumulative assessments of the available intelligence indicators. Had the intelligence community systematically prepared and periodically presented compilations of accumulated indicators, this would have permitted appropriate policy-level consideration of developments in Cuba and of alternative courses of action as required. The practice followed in the Cuba situation of providing White House

TOP SECRET

- 6 -

staff members with some of the raw indicator reports was not an acceptable substitute for professional analytical reporting on a developing crisis situation. While raw intelligence reports were used effectively in targeting the October 14 U-2 mission which led to the discovery of offensive missiles in Cuba, the significance of the important indicators involved was not communicated to the President.

(3) Despite the intelligence indicators which were accumulating even before the U-2 discovery on October 14, the intelligence community did not produce for the benefit of policy-level consumers a revision of its erroneous National Intelligence Estimate of September 19.

We believe a further and exhaustive examination, not limited to Cuba, should be made by the intelligence community of the complex analytic process employed throughout the community in the assessment of intelligence indicators. We base this belief on the nature of the indicator-type data which our review discloses was available during the period from May to October 1962.

Thirty five examples of such available indicators are set forth in Annex A to this report. In cataloging such examples we appreciate fully that we have the benefit of a perspective which was not then possessed by the intelligence community. We are also aware that the illustrations listed are but a small number taken from the great volume of reports which were received and which included some demonstrably erroneous information. We urge that the annexed illustrations be read not only for their individual content but also for the purpose of noting the cumulative significance of the information being received. These indicators were acquired from a variety of intelligence sources, such as [redacted] refugees, clandestine agents, and friendly foreign diplomats. They dealt with various aspects of the Soviet military build-up in Cuba, including the introduction of high-ranking Soviet military personalities who were specialists in the fields of military construction, engineering, electronics, jet pilot training, surface-to-air missile defenses, and Soviet long-range air and strategic striking forces; the assignment to Cuba of Soviet specialists in rocketry and atomic arms; the statements made by persons highly placed in the Castro regime concerning expectations that a nuclear delivery capability would be established in Cuba; the sightings by ground observers of offensive missiles being deployed under strict Soviet control

and under conditions of great secrecy; and the introduction on a progressively increasing scale of Soviet troops, arms, and military equipment and materiel in large volume and, in a number of instances, under strict security conditions. (On the latter subject we note from other materials which we have reviewed that the number of Soviet Bloc ships arriving in Cuba increased from an average of 30 a month in the first seven months of 1962 to a peak of 67 arrivals in September.)

Intelligence Reporting

Our review of the intelligence reporting process reveals that limitations which were placed on the publication and dissemination of reports and information concerning the situation in Cuba were either misinterpreted or misapplied. This inhibited the flow of significant data.

One such limitation was imposed by the Director of Central Intelligence in May 1962. Because of the Director's reservations concerning estimates on Cuban order of battle, he instructed CIA analysts to check out with the National Photographic Interpretation Center (NPIC) any report that was susceptible of photographic verification. The purpose was to establish by all available means the authenticity of refugee and agent reports. However, according to the Director of Central Intelligence, it operated as a limitation on publication because the instruction was interpreted by CIA analysts as a restriction against publishing anything that could not be verified by the NPIC. One consequence was that during the pre-October 14 period as information became available on the offensive build-up in Cuba, it was not published by the CIA even in the President's Intelligence Checklist.

On August 31 another limitation was imposed. The President placed limitations on the publication of reports on weapons which might be offensive, pending receipt of further information concerning a suspected missile installation at Banes. On October 9 these instructions were reiterated by the President who emphasized the importance of maintaining the tightest possible control of all information relating to offensive weapons.

The President made clear that he wished to impose no limitation whatever on the collection and analysis of intelligence relating to offensive weapons and he emphasized that he wanted all such information collected, analyzed, and promptly reported to officials having a real need to know. However, the United

States Intelligence Board interpreted the Presidential instructions as an injunction not to print any information on offensive weapons in Cuba in any intelligence publication. Although the Director of Central Intelligence exempted CIA's Presidential Intelligence Checklist from this injunction, the Checklist issues prepared subsequent to the President's instructions failed to include information from any of the refugee or agent reports on the sightings of offensive missiles in Cuba.

The President's directive restricting the publication of intelligence on offensive weapons was clearly wise, necessary, and essential to the national interest. The misinterpretations of this directive endangered the necessary flow of information and serve as a warning that in future situations requiring such restrictions attention must be given to establishing secure channels for transmission of vital information to officials having a clear need to know.

Emergency Planning

The Cuba experience points up the need for advance planning to ensure that our human and material intelligence resources are sufficient, and are adequately organized, to meet the demands of an emergency such as that which confronted our Government in this instance.

When the President found it necessary to restrict the publication of information on offensive missiles in Cuba and to confine such information to designated categories of recipients, the intelligence community did not have in readiness a plan to meet the reporting requirements of such an emergency. As a result, significant information did not reach some elements of the Government, both in Washington and the military commands, and in some instances important intelligence was not brought to the attention of the President and some other high officials. Two examples of the consequences which followed were (1) officials who checked in normal places concerning such matters as the October 10 speech of Senator Keating were told that there was no evidence of offensive weapons, although in fact raw intelligence had already led to the targeting of the San Cristobal area where offensive missile installations were subsequently found through U-2 photography on October 14, and (2) for a brief period the limitation on publication operated in such fashion as to preclude the Defense Intelligence Agency from disseminating outside the Washington area intelligence publications on the developing Cuba situation. As a consequence, it was necessary to call in certain military commanders from the field

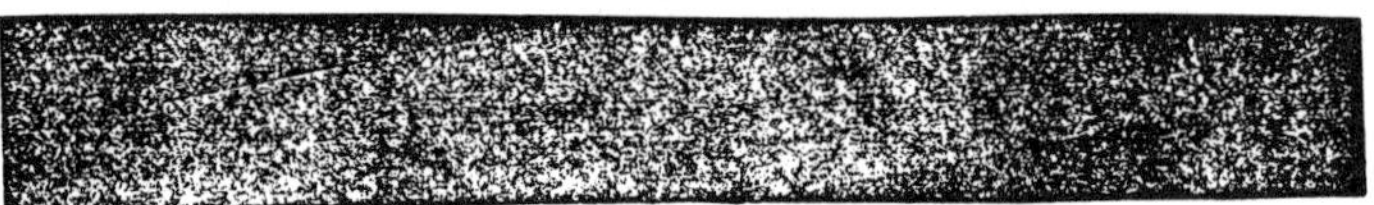

111. *(Continued)*

~~TOP~~-SECRET

and give them oral briefings on the subject. The restriction served to hamper the commanders in their planning for possible military action involving Cuba.

We note next that when U-2 overflights of Cuba began on an accelerated basis on October 14, no more than a 10-day supply of photographic film was on hand in the entire country to meet the demands resulting from the sudden step-up of aerial reconnaissance operations. Moreover, in the absence of a central processing facility for developing photographic film in quantity, under appropriate security safeguards, it was necessary to make use of film laboratories at scattered locations considerably removed from Washington.

* * *

Throughout our review, we have been mindful of public charges to the effect that during the period of the Soviet military build-up in Cuba, the U. S. intelligence process was in some manner manipulated for partisan political purposes. We find no evidence whatsoever to support such charges.

James R. Killian, Jr.

James R. Killian, Jr., Chairman
President's Foreign Intelligence
Advisory Board

William O. Baker, Member
Clark Clifford "
James Doolittle "
Gordon Gray "
Edwin H. Land "
William L. Langer "
Robert D. Murphy "
Frank Pace, Jr. "

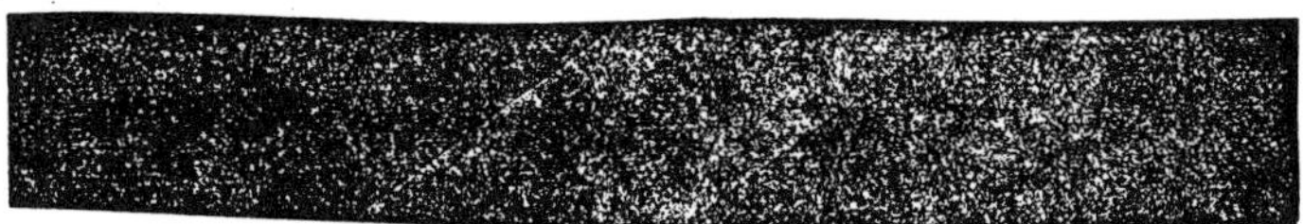

~~TOP~~ SECRET

- 10 -

112. *McCone, Memorandum for the President, 28 February 1963, and "Conclusions" (attached)*

28 February 1963

MEMORANDUM FOR: The President
The White House

I am returning the report of the President's Foreign Intelligence Advisory Board dated February 4th commenting on the intelligence community's actions in connection with the Cuban crisis. I will not attempt to comment on the specifics of the report. It is my understanding that the Board will make recommendations to you for corrective measures which they feel should be taken within the intelligence community. When these recommendations are received, I would hope for an opportunity to comment upon them as I did on the recommendations contained in their interim report of December 28th.

When I appeared before the Board on November 7th, December 9th, and December 28th, I stated that there was an understandable reluctance or timidity in programming U-2 overflights over Cuba after we had discovered the presence of surface-to-air missile installations. This caution was understandable not only because of the extremely severe criticism of "U-2 incidents" dating back to the Powers' incident on May 1, 1960, but also because of the more recent loss of a Chinat U-2 and a U-2 intrusion over Sakhalin in early September. This same attitude apparently dictated the Secretary of State's action in revising a CIA-proposed flight at the Special Group meeting held in Mr. Bundy's office on September 10th. It was, I believe, the same attitude that caused the Special Group in considering my request on October 4th for extensive Cuban reconnaissance to ask [illegible] JCS, and CIA to study all alternative means of conducting aerial reconnaissance and to report back on October 9th. In retrospect, it might be contended that there was a failure to exercise sufficient urgency in proposing U-2 reconnaissance missions; however, I am inclined to believe that any one reaching such a conclusion must first carefully weigh the serious considerations that enter into a decision to overfly denied territory.

I further advised the Board that I felt the analysts, both in the intelligence community and elsewhere in Government, including the

~~TOP SECRET~~

TOP SECRET

State Department, were so convinced that the Soviets would not accept the inevitable confrontation resulting from placement of offensive missiles in Cuba, that they were inclined to dismiss such evidence as there was to the contrary. This, I find, is one of the difficulties of dealing with the imponderables of what the other fellow will or will not do. With particular reference to the Cuban situation, it should be noted that for two years the intelligence community had been surfeited with reports of "missiles in Cuba," all of which proved to be incorrect prior to those which we received on or about September 20th. Nevertheless, one can now readily conclude that greater emphasis should have been placed by the estimators on certain of the "Intelligence Indicators" attached as Annex A to the Board report. About 3,500 agent and refugee reports were analyzed in the preparation of my report to the Killian Board and of this number, only eight in retrospect were considered as reasonably valid indicators of the deployment of offensive missiles to Cuba.

I continue to feel that the intelligence community performed well. I have examined this performance personally and in depth, and incidentally with a critical eye. As you know, my own views differed from those of the community. I believe that the conclusions reached from my study made for the Board at your request reflect a more reasonable judgment of the performance of the intelligence community in the six months' period prior to the October crisis. A copy of these conclusions is attached.

John A. McCone
Director

Attachment

JAM:mfb:bd (28 Feb 63)
Orig - Addressee
1 - DCI White House
1 - DCI Chrono
1 - IG
1 - WE

TOP SECRET

112. *(Continued)*

TOP SECRET [redacted]

CONCLUSIONS

1. Although the intelligence community's inquiry into its actions during the Cuban crisis revealed certain areas where shortcomings existed and where improvements should be made in various areas of intelligence collection and processing, the intelligence community operated extensively and well in connection with Cuba. Every major weapons system introduced into Cuba by the Soviets was detected, identified, and reported (with respect to numbers, location and operational characteristics) before any one of these systems attained an operational capability.

2. A relatively short period of time ensued between the introduction of strategic weapons into Cuba, particularly strategic missiles, and the commencement of the flow, although meager, of tangible reports of their presence; detection of their possible presence and targeting of the suspect areas of their location was accomplished in a compressed time frame; and the intelligence cycle did move with extraordinary rapidity through the stages of collection, analysis, targeting for verification, and positive identification.

3. The very substantial effort directed toward Cuba was originated by an earlier concern with the situation in Cuba and the effort, already well under way, contributed to the detection and analysis of the Soviet build-up.

4. Information was disseminated and used.

5. Aerial photography was very effective and our best means of establishing hard intelligence.

6. The procedures adopted in September delayed photographic intelligence, but this delay was not critical, because photography obtained prior to about 17 October would not have been sufficient to warrant action of a type which would require support from Western Hemisphere NATO allies.

TOP SECRET [redacted]

TOP SECRET [redacted]

7. Agent reports helped materially; however, none giving significant information on offensive missiles reached the intelligence community or policy-makers until after mid-September. When received, they were used in directing aerial photography.

8. Some restrictions were placed on dissemination of information, but there is no indication that these restrictions necessarily affected analytical work or actions by policy-makers.

9. The 19 September estimate, while indicating the improbability that the Soviet Union would place MRBM's and IRBM's in Cuba, did state that "this contingency must be examined carefully, even though it would run counter to current Soviet policy"; the estimators in preparing the 19 September estimate gave great weight to the philosophical argument concerning Soviet intentions and thus did not fully weigh the many indicators.

10. The estimate of 19 October on probable Soviet reactions was correct.

TOP SECRET [redacted]